Human Rights in Develo
Yearbook 1998

# Human Rights in Development
# Yearbook 1998

## Global Perspectives and Local Issues

Edited by

*Hugo Stokke and Arne Tostensen*

A Human Rights Project involving the following institutions:

*Chr. Michelsen Institute*, Bergen, Norway
*Danish Centre for Human Rights*, Copenhagen, Denmark
*Icelandic Human Rights Center*, Reykjavik, Iceland
*Ludwig Boltzmann Institute of Human Rights (BIM)*, Vienna, Austria
*Netherlands Institute of Human Rights (SIM)*, Utrecht, The Netherlands
*Norwegian Institute of Human Rights*, Oslo, Norway
*Raoul Wallenberg Institute of Human Rights
and Humanitarian Law*, Lund, Sweden

## Kluwer Law International
The Hague / London / Boston

## Nordic Human Rights Publications
Oslo

A C.I.P. Catalogue record for this book is available from the Library of Congress.

ISSN 0801–8049
ISBN 90-411-1297-9

Published by Kluwer Law International,
P.O. Box 85889, 2508 CN The Hague, The Netherlands.

Sold and distributed in North, Central and South America
by Kluwer Law International,
675 Massachusetts Avenue, Cambridge, MA 02139, U.S.A.

In all other countries, sold and distributed
by Kluwer Law International,
P.O. Box 85899, 2508 CN The Hague, The Netherlands.

*Distribution in Scandinavia*
Norwegian Institute of Human Rights
Grensen 18
N-0159 Oslo
Norway
Tel. 47-22-42-1360
Fax. 47-22-42-2542

*Printed on acid-free paper*

Printed in the Netherlands.

# PREFACE

The Yearbook on Human Rights in Development is a joint project of the Chr. Michelsen Institute, Bergen; the Danish Centre for Human Rights, Copenhagen; the Icelandic Human Rights Centre, Reykjavik; the Ludwig Boltzman Institute of Human Rights, Vienna; the Netherlands Institute of Human Rights, Utrecht; the Norwegian Institute of Human Rights, Oslo; and the Raoul Wallenberg Institute of Human Rights and Humanitarian Law, Lund. The Chr. Michelsen Institute currently holds the editorship on behalf of the collaborating institutions. This year's edition is the eleventh in a series, which was first launched in 1985 by the Norwegian Human Rights Project and the Chr. Michelsen Institute.

The Yearbook is geared to a broad readership, including government agencies, donors, embassies, the mass media, non-governmental organisations, the academic community, and the interested public.

This year's volume differs from previous editions in that it contains no case studies monitoring developments in the human rights situation of specific countries. The conventional country reports is a format that has been overtaken by events and left behind in this age of electronic communication and the Internet. There are many agencies and NGOs providing reliable and updated information on human rights conditions around the globe – virtually all available instantaneously via the Internet. Most of this information deals with the civil and political rights. Comparatively less material is available on economic, social and cultural rights. It is regrettable that the latter set of rights continues to be underreported.

The present edition goes some way towards realising some of the ambitions set in the preface to the 1997 edition: less emphasis on country reporting; sharper focus on themes and issues; and more attention to self-monitoring of the policies and actions of Northern stakeholders. However, more needs to be done in this direction.

Although drawing on empirical realities – be they country-specific or not – all seven contributions address a topical theme. The first five articles all discuss in various ways *the promotion of human rights*. While protection of human rights has been a paramount concern, promotion of human rights has received comparatively less attention. The articles by Jerve, Hey/Lasbrey and Stokke discuss how human rights may be promoted by means of development assistance and technical co-operation. Lindsnæs and Lindholdt find that national human rights institutions have promotional as well as protective tasks. Finally, Oo and Grieg assess how the incentive and disincentive policies, respectively, of the regional associations ASEAN and EU promote human rights in Burma. A common denominator of the last two articles is *local conflict*. In Ekern's contribution, local communities in Latin America find themselves caught up in nation-wide civil wars between the government and guerrilla forces espousing rival political ideologies and being forced to take sides. Andreassen holds that local ethnic tension raises fundamental constitutional issues that need to be resolved before political stability can be attained in Kenya.

The first contribution by Birgit Lindsnæs and Lone Lindholdt discusses the emergence and achievements of national human rights institutions. These institutions are broadly mandated, independent bodies, established by law and reflecting the pluralism of civil society. The article traces the evolution of principles and guidelines governing these institutions' behaviour in UN fora, and assesses their legal basis, political and financial independence from the government as well as their composition in terms of professional legal expertise and pluralist representation. In reviewing reports from national institutions in operation, examples are given as to how they divide their labour between protective and promotional tasks and what specific human rights foci they have developed, whether related to non-discrimination, vulnerable groups or specific civil, political, economic and social rights. In accounting for their achievements, two sets of explanatory factors are singled out. First, the institutional framework has a determining influence on outputs and achievements. Second, and no less important, the character of the political regime and its state institutions also exerts a strong influence on the operations and achievements of these institutions.

In his contribution Alf Morten Jerve raises the question of negative social impact of development in a human rights perspective. Although human rights are generally considered interrelated, interdependent and indivisible in real life situations practitioners are often confronted with difficult trade-offs. Jerve discusses the social consequences of development interventions and highlights two sets of problems. One relates to rehabilitation of livelihoods where development projects temporarily cause adverse effects, i.e. how those affected are to be compensated so that the 'do no harm' rule of thumb be observed. The other concerns the sharing of benefits deriving from development activities, i.e. how they may contribute to the progressive realisation of economic, social and cultural rights. This problematique is discussed in light of the World Bank's experiences – in setting standards and in enforcing them.

Hilde Hey and Carol Lasbrey argue the case for increased attention to the promotional aspects of human rights, particularly through development assistance. The promotion of civil and political rights has been recognised as an important objective in Dutch development policy in the 1990s and human rights are now securely integrated with other objectives of foreign policy. The conclusion of a peace agreement in Guatemala in 1996 between the government and the guerrilla forces has offered an opportunity for realising this objective. The article reviews two projects, one relating to education for the Maya indigenous community, and the other one supporting a forensic association which assists in the identification of victims of killings during the civil war in Guatemala. Both projects are found to have made significant contributions to the promotion of various human rights. The article ends with a plea that development projects be justified as promotional means, not only as vehicles for protecting human rights.

Zaw Oo and Kai Grieg scrutinise the 'statecraft' of regional groupings like the EU and the ASEAN, respectively, in their attempts to influence the Burmese military regime to mend its ways and embark on a path towards democratisation and respect for human rights. They examine the pros and cons of so-called incentive and disincentive policies, and discuss the conditions under which they are likely to succeed. Detailed historical and contemporary background factors are considered – in the sender and target states alike. Yet, on the face of it, the incumbent Burmese regime appears to be as intransigent as ever in the face of external pressure and domestic opposition.

The struggle against child labour is the subject of Hugo Stokke's article, which focuses on the dual role of the International Labour Organisation in this regard. On the one hand, the ILO has a standard-setting function in adopting tripartite labour conventions, to which governments, trade unions and employers' associations subscribe. On the other hand, the Organisation also has an enforcement task, which comes to the fore in its operational activities, in this case the International Programme to Eliminate Child Labour (IPEC). Stokke takes an institutional approach to the problems at hand. He sees the ILO's behaviour as being determined by its internal and external environments, i.e. the various stakeholders within the organisation and outside it. The empirical cases are drawn from the South Asia region, in particular Nepal.

Stener Ekern analyses how local communities get caught up in nation-wide civil wars between government and guerrilla forces. Individuals from these communities find themselves pulled between the grand narrative of wars in the name of competing ideologies and the little narrative of community rights and obligations. Drawing upon his own experience while working for the Truth Commission in El Salvador and written accounts from Peru and Guatemala, Ekern shows what meanings these conflicts have for local communities in these countries. They accentuate the difference between nationally codified law and local customary law, and highlight the dual identities of individuals as state citizens and community members. Caught between state and community demands, individuals face a quandary from which there is no easy way out.

The contribution by Bård-Anders Andreassen addresses the vexing issue of how to accommodate ethnic interests and their right to self-determination within the constitutional dispensation of an African territorial state, viz. Kenya. He traces the historical roots of the ethnicisation of Kenyan politics to the independence negotiations in the early 1960s, and argues that ethnic politics have been the order of the day throughout the post-independence period despite appearances to the contrary. However, ethnic sentiments have taken new forms in the multi-party era of the 1990s, in some cases leading to violent ethnic clashes. The current constitutional debate in Kenya is searching for constitutional arrangements that may help ease ethnic tension. In looking for solutions Andreassen points to devolution of decision-making authority and elements of federalism cutting across ethnic constellations in order to discourage the persistence of ethnicity as the predominant cleavage in the political game.

A novel feature of this year's edition of the Yearbook is a book review section. A review essay by Kenneth Christie discusses a number of books, which deal with the Asia-Pacific value debate as it relates to rights and democracy. Helmut Sax reviews a collection of essays on cultural internationalism and the world order. We hope to expand the book review section in next year's edition.

On behalf of the authors, as well as ourselves, we would like to thank all experts who have refereed and commented upon drafts at various stages of completion. The editors would also like to extend their heartfelt thanks to Inger A. Nygaard for her meticulous efforts in turning the manuscripts into camera-ready copy. Further thanks are due to Richard Moorsom who once gain has taken a firm and competent grasp of the final language editing. We also express our gratitude to Kluwer Law International for publishing the Yearbook yet again.

Without the financial support of the Danish Ministry of Foreign Affairs (Danida), the Hermann and Marianne Straniak Foundation in Switzerland, the Netherlands Ministry of Foreign Affairs, and the Norwegian Ministry of Foreign Affairs this publication would not have materialised. Notwithstanding financial sponsorship, no donor has ever attempted to influence the analyses and assessments made in the various chapters.

The usual disclaimer applies: no inference, viewpoint or assessment should be interpreted to reflect the policies of the donors. The authors are themselves responsible for the contents of their contributions. Similarly, although the editors have reviewed all contributions, offered comments and can vouch for the academic quality of the end product, the editorial team does not necessarily share the views expressed. For the benefit of future editions under our editorship, we welcome critical and constructive criticism on any one of the contributions or the Yearbook as a whole.


HUGO STOKKE
ARNE TOSTENSEN

Bergen, July 1999

# TABLE OF CONTENTS

# National Human Rights Institutions: Standard-Setting and Achievements

*Birgit Lindsnæs and Lone Lindholt*

# INTRODUCTION

Since 1946 a new type of institution has evolved: the national institution for the promotion and protection of human rights. This type of institution has – although established nationally – been defined in the framework of United Nations with the primary aim of improving national human rights performance. Thus, as an institutional type national institutions are new in history and unique in focussing only on human rights promotion and protection.

The question that needs to be examined is whether this type of institution is likely to influence national human rights agendas and, in a long-term perspective, the protection of human rights in states with differing political systems. It is, however, not possible to make such an exhaustive analysis in one article. Therefore, the article aims at making a preliminary study of a number of selected elements relevant to an overall analysis.

The aim of this article is to review the development of standard-setting for national institutions, to examine the institutional framework that has a bearing on organisational performance and to provide some examples of achievements in implementing human rights at the national level.

The article looks at four areas: 1) the background for the development of the United Nations' so-called Paris Principles of 1991 for the establishment and functioning of national institutions,[1] 2) the character of national institutions established before and after the adoption of the Paris Principles; 3) the contents of the Paris Principles in relation to the institutional framework and outputs of national institutions; and 4) examples of resulting achievements.

The focus will be on the types of national institutions having a mandate in line with the framework laid down in the Paris Principles. They are characterized by a) having broadly defined mandates with emphasis on the national implementation of international human rights standards, b) being established by legislative means, c) being independent of the state in decision-making procedures, d) having a pluralist representation of civil society and vulnerable groups in the governing bodies, and, in relevant cases, e) handling individual complaints.[2]

According to the Paris Principles "the ombudsmen, mediators and similar institutions form other bodies" and are thus not defined as a national institution.[3] The authors agree with this conceptual segregation because most ombudsmen institutions

---

[1] The Paris Principles were defined at the International Workshop on National Institutions for the Promotion and Protection of Human Rights, Paris, 7-9 October 1991 (E/CN.4/1992/43 of 16 December 1991). They were further codified by the United Nations Commission on Human Rights in Resolution 1992/54, 1992, and in General Assembly resolution 48/134, 1993. They are included as an Annex to the *United Nations Handbook on the Establishment and Strengthening of National Institutions*, Professional Training Series No. 4, United Nations Centre for Human Rights, 1995 (hereinafter UN Handbook, 1995).

[2] See for example Brian Burdekin, *Human Rights Commissions, Workshop in Paris, 2nd European Meeting of National Institutions*, 1991, pp.103-113; Morten Kjaerum, Council of Europe and Danish Centre for Human Rights, January 1997, pp. 41-57.

[3] Commission on Human Rights Resolution 1992/54, 1992, General Assembly Resolution 48/134, 1993, UN Handbook, 1995.

are rather specialised and do not meet the criteria of having "as broad a mandate as possible".[4] The article will therefore not include institutions focussing on narrowly defined human rights issues or at specific target groups. This includes institutions such as the European type of ombudsman institution,[5] and commissions and councils concerned with issues such as equal opportunities, women, minorities, persons with disabilities, indigenous peoples and refugees.

Nor will the article include human rights commissions that are political in nature in the definition of national institutions. This type of human rights commission is formed by governments as well but serves as an integrated part of the state and parliamentary structure with parliamentarians as the main group of members. This type of commission or committee is often confused with the independent national institution frequently called a commission.

In relation to the normative framework established by the United Nations the main sources used in this article are documents and reports adopted by the various organs. The empirical part is based on legal texts and annual reports of the institutions themselves. From a methodological point of view it has only been possible to make an indirect assessment of the achievements of the national institutions reviewed due to lack of access to evaluation reports on most institutions. Also, field work has not been carried out.

Starting out from the Paris Principles, the article analyses the institutional framework which is the foundation for establishing and running national institutions. This encompasses analyses of the legal foundation, mandate and powers of the institutions, the conditions for appointment of leading members, e.g. commissioners and board members, the degree of transparency and independency in decision-making procedures, and the degree to which the actual institutional framework relates to the output of national institutions.[6]

The hypothesis behind an institutional framework approach is that the degree of political consensus behind creating such a type of institution (including such elements as political autonomy, independency in decision-making procedures, the professional approach to analyse human rights standards and national issues, the content of the mandate and powers of the institutions, the constituency and stakeholders behind and

---

[4]   The UN Handbook, para 41, p. 7 enlarges the Paris Principles and includes the ombudsmen and similar institutions in the concept of national institutions. Although the arguments for widening the concept seem logical, because of similarities in complaints handling procedures, in this context it would be more meaningful to keep the two concepts distinct.

[5]   Most European ombudsman institutions focus on the legality of administrative proceedings in the state administration, or on issues such as consumer protection or other specialised areas, in combination with complaints handling. See for example the International Ombudsman Yearbook, Linda C. Reif (ed.), *The International Ombudsmann Yearbook*, vol. 1, 1997, Kluwer Law International.

[6]   Experience shows that there is a strong relationship between a thoroughly considered institutional framework and the output and impact of an institution. See for example David Korten, *Getting to the 21st Century. Voluntary Action and the Global Agenda*, Connecticut: Kumarian press, 1990; Kristina Hedlund Thulin, *Evaluation of the Legal Information Centre for Human Rights in Tallinn, Estonia*, Danish Centre for Human Rights, 1996; Birgit Lindsnaes, "Human Rights and Capacity Building—Experiences from Malawi and Estonia" (in Danish), i *Den Ny Verden*, No. 2, Center for Development Research, 1998.

the actual size and capacity) is decisive for the achievements to be obtained by national institutions.

Even though it is difficult to set up benchmarks for the achievements of national institutions, at least some indicators can be set up for the majority of these institutions. This includes registering the number of complaints handled and solved by complaints handling national institutions and the number of cases that led to change in laws. This type of indicator has been included in the article to the extent possible at this stage.

## THE DEVELOPMENT OF THE CONCEPT OF NATIONAL HUMAN RIGHTS INSTITUTIONS

The historical process of external endorsement of national human rights institutions goes as far back as 1946, to the second session of the United Nations Economic and Social Council (ECOSOC). Here it was decided to invite member states to "consider the desirability" of establishing local bodies in the form of "information groups or local human rights committees" to function as vehicles for collaboration with the United Nations Commission on Human Rights.[7]

In 1960, the issue was raised again, this time indicating a sharpening of the mandate of these institutions beyond being mere agencies of information and encouraging them to enter into the field of active participation and monitoring.[8] The trend continued, in the wake of the growing recognition that with the continued expansion of human rights instruments during the 1960s and 1970s, there was an increasing need for mechanisms to ensure national implementation of these instruments as well. In this context, national institutions could obviously play a significant role, but since their number was still limited and experiences scattered, it was decided to convene a "Seminar on National and Local Institutions for the Promotion and Protection of Human Rights" in Geneva in September 1978.[9]

The seminar adopted the first set of guidelines outlining the general functions of national institutions. According to these guidelines, national institutions should fall into one of two categories, the first of which would be occupied with the general promotion of human rights (information and awareness-raising). The other would take direct action in the form of reviewing national policy (legislative, judicial and administrative steps and decisions), reporting and making recommendations to the state. With regard to the organisational structure, it was recommended that national institutions should be composed in a manner reflecting a cross-section of society with a view to facilitate popular participation. In addition, they should be immediately accessible to members of the public, function on a regular basis, and in appropriate cases be assisted by local or national advisory organs.[10]

The guidelines were endorsed by the United Nations Human Rights Commission and the General Assembly,[11] which urged member states to comment on the

---

[7]   ECOSOC Resolution 2/9 of 21 June 1946.
[8]   ECOSOC Resolution 772 B (XXX) of 25 July 1960.
[9]   St/HR/SER.A/2, chapter V.
[10]   *United Nations Action in the Field of Human Rights*, United Nations, 1988, para. 83ff.
[11]   A/RES/33/46 of 14 December 1978.

guidelines, and to provide the Secretary General with relevant information relating to their own experience of establishing national human rights institutions.

The General Assembly raised the matter again in 1979, recommending the member states to take the necessary steps to create and improve conditions for the establishment of national institutions, bearing in mind the guidelines adopted the previous year, and emphasizing the importance of ensuring the integrity and independence in accordance with national legislation.[12] Finally, the constructive role to be played by non-governmental organisations (NGOs) was brought to the attention of the states.

By virtue of these resolutions the United Nations Secretary General was requested to report to the Commission on a survey of national institutions, which he continued to do the following years.[13]

In the General Assembly's Resolution from 1981,[14] a section on the conceptual human rights foundation on which national institutions should be based is outlined. The Resolution further states that "all human rights and fundamental freedoms are indivisible and interdependent, and that equal attention and urgent consideration should be given to the implementation, promotion and protection of both civil and political, and economic, social and cultural rights". This statement and the underlying holistic approach to human rights, which we later find clearly expressed in the Preamble to the Declaration on the Right to Development from 1986[15] and in section 5 of the Vienna Declaration and Programme of Action from 1993,[16] stands out as distinct from most other human rights instruments in force at that time.[17]

Regardless of the reasons behind the inclusion of the formulation in the 1981 Resolution, the outcome is interesting. For the first time, there was a direct indication that national human rights institutions were not meant to occupy themselves merely with the judicial procedures and respect for civil and political rights. The monitoring of the implementation of the entire scope of human rights would fall within the scope of the national human rights institutions. This corresponds to the broad nature of the Secretary General's early reports and is in conformity with his obligation to take into account "differing social and legal systems" (section 9 of the Resolution).

---

[12] A/RES/34/49 of 23 November 1979.

[13] Examples hereof are A/36/440 (1981) and A/38/416 (1983).

[14] A/RES/36/134 of 14 December 1981.

[15] The Declaration reads "... and considering that all human rights and fundamental freedoms are indivisible and interdependent and that, in order to promote development, equal attention and urgent consideration should be given to the implementation, promotion and protection of civil, political, economic, social and cultural rights", United Nations General Assembly Resolution 41/128 of 4 December 1986.

[16] "All human rights are universal, indivisible and interdependent and interrelated. The international community must treat human rights globally in a fair and equal manner, on the same footing, and with the same emphasis."

[17] The Proclamation of Teheran by the International Conference on Human Rights in May 1968 expressed a similar notion: "Since human rights and fundamental freedoms are indivisible, the full realization of civil and political rights without the enjoyment of economic, social and cultural rights is impossible" (section 13).

In the first and second reports of the Secretary General from 1981 and 1983,[18] the mandate was perceived in the broadest possible manner, encompassing the examination of almost all varieties of institutions even remotely concerned with human rights. As such, the reports reveal a lack of definite limitations on the scope of institutions to fall under the category of national human rights institutions. On the basis of information provided by individual states, the report broadly categorise the activities rather than specify the framework of the institutions themselves.

The mandate is twofold: the function of protection on one hand and the function of promotion on the other hand. The former includes the hearing of complaints, seeking of amicable settlements, bringing matters to the attention of the Courts or prosecutors' offices, providing legal counselling or instituting petition or inquiry procedures before national parliaments. However, it excludes the issuing of independent and final decisions and does not mention the more pro-active methods of investigation. In addition, a tentative distinction is made between judicial and non-judicial institutions where the latter category encompasses ombudsmen and similar bodies particular to each region, endowed with an independent status and the ability to hear complaints. Distinct from these bodies, the so-called 'national and local bodies for the protection of human rights, which report to the executive branch', are mentioned, giving as examples a number of national human rights commissions and committees.

In relation to promotional activities, the reports are extremely broad, listing those activities directly related to human rights and legislation, such as participation in the legislative process, the work of electoral commissions, the dissemination of information and public awareness campaigns. They also include functions carried out by educational institutions and those dealing with health care, social security, employment, working conditions, race relations and the rights of special groups such as children and young persons.

We can *conclude* that during this initial phase there were virtually no limitations on the definition of a national human rights institution. The bodies defining the scope and role of national institutions seemed to perceive this broad all-encompassing scope as a strength rather than a weakness in order to include as many tentative institutions as possible. The mandate of the individual institution was therefore not narrowly described. The earliest resolutions even saw the institutions as a service organ of the United Nations in distributing materials, perceiving them as a resource for the United Nations rather than the other way around.

During the 1980s the United Nations Commission on Human Rights continued to place the question of national institutions on the agenda of its annual session, resulting in a series of resolutions subsequently endorsed by the General Assembly.[19]

---

[18]  A/36/440 of 9 October 1981 and A/38/416 of 24 October 1983.

[19]  The resolutions from 1986 to 1991 stress that the issue should be given high priority, that funding and technical assistance should be ensured, and that the UN should play "a catalytic role in assisting the development of national human rights institutions by acting as a clearing house for the exchange of information and experience". In return, the original intention that national institutions should serve as focal points for the dissemination of UN materials, is maintained. The need for a handbook on national institutions, based on and supplementing the demand for publication and dissemination of the

In addition, regional cooperation in the field was encouraged and resulted in the holding of workshops for Africa (Lome, April 1988) and Asia-Pacific (Manila, May 1990).[20] These fora were mainly directed towards the exchange of ideas and experiences and distinguish themselves from later initiatives, which were meetings *of* rather than *on* national institutions.[21]

## THE PARIS CONFERENCE: LAYING DOWN THE GENERAL PRINCIPLES

A step of major significance was the holding of the first International Workshop on National Institutions for the Promotion and Protection of Human Rights in Paris, 7-9 October 1991.[22] The Workshop had a double basis: the resolutions of the Human Rights Commission as listed above and the need for implementation of the United Nations Programme of Advisory Services.

The output was a set of recommendations and principles entitled the *Paris Principles,* which were adopted and acclaimed by the Human Rights Commission the following year.[23]

The Paris Principles focus on three general areas: i) the *competence and responsibilities* of national institutions, concerning their legislative foundation as well as their primary tasks, ii) the *composition* of national institutions *and the guarantees of independence and pluralism,* listing criteria for appointment designed to ensure plurality of representation as well as financial independence; and iii) the *methods of operation* of national institutions including the mandate to take up matters as well as their cooperation with civil society. Finally, a specific section was added iv) relating particularly to those institutions with *quasi-judicial*[24] competence, i.e. the competence to hear, transmit and settle individual complaints.

---

Secretary Generals' reports, is also voiced; Commission on Human Rights Resolution 1988/72 of 10 March 1988 and later resolutions by the General Assembly and the Commission.

20  See Human Rights Commission Resolutions 1989/52 of 7 March 1989 and 1991/27 of 5 March 1991.

21  Since the Vienna Conference in 1993 a number of regional and international workshops of human rights institutions and ombudsmen have taken place. Examples hereof are the First and Second European meetings of National Institutions (Strasbourg, 1994; Copenhagen, 1997); the First and Second Conferences of African National Human Rights Institutions (Cameroon, 1996; South Africa, 1998); the First and Second Asia-Pacific Regional Workshops (Australia, 1996; New Delhi, 1997); Human Dimension Seminar on Ombudsman and National Institutions (Poland, 1998); the Third International Workshop on Ombudsman and National Human Rights Institutions (Latvia, 1997); the First Meeting of Mediterranean National Institutions (Marrakesh, 1998), and the Second, Third and Fourth International Workshops of National Human Rights Institutions (Tunis, 1993; Manila, 1995; Mexico, 1997).

22  About 35 countries with an almost equal distribution between developed and developing countries were represented. The dominance of European and Latin American countries is striking, with only five Asia-Pacific countries (Australia, New Zealand, Japan, Philippines and Thailand) present as well as five from Sub-Saharan Africa (Benin, Uganda, Senegal, Togo and Namibia). The seminar had observers from the European Court as well as from the Inter-American Court and Commission, but none from the African Commission on Human and Peoples Rights.

23  Human Rights Commission Resolution 1992/54 of 3 March 1992. The paper on 'Human Rights Commissions' (see note 2 above) was a significant contribution to the development of the Principles as well as to later United Nations initiatives in the field.

24  The headline in the original Paris Principles, contained in the original report of the workshop (E/CN.4/1992/43), reads quasi-*jurisdictional* rather than quasi-*judicial*. This creates a sense that

8

The Commission on Human Rights decided to publish the proceedings, and the UN Handbook 1995 is a result hereof.

The process of formulation and elaboration of the concept of national human rights institution did not stop with the formulation of the Paris Principles; They became the starting point for further exploration and dialogue at the United Nations as well as various regional levels. One example is the transmission of the Principles to the Preparatory Committee for the World Conference on Human Rights in Vienna for consideration, leading to a stressing of the constructive role to be played by national institutions at the Vienna Declaration and Programme of Action (art. 36).[25] The Vienna conference in 1993 as well as the United Nations Commission on Human Rights in 1995 requested the Secretary General to accord high priority to requests from member states for assistance in establishing and strengthening national institutions.[26] The High Commissioner for Human Rights soon thereafter prioritised the strengthening of national institutions through technical assistance.[27]

Finally, the United Nations Secretary General and the Commission on Human Rights continued to focus on the subject, resulting in a number of reports and annual resolutions. In later years, the main themes have been cooperation between the various institutions through the establishment of a Coordinating Committee as well as with the United Nations in relation to technical cooperation.[28] The continuing work to enable the national institutions to represent themselves in international fora has moved forward in recent years, reaching a point where the national human rights

---

something went amiss in the process, given that the contents of the section in the Paris Principles correspond to the definition of quasi-judicial, in "describing a function that resembles the judicial function in that it involves deciding a dispute and ascertaining the facts and any relevant law, but differs in that it depends ultimately on the exercise on an executive discretion rather than in the application of the law" (*The Concise Dictionary of Law*, Oxford University Press, 1986). This would have been consistent with the text in the report which speaks solely of "quasi-judicial powers" (table of contents and sec. 188-200) and of "jurisdiction" - but no reference is found to the term "quasi-jurisdictional". The power of precedence, however, is strong, since the headline is uncritically reproduced in different versions of the Principles, as found both in the a Annex to Human Rights Commission Resolution 1992/54 of 3 March 1992 affirming the Paris Principles, in the 1995 United Nations Handbook and in the United Nations Fact Sheet No. 19 on National Institutions for the Promotion and Protection of Human Rights from 1993.

[25] See para. 18, 36, 74 including section C, Co-operation, Development and Strengthening Human Rights in the Vienna Declaration and Programme of Action, 1993.

[26] Commission on Human Rights Resolution 1997/40. *National Human Rights Commissions - National and International Perspectives*. Prepared for the Commonwealth Secretariat by the Special Adviser to the United Nations High Commissioner for Human Rights on National Institutions, Brian Burdekin, undated, p. 8.

[27] *Ibid.* The Office focuses on holding regional seminars and giving advice on national establishment. A Special Adviser to the High Commissioner of Human Rights gives technical assistance to governments on draft legislation, institutional set-up and counselling of national institutions, including ombudsmen. Funding is provided by the UN Voluntary Fund. In 1997, the total expenditures of the Fund were USD 5.6 mn. on these activities. ECOSOC E/CN.4/1998/92. March 1998.

[28] Reports of the Secretary General E/CN.4/1995/48, E/CN.4/1996/48, E/CN.4/1997/41 and E/CN.4/1998/47, and resolutions from the UN Human Rights Commission 1995/50, 1996/50, 1997/40 and 1998/55.

9

institutions are given the opportunity to speak independently at the sessions of the United Nations bodies.[29]

## IMPLEMENTATION OF THE PARIS PRINCIPLES

Between 1948 and 1990 only a few national institutions embody the later Paris Principles were established. The first ones were established in France (1948[30]), New Zealand (1978), Canada (1978), Australia (1981, re-established in 1986), the Philippines (1987) and Denmark (1987). In addition, a number of government commissions were established in various countries. After the adoption of the Paris Principles in 1991 and the Vienna Declaration in 1993, making national institutions the focal point for implementation of human rights standards, such national institutions have mushroomed.

In the 1990s broadly mandated national institutions on the African continent have been set up in Cameroon (1991), Chad (1994) Ghana (1993), Nigeria (1996), Senegal (1997), South Africa (1995), Uganda (1996) and Zambia (1997).[31] Three have been established in the Asia-Pacific region: India (1993), Indonesia (1994) and Sri Lanka (1997). In the American region, at least two national institutions have been set up in Mexico (1990) and Costa Rica (1993), respectively. In Europe, one national institution has been established in Latvia (1995). Similar broadly mandated institutions have been set up in CIS countries[32] such as Kazakstan (1996) and Georgia (1997). In addition, plans to establish national institutions are evolving in Bangladesh, Ethiopia, the Federal Republic of Germany, Fiji, Ireland, Kyrgyzstan, Liberia, Malawi, Mongolia, Nepal, Pakistan, Papua New Guinea, Rwanda, Tanzania, Thailand and Uzbekistan.

In the following discussion the various sections of the Paris Principles will be analysed with examples of their implementation by some of these national institutions.

### Independence and capacity

The Paris Principles state that national institutions should be vested with competence, founded on a legislative or constitutional basis and be given as broad a mandate as possible. The Principles address the question of composition, in the form of guarantees of pluralism in representation and composition, fixed terms of mandate for its members and of a suitable infrastructure with staff and premises. In addition, the

---

[29]  See UN Human Rights Commission 1998 Resolution 1998/55 and report of the Secretary-General concerning the Participation of National Institutions in UN meetings E7CN.4/1998/47.

[30]  The French Commission was established as a consultative body to the Government by initiative of René Cassin, judicial adviser of Général de Gaulle. In 1984 the Commission was reactivated and in 1993 the Commission achieved 'independent' status by constitutional decree. See the Annual Report, République Francaise, Premier Ministre, Commission Nationale Consultative des Droits de L'Homme, 1997.

[31]  According to "Report of the chairman of the Co-ordinating Committee of African National Institutions for the Second Conference of African National Institutions", by Dr. Solomon Nfor Gwei, Durban, South Africa, 1-3 July 1998 there are about 20 African national institutions.

[32]  Commonwealth of Independent States of the former Soviet Union.

national human rights institutions should be ensured guaranteed independence of decision-makers by having their own budget and not be subjected to financial restraints. Finally, the Principles address the methods of operation.

These requirements serve two purposes; to guarantee the independent functioning of national institutions and to limit their vulnerability to undue pressure or coercion from outside interests, typically the government; and to ensure the capacity and the effectiveness of the institutions.

## Legal foundation

According to the Paris Principles, one of the most critical criteria for establishing national institutions is that the institutions "shall be given as broad a mandate as possible, which shall be clearly set forth in a constitutional or legislative text, specifying its composition and its sphere of competence."[33] The broadly mandated national institutions reviewed here have been established in three ways: i) by constitution or constitutional amendment; ii) by law or act of parliament; or iii) by presidential decree.

The establishment of national institutions within the constitution would normally be the most powerful option because the procedural requirements for changing constitutions in many countries are far stricter than requirements for changes of laws. National institutions established by constitution (in addition often also by law) are mainly found in countries which have recently undergone constitutional reforms and which have been marked by grave human rights violations in the past.[34] In the 1980s a national institution was established by the Constitution in the Philippines.[35] In the 1990s, national institutions have been established by constitution in Ghana, Georgia, South Africa, Uganda and Zambia. One is in the process of being established in Malawi.

The majority of national institutions are established by law or act of parliament in countries such as Australia, Benin, Canada, Chad, Denmark, India, Latvia, Mexico,[36] New Zealand, Senegal, Sri Lanka and Togo. Further, legislation to establish national institutions has been adopted in Nepal, Rwanda and Uzbekistan.

National institutions established by presidential decree are found in countries such as Cameroon, France, Indonesia, Kazakstan and Nigeria. They are in the pipeline in Kyrgyzstan. Even though they may live up to the Paris Principles,[37] the fact that these

---

[33]  UN Handbook, Annex, 1992/54.

[34]  Establishment by constitution also depends on traditions for changing and amending constitutions. In Denmark, for example, the Parliament is very hesitant to make constitutional changes. The Constitution was adopted in 1849 and amended most recently in 1953.

[35]  Executive Order no. 163 of 5 May 1987, art. XIII section 17 of the Constitution of the Philippines.

[36]  Despite the fact that the Mexican Commission is established as a legally independent entity, it is structurally located as a department in the Ministry of Interior. *Human Rights Commissions*, Workshop in Paris, Brian Burdekin, 1991, p. 129. See also the "Law on the National Commission for Human Rights" (23 June 1992), temporary articles, art. 4, which states "[...] the national commission for human rights [...] is a semi-autonomous agency of the Ministry of Interior."

[37]  In the *UN Handbook on the Establishment and Strengthening of National Institutions*, 1995, para. 39, the legal conditions for establishment includes the wording 'by law or decree'.

11

institutions have not been established by act of parliament may make them less than fully supported by a majority in parliament, and thus less independent of the executive. However, there is no evidence that these institutions are less independent than institutions established by parliament. There are also indications that establishment by decree in Kazakstan and Kyrgyzstan has been the only feasible political option because the parliaments were thought not to approve the establishment of this type of institution.[38]

One of the early commissions illustrates the strengths and weaknesses of what was then characterized as a national institution. In the case of *El Salvador*, the Commission has been characterized as "not addressing what is now the main human rights issues [e.g. unlawful disappearances and death squads] in El Salvador, but, within the limited sphere in which it works, for being a constructive force."[39] The functions of the Commission have been contradictory. "Since February of 1984, the Commission staff has had a regular program of visits to prisons and detention facilities, and has been increasingly successful in locating detainees and prompting their transfer to courts or their release ... While there is marked improvement in the performance ... other actions are less useful ... [such as] ... the misleading nature of its public statements."[40] A similar pattern seems to be developing in *Nigeria* where many political prisoners have been released recently.[41] The newly established Commission has surprised observers[42] by carrying out serious training activities, initiating studies and a comprehensive plan of action for 1998, even though it can still be regarded as an institution depending on political goodwill as reflected in its relatively restrained criticism of the governments human rights performance.[43] In *Indonesia*, the priorities given in the plan of action of 1998 to ratify international conventions should be noted. Whereas the International Covenant on Economic, Social and Cultural rights, and the conventions against torture, elimination of discrimination, etc, are to be ratified in year one to four, the Covenant on Civil and Political Rights is to be ratified in year five. It follows in the plan of action that research into and harmonization of domestic laws in line with the ratified conventions will be carried out. The plan of action can be analysed in light of the fact that there still are political prisoners in Indonesia,[44] and that the one thousand man Peoples

---

[38] Lis Dhundale and Peter Vedel Kessing, *Report of missions to Kazakstan and Kyrgyzstan,* Danish Centre for Human Rights, OSCE/ODHIR, 1998.

[39] The Americas Watch Committee, El Salvador reports, January, 1984, August, 1984, March, 1985, quoted in the Human Rights Internet/Directory. 15.004. For an elaboration of the human rights violations in El Salvador, see Human Rights Watch Americas: *El Salvador – Darkening Horizons: Human Rights on the Eve of the March 1994 Elections,* vol VI, no 4, March 1994.

[40] *Ibid.*

[41] Amnesty International, Press Release, 4 June, 1998.

[42] "Making human rights treaty obligations a reality at the national level: Identifying and working with new actors and partners", Anne Gallagher in Alston and Crawford (eds.), *The Future of the United Nations Human Rights Treaty System* (forthcoming).

[43] Human Rights Newsletter, vol 1, No 3, 1998; National Plan for 1998; *Briefs on the National Human Rights Commission of Nigeria; Nigerian Human Rights Commission.* Training Workshop for Lower Court Judges in Cooperation with Civil Liberties Organisation and The Danish Centre for Human Rights, 1998.

[44] Amnesty International, Press Release, 4 June 1998.

Advisory Council does not support political reforms.[45] The order of priority, however, shows that the Indonesian military government apparently does pay attention to the question of ratification and implementation of human rights law.[46]

## Composition

### Appointment and dismissals of leading members

The Paris Principles deal with criteria for the appointment of leading members in a general way. They state that "in order to ensure a stable mandate for the members of the institution, without which there can be no real independence, their appointment shall be effected by an official act which shall establish the specific duration of the mandate".[47] However, more specific criteria for appointment are crucial in guaranteeing the independence in decision-making procedures, the professional level of commissioners and staff, and, not least, public credibility. The terms of appointment should include definition of "method of appointment, criteria for appointment such as nationality, profession and qualifications, duration of appointment, whether members can be reappointed, who may dismiss members and for what reasons, privileges and immunities".[48]

Laws and statutes of national institutions examined deal with the above sets of conditions and criteria in different ways. They can be divided into three models: 1) Objective appointment criteria combined with appointment by president or parliament in which appointments depend on professional qualifications (academic degree, judge, etc) and institutional affiliation (e.g. courts, universities, NGOs, etc); 2) Objective appointment criteria in which leading members are appointed by the institutions they represent and not by president or parliament, and 3) absent or weak objective appointment criteria combined with appointment by president or parliament.

With regard to the first model, the *Indian National Human Rights Commission* is probably applying the most elaborate and strict criteria. Although commissioners are appointed by the President, the three leading members of the Commission are recruited from the highest levels of the judiciary, and two members are to be knowledgeable of human rights. For certain functions of the commission, the chairpersons of the national commissions for minorities, the scheduled castes and

---

[45]   This Council is appointed under the governance of the former dictator Suharto and includes representatives of the military. *Politiken*, Newspaper, 12 and 18 November, 1998.

[46]   The President's recent announcement accepting the Commission's request to replace twelve members without the president's approval supports this argument. There are indications that the military government's attention to human rights is due to pressure from intergovernmental bodies such as United Nations and the European Union, and embassies located in the country. *The Indonesian National Plan of Action on Human Rights*, 1998-2003, June 1998; *Report from Conference about human rights*, European Union, Indonesia, Diego Bang, the Danish Centre for Human Rights, October, 1998, pp. 28-29.

[47]   UN Handbook, para. 78 and 79. In this aspect the UN Handbook strengthens the criteria agreed upon in the Paris Principles.

[48]   *Ibid.*

13

tribes, and women's affairs shall be members.[49] A commissioner may be removed from office if he "engages during his term of office in any paid employment outside the duties of his office."[50] In addition, "on ceasing to hold office, a chairperson or a member shall be ineligible for further employment under the governments of India."[51] The strict conditions of employment ensure the accountability of the commissioners towards the public, the full time engagement in work *inside* and not *outside* the commission[52] and that commissioners can neither be corrupted by nor be dependent on the public sector. In this respect the Indian Commission goes beyond the requirements of the Paris Principles. A number of countries such as Ghana, Uganda and Nigeria apply similar criteria but not to the same extent as found in the mandate of the Indian Commission.

Denmark seems to be the only country applying the second model. At the *Danish Centre for Human Rights*, half of the Board members are appointed directly by institutions with the right to a seat on the Board. The other half is appointed by a Council consisting of a wide range of non-governmental organisations, representatives of all political parties and individuals with specific knowledge and commitment in the field. In practice, the Board is composed of six university representatives, a member of the bar association, three members representing non-governmental organisations and two members of parliament.[53] The chairperson is elected among the twelve members. The centre has no commissioner but a Director who represents the centre publicly.

The third model is applied in most countries reviewed. According to the mandates, only few national institutions apply appointment criteria that go beyond requiring that the parliament, president or governor must pay regard to "their personal attributes ... and having knowledge of or experience in the different aspects of matters likely to come before the Commission"[54] or "knowledge of human rights". Despite this, well established national institutions seem, in practice, to recruit members according to informal professional criteria.

In 1982, the responsible authority for the decision-making and priority setting procedures of the *El Salvadorian Commission* was noted as having had a direct involvement in human rights abuses. While the "Commission was headed by a lawyer who seemed sincere about human rights, ... the governments representative on the Commission was head of the National Police, which has committed many of the most serious violations."[55] Such a composition must be said to be in contradiction with the later standards. In the 1980s, in *Guatemala*, a multi-party composition model was

---

[49]   Too strict criteria for professional background required for recruitment has a resource aspect. The fact that three commissioners mustbe former judges is hindering the establishment of national institutions in some Indian states because of the non-availability of judges. National Human Rights Commission, India, *Annual Report 1996-97*, p. 57. Similarly, in many developing countries there is a tremendous lack of jurists and judges.

[50]   The Protection of Human Rights Act, National Human Rights Commission, India, 1993.

[51]   *Ibid.*

[52]   A number of commissions allow for academic work only outside the institution.

[53]   Mandate of the Danish Centre for Human Rights, 1987, revised in 1998.

[54]   New Zealand, Human Rights Commission Act, 1977.

[55]   Americas Watch Committee, El Salvador report, 1982.

established which "appears to have politicized the Commission, and reduced its effectiveness".[56] With the adoption of the Paris Principles, these two Commissions would probably not qualify as national institutions.

However, as late as in the 1990s, institutions have been established which do not apply any professional or institutional criteria for appointment of leading members. One example is the *Latvian National Human Rights Office* where the director shall be appointed by the parliament upon recommendation of the Cabinet of Ministers. The statutes also read "The Director may be discharged ... in the event he/she is elected to leadership of a political party or its auditing structure."[57] The present Director has been appointed *from* members of the parliament. Even though a politically appointed Director can be - and seem to be – qualified for the position, it follows from this lack of objective appointment procedures, combined with a lack of demand for political neutrality, that the risk of politicisation of the position becomes high. This allegation in fact can be deduced from the change in leadership of the Latvian National Human Rights Office that led to a change in the interpretation of the right to citizenship. In its Activity Report of the first quarter of 1998, it reads that "the Office especially supports granting of citizenship to those children born in Latvia whose parents are permanent residents, because the rights of children to citizenship are absolute ... ." In the later Activity Report issued after the appointment of the present Director, the Latvian Government is advised to "delete the norm providing for citizenship for all children ... at birth." It further reads: "The UN Convention on Children's Rights provides that a child is entitled to citizenship at birth. This norm does not ... provide that a child should be granted citizenship immediately after birth ... ."[58]

The Paris Principles do not specify criteria for dismissals of leading members, but principles for dismissals have been elaborated on in the UN Handbook.[59] In the mandates of almost all the national institutions reviewed these criteria have been applied. In Denmark, where these principle are not formulated in the statutes of the Centre, the principles protecting government officials apply.

*Pluralistic reflection of society*

In order to ensure their independence, national institutions shall in their composition "ensure the pluralist representation of the social forces"[60] actively engaged in the promotion and protection of human rights, by ensuring cooperation with, or the presence of, wide sections of civil society. This includes non-governmental organisations, trade unions, social and professional organisations as well as those with a particular focus on vulnerable groups, representatives of "trends in philosophical or

---

[56]  Amnesty International Report, *Human Rights Violations Under the Civilian Government*, 1989.
[57]  Law on the Latvian National Human Rights Office, 1995.
[58]  Activity Report/Newsletter, January-March, 1998; p. 6; Activity Report, April-June,1998, pp. 2 and 4.
[59]  UN Handbook, sec. 80, 1995.
[60]  Paris Principles, UN Handbook, 1995.

religious thought",[61] universities and qualified experts. To these groups the Paris Principles add representatives of parliaments as well as of government departments, the latter, however, only in an advisory capacity in order not to endanger the independence of the institution. The composition of national institutions should be a reflection of its society, and accordingly its members should reflect diversity in sex, ethnic origin, language and political affiliation as appropriate.

The statutes of the majority of institutions reviewed ensures pluralistic representation in two ways. One model, applied in Australia, India and New Zealand, is to appoint commissioners representing specific vulnerable groups such as minorities and women. Another model, applied in Denmark and France, ensures that non-governmental organisations in the governing bodies represent vulnerable groups in society. Neither of the models applied ensure representation of all major vulnerable groups in society. This, however, would realistically speaking not be possible in any case without creating an unmanageably large governing body.

**Financial autonomy and capacity**

According to the Paris Principles, a key factor securing independence and accountability is the provision of 'adequate funding', e.g. that the institutions must be able to function independently according to their aims without any state interference or 'financial control which might affect its independence.[62] This condition poses two questions. The first, is whether the funding is secured in such a way that political discussion of the priorities set by the members of national institutions can be avoided – otherwise the consequence could be that the politicians or responsible ministries set the priorities instead of the national institution themselves. The second, is whether the funding is sufficient to secure a high level of activity and professionalism.

All national institutions examined are in principle financed by the state, but, many of them are also subsidised by donor funding. This is done in some countries by establishing a trust fund independent of the state's interests. The majority are funded directly by the finance act of the parliament, while others have funds allocated by a ministry approving the proposed budget. Funding through the parliament is believed to give the highest degree of independence in decision-making whereas funding through a ministry creates room for interference by political interests.

In the second and third annual reports of the *Commission on Human Rights and Administrative Justice, Ghana*, the Commission raised the view that it could only be fully independent if it could submit its budget directly to the parliament instead of to the Ministry of Finance and Planning, which can cut the budget "after a lengthy and cumbersome vetting process undermining the Commission's independence as provided for in article 222 of the Constitution".[63] The South African Human Rights Commission criticises the allocation of funding for the Commission by the Ministry of Justice. It argues that the budget of the Commission is given a lower priority than

---

[61]  *Ibid.*
[62]  E/1992/22. General Assembly Resolution 48/134, 20 December, 1993.
[63]  Second and Third Annual Reports, Commission on Human Rights and Administrative Justice – Ghana, 1995 and 1996.

other activities of the Ministry and concludes that funding for the Commission should be granted directly by the Parliament.[64]

The question of resources is closely connected to the question of whether the institutions have sufficient staff members. Figures reveal that national institutions are differently staffed in total numbers. In *Australia*, there has been a substantial decrease in staff due to a reduction of about 40 percent of the Commission's budget. Today there are about 100 staff members plus eight staff in regional offices.[65] The population figure is 18.2 million. In *Ghana*, there are about 450 staff members and 38 district offices in ten regional capitals.[66] There are 17.5 million inhabitants in the country. The *Indian* National Human Rights Commission has 300 employees and seven state commissions. The population figure is 1 billion inhabitants. The *Latvian* Human Rights Office has one office and about ten staff members. There are 2.5 million inhabitants in the country. In *South Africa*, there are about 60 staff members, one national and two regional offices. For the financial year 1998/99, the South African Human Rights Commission has been granted funding to establish six regional offices.[67] There are 49 million inhabitants in the country. The *New Zealand* Commission has 42 staff members and six commissioners in a country of 3,5 million people.[68] The *Ugandan* Commission has 1 office and about 30 staff members. There are plans to establish regional offices if funding is provided. There are 20 million inhabitants in the country. The *French* Commission has one office, four full time staff members and one part time president in a country with 58 million inhabitants. The *Danish* Centre for Human Rights has 65 staff members, a board of twelve members and one office in a country of five million people. The last two institutions are not handling complaints and both focus on human rights nationally as well as internationally.[69]

## Mandate

### Promotion

Although there might be slight differences in the wording of the legal foundations of the national institutions, they all have very similar mandates in line with the Paris

---

[64] B. Pityana., *National Institutions at work: The case of the South African Human Rights Commission*, British Council Seminar, Belfast, May 1998.

[65] Human Rights and Equal Opportunity Commission, Australia, *Annual Report 1997-98*, pp. 22, 160 and 167.

[66] Annual Report, 1996, Ghana.

[67] The Commission has nine commissioners (five full time, two vacancies and two part time) while there seems to be a lack of staff. In this context it might be relevant to examine the distribution of resources between commissioners and staff. This discussion has taken place in Ghana, where, for lack of resources, the Consultative Assembly decided in 1992 to fuse the then existing ombudsman institution into the now established national institution. *Working plan of the SAHRC 1998/99*, The Commission on Human Rights and Administrative Justice in Ghana, Emile Francis Short, West African Human Rights Forum, Dakar 16-18 April, 1998.

[68] *Annual Report 1997*, New Zealand, p. 7.

[69] The population figures are from the *World Fact Book*, 1997. USA Central Intelligence Agency, Washington DC, http://ciapubs.bilkent.edu.tr/publications/factbook.

Principles. They are usually commissioned to carry out promotion, information, education, documentation and research or analyses on human rights. They must promote ratification of international instruments, review national legislation's compliance with international law, report or make recommendations to governments or parliaments on legal changes or policy issues and cooperate with United Nations and regional agencies, including assisting governments in drafting state reports or themselves draft the so-called 'shadow reports' that serve to counter balance government reports to the United Nations system.[70]

*Protection*

The main difference between the mandates of national institutions is whether or not they are mandated to handle individual complaints. To the generally applicable Paris Principles is added a section on institutions with quasi-judicial competence. The findings at the Paris Workshop indicate that while such functions of protection would be appropriate in some states, it would not be the case in others, where this power was vested in other national bodies. In practice, only a few national institutions lack this competence (the Danish and the French).

The issue is the reverse in European countries that have not established broadly mandated national institutions. Most of these countries have established ombudsmen and similar bodies to handle individual complaints but do not have a broadly based national institution to monitor and review human rights issues in a strategic and structured way.

The review reveals major differences in the power of national institutions to handle individual complaints. As a minimum national institutions handling complaints are vested with the rights of *investigation, conducting hearings, settling of disputes, conciliation* and the right of deciding *not to proceed* with a complaint. These powers are found in combination with other powers in the mandate of various national institutions. They can include the entitlement to *request any relevant documentation* from state agencies, to *summon witnesses*, to *inspect private or public offices*, to *inspect police detentions, prisons and other institutions restricting freedom of movement* such as mental hospitals and to *investigate the acts of state agencies* such as the police and the army.

Whether national institutions can initiate investigation or inspection on their *own initiative* or if a *formal complaint must be lodged* varies. The investigative power might be compared to that of the police or the prosecution. One reason to justify the vesting of such extensive powers with national institutions is probably the need to have an independent investigative body to examine violations committed by the institutions that normally carry out this function such as the police and the prosecution.

Complaints-handling national institutions vested with all or part of the above listed powers normally do *not have the judicially binding power of the courts to enforce*

---

[70]  See Anne Gallagher, *op. cit.*, who rightly points out that "the functions commonly assigned to human rights institutions – clearly indicate the links which exist – or should exist – between these bodies and the human rights treaty system."

their recommendations. They can recommend settlements of disputes or make decisions on complaints that are, however, not legally binding on the involved parties or the government. This is the case for the majority of national institutions, including Australia, Canada, Ghana, India, Latvia, Mexico, New Zealand and South Africa.

The advantage of this quasi-judicial mode of complaints-handling is that the procedures are less time consuming, more flexible, informal, non-confrontational, inexpensive and thus more accessible to vulnerable groups, than the courts.[71] Furthermore, "such power of a national institution may discourage acts or practices inimical to the enjoyment of human rights".[72] However, as the New Zealand Human Rights Commission pointed out in its Annual Report, "dealing with complaints can only be a stop-gap measure. It is like treating the symptoms of a disease rather than eradicating the cause."[73]

The power of the quasi-judicial bodies in general does not overlap with those of the courts. The majority of the complaints handling national institutions are vested with the power to *refer complaints to alternate redress such as complaints tribunals or courts*. In these cases, the recommendations of these institutions can be very strongly enforced. This has been experienced in *Ghana* where the former Ombudsman did not have the power of enforcement of his decisions, and the result was that his decisions were often neglected.[74] The later established Commission on Human Rights and Administrative Justice has been vested with this power and can reportedly enforce its decisions in the majority of cases. Since 1993, the commission has only referred thirteen cases to court action.[75] In *India*, the National Human Rights Commission uses this power to enforce decisions that state governments have not consented to carry out. The Commission reports that in 1996-97 there was only one such case, in Tamil Nadu. The case "related to the payment of compensation to a victim of police atrocities. The Commission has sought the intervention of the appropriate Court to have its recommendations implemented by the State Government."[76]

Other powers vested in national institutions are the right of issuing *administrative fines* to witnesses failing to appear before a hearing (Latvia), and the right to recommend *compensation* to victims or members of his family (Australia, Canada, Ghana, India, New Zealand, Nigeria, Phillippines, South Africa and Uganda). In India, this power does not extend to recommending compensation to settle grievances

---

[71] Brian Burdekin, Human Rights Commission, Workshop in Paris, 1991, p. 120; E.V.O. Dankwa, *Promotion of Human Rights and National Institutions, An Example from Ghana*, July-September, 1997.

[72] Brian Burdekin, *National Human Rights Commissions - National and International Perspectives*. Prepared for the Commonwealth Secretariat by the Special Adviser to the United Nations High Commissioner for Human Rights on National Institutions, undated, unpublished, p. 3.

[73] *Annual Report of the Human Rights Commission for the year ended 31 March 1979*, New Zealand, p. 3.

[74] In Denmark, as in other European countries, the power of the ombudsman is only advisory. However, the customary practice of the parliament and other state institutions is to follow the recommendations of the ombudsman.

[75] Emile Francis Short, *The Commission on Human Rights and Administrative Justice in Ghana*, April, 1998.

[76] National Human Rights Commission, India, *Annual Report 1996-97*, p. 60.

brought under the complaint.[77] An example is a complaint lodged with the Indian National Human Rights Commission by the family of an inmate who died in police custody. The Commission found that the inmate had been subject to torture by the police only few hours before he committed suicide. On the basis of its recommendations, the family of the deceased was paid compensation of Rs. 100,000 and the Home Department, of the Government of Kerala asked the Director General of the police to register a case against the police officers responsible for torturing the deceased.[78]

At least two national institutions are vested with the power, however limited, of a civil court. The *Indian National Human Rights Commission* while inquiring into complaints has the powers of a civil court trying a suit under the Code of Civil Procedure.[79] The power mainly concerns omission to answer inquiries, produce documents and sign statements requested by the Commission, against which the Commission can take steps to prosecute persons refusing to cooperate by bringing the case to the Magistrate.[80] The *Ugandan Human Rights Commission* may under section 53(2) of the Constitution, in case of infringement of human rights, order the release of a detained person, payment of compensation or any other legal remedy or redress. Section 53(3) provides that orders made by the Commission can be appealed to the High Court.[81]

As a last resort, the most powerful tool of enforcing human rights standards is a court decision. A small number of national institutions can *intervene in court proceedings* (Australia, Canada, India). In 1990, the Australian Commission formally resolved to seek leave to intervene in one case only. "In this case, the Commission presented oral submissions and assisted the court in the role of *amicus curiae*, or 'friend of the Court'. ... The parents of a young girl with an intellectual disability had applied to the Court for appropriate orders relating to the authorisation of surgery for the sterilisation of the child."[82] However, in 1997 and 1998 the Australian Government announced the Human Rights Legislation Amendment Bill (one and two), intending to change the legislation governing the Commission. One of the proposed changes is to make the Commission's power to intervene in court proceedings subject to approval by the Attorney-General. The Commission responded to this proposal by presenting "a submission to the Senate Legal and Constitutional Legislation Committee which argues that the removal of the Commission's power to intervene in proceedings before the Courts and the failure to provide transitional provisions compromise the Commission's independence and integrity."[83] The draft

---

[77]  Letter from Justice V.S. Malimath, Member of the Indian National Human Rights Commission, 28 December 1998.
[78]  Indian National Human Rights Commission, *Annual Report 1996-97*.
[79]  The Protection of Human Rights Act, National Human Rights Commission, India,1993, chapter III, art. 13, 1.
[80]  Letter from Justice V.S. Malimath, *Annual Report 1996-97*.
[81]  Ugandan Constitution, 1995, section 53(2) and 53(3).
[82]  Human Rights and Equal Opportunity Commission, Australia, *Annual Report 1989-90*, p. 35.
[83]  Human Rights and Equal Opportunity Commission, Australia, *Annual Report 1997-98*, pp. 24, 70 and 71.

also contains a proposal for an extension of the power of the Commission by suggesting the creation of the role of amicus curiae for all commissioners in proceedings under the amended legislation that are before the Federal Court.[84] In 1996-97, the Indian Commission asked for permission to intervene in court proceedings in a case on alleged abduction and killing of an advocate by security forces. "The High Court of Jammu and Kashmir permitted the Commission to intervene in the pending proceedings and, since then, the Commission has placed the report of its team before the High Court ... The case is pending."[85]

In a few countries, tribunals are established in relation to national institutions. In Canada and New Zealand, the Human Rights Act's provide for the establishment of Human Rights or Equal Opportunity Tribunals that work closely with the commissions.[86] In *Canada* the Canadian human rights tribunals and courts ordered in 1993 a number of civil organisations to stop making available to the general public recorded hate messages concerning "recent immigrants, jews, lesbians and gay men. When some of those responsible refused to comply with a court order, they were sent to jail."[87] Their imprisonment was enacted by the court following from their lack of compliance with a decision by the Tribunal which has the force of a court order. Whether the goal of stopping the activities of such groups has been achieved can, however, be questioned. Reportedly, "after a lengthy proceeding initiated by the Commission, one of these groups announced the closure of its Toronto-based telephone hotline. It has, however, announced its intention to utilize the Internet to continue disseminating its message."[88]

## EXAMPLES OF SPECIFIC HUMAN RIGHTS FOCUS

The focus of national institutions varies to some degree. Concentration on civil and political rights and the rule of law is found in all countries examined. Specific focus on economic, social and cultural rights is only clearly expressed in the mandate of a few national institutions such as the Indian, Ghanaian and South African commissions. A particularly strong focus on non-discrimination, equal opportunities and vulnerable groups' rights, reflected in the legislation of the institutions, is found in countries with a history of institutionalised discrimination or systems of inequity (Australia, Canada, India, and New Zealand).

While the concrete outputs of the activities of national institutions can be easily verified, the long term achievements and impact on state, laws and society are difficult to assess because numerous other factors influence the developments in this field. In the following, we give examples of outputs and results achieved by various national institutions, structured according to categories of human rights. This exercise

---

[84]  *Ibid*, p. 71.
[85]  National Human Rights Commission, India, *Annual Report 1996-97*, p. 80.
[86]  The Canadian Human Rights Act , RSC., 1985, c. H-6, June 1998, art. 48 (1) and The New Zealand Human Rights Act 1993.
[87]  Human Rights and the Canadian Human Rights Commission, *Equality*, 1996, p. 17; *Annual Report 1997*, p. 13.
[88]  *Ibid*, p. 13.

aims at indicating differences in performance that can partly be derived from differences in the mandate and institutional framework. It does not, however, pretend to be exhaustive or conclusive.

### *Examples of focus on non-discrimination and equal opportunity*

National institutions in Australia, Canada and New Zealand focus particularly on non-discrimination, equal opportunity rights and vulnerable groups such as indigenous peoples. While the Commissions of Australia and New Zealand rely on international law, the Canadian Commission relies on domestic legislation.[89] The powers of the Australian Commission take their point of departure in the Racial Discrimination Act 1975, the Sex Discrimination Act 1984, the Human Rights and Equal Opportunity Commission Act 1986 and the Disability Discrimination Act 1992. In the jurisdiction of the Australian Commission, nineteen grounds for resolving complaints of discrimination in employment and occupation are listed.[90] The powers of the New Zealand Commission are defined in the Human Rights Act 1993 listing grounds for unlawful discrimination. In addition, it provides for positive measures that can be taken to ensure equality.[91] In the Canadian legislation, grounds for discrimination are more explicitly spelled out than the formulations in most international instruments. Types discrimination, listed in international standards, are sometimes excluded. However, such clear-cut legislation establishes a precise field of competence of complaints handling national institutions by which precedence in individual and principal cases can be established. Supported by a strong institutional framework, this will eventually result in standard setting and thus make an impact on state and society.

In the Canadian Human Rights Act, by which the *Canadian Human Rights Commission* is established, the prohibited grounds for discrimination are very clearly defined. They include, beyond grounds normally defined in international human rights law, 'age', 'sexual orientation', 'marital status', 'family status' and 'disability'. However, 'language', 'political or other opinion', 'social origin', 'property' and 'birth' (as found for instance in article 2.1 of the Universal Declaration and article 2.1 in the International Covenant of Economic, Social and Cultural Rights) are not included in this Act.[92] Most of these rights (except 'property' and 'birth') are, however, prohibited grounds in a number of or in all the ten provinces and two territories depending on the specific issue dealt with. There are, in other words, differences between those grounds for discrimination prohibited explicitly in relation to different areas covered and the standard setting in the provinces. 'Language' is, for example, accepted as a prohibited ground for discrimination in employment in two provinces, whereas disability is a prohibited ground in general.[93]

---

89 The Canadian Human Rights Act, R.S. C., 1985, c. H-6. June 1998 is by one author described as 'purely domestic legislation' but with expressed clear recognition of the relevance of international instruments. Brian Burdekin, *Human Rights Commissions*, Workshop in Paris, 1991, p. 114.

90 Human Rights and Equal Opportunity Commission, Australia, *Annual Report 1989-90*, p. 29.

91 Section 73 of the Human Rights Act 1993 provides measures to ensure equality.

92 Canadian Human Rights Act, RS.Co, 1985, c. H-6. June, 1998.

93 In the jurisdiction of the Australian Commission, nineteen grounds for resolving complaints of discrimination in employment and occupation are outlined. Human Rights and Equal Opportunity

In 1997, the Canadian Commission completed 2,025 complaints. Some 300 were referred to alternate redress mechanisms, 200 were settled, some with the assistance of a conciliator, and 24 complaints were referred to a hearing before the Canadian Human Rights Tribunal. The remaining 1,500 were unfounded, withdrawn, or not treated for other reasons.[94] Another achievement in 1997 was the Human Rights Tribunal's decision that "found evidence of systemic discrimination in one federal department."[95] While no immediate effect on the conduct of the federal department has been documented, the Commission reports that it "expects to see improvements in the government's record, particularly in light of the new Employment Equity Act."[96]

On the impact side, in 1995, "a Human Rights Tribunal ruled that a federal department discriminated against two scientists of Asian descent who applied for positions as drug evaluators. The Tribunal found that the men had been discriminated against on the ground of race. In its decision, the Tribunal said both were qualified for the jobs and after the department refused to hire them, it continued to look for applicants that had the same qualifications as the two candidates."[97] The two complainants were awarded lost wages and directed that they be given the first available jobs as drug evaluators.[98] An example of a structural change brought about by a decision of the Human Rights Tribunal is the change of the Elections Act in 1992. The Act sets standards for the participation of people with disabilities in elections. According to the Act, "all polling stations and polling booths must be accessible to people with disabilities."[99]

## *Examples of focus on vulnerable groups' rights*

A number of national institutions such as the Australian Commission and the Danish Centre regularly analysis the human rights situation of vulnerable groups such as children, the aged, those senile dementia, minorities, indigenous peoples, migrant workers, asylum seekers and refugees.

*The Australian Human Rights and Equal Opportunity Commission* deals directly with legislation based on and incorporating international human rights instruments.[100] This includes conventions as well as declarations such as the Covenant on Civil and Political Rights, the Convention on the Elimination of Racial Discrimination, the Convention on the Rights of the Child, the Convention on the Elimination of all

---

Commission, *Annual Report 1989-90*, p. 29. The powers of the New Zealand Commission are set out in the Human Rights Act 1993. After its establishment in 1978, the Commission emphasized discrimination against the individual citizen and women. The Commission in its first annual report emphasized that the women's movement recommended the establishment of the body. *Annual Report of the Human Rights Commission for the year ended March 1979*, New Zealand, p. 4.

[94] Canadian Human Rights Act, R.S., 1985, c. H-6. July, 1996.
[95] Canadian Human Rights Commission, *Celebrating our Progress, Facing our Future*, 1998, p. 3.
[96] *Ibid.* p. 3.
[97] Human Rights and the Canadian Human Rights Commission, *Equality*, 1996, p. 16.
[98] *Ibid.* p. 16.
[99] *Ibid.* p. 17.
[100] Brian Burdekin, *Human Rights Commissions*, Workshop Paris, 1991, p. 110.

23

Forms of Discrimination Against Women, the Declarations on the Rights of Persons with Disabilities, including persons with mental disabilities, the Declaration on the Elimination of All Forms of Intolerance and Discrimination Based on Religion or Belief and the ILO Convention against discrimination in employment and occupation.[101] The Commission carries out education, information and promotional activities and is empowered to hear individual complaints and to intervene in court hearings.

One specific characteristic of the Australian Commission is that it has developed a profound tradition of convening public inquiries focussing on vulnerable groups. Prior to the holding of the inquiries extensive research and consultations with individuals and organisations are conducted. The subjects have included a national inquiry into homeless children, a local inquiry on lack of services to particular Aboriginal communities, an inquiry on racist violence, a localised inquiry on health services to an Aboriginal community and a national inquiry on the rights of people with mental illness.[102] The output of these hearings has been a series of reports with recommendations to the Australian Government and local authorities on measures to be taken to remedy the shortcomings of rights and access to services. In the Annual Report of 1989-90, the Australian Commission reports significant initiatives announced by the Federal Government as a result of the inquiry into homeless children. Its 1989-90 budget, outlined in the report 'Towards Social Justice for Young Australians' "commits the government to an expenditure of $100 million over four years for services and accommodation for homeless and disadvantaged young people."[103] In its Annual Report of 1997-98, as the result of another series of hearings, the Commission reports that the Minister for Aboriginal and Torres Strait Islander Affairs in 1997 announced "a package providing $63 million to be delivered over four years. The response targeted health, counselling services and family reunions [children with their families. Authors note]."[104]

In relation to vulnerable groups, *the Danish Centre for Human Rights* has in a number of cases successfully managed to impact the adoption and amendment of laws. One example thereof is a memorandum submitted to the Ministry of Justice in 1997 on two laws concerning the law on names and the law on adoption in relation to the hearing of children and minors. Here, the Centre stressed the need to ensure compliance with all relevant sections of the Convention on the Rights of the Child to which Denmark is a party. The Ministry directly referred to the intervention of the Danish Centre in the *travaux préparatoires* to the Bill covering these amendments.[105] Another example, also from 1997, relates to a similar memorandum relating to the appointment of legal guardians for persons suffering from mental disorders. In this case the Centre stressed that in order to ensure compliance with fundamental human rights principles the point of view of individuals should actively be sought by the

---

[101] *Ibid.*
[102] *Ibid*, pp. 124-125.
[103] Human Rights and Equal Opportunity Commission, Australia, *Annual Report 1989*-90, p. 26.
[104] Human Rights and Equal Opportunity Commission, Australia, *Annual Report 1997-98*, pp. 25-26.
[105] *Report of the Expert Committee on Childrens' Law under the Ministry of Justice, (Børnelovsudvalgets Betænkning)* no. 1350, Copenhagen, 1997.

administration in spite of their health condition. The recommendations were followed by the Directorate for Civil Law.

The Danish Centre for Human Rights has also been active through its researchers in relation to administrative preventive detention of asylum seekers in Denmark. Following the arrival of an increased number of asylum seekers from Eastern Europe, which caused problems at the asylum centres and in the community, the police restricted the freedom of movement of a number of them, primarily young men. This practice was authorised by the municipal Court as well as by the High Court of Eastern Denmark, in spite of the fact that the relevant law pertaining to asylum seekers did not provide for this. The Centre's researchers addressed the issue in a memorandum to the Ministry of Justice in March 1995, questioning the practice as a violation of section 5 on the right to personal liberty and section 14 on freedom from discrimination in the European Convention on Human Rights.[106] Following this argumentation by the advocates that the practice went beyond the limits of the law in these cases, the High Court changed its position accordingly and declared the practice invalid in January 1995. As a consequence, the Parliament introduced the necessary legislation in 1995[107] without solving the basic conflict with the European Convention on Human Rights. The issue is still being addressed by the Centre.

Another area, also in relation to the laws concerning asylum seekers, where The Danish Centre for Human Rights has played an important role, concerns the introduction of the so-called "lunch box arrangements" in July 1998.[108] According to this arrangement, asylum seekers deemed unwilling to document their identity shall be "motivated" to do so. The chosen method involves keeping them on a tight leash by providing them twice a month with a box of food and essential toiletries, instead of a financial allowance including pocket money which is normally given to asylum seekers and consistent with basic respect for individual dignity, privacy and choice. An example of its application was in relation to an asylum seeker suffering from the consequences of "ethnic cleansing" in former Yugoslavia, who simply lacked a passport, and was therefore deemed to be "uncooperative". A newspaper article by the DCHR researcher in July 1998 led to the raising of the issue in Parliament, where the Minister of the Interior was asked to comment on it. He replied in September 1998 that the duty of cooperation only entered into force upon arrival and that examples such as the one mentioned above did not constitute sufficient grounds for assuming lack of cooperation, hereby contradicting the position taken by the authorities in the initial cases. The very same day the Ministry reviewed a case on this matter and changed its decision so as to conform to the recommended approach.

---

[106] "Note concerning administrative detention of asylum seekers from Eastern Europe" (in Danish), The Danish Centre for Human Rights, March 1995; see also Kim Kjær in *Ugeskrift for Retsvæsen*, 94B, p. 457ff.

[107] Law no. 282 of 14 June 1995.

[108] Law no. 473 of 1 July 1998.

## Examples of focus on civil and political rights

The *Mexican National Commission for Human Rights* has as its primary focus the civil and political rights, even though it is not competent to deal with electoral questions, but also to a lesser extent occupies itself with other rights. The Commission is a good example of a national institution which gets results as well as has an impact. Still, it can only issue recommendations for administrative investigative action and, depending on the result, ask that a preliminary verification is processed by the Prosecutors' Office which can then bring the matter before the judge.[109]

In the Annual Report 1997/98, the Commission reports that it has issued 1,315 recommendations during the last eight years, of which 931 have been complied with by the authorities, which should be seen in light of the fact that during the same period the authorities have taken actions against 3,029 public servants. The Commission also criticises governments of various states for failing to comply with its recommendations, stating that "this aids and abets impunity; it protects, covers, ignores or tolerates the public servants who, (...) fail to keep to their legal mandate".[110]

In 1997/98 the Commission reports that it completed six studies[111] and concluded 8,706 complaints. The main reasons given for the complaints were "unjustified denial of the benefits of the law to inmates of prisons, delay or administrative negligence in the jurisdictional process, refusal of the right to petition, illegal exercise of public power and arbitrary arrests."[112] 58 complaints concerned torture where, as a "result of the recommendations issued on this matter (...) 24 public servants were handed over to a judge". "In compliance with the recommendations of the commission, sanctions or criminal action has been brought against 287 public servants."[113] Out of these, 48 public servants were handed over to a judge.[114]

In cases of alleged disappearances, the Commission reportedly made field trips to 28 states. 64 cases were cleared up out of which 51 reported disappeared persons were found alive. There is evidence that the remaining are dead. The Commission reported their findings to the United Nations Working Group on Forced or Involuntary Disappearances.[115] In addition, the Commission carried out inspections on its own initiative and visited detentions and psychiatric hospitals. As a result of these visits, a number of recommendations were issued to various public authorities. The

---

[109] Letter from the Executive Secretary, Mr. Ricardo Camara, Mexico City, March 2, 1999.

[110] National Commission for Human Rights, *Annual Report of Activities*, Mexico City, May 1997-May 1998. Please note that quotations are taken from a synthesis and that the notes therefore do not coincide with those in the final Annual Report.

[111] On Mexican migrant Women; Elderly People; Latin American laws on the rights of the indigenous peoples in 16 countries; draft bill for setting up a Centre for victims of Crime; draft bill on Reforms to the Penal Code for the Federal District in matters of Common Law; Comparative analysis of local and international legislation on women and children.

[112] *Ibid.*

[113] *Ibid.*

[114] Out of the 48 public employees, 22 were members of the Federal Judicial Police, 12 of the State judicial Police, six military personnel, three of the Federal Highway Police, two of the Prosecutor's office for State law, two from the Institute for Social Security and a former Mayor. *Ibid.*

[115] *Ibid.*

cooperation with the prison authorities on a programme of visit resulted in the release of 95 prisoners who had the right to an early release.[116]

The Commission seems to have attempted to play a role in relation to conflict resolution. In the troubled Chiapas province, the local office of the Commission in the last year processed 364 complaints, "of which 300 were concluded, for the most part through conciliation ... in favour of victims of human rights violations".[117]. The Commission recommended measures that all "were accepted by the state authorities" of Chiapas.[118] They included removal of twelve public higher level servants and proceedings started against them, indemnification of the victims or their relatives and compensation, the initiation of support to food productivity, health care, education etc., an administrative audit of the State Attorney General for Justice, and the judicial authorities issuing 111 arrest warrants out of which 101 were executed before May 1998.[119]

*Examples of focus on economic, social and cultural rights*

The *Indian National Human Right Commission, The Danish Centre for Human Rights* and *The South African Human Rights Commission* focus on civil and political rights,[120] vulnerable groups rights[121] as well as on monitoring the implementation of economic, social and cultural rights. While results of remedying acts of discrimination against individuals and of violations of civil and political rights can be measured immediately, fulfilment of economic, social and cultural rights primarily depend on political will and initiatives and on long term investments. The matter in this area is therefore far more difficult to evaluate. Judicially oriented national institutions primarily deal with these types of rights in the form of recommending political initiatives to be taken on an overall level. This includes providing access to education, health and housing as well as recommending changes of laws, rules and regulations for certain groups in society or giving them access to these rights. Until now, it seems that individual cases on economic and social rights have only rarely been dealt with by complaints handling national institutions.[122]

---

[116] Mexican National Commission for Rights Commission, *Annual Report May 1997 -May 1998*, Mexico City 1998.

[117] *Ibid.*

[118] Recommendation 1/98 sent to Governor of the State of Chiapas and to the Attorney General of the Republic, letter from the Executive Secretary, and Annual report.

[119] *Ibid.*

[120] In 1996-97, the Indian Commission completed 16,823 complaints. Out of 6,394 complaints considered, 888 were on custody and 1,643 on the police. The remaining complaints were unfounded, withdrawn, or not treated because of lack of evidence. An example of an outcome is that out of 259 cases registered against members of the border security force and the army, 81 were punished, including 29 officers. The Commission also drafts laws (such as a model prison bill), carries out education, and, in relation to complaints handling, has the power of a court. *op. cit.*, p. 12 and p. 136.

[121] Which is particularly dealt with by the National Commissions for Minorities, for Scheduled Castes and Scheduled Tribes, and Women, all members of the Indian National Human Rights Commission.

[122] Regional and national courts are increasingly dealing with this type of cases. See Asbjørn Eide, Catarina Krause and Allan Rosas (eds.), *Economic, Social and Cultural Rights, A Textbook*, Martinus Nijhoff Publishers, 1995.

*The National Human Rights Commission of India* is probably one of the national institutions that have given most consideration to economic and social rights.[123] The Commission links the issue of child labour with the right to compulsory education free of charge based on a supreme court decision in the state of Andhra Pradesh which has made the right to education judiciable.[124] In addition, another Supreme Court decision in Tamil Nadu confirmed this decision and added a set of recommendations for the implementation of these decisions, including a fine for employers using child labour.[125] On the basis of these court decisions as well as on reports on government officials employing child labour as domestic servants, the Commission in its Annual Report 1996-97 recommended to the Central and State Governments that they incorporate and prohibit such employment in the rules of conduct of government servants. Eight states agreed to this recommendation and prohibited employment of child labour as domestic servants. So far the Central Government has not agreed to the recommendation. It has, however, on renewed request from the Commission agreed to re-examine the matter.[126] The combination of the High Courts' decisions and the Commission's recommendations, reflecting a strategy of reaction as well as prevention, has beyond any doubt lead to extremely significant results.

*The Danish Centre for Human Rights* has included as one of four areas of competence in its newly adopted Strategic Plan of Action "Human rights and cultural practices". In addition a senior researcher has been appointed to cover the area of economic, social and cultural rights.

The *South African Human Rights Commission* is explicitly mandated to monitor economic, social and cultural rights, i.e. the right to access to education, housing, health care, food, water, social security and a clean environment.[127] In reinforcing the protection of these rights, the Commission must investigate, report and carry out research on the observance of economic and social rights, take steps to secure appropriate redress where these rights have been violated and educate organs of state and members of the public on the need for the protection and promotion of these rights. In addition, the Commission must, each year, request relevant organs of state to provide it with information on the measures they have taken towards the realisation of socio-economic rights.[128]

In relation to the monitoring process in 1997/98 the newly established Commission developed questionnaires and guidelines in order to assist state organs in fulfilling their reporting obligations. The Commission analysed the responses and made a report on the state's realisation of economic and social rights in South Africa. In

---

[123] The Annual Report of the National Human Rights Commission of India mainly emphasises problems faced and makes recommendations to the central and state governments. Thus, it does not emphasize results obtained.

[124] Andra Pradesh Supreme Court, 1993-ISC645. "Article 45 of the Constitution, directing the providing of free and compulsory education for all of the children of India until completion of the age of 14 years, [must] be treated as an enforceable fundamental right." National Human Rights Commission, India, *Annual Report 1996/97*, p. 38.

[125] Tamil Nadu Supreme Court, AIR 1997 SC 699. *Ibid*, p. 38.

[126] Letter from Justice V.S.Malimath, *ibid*.

[127] Sections 24, 26, 27, 29, 28 (1c), 35 (2e) of the Constitution of the Republic of South Africa of 1996.

[128] *Ibid*, Section 184.

addition, the Commission conducted a survey on the public perception of social and economic rights in South Africa and held public 'poverty hearings' in many parts of the country. It also held several consultative and educational workshops for government official and civil society organisations. Internally, the Commission has established a disability committee and a committee on children's rights.

Since the Commission's monitoring of economic and social rights is new, it is not possible to measure the output of this specific function of the Commission. So far, complaints relating to economic and social rights have not been subject to legal procedure and the work has mainly focussed on the research and educational aspects.

### Examples of focus on civil, political, economic, social and cultural rights

*The Commission on Human Rights and Administrative Justice in Ghana* focuses primarily on investigation of complaints, on education in human rights and on making proposals for the Government on improvements in legislation. It is interesting to note that the emphasis in its Constitution is on both civil and political rights and on economic, social and cultural rights. The outputs reflect a focus on both types of rights such as labour rights and cultural practice in conjunction. The power of investigation is rather wide and encompasses the public sector, including the armed forces, the police and prison service, the investigation of corruption, and the private sector. In addition, the Commission has the power to restore "to any person any property confiscated by or under the authority of the Armed Forces Revolutionary Council and the Provisional National Defence Council under certain specified conditions."[129] If a decision of the Commission is not complied with, it also has the power within three months to approach any Court on the matter.

Since 1993, the Commission has dealt with 8,775 cases out of 12,409 received. Among these, 40-50 percent are resolved by mediation. In the vast majority of the remaining cases, the recommendations of the Commission reportedly are accepted and implemented by the respondents. In 1996, the Commission received 5,200 petitions out of which 2,209 were labour-related[130] such as dismissals, salary issues, and termination of employment. The Commission has intervened in a number of cases of unlawful detention, confiscation of property by the Government without due compensation, gender discrimination, and women's and children's rights issues. It conducted a nationwide inspection of police cells and prisons, and issued a report on its findings. Reportedly, following the recommendations of the Commission, significant reforms were introduced by the Government, such as the increasing of feeding allowances for prisoners by 300 percent, the transfer of children to other institutions and the reviewing of sentences of selected inmates. With regard to a customary practice of keeping old women considered to be witches in so-called 'witches' homes', the Commission has undertaken educational programmes in the relevant local communities. Finally, the Commission investigated allegations of corruption (illegally amassed wealth) against top government officials. As a result,

---

[129] *Third Annual Report*, Ghana, 1996.
[130] Emile Francis Short, *The Commission on Human Rights and Administrative Justice in Ghana*, April 1998, p. 12.

two ministers and a staff member of the presidential office resigned and an investigation of another two was still pending in April 1998.[131]

## CONCLUSION

In choosing our methodology two factors have been particularly important, namely the availability of material as well as the issues raised by the contents. In relation to the first factor, the normative aspect has been reviewed through various United Nations materials, handbooks, resolutions and reports. The illustrative examples of shortcomings and achievements have been taken from materials produced by the various institutions themselves, recognising that an objective statistical and in-depth study could not be carried out on this basis.

With regard to the second factor, we have chosen to focus primarily on the section in the Paris Principles addressing the issue of independence of the national institutions, including criteria for appointment of staff, pluralism in their representation and financial autonomy. In addition, we have looked at other sections of the Principles addressing the legal foundation, activities and areas of competence and powers in relation to reception and treatment of complaints by the national institutions. Finally, we have examined the focus of the institutions on various categories of human rights.

The background for the development of national human rights institution was the United Nations' and its member states' need for an institution instrumental in servicing the United Nations system with information and, with the development of the Paris Principles, in promoting and protecting human rights standards at the national level. At the Vienna Conference in 1993, the importance of implementation through national institutions was further recognised and expressed in the Vienna Declaration and Programme of Action. Since its establishment in 1995, the Office of the High Commissioner for Human Rights has played a central role - through the position of a Special Adviser – in promoting the states' establishments of these institutions.

Between 1946 and 1993, a smaller number of national institutions and human rights commissions were established, parallel to the development of the Paris Principles. There was at this stage no clear distinction between the various types of institutions concerned with human rights established by the state. The efforts of evolving the criteria during this period is reflected by the fact that in the later part of this period, more institutions independent in their decision-making powers were established by constitution, by law or act of parliament, or by decree. A few institutions such as the French Commission were re-established to conform to the Principles. The examples indicate that even though the legislative foundation is important to ensure the autonomy of the institutions, establishment by decree in itself does not exclude that the Commissions are functioning well. On the contrary, the examples of Nigeria and Indonesia indicate that these institutions seem to function well given the very difficult political environments.

---

[131]  *Ibid*, pp. 1-19.

The development and normative changes following from the Paris Principles are reflected in the strengthening of the appointment procedures of leading members. Examples are the Commissions in El Salvador and Guatemala which had among their leading members in the 1980s representatives of state institutions which themselves had violated human rights. These commissions today would not meet the standards as formulated in the later Paris Principles. As the examples show, national institutions such as the Indian, the Ghanian and the Nigerian have proven able to address human rights issues in a professional manner. One reason for the success is the objective and professional appointment procedures combined with the institutions' independence in decision making procedures. It is also shown that new national institutions such as the Latvian with no objective appointment procedures tend to make rather political appointments leading to a more politicised human rights approach.

The preliminary review indicates that there is a strong relationship between the institutional framework and capacity on the one hand and the output of these institutions on the other hand. Criteria for appointment and dismissal of leading members and staff, representation of civil society and vulnerable groups in the governing bodies, guarantees of independent, objective and professional decision-making procedures, financial autonomy, combined with courage and vision, are determining factors for the likely outputs and achievements. The examples of Nigeria and Indonesia are illustrative of national institutions that no observers expected to be able to function according to their mandates but which actually do professional work and seem to fulfil the Paris Principles.

Still, this depends to some extent on the type of government and state institutions in the particular countries. The political and historical context of any state establishes outer limitations to the functioning of national institutions; they would rarely be found and be seen to be effective and autonomous in a society with no traces of pluralistic governance and rule of law. Consequently, no national institutions are found in countries with no separation of powers such as the remaining communist states. Another important condition for a well-functioning national institution is the existence of a vibrant civil society that can cooperate with but also act as a watch-dog over national institutions. While almost all institutions examined fulfil the criteria of the Paris Principles, there is still room left for adaptation to the particular context. It is therefore not possible to conclude that one model is better than another: a margin of choice should be left to the individual state to establish an institution suited to the particular context.

We can conclude that the institutional framework of the early established national institutions has served as a model and a source of inspiration for the development of the Paris Principles – in particular the Australian Commission; that some of the early established national institutions have developed quite elaborate criteria while some of the newly established ones have not; and that objective appointment procedures for leading members ensure greater independence in decision-making from party politics and political interests. With regard to a pluralistic representation of society in the leading bodies this representation usually is indirect so that vulnerable groups most often are not directly represented but indirectly through a commissioner appointed by the state or through non-governmental organisations looking after their interests. Also, not all major types of vulnerable group are represented in the governing bodies of any national institution (the homeless, children, etc.).

While financial autonomy of national institutions is crucial for their ability to be independent in decision-making of government interests, the autonomy in itself does not ensure a high quality of work seen in relation to the resources allocated. The material reviewed does not indicate that funding channelled through the parliament, a trust fund or through a ministry alone secures more or less independence in decision-making, which can also be said for the sufficiency of funding in itself. On the contrary, compared to similar institutions in other countries, institutions critical towards receiving funding through ministries, in fact seem to be relatively well funded in terms of the number of staff members. Independence in decision-making relies as much on the professional capacity and accountability of leading members and staff, and, in particular, detachment from politics. Sufficient basic funding, however, is still a necessary precondition.

National institutions focus on a broad range of promotional activities and on the creation of conditions for implementing human rights at the national level. Here, they differ from traditional international non-governmental organisations such as Amnesty International, Human Rights Watch, etc., which concentrate exclusively on monitoring human rights violations. In this context, it should be noted that the word 'monitoring' is not used in the Paris Principles or in the various United Nations declarations and documents in this field - perhaps in order to avoid national institutions concentrating their efforts on documenting human rights abuses instead of on implementation. It could, however, also to be seen as a reflection of the fear states may have of criticism from such institutions.

The function of protection includes the power to receive, investigate and settle disputes and claims of human rights violations. Most institutions examined have that capacity. They differ in that some institutions have a mandate to go beyond recommending settlements and into passing legally binding decisions. National institutions in many cases provide a vehicle for conflict resolution which is cheaper, faster, more accessible, and thus more effective for the individual as well as for society.

Focus on civil and political rights, non-discrimination and equal opportunities for various vulnerable groups show the most immediate results, for example in relation to the number of persons held legally responsible for human rights violations. National institutions mainly seem to resolve the immediate conflicts by mediation, pinpointing structural or legal problems or, in a limited number of cases, by bringing cases to courts. However, there are also examples (Australia, Mexico and India) where the efforts of national institutions have led to major government initiatives directed at structurally changing the situation of vulnerable groups.

Focus on economic, social and cultural rights is perhaps the weakest part of the efforts of national institutions. Except in a few countries such as Australia, Denmark, Ghana and India, documentation of outputs or achievements in this area is not found. However, the documentation indicates that national institutions have a potential for influencing the development in this field through promoting these rights as mandatory and absolute. In this work they have used public hearings, research, dialogue with the authorities or court decisions - making these rights judiciable – to underpin their efforts.

Finally, there is a number of relevant questions that cannot be dealt with within the limits of this article. They include questions such as the degree of access of vulnerable groups and the public to the national institutions, which are not specifically addressed in the Paris Principles, but which in the concrete situation will have a decisive influence on the functioning of the institutions in their respective societies.

It is difficult to sum up the main achievements of national institutions because of their very different history and the context in which they operate. Each institution has chosen a broader or narrower focus, dealing with very different problems and on the basis of various rights and standards. Nonetheless, it is possible to conclude that not only has their number increased in later years, and will probably continue to do so in the near future, but most of them have also been able to show concrete and constructive results from their work. By keeping the dialogue on how to improve human rights constantly open, this has had an immediate effect on those groups and individuals directly involved but also on their society. The next decades will show how much impact national institutions can make on the states' protection and promotion of human rights.

# Social Consequences of Development in a Human Rights Perspective: Lessons from the World Bank

*Alf Morten Jerve*

# INTRODUCTION[1]

It would be fair to say that the International Covenant on Economic, Social and Cultural Rights (ICESCR), ever since it was adopted in 1966 and entered into force ten years later, has been living a life in the shadow of the covenant on civil and political rights. Lately, however, there has been a certain resuscitation in the focus on economic, social and cultural human rights (ESCR). A main reason for this has been a growing concern about negative social consequences of development. While for a long time, ESCR were seen by most human rights experts as expressions of *aspirations* in nations' struggle for "progressive realisation" – as the term goes – of improved living standards, this mutual relationship between development efforts and ESCR is now being questioned. Planned development, in fact, might also violate human rights.

This paper looks at experiences from World Bank operations in setting standards for rectifying the adverse social impacts of development projects. The main purpose is to explore the possibilities for linking these experiences to the general concern about lack of operational clarity on what constitutes violation of ESCR. The discourse in the World Bank has mostly focused on the practical requirements needed to obtain what is referred to as environmental clearance of development investment proposals. There has been a growing trend in recent years to incorporate social issues in national environmental laws and procedures for environmental assessment. The focus of the World Bank has undoubtedly been reinforced by the vigilant attention of environmentalist groups towards projects that it finances. Although there is hardly any reference to human rights in environmental laws and assessments, our argument is that the experience of the World Bank has generated important lessons useful to the work of the UN Commission on Human Rights in defining violation of ESCR. In the same way, we would suggest that the operational policies of the international finance institutions would benefit from carrying explicit references to human rights dimensions, where appropriate.

The usefulness of the World Bank experience stems from two underlying principles in its policy directives on social impact: (1) 'Do no harm', or, as it is often phrased in the Bank, 'nobody should be made worse off'; and (2) vulnerable groups shall have a share in project benefits. Practising the two principles inevitably involves conceptualising basic rights: The rights of whom, and to what. And as developers commonly ask: 'How much is enough', which implies setting standards.

We are focusing on the problem of setting standards of conduct for a developer and principles of rehabilitation and involvement of affected people, where

---

[1]  This paper is based on the experiences of the author working for the World Bank Group as a staff member or consultant since 1992 on issues related to the social impacts of infrastructural and industrial projects. It is inspired by many stimulating discussions on the principles of managing development-induced impact with colleagues working in the Social Development units of the Bank. Parts of the paper draw upon a draft report prepared by the Chr. Michelsen Institute (CMI) and commissioned by the World Bank (Alf Morten Jerve and Rashid Sumaila, *Compensation for Loss of Land and Land-based Fixed Assets: Valuation of Replacement Cost in Indonesia and India*, Draft, Chr. Michelsen Institute, Bergen, April 1997). Special thanks to Hugo Stokke at CMI for advice and assistance in identifying relevant human rights literature.

development interventions will change status quo. It is our argument that it is principles of *violation* of ESCR that can be operationalised most successfully in such circumstances, i.e. areas where a state directly can be held directly responsible for adverse changes in peoples' living conditions. It is definitely easier to conceptualise, as well as monitor, basic rights, including human rights, in situations of induced social *change*, compared to cases where states fail to *improve* living conditions to certain prescribed standards, or even worse, where states fail to attain a non-defined measure of incremental improvement.

This paper starts by discussing some commonalties in development and human rights theories, leading up to a presentation of what the UN Commission on Human Rights have said about adverse social impacts of planned development (section 2). This is followed by a presentation of relevant World Bank policies (section 3), focusing on two main principles: rehabilitation of livelihoods and sharing in project benefits. As a contribution to the ongoing work on defining criteria for violation of ESCR, we shall conclude by summarising some salient features of mitigating impacts of transport infrastructure projects in Bangladesh, which illustrate difficulties and controversies in dealing with the 'right' not to be deprived of one's own means of subsistence, like for landless people in rural areas (section 4). Finally, the rights of particularly vulnerable groups, such as tribal minorities, are discussed in the context of mining development in India (section 5).

## DEVELOPMENT AND HUMAN RIGHTS

At the basis of development policies are concepts of the 'good' society and ways to get there. While most governments emphasise aggregate growth – in wealth, production, public services, consumption etc – others stress distributional aspects as well – i.e. ensuring minimum standards of quality of life throughout the population. The latter perspective dominates policies of development aid agencies today – both bilateral and multilateral. The goal expressed is poverty reduction, where poverty is broadly understood as the 'lack of' a series of basic human needs. Human rights lawyers struggling to formulate operational criteria for determining violations of ESCR carry a similar perspective, where basic needs have to be expressed in terms of rights.

### Poverty reduction in a rights perspective

The concept of poverty is not only limited to a person's pure material requirements, such as food, clean water and adequate housing, but includes his or her access to community-based services like education and health services, as well as the opportunities of benefiting from labour and commodity markets. Moreover, it is a growing consensus that poverty also includes more immaterial aspects of life, such as lack of personal security, access to information, and ability to influence political decisions. Within this multidimensional perspective, poverty reduction will have to address not only improvements in livelihoods, but also improvement in access to resources, expansion of knowledge and increased empowerment.

The work on human rights instruments, similarly, is motivated by the need to establish universally accepted norms for quality of human life. Therefore, poverty reduction can also be seen as a development strategy for fulfilling basic human rights – covering the full range from civil and political rights to social, economic and cultural rights. Where development policy-makers emphasise setting goals for incremental improvements, however, the challenge of the human rights experts is how to define minimum acceptable standards – i.e. definitions of violations of human rights.

In recent years, there has been a movement in the development rhetoric on poverty reduction from an emphasis on 'basic needs' to one on 'basic rights', or in other words, that people have a 'right not to be poor'. This, conceptually, has created a meeting place with the human rights agenda. Some would argue that this convergence in rhetoric complicates both agendas. By taking on board notions of rights, development work may unduly focus on minimal requirements and negative aspects of development. As a result, critics say, creativity will suffer – i.e. losing out on opportunities for what *can be done for* people and for stimulating people's creativity. Many human rights lawyers and activists, similarly, are concerned that steadily broadening human rights to incorporate more dimensions of human life may cause the legitimacy of the human rights conventions as international law to suffer. They will more and more become declarations of intent – based on aspirations – rather than enforceable standards. The effectiveness of the human rights instruments, it is argued, rests fundamentally on the ability to define and monitor, in unambiguous ways, what should *not be done to* people.

## Not making people worse off

It can also be argued, however, as this paper will show, that the new meeting place creates an opportunity that might help in advancing the work on what should not be done – i.e. establish standards for what constitutes *violation of rights*. What appears to be initially the most promising approach relates to the 'do no harm' principle. The right not to be poor, as a first line of defence, should be interpreted as 'the right not to become poorer'. As for the human rights norms, these would be applicable to situations where a state is responsible, directly or indirectly, and can be made accountable.

An international consensus has emanated that no development programme and project can be justified if it is known that, as a consequence, some people will be made worse off. The notion that it is politically and morally unacceptable to cause further poverty as a means, even temporary, to achieve a development goal, is tantamount to formulating people's 'right' to protection of their quality of life. Development-induced deterioration of living standards is not acceptable. Although this 'do no harm' principle is not directly codified in any of the human rights articles, it indirectly addresses the same problems of defining social and economic standards. What is 'harmful', and how to measure it? For the state or any other developer authorised by the state to avoid or minimise adverse social impacts, this must be answered in fairly concrete terms.

It is important to note, of course, that this 'right' to protection of quality of life, does not remove the right of states to effect changes in the status quo, including cases where this might be involuntarily forced upon some people. This is legally enshrined in all national constitutions, in what is called a state's right of eminent domain. The principle implies, however, that where such change is unavoidable in the public interest, the state carries the responsibility to ensure that unavoidable adverse social impacts are mitigated, and culturally acceptable forms of restoration of livelihood are effectively implemented. This obligation raises another question with respect to social and economic standards. When 'acceptable' harm is done, what constitutes adequate restoration? For a developer it is important to know how much is enough.

We have seen that the pressure for defining adverse social impacts and adequate restoration measures has been far greater than defining violations of the economic, social and cultural rights. The reason is that many countries, during the last decade or so, have passed legislation that introduces a screening and clearance mechanism for development projects, which includes social consequences. In most cases, this mechanism is part of broader environmental legislation, introducing mandatory environmental impact assessments, environmental approval, and environmental audit. There has been a similar trend in development aid. All major bilateral donor agencies and all the multilateral finance institutions have endorsed policy directives based on the same principles.

The introduction of a mandatory environmental clearance to be issued by semi-autonomous technical offices, as the World Bank did in 1989, created formidable pressure for defining what is an adverse impact and what is satisfactory mitigation. There are now several cases where international aid projects have been modified, delayed and even abandoned as a consequence of the environmental and social approval process. Similarly, private sector investments are increasingly subject to the same scrutiny. Knowing that the signature on the social clearance is, in some cases, the tiny cork that holds back a multi-billion dollar investment, the pressure for improved formulation of standards and criteria is understandable.

The one issue that has received most attention in recent years is the expropriation by states of private or communally held property, especially land, resulting in the *involuntary resettlement* of people. The World Bank, in particular, has been in the forefront on this issue, both as the alleged perpetrator, the judge and recently also the defender of the affected party. Below, we shall reflect on experiences of applying the do-no-harm principle on this issue. But first let us explore how the human rights instruments treat social consequences.

## What is adverse social impact?

Agreeing on what *not* to do to people in terms of economic, social and cultural change is far from straightforward. Development is inherently a process of social transformation, and it is a well-known fact that people evaluate changes in society differently. The same type of development may be perceived by one group as beneficial, while another group see it as deterioration in their quality of life. Social impact is indeed a very broad term. A group of impact assessment specialists formulated in 1995 a set of guidelines for social impact assessment (SIA),[2] where social impacts are defined as consequences to human populations that alter the way people

- live,
- work,
- play,
- relate to one another,
- organise to meet their needs, and
- generally cope as members of society.

These points cover all possible aspects of social change. A social impact assessment is meant to be an analytical as well as participatory process that identifies which aspects are the most important in a particular case. The purpose is to ensure that the design of projects is sensitive to both estimated real and perceived social change, involving all potentially affected parties. This includes both negative and positive impacts, and implies dealing with the problem of defining what is negative and positive, and weighing the two. This is a process of democracy at work, guided by social science input. The result is judgmental – i.e. an *assessment* of the social feasibility of the project, which together with analyses of economic, technical and environmental feasibility, constitute, ideally, the main elements for political decisions on how to proceed. An important by-product of the SIA would be policies and plans on how to mitigate unavoidable adverse social impacts, if the project moves ahead.

A reference to human rights is relevant on two accounts in this assessment process.

- Firstly, do any of the human rights conventions contain clauses that would render particular development interventions illegal, as per international law?
- And secondly, do we find principles that should guide the content of mitigation policies?

There is an important distinction between the two questions. The first refers to situations that cannot be remedied through compensation or other mitigation measures, or in other words, that potentially affected persons or groups, with reference to human rights, can demand the project be stopped or dramatically redesigned. The second question, is based on the assumption that the state legitimately can intervene as proposed, but carries a responsibility for proper restitution.

It is in the treatment of *forced population transfers* where we find the most explicit references to development-induced impacts. In such cases, the answer to the first question, to date, has been no. Human rights instruments have not

---

[2]  International Committee for Guidelines and Pronciples for SIA (ICGPS), "Guideline and Principles for Social Impact Assessment", *Environmental Impact Assessment Review*, No. 15, pp. 11-43, 1995.

effectively limited the right of states to acquire private or communal property in the public interest. It is accepted that workplaces and livelihood systems can be removed and altered. The ICESCR has yielded little protection of people's rights in this regard. Hopefully it can work better in setting standards for proper restitution.

## Aspirations versus minimum standards

Of the two human rights covenants, it is the ICESCR which has proved to be the most difficult to implement. It has been difficult to define, in more precise terms, the limits of acceptable conduct of states that have ratified the covenant, not to mention mechanisms for effective reporting against trespassing against such limits. The distinction between a development objective (e.g., people's housing standard shall be improved) and a defined minimum universally acceptable standard (e.g., the state shall guarantee that all citizens at least have adequate housing) has been hard to draw. One comes up against a whole range of definitional problems, where notions of what is adequate and acceptable vary among countries and groups within countries. Furthermore, it generally takes more than political will to ensure economic and social rights. Implementation is directly dependent on a state's economic strength and institutional capacity.

In an article outlining a 'violations approach' for monitoring compliance with the ICESCR, Audrey R. Chapman argues that the current paradigm of 'progressive realisation' is highly ineffective. It has not been possible to formulate appropriate indicators of progressive realisation, let alone furnish the monitoring body – the UN Committee on Economic, Social and Cultural Rights, with the sophisticated statistical data required to record incremental changes in the quality of life of different social groups. The absence of operational standards, translating abstract legal norms into minimum core obligations, makes it methodologically very difficult for states to assess their own performance, and "without effective monitoring, states cannot be held accountable for implementation of, or be made liable of violation of, these rights".[3]

The problem is further compounded by the term used in Article 2(1) of the Covenant, that a state party shall take steps "to the *maximum of its available resources* [emphasis added], with a view to achieving progressively the full realisation of the rights".[4] While 'maximum' sets a normative standard, the word 'available' creates scope for considerable pragmatism and opportunistic interpretation of a state's performance.

A 'violations approach', according to Chapman, based on "delineation of performance standards related to each of these components [of the enumerated rights], including the identification of potential major violations", has distinct advantages from an operational point of view.[5] The "disadvantage", of course, is that few of the 130 countries that have ratified the Covenant seem to share the concern of lack of operational clarity. The international community, typically,

---

[3]    Chapman, Audrey R., "A 'Violations Approach' for Monitoring the International Covenant on Economic, Social and Cutural Righta", *Human Rights Quarterly*, 18, 1996, p. 23.
[4]    International Covenant on Economic and Social and Cultural Rights, Article 2(1).
[5]    Chapman, *op.cit*, p. 29.

shies away from the language of rights, preferring aspiratory statements when discussing economic and social development. This was clearly demonstrated at the 1995 Social Summit in Copenhagen. The concluding document – the Copenhagen Declaration on Social Development – bears no reference to the ICESCR.

We have to accept that grey zones will remain between declarations of intent and the setting of minimum standards, and between the will and the ability to act, in the implementation of economic, social and cultural rights. But at least in one area there has been progress in recent years in terms of formulating 'basic rights' of development, namely in the area of *adverse social consequences* of planned development, where the basic approach has been to prevent affected people from becoming poorer.

## Social impact in a rights perspective

In 1986 the UN Committee on Economic, Social and Cultural Rights adopted the so-called Limburg Principles[6] and, on the tenth anniversary of these principles, a group of international human rights experts meeting in Maastricht prepared a set of guidelines (the Maastricht guidelines) to further elaborate principles for understanding and determining what constitutes violations of ICESCR. These principles and guidelines represent a significant legal development, but formulated in the abstract language of international law, they provide little guidance on how to identify and actually measure concrete violations in their social and political context.

In her work on the 'violations approach', Audrey Chapman attempts to move the agenda further. She distinguishes between three types of violations:

1. Violations resulting from specific state actions – i.e. commissioning of legislation, policies and activities that contravene standards.
2. Violations related to patterns of discrimination – i.e. cumulative effects of various policies and developments, requiring both measures to prevent further discrimination against groups based on gender, race, ethnicity, social status etc., and 'affirmative action'-type initiatives to compensate for past discrimination.
3. Violations taking place due to a state's failure to fulfil the core minimum obligations contained in the Covenant – i.e. acts of omission on the part of the state.

If we analyse development-induced impact and the 'do no harm' principle in the light of this conceptual scheme, we find that all three types of violations might take place. First of all, we are at the outset dealing with an act of commission (type 1) which may or may not contravene established standards. A particular development intervention may be considered completely unacceptable from a human rights perspective, or alternatively, on the condition that appropriate compensatory and remedial measures are taken, might be accepted. In the latter case, the two other types become relevant. Rehabilitation of affected persons has

---

[6]  Reprinted in *Human Rights Quarterly,* vol. 9, 1987, pp. 122-35.

to respect the principle of non-discrimination (type 2), including the obligation of the state to use this opportunity to reduce established patterns of discrimination. The type 3 violation becomes relevant in setting standards for rehabilitation measures. It would be an act of omission if the post-intervention outcome, in terms of people's standard of living after receiving compensation and rehabilitation support, contravenes norms of minimum standards. This refers in particular to Article 11 of the Covenant on the right of everyone to an adequate standard of living, including food, clothing, and housing.

From this we see that pursuing the 'do no harm' principle in development work represents actual field-testing of the 'violations approach'. The principle, as such, is not mentioned by Chapman, and surprisingly, despite all the public attention surrounding this issue, we also find no direct reference to it either in the Limburg Principles or in the Maastricht Guidelines. The closest is the statement in the Limburg Principles that a state will be in violation of the Covenant if:

> it deliberately *retards* [emphasis added]or halts the progressive realization of a right, unless it is acting within a limitation permitted by the Covenant or it does so due to a lack of available resources or *force majeure*.[7]

The same is reiterated in the Maastricht Guidelines, adding, as an example of violations through acts of commission:

> The reduction or diversion of specific public expenditure, when such reduction or diversion results in the non-enjoyment of such rights and is not accompanied by adequate measures to ensure minimum subsistence rights for everyone.[8]

Moreover, the Guidelines instruct international finance institutions "to correct their policies and practices so that they do not result in deprivation of economic, social and cultural rights".[9] These thoughts are further developed in reports from the UN Commission on Human Rights.

### Illegal and legal forced eviction

In a recent resolution the Sub-Commission on Prevention of Discrimination and Protection of Minorities, clearly states that development-induced forced evictions are "*prima facie*, incompatible with the requirements of the International Covenant on Economic, Social and Cultural Rights and could only be justified in the most exceptional circumstances, and in accordance with the relevant principles of international law".[10] The resolution reaffirmed the statement adopted at the UN Conference on Human Settlement (Habitat II) in 1996, saying that:

---

[7] The quote is from "The Maastricht Guidelines on Violations of Economic, Social and Cultural Rights", *Human Rights Quarterly* 20 (1998), p.693.

[8] *Ibid.*, p.697.

[9] *Ibid.*, p.698.

[10] UN High Commissioner for Human Rights, *Forced evictions. Sub-Commission resolution 1998/9.* Geneva, 20 August 1998.

the practice of forced eviction constitutes a gross violation of a broad range of human rights, in particular
- the right to adequate housing,
- the right to remain,
- the right to freedom of movement,
- the right to privacy,
- the right to property,
- the right to an adequate standard of living,
- the right to security of the home,
- the right to security of the person,
- the right to security of tenure and
- the right to equality of treatment.[11]

An expert seminar, convened in June 1997 at the request of the UN Secretary-General, prepared a set of 'Comprehensive human rights guidelines on development-based displacement'.[12] The guidelines apply to:

instances of forced evictions in which there are
- acts and/or omissions involving the coerced and involuntary removal of individuals, groups and communities from their homes and/or lands and common property resources they occupy or are dependent upon, thus
- eliminating or limiting the possibility of an individual, group or community residing or working in a particular dwelling, residence or place.[13]

With this comprehensive definition and the long list of rights that are potentially violated, it is difficult to imagine any instance of forced eviction that would be legal. Nevertheless, development-based displacement takes place on a broad scale, and commonly it is claimed that neither national nor international laws are broken. How is this possible? The answer, if any, has to be found in the following questions:

- Under what circumstances will development-induced eviction no longer be called 'coerced and involuntary'?
- Subject to which conditions can the element of force be legally justified?

The ways out of this seemingly intractable contradiction between individual and group rights, on the one hand, and the right of the state to eminent domain, on the other, are to be found in a process of free and fair negotiation and the provision of adequate compensation and resettlement support. According to Awn Shawkat Al-Khasawneh, Special Rapporteur of the Commission on Human Rights, population transfers in the context of development programmes would be *lawful*

if they are non-discriminatory and are based upon the will of the people, and do not deprive a 'people' of their means of subsistence. The general consent of the population sought to be transferred must be obtained by means of dialogue and

---

[11]  *Ibid.*
[12]  UN Economic and Social Council, Commission on Human Rights, *The realization of economic, social and cultural rights. Expert seminar on the practice of forced evictions.* Geneva, 2 July 1997.
[13]  *Ibid.*, p.4

negotiations with the elected representatives of the population on terms of equality, fairness and transparency, and equivalent land, housing, occupation and employment, in addition to adequate monetary compensation, must be provided. Moreover, such transfers are justified by the public interest.[14]

It can be inferred from this statement that the eviction of people is illegal unless a 'general consent' is obtained from the people to be displaced. It is, however, quite likely that people in many instances will not give their consent, not even at the promise of the most lavish form of compensation. We have seen this with indigenous peoples objecting in principle to departure from their ancestral lands. What principle should prevail in these cases – the right not to be expelled from one's homeland,[15] or the right of the state through democratic decision-making ('the will of the people') to act in the public interest? Unfortunately, there is no guidance on this dilemma in the UN documents surveyed. The Commission on Human Rights endorse both principles. The guidelines referred to above declare that "states should refrain, to the maximum extent possible, from compulsory acquiring housing or land".[16] As a last resort, however, forced eviction can be accepted if it is solely for the purpose of protecting the general welfare in a democratic society, is reasonable and proportional, and follows laws and norms with respect to fair hearing, legal counsel and effective rehabilitation.

It seems evident that these ambiguities cannot be resolved at the level of principles and general guidelines. Each case has to be judged individually. This counts for decisions to 'legalise' the use of forced eviction, in the first place, and subsequently, as well, determining the adequacy of remedial measures. The experience of the World Bank amply illustrates the complexity in handling these issues in concrete cases.

## WORLD BANK POLICY ON DEVELOPMENT-INDUCED IMPACT

The World Bank from its early days, supporting post-war reconstruction in Europe (through the International Bank of Reconstruction and Development – IBRD), declared poverty reduction and improvement of living standards as its primary rationale. These objectives were initially to be met through a series of development investments that over time generated enough economic growth to broaden employment and other income opportunities. In the same manner, the state revenue would improve, creating a financial basis for the introduction of welfare measures. With these economic growth theories, social responsibility was formulated as an indirect effect of successful growth, rather than a commitment that would lead directly to certain investments and exclude others.

---

[14]   UN Economic and Social Council, Commission on Human Rights, *Freedom of movement. Human rights and population transfer. Final report of the Special Rapporteur, Mr. Al-Khasawneh,* Geneva, 27 June 1997, p.15.

[15]   The former UN High Commissioner for Human Rights, Mr. José Ayala-Lasso, stated on 28 May 1995 that "the right not to be expelled from one's homeland is a fundamental human right". *Ibid.,* p.4.

[16]   UN Economic and Social Council, Commission on Human Rights, *The realization of economic, social and cultural rights. Expert seminar on the practice of forced evictions.* Geneva, 2 July 1997, p. 6.

Whereas the international development debate fluctuated between indirect approaches to poverty alleviation – e.g. typically illustrated by the term 'trickle down', and interventions aiming directly at the poor – e.g. illustrated by the basic needs approach of the 1970s, there was virtually no debate about whether the Bank would carry any responsibility for the failure of any of these approaches. In other words, how should the Bank respond to documented losses of living standards as a direct consequence of Bank-supported development policies and projects. Although no measure of clever theorising and careful planning can provide guarantees that well-intended development objectives are ultimately achieved, there are also numerous examples of negligence in planning and at times outright and deliberate disregard of the interests of particular vulnerable groups. The explanation often heard is that there can be no development without a measure of sacrifice and suffering. This was the tough lesson of the industrialised countries, it is claimed, and the developing countries of today cannot expect it to be any different.

Such arguments are no longer acceptable in a world where interest groups can join forces effectively across continents. Besides, moral values have changed over the century. What was seen as inevitable in 19$^{th}$ century Europe is not acceptable in the developing world of the 20$^{th}$ century. But it was not until civil unrest in protest against the resettlement of people in connection with large dams, during the late 1970s and early 1980s, that the 'do no harm' debate entered the Board room of the World Bank. Social obligation could no longer only be formulated in terms of virtuous development objectives. It would also be a social obligation of the Bank to prevent induced development from worsening the condition of people.

In the wake of the so-called 'lost decade', especially of Africa, with an emphasis on macroeconomic structural adjustment, the beginning of the 1990s saw a renewed focus on poverty reduction in World Bank rhetoric, advocating the need for poverty targeted interventions, primarily in the social sectors, and social safety nets. Economic growth remained the means to make this possible, but from now on improving the lot of the poor was explicitly formulated as the *raison d'être* of all work of the Bank. With this emphasis on poverty and social justice, the advocates of new policies on social impacts had an easier task, but had to use a back door.

**Riding the wave of environmental concern**

Initially, environmental guidelines for development projects focussed exclusively on the biological and physical environment, but soon it was advocated that social impacts also had to be counted as 'environmental' and be addressed through the new Environmental Assessment (EA) processes being developed. Several factors pulled in this direction at the end of the 1980s.

The Brundtland Commission had convincingly argued that poverty constituted one of the key threats to environmental sustainability in many developing countries, and by implication environmental and social and economic analyses have to go together. This was also the time when the World Bank in particular received a lot of flak for its involvement in some controversial large-scale infrastructure projects, the Narmada (also called Sardar Sarovar) hydropower and

47

irrigation project in India being the most pronounced. The key issue was the involuntary resettlement and forced eviction of tribal communities. This triggered a debate about how to weigh social costs against economic benefits, and more particularly what rights of protection and rights to restitution do people have vis-à-vis international finance institutions and their national borrowers. In retrospect it can be argued that it would have been more logical to place this debate in the context of ICESCR, rather than making it an extension, and in many ways an appendix, to the EA concept. Strategically, however, this was not an avenue that at the time had much prospect of success.

It was in fact a smarter move to jump onto the bandwagon of the environmental train, which by then was really gaining speed. Three important decisions were made by the Board of Directors of the World Bank when the new Operational Directive on Environmental Assessment was approved, which strongly impacted on the way social issues were treated.[17]

First and most importantly, it was decided to introduce a *mandatory* and independent (i.e. independent of the operational departments within the Bank managing the planning and preparation of new projects) environmental clearance of all Staff Appraisal Reports (i.e. the document forming the basis for the subsequent loan agreement). While most Operational Directives in the Bank had functioned mainly as guidelines, and were not linked to strong policing mechanisms, on the issue of environment the Bank was instructed to establish internal watchdogs in the form of technical experts on environmental and social impact. The operational departments and their project officers (the so-called task managers) from now on had to obtain a formal letter of environmental clearance from these technical departments before they could enter final negotiations with the borrowing government.

The second decision related directly to social impacts. Separate Operational Directives had recently been formulated on the issues of involuntary resettlement, indigenous peoples and cultural heritage, and the Board decided to make compliance with these directives a component of the environmental clearance as well.[18]

The third decision concerned public consultation and public disclosure of project documents. The EA debate opened new doors in the Bank on these issues. The borrower, according to the directive, is expected "to take the view of affected groups and local NGOs fully into account."[19] Relevant information on the project, as well as the EA report itself, should be made available to the general public and disseminated "in a form that is meaningful for, and accessible to, the groups being consulted."[20]

---

[17] This took place in two rounds. In October 1989 Operation Directive 4.00 was approved. This was revised in 1991 and issued as World Bank, *Operational Directive 4.01: Environmental Assessment*, Washington, October 1991.

[18] World Bank, *Operational Directive on Involuntary Resettlement* (OD 4.30), June 1990; *Operational Directive on Indigenous Peoples* (OD 4.20), September 1991; and *Management of Cultural Property in Bank-Financed Projects* (OPN 11.03). OD 4.30 is currently under revison and will be reissued as a new Operational Policy document in the course of 1999.

[19] World Bank, OD 4.01, *op.cit.*, para. 19.

[20] World Bank, OD 4.01, *ibid.*, para. 21.

All three decisions were clearly a political concession to strong environmental lobby groups in the US and Europe, and their implementation in practice naturally was closely monitored by the same groups. The Bank soon had to struggle with defining operational criteria for what constituted compliance, or the reverse – violation – of its new policies. And political interest and objective needs to move projects forward, closely watched by the many organisations critical of the Bank's environmental track record, created pressure for precise and unambiguous definitions of adverse social impact and how much is enough with regard to mitigation and reparation.

No similar pressure can be found in relation to human rights law on how to operationalise ICESCR. The international EA agenda, therefore, because it came to harbour some critical social issues, and gained prominence in the operations of the international development banks, is now in the forefront of interpreting social, cultural and economic rights.

### From commitment to results: a long haul

The mandatory environmental clearance of projects, formulated in the Bank's Operational Directive 4.01, is based on an initial screening of all projects in three categories:[21]

- Category A projects are those that are "likely to have significant adverse impacts that may be sensitive, irreversible and diverse". Mineral development falls in this category, and so do projects necessitating "[R]esettlement and all projects with potentially major impacts on people". A full Environmental Impact Assessment is required.
- Category B projects are those that "may have adverse environmental impacts that are less significant than category A impacts. Few if any of these impacts are irreversible." A separate EA is not required. Preparation of a mitigation plan would normally suffice.
- Category C projects are those that "are unlikely to have adverse impacts". Social sector and institutional development projects would normally be in this category.

The EA is to be prepared by the borrower, although in most cases the Bank has a heavy hand in coaching the work. The quality of the analysis and the content of proposed mitigation policies and plans are subsequently reviewed by technical specialists of the Bank. In many cases, the assessments presented to the Bank have been negative, which has confronted the Bank with its dual mandate. As a bank it is supposed to finance projects that would yield an economic return to the borrower, while as a development agency it is supposed to think long-term, take risks, and contribute to putting in place the preconditions for economic development. Should it turn down project proposals that appeared socially inappropriate, or should it intervene and try to change project design and

---

[21]  See Annex E of OD 4.01, World Bank, October 1991

governments' own policies and practices on social impacts, and aim for incremental improvements? The latter became the common approach.

Some critics argue, therefore, that the World Bank's concern for minimising adverse social consequences of development projects is just another tactical manoeuvre by the 'masters of illusion'.[22] Yet it remains a fact that the Bank is in the forefront among international development agencies in conceptualising an operational policy on the matter, but still there is a long way to go before actual practice is satisfactory.

Avoiding the use of normative arguments, such as a rights perspective, the Bank has sought to justify its social policies in terms of development efficiency; it is good economics to be environmentally and socially responsible. Failing to take account of adverse effects will be costly. It may cause project delays or, in the worse case, abandonment of the idea. The weakness of this economic rationale and the efficiency paradigm, however, is that it goes along with the general trend of the Bank to emphasise quality of planning at the expense of monitoring actual impacts. The new operational polices on social issues undoubtedly enhanced 'quality at entry' – as the slogan goes in the Bank, which is confirmed in a Bank report on its experiences with environmental assessment: "Category A projects, which require a full environmental assessment, have a better track record on average in terms of their implementation than other Bank projects".[23] While the report suggests that EAs play a positive role in improving project plans, it also underscores a main finding of the review that the Bank's supervision of projects during implementation is generally insufficient. Hence, the information on actual environmental impacts, as opposed to quality of plans, is often incomplete.

A fresh Bank review of experiences with involuntary resettlement paints the same picture: "The main failings were not due so much to the lack of Bank attention as to the difficulty in reaching Bank objectives using 'plans' rather than 'results' as the touchstone of quality management."[24] "[T]he Bank exits the project before staff can determine the probability of reaching the Bank's overarching objective of restoring or improving incomes and standards of living."[25] It is, therefore, gradually realised that commitment and 'progressive realisation' are not enough. A moral imperative has to come to the fore, linking the do-no-harm approach to norms defining the basic rights of project-affected people. Let us look at the operationalisation of the two norms mentioned above – viz. the 'right' to rehabilitation and the 'right' to benefits.

---

[22] Referring to the title of the book by Catherine Caufield, *Masters of Illusion. The World Bank and the poverty of nations*, Pan Books: London, 1998. The book is about, according to the author, how "the Bank has survived more than half a century of dramatic global economic and political changes…due largely to its ability to redefine itself" (p. 2).

[23] World Bank, *The Impact of Environmental Assessment. The World Bank's Experience*, Environment Department, Washington, 1996, p. xv.

[24] World Bank, *Recent Experience With Involuntary Resettlement*, Operations Evaluation Department, Washington, 1998, p. 6.

[25] *Ibid.*, p.3.

## THE 'RIGHT' TO REHABILITATION

In the Operational Directive on involuntary resettlement the Bank states that "[d]isplaced persons should be ...assisted in their efforts to improve their former living standards, income earning capacity, and production levels, or at least to restore them".[26] Since this was written there has been much debate and some precedence established on how to interpret the term 'displacement' – i.e. the effect, or type of impacts covered by the policy; the types of interventions that would be recognised as causing displacement; and principles of rehabilitation, as well. Let us first look at the causes.

### What causes development induced displacement?

There are obviously many forces in a society that can affect a person socially and economically, and a specific project can contribute to any of these. OD 4.30 is, however, limited to situations where we have adverse impacts on people caused by changes in land use directly induced by a project. This may involve changes in land rights as well. Transfer of ownership and user rights can take different forms, based on voluntary settlement, market transaction, or involuntary acquisition. The term acquisition refers to situations where the original holders of rights have no option but to relinquish these. The following situations have been identified:

- The most obvious cases are whenever a government decides to expropriate or acquire private land and immobile assets on that land, to implement a project. This is typically done for dams, new towns and ports, housing projects, water and sanitation infrastructure, mining, industrial plants, railways and highways, airports and irrigation canals.
- The directive is, however, not limited only to legal acquisition of private properties by the state. It applies equally to situations where the state decides to change the use of land already owned, or claimed to be owned, by the state. There are many countries that do not recognise private ownership of land, or only in a limited way (like China). In most countries large tracts of land have been placed under the custody of the state (e.g. national parks, forests, water bodies), but people may still be making use of the land.
- Most state agencies are major real estate owners, and changes in the use of such properties may also cause resettlement.
- Furthermore, there are projects that do not cause complete change in ownership or use of land, but introduce new restrictions on current land use, as for instance in the case of nature conservation projects and power transmission lines.
- Finally, there are projects that indirectly affect the land use in the impact area, due to noise, air and water pollution, and erosion. Where such impacts are envisaged during the design of the project, efforts to minimise the effects will be taken, but nevertheless restrictions on land use might be unavoidable. The responsibility for any unforeseen displacement rests with the developer.

---

[26]    World Bank, OD 4.30, *op.cit.*, para 3.

There is one situation where the interpretation of the directive is not clear, namely impacts from the purchase of land. Although a market transaction in land involves a willing seller and a willing buyer (assuming the seller is not coerced), it is quite possible that a third party could be adversely affected – e.g., a tenant or a person with customary access. Insofar as one cannot assume that existing laws regulating acquisition of land adequately protect the rights of the affected party vis-à-vis government, one cannot assume that existing land laws and tenancy laws safeguard the interests of a third party vis-à-vis a private owner. This is an area the Bank has tried to avoid so far, but the issue has been raised particularly in connection with programmes built on public sector intermediaries on-lending to private enterprises.

The power of the state to expropriate land forms part of all modern constitutions, but the obligations of the state towards the affected parties to such acquisitions is often less codified. The same applies to the definition of what is acceptable in the 'public interest'. Typically, ambiguities in this regard go together with poorly developed or ineffective legal appeal mechanisms, lack of public consultation and participation in the decision-making process, and authoritarian approaches to restitution.

The World Bank is a financing agency, and its policy translates into obligations on the part of the project sponsor – the borrower, normally a government institution. First of all, it is an obligation to minimize adverse social impacts, by reducing the area to be acquired and avoiding productive and settled land. It is often found, however, especially in countries where the cost to government of land acquisition is low and people have poor legal recourse to defend their interests, that governments tend to consider social impacts as no obstacle.

Besides controversies over projects as such and how to minimize impacts, struggles have revolved around two other general questions. Firstly, who is recognised as displaced and what kind of losses are acknowledged; and secondly, how to determine the level and quality of compensation and rehabilitation measures?

**Bangladesh: whose losses are counted?**

The terms 'displaced person' and 'resettler' have to be broadly understood. Normally one associates resettlement with physical relocation, but in the case of OD 4.30 it is precedence for recognising a displaced person, or project affected person (PAP), as someone who will lose

(a) land or any other immobile properties,
(b) his/her place of residence, and/or
(c) a vital source of livelihood or income

where such losses are directly related to changes in land use caused by the project. Whether the person actually resettles is a practical issue, not a matter of principle.

The potential losses of a displaced person, similarly, exhibit a broad range. The nature of rights to land span from legally guaranteed private ownership, to customary rights and temporary access to public lands. Acquisition of land in most cases causes loss of fixed assets as well, like irrigation facilities, buildings and trees. In addition there is likely to be loss of employment and income, access to services and a place of residence for some. Some may have to relocate, not because the house as such is acquired, but because they have to find new sources of income.

The problems involved in defining an 'affected' person and his/her losses are amply illustrated in the case of Bangladesh. The country is situated in the delta of three big rivers – Brahmaputra, Ganges and Meghna. The monsoon floods regularly deposit fertile sediments on the river plain, and combined with access to water throughout the year, the country enjoys one of the most productive agricultural systems in the world. This explains why it is possible to sustain a population of 125 million, with the highest population density in the world (except city-states) of 920 people per km², the existence of widespread poverty notwithstanding. Under these conditions of high soil fertility and extreme population pressure, agricultural land obviously is a scarce and critical resource. In Bangladesh, there is, in fact, hardly a piece of land that is not cultivable in one form or another.

The natural ecosystem that is beneficial to agriculture at the same time presents severe difficulties for the development of the kind infrastructure associated with development. Because of seasonal floods, that at times are more destructive than benevolent, buildings, roads and railways have to be elevated to flood-safe levels. Large earth embankments are constructed to reduce flood damage. The physical masses needed for these structures have to be dug from nearby fields. There is no 'surplus' anywhere – no barren soils or mountains to be used as construction material. The rivers, on the one side, arteries of natural fertilisation, also represent impediments to modern transport, especially the growing road network. The unit costs of road construction in Bangladesh, including bridges and ferries, are amongst the highest in the world.

The conflict between agriculture and modern infrastructural development has existed for decades. It is also a conflict that mirrored the power structures of the society – i.e. rural poor that gradually lost their land and agriculture-based livelihood, at the expense of a development path that benefited mostly an urban elite. The state had institutionalised a legal system and administrative set-up that effectively served the interests of the developers – codified in the Land Acquisition Law. Despite legal assurance of due process and fair compensation, the slums of the capital Dhaka continue to receive victims of public and private development projects.

The land acquisition law until recently gave recognition only to registered owners of land and land-based assets. Tenant farmers were not recognised.[27] In a country where landlessness in rural areas is widespread, the renting of land is, for many, the basis of the family economy. There is large variation in types of tenancy contracts, from those based on sharecropping to forms of leasehold. Common to most is that there is no form of registered contract. The same applies to tenancy in

---

[27] The law was modified in 1995 to recognise persons with documented sharecropping and tenancy contracts. The implementation of this reform, however, is fraught with practical difficulties and outright resistance in the land administration.

connection with petty trade and semi-urban/urban housing. Loss of employment, like for agricultural workers, is not recognised by the law.

Bangladesh has a huge problem of homeless people, who have been forced to encroach on public land. Squatters typically are found alongside roads, railways and canals, and on vacant urban plots. In the floodplains, where land erosion is common, there is a traditional institution allowing flood and erosion victims (called *uthuli*) to stay temporarily on private land. Squatters and erosion victims likewise have no rights to compensation.

In 1993, a survey was conducted of the population to be affected by land acquisition for the large Jamuna Bridge project.[28] The survey distinguished between directly affected households – i.e. land losers recognised by the law, and indirectly affected households, such as tenants, workers and squatters. The distribution between the two categories was almost exactly 50-50.[29] This shows that a substantial portion of the affected population falls outside existing systems of dealing with development-induced displacement.

The external financing institutions, led by the World Bank, entered into intensive negotiations with the Government to improve this situation. While the government was reluctant to change the legislation, a project-specific policy for the Jamuna Bridge was accepted. In this policy the following types of loss were recognised:[30]

1. Loss of agricultural land
2. Loss of homestead land
3. Loss of living quarters and other physical structures
4. Loss of economically valuable perennials (especially fruit trees)
5. Loss of occupied homestead land (illegally – i.e. squatters, or with permission of owner – i.e. *uthulis*)
6. Loss of tenant contracts for farming
7. Loss of wage income
8. Loss of plots for commercial activity
9. Loss of structures used for commercial or industrial activity
10. Displacement from rented/occupied commercial premises
11. Loss of standing crops
12. Losses incurred by persons who have already parted with properties and have relocated elsewhere (refers to cases of expropriation completed before the policy took effect)
13. Adverse impacts on the host population from development of resettlement sites
14. Losses to people adversely affected by bridge construction, i.e. change in water levels upstream or downstream, or in unforeseeable ways

---

[28] The bridge, crossing the Brahmaputra, opened in 1998 and is the largest project ever undertaken in the country. The project was cofinanced by Government of Bangladesh, World Bank, Asian Development Bank and Japan.

[29] Data from the survey undertaken by BRAC is presented in M.Q. Zaman, "Development and displacement in Bangladesh", *Asian Survey*, Vol. 36, No. 7, 1996.

[30] Jamuna Multipurpose Bridge Authority, *Resettlement: Compensation and Rehabilitation Policy.*

Broadening the types of losses recognised and the definition of people entitled to some form of compensation take us only part of the way towards realising the right to rehabilitation. It remains to ensure that the value and form of compensation provided actually will enable the affected persons to fully restore their social and economic position.

## Compensation or rehabilitation?

Whereas most national legal regimes are based on concepts of compensation, OD 4.30 goes a step further to say that the aim is to improve or at least to restore livelihood. This takes the responsibility of the state to a new level – i.e. rehabilitation. Compensation should not only be fair in relation to the loss; it should enable the social unit receiving the compensation (i.e., not only the individual receiving the compensation) to re-establish its livelihood in a manner qualitatively comparable to or better than what it enjoyed before the project. The concept of replacement differs from the concept of compensation in some important ways:

- The principle of compensation is based on the notion that government is released from any further obligation after full payment. The principle of rehabilitation, on the other hand, implies that the obligations of government are only released when it can be demonstrated that people have successfully recovered from the losses they had suffered. This principle is more comprehensive, but also more difficult to quantify for the purpose of defining rights to entitlement. In some countries laws have been passed which expand the rights of affected people to include opportunities to regain and enhance the standard of living they enjoyed prior to the project. "This is tantamount to an entitlement to rehabilitation".[31] We are not aware, however, of any legislation aiming at guaranteeing a prescribed standard of living.
- The two principles also differ in their relationship to time. Whereas compensation is generally provided up front, simulating a market transaction, rehabilitation constitutes a series of activities over time. In a policy for rehabilitation the element of risk is higher. It is necessary to allow for factors external to the project. The ingenuity of the affected persons themselves is a key issue in rehabilitation. The general economic and political development of the area is, of course, also a main factor determining changes in individual welfare.
- Finally, the two principles tend to generate different assessments of what constitutes the impact of a project. The right to compensation is generally pegged to loss of physical assets and sometimes also to direct losses of income. The rehabilitation perspective opens the way for the recognition of a broader set of impacts related, for example, to social networks and access to communal resources and public services.

---

[31] I. Shihata, *The World Bank in a Changing World,* Martinus Nijhoff Publishers, London 1991, p. 191.

In debating these principles some governments argue they cannot afford 'lavish' entitlements to rehabilitation. This is the prerogative of rich nations, which can finance welfare systems and social safety nets that can also capture displaced persons. Others argue that rehabilitation is meaningless as a legal provision, as it is too difficult to quantify. In recent years, thanks largely to OD 4.30, the position among most international aid agencies has been that the two principles can co-exist. In practical terms, this mean that in situations where existing compensation cannot be replaced by new and improved national policies based on the principle of rehabilitation, the owner of the aid-financed project will have to supplement or top up the compensation.

Still, the question remains: how much is enough? Admittedly, income and livelihood are difficult to measure in any exact way. It is also impossible for any government to guarantee the social and economic status of a person several years into the future. Peoples' livelihoods are influenced by many factors, positively and negatively, a development project being only one of several. There are cases where affected people are better off some years down the road despite poor compensation and no proper resettlement support, because other factors compensated for this. And the other way around, excellent resettlement support cannot compensate for general economic decline. The challenge to the borrower and the World Bank, therefore, is to develop a compensation policy that to the best of their judgement gives the affected people a realistic chance to restore or improve their livelihood.

### How much is enough?

There is obviously no blueprint for adequate compensation and successful rehabilitation. A policy has to be tailored to the conditions of a specific country and project area. From the Bank's directive and its world-wide experience, some general principles have emerged, which have become benchmarks for evaluating resettlement policies:

- Properties should be compensated at *replacement cost*. The affected person should be in the position to replace the asset lost, if he or she so desires. This refers to productivity in terms of land (or other productive assets), and standard in terms of housing.
- The *absence of formal legal title* to land of some affected groups should not be a bar to compensation.
- The primary focus of the policy should be on those whose *income stream* is affected (not merely property). As far as possible one should compensate loss of productive assets in kind, i.e. farmers should be given new farmland. Income losers should be given realistic options for seeking alternative sources of income.
- Access to means and measures of economic rehabilitation (education, extension service, job reservation, credit, grants, etc.) should be formulated as rights in the form of *entitlements*.

- Particular attention should be paid to *vulnerable* households and groups, such as indigenous people and ethnic minorities, and in many societies female-headed households.
- For those who will have to move, all costs associated with *relocation* should be covered.
- Special measures have to be taken to assist people during the *transition* period, whether it is a transition to a new income-generating activity or a new place to live.
- Compensation must be provided *in time* for people to manage the transition to a new life situation. Which means that the start of civil works is dependent on timely and successful implementation of the resettlement policy.
- *Communal* infrastructure and services that are affected should be replaced.
- The *host population* should be assisted to help them accommodate resettlers.

In principle, one can distinguish between three alternative ways of providing rehabilitation: (1) monetary compensation at replacement cost; (2) physical replacement of the asset lost – e.g., land-for-land or house-for-house; or (3) provision of alternative rehabilitation measures acceptable to the affected person. Well-designed resettlement programmes will often have to include a mixture of all three, but most project owners would prefer to rely solely on monetary compensation. This is the easiest way out. As a consequence of this emphasis on monetary approaches (the first alternative) the Bank has become involved in a lot of wrangling over the concept of *replacement cost*.

## What is replacement?

Assets lost can rarely be replaced with a close to identical substitute. Besides, an affected person frequently takes the opportunity to go for some changes in life, whether housing standard or economic adaptation. Therefore, valuation of replacement cost refers to the level of valuation for expropriated property sufficient to allow actual replacement of lost assets, or to acquire substitutes of equal value or comparable utility, inclusive of all associated relocation and transaction costs.

From the economic point of view, a proper theoretical calculation of the cost/value of full restitution of a displaced person would include replacement cost of both market and non-market assets; and income compensation for the whole adjustment period, including compensation for forgone growth of past income. The latter is supposed to make up for losses incurred during the adjustment period due to the disturbance to the natural course of development in property values.

Different approaches can be applied, depending on the type of loss and the information available. To various extents these approaches internalise all or some of the dimensions of impact indicated above:[32]

---

[32] The author is indebted to Rashid Sumaila, Chr. Michelsen Institute, for this perspective on replacement cost.

- For land, the most common approach is market value, and the methodology is based on comparing recent market transactions in the area. The market price of a property may be defined as the price at which the property would change hands between a 'willing buyer' and a 'willing seller'. There are many cases where a market value is not easily obtainable. This problem is not restricted to remote rural areas. It is also found in many urban situations. There are assets for which there is no real demand, because of social and cultural norms, or quality considerations.
- The concept of strategic value attempts to capture the future expected value of a given property. For instance, land which is agricultural at the date of acquisition would have a certain value on that date. Now, if the land is to be used to construct, say, a five star hotel, then clearly the value of the same land would be strategically higher than its agricultural value at acquisition. The argument is that the landowner should benefit from this strategic value by getting a higher compensation for this land. In a well functioning property market, the strategic value would automatically be i'ternalized in the going market price for the land.
- The 'negotiated' price for acquired property is the price arrived at through negotiation between the public agency responsible for the acquisition and the private entity that owns the land. The problem with using negotiation to determined the compensation for acquired property is that the negotiating parties are usually not equal: the government agency usually has the bigger bargaining power, hence it is able to turn the negotiations in its favour.
- For productive assets, in some cases the productive value is estimated, based on a calculation of the benefit flow from the asset lost for a certain period of time plus initial investment costs. For example, a mature fruit-bearing tree will be compensated at the cost of bringing a tree of this species to fruit-bearing age plus the net returns from the tree for a period which equals the time it takes to reach fruit-bearing of equal productivity as at the time of acquisition.
- Buildings and other infrastructural investments can be physically replaced, and the actual costs of new structures of comparable utility can be used as the replacement cost.
- A theoretically more sophisticated approach is related to contingent valuation, based on methods of determining 'willingness to accept compensation'.[33] The approach recognises that market prices do not capture the full personal and cultural benefits of an asset.

In practice, it has not been possible to introduce a uniform approach to compensation. The World Bank has accepted monetary compensation for individual assets at rates definitely below replacement cost in cases where the project owner has convinced the Bank that the total compensation package, including other elements, is likely to be sufficient for rehabilitation. Moreover, the

---

[33] See D. Pearce (1993), *The Economics of Involuntary Resettlement. A Report to the World Bank*, University College London, for a more elaborate theoretical discussion on this concept in the context of land acquisition.

adequacy of a compensation policy in terms of rehabilitation is also dependent on the efficiency of delivery.

## Implementation – a main bottleneck

In theory, the concept of replacement cost is not difficult to grasp. The main problem arises when the concept is to be applied in the field. In this case, important questions such as what are we trying to replace become crucial. Is it the physical loss, for example land, that we want to replace or the standard of living supported by the land? Another relevant question is, are we seeking to restore the post-project standard of living, or is it that we want to give people the necessary platforms, opportunities and chances of restoring their livelihood?

The best chance for the operationalisation of the concept of replacement cost lies precisely in the use of a combination of different elements, viz.,

- cash compensation directly connected to the value of the property lost;
- topping-up packages, and
- rehabilitation and resettlement programmes for affected people, especially the economically weak among them.

The justification for the three-layered approach outlined above is the following. The first element – compensation – is to cover the physical loss. The second, that is the solatium, is to compensate for the forced nature of the displacement. And the third is meant to account for other losses related to loss of property, for example, cultural attachment, social ties and common property grazing land. This compensation can also be seen as part of Bank policy to see involuntary replacement as a development opportunity, especially for the poor among the affected persons.

The final assessment of whether this is adequate will have to incorporate other dimensions as well, taking existing legal provisions as a starting point; are all the assets involved recognised and properly registered by the state itself; are the owners' identities known through existing formal registration; and can the losses to be incurred be quantified? The Bank's experience has revealed the following main problems during implementation:

- Lack of institutional capacity and actual commitment of the compensation/ resettlement agency results in incomplete registration of losses and entitled persons.
- Crude methods of valuation of assets combined with lack of reliable information tend to work to the detriment of the affected person.
- People are not able to get their grievances heard.
- People receiving monetary compensation are not able to use the money to replace the assets lost because the assets concerned are not easily available in the market.

- The mechanisms of delivery of compensation entail unacceptable costs on the part of the affected persons, due to time delays, administrative and transport costs, and bribery.

It follows from these problems that it is important at an early stage in preparation of a compensation policy to determine the extent to which compensation in cash and self-management of the cash is an appropriate vehicle. A key issue is the appropriateness of cash compensation in areas or for types of losses where the market is poorly developed. Firstly, it must be established how effectively affected people can make use of cash in their rehabilitation efforts, and secondly how a realistic replacement value of an asset can be determined when a market value is not easily obtainable. These problems are not restricted to remote rural areas. They are also found in many urban situations. Obviously, the absence of a well-developed market is not only a demand-related issue. It relates, as well, to national legislation and policies, social and cultural norms, and other factors constraining the supply to the market of a particular asset (i.e. good agricultural land or housing plots).

## THE 'RIGHT' TO BENEFITS FROM DEVELOPMENT

The directive on involuntary resettlement states up front that the objective is "to ensure that the population displaced by a project receives benefits from it".[34] This perspective of linking adverse social impact with a right to benefit from the intervention causing the impact is further developed in the Bank's operational directive on indigenous peoples. Starting from a concern for isolated tribal communities, the interpretation of this principle has come to embrace also other vulnerable groups.

### Who shall benefit?

In 1982 the World Bank issued its first operational policy on what was then labelled 'tribal people'. The primary objective was to ensure that "whenever tribal peoples may be affected, the design of projects should include measures or components necessary to safeguard their interests, and, whenever feasible, to enhance their well-being."[35] The definition of tribal was fairly narrow, and referred to ethnic groups exhibiting in various degrees the following characteristics:

1. Geographically isolated or semi-isolated;
2. Unacculturated or only partially acculturated into the societal norms of the dominant society;
3. Non-monetised, or only partially monetised; production largely for subsistence, and independent of the national economic system;
4. Ethnically distinct from the national society;
5. Non-literate and without a written language;

---

[34] World Bank, OD 4.30, *op.cit.*, para 3.
[35] World Bank, Operational Manual Statement 2.34, February 1982, para. 4.

6. Linguistically distinct from the wider society;
7. Identifying closely with one particular territory;
8. Having an economic lifestyle largely dependent on the specific natural environment;
9. Possessing indigenous leadership, but little or no national representation; and
10. Having loose tenure over their traditional lands.[36]

The directive carries notions of both protection and integration of tribal people, and is imbued with an implicit paternalistic concern for a slow and gradual acculturation process. A five-year implementation review, issued in 1987, confirmed that the directive generally had been applied to relatively small, isolated, unacculturated ethnic minorities such as the rainforest Indians of South America and the pygmies in Central Africa.

It recommended that the focus be broadened to include larger and more heterogeneous populations where certain groups possess socio-cultural systems and modes of production clearly distinct, but not isolated, from the dominant society, such as pastoralist groups in the Sahel and scheduled tribes in India.

Facing mounting criticism of several Bank-financed projects, not least in the Amazon region of Brazil (the Polonoroeste projects), the Bank issued a revised directive in 1981 (Operational Directive 4.20) which differed from its predecessor on two main points. Firstly, the definition of 'indigenous people' is made broader than the one of 'tribal people', referring to "social groups with a social and cultural identity distinct from the dominant society that makes them vulnerable to being disadvantaged in the development process."[37] Secondly, the obligation to develop is made more explicit – "to ensure that ... they receive culturally compatible social and economic benefits."[38] This objective is further reinforced by what Shelton Davis calls a main innovation, namely the mandatory requirement that the borrower shall prepare a special Indigenous Peoples Development Plan if the project affects the lands, resources and cultures of indigenous peoples.[39]

The directive gives elaborate guidelines on the preparation of such plans, emphasising, most importantly, the involvement of the affected people through a process of "informed participation". The concern is to "foster full respect for their dignity, human rights, and cultural uniqueness". The primary strategy is to give these people a voice, and decisions should be based on participation of the people themselves. It follows that the Bank should show more restraint when it comes to accepting land acquisition and resettlement, if and when such groups oppose the project.

The drafting of OD 4.20 was heavily influenced by the Bank's experiences in Latin America. On the other continents it is anthropologically far more difficult, and also politically more contentious, to determine who is indigenous. The answer of the Bank is that the OD is not meant to resolve issues of indigenous rights. Its

---

[36] Taken from Shelton H. Davis, "The World Bank and Indigenous Peoples", paper presented at University of Denver Law School, April 1993, mimeo, Environment Department, World Bank.
[37] World Bank, "Indigenous peoples", Operational Directive 4.20, September 1991, para. 3.
[38] *Ibid.*, para. 6.
[39] Shelton, *op.cit.*, p.24.

61

concern is vulnerability. The term 'indigenous' refers to any culturally distinct group – e.g., ethnic minorities, tribes or scheduled tribes (in India), that is *vulnerable and disadvantaged* in the development process. Where a country's legal framework does not provide an acceptable basis for identifying such groups, a careful social-anthropological and political analysis would be required.

### India: Who pays the price of industrialisation?

India has a dramatic history of forced displacement of people in recent decades. From 1950 to 1991 an estimated 21 million people were resettled from state-financed dams, mines, wildlife sanctuaries and industries, and 75 per cent of those are still not cared for.[40] The national public debate on involuntary resettlement is currently gaining a strong momentum. Several states and parastatal corporations have formulated specific resettlement and rehabilitation (R&R) policies,[41] complementing the national Land Acquisition Act, and several lobby groups are pressing to have the act revised. The Ministry of Rural Development is drafting a National Policy for Development-Induced Displacement and Rehabilitation of Persons Displaced as Consequence of Land Acquisition.

The main issues in contention are:

- The demand for a more restrictive definition of "public purpose" that can justify expropriation of land. Project developers should buy land directly from the owners, rather than use the state machinery.
- The need to establish rights to compensation for people with ancestral claims and communal property rights to land claimed as state property. Large tribal populations have no registered title to their land.
- That Government should formulate procedures that force project developers to look for alternatives that avoid or minimise resettlement.
- That the right and access to information must be improved.
- That compensation should be based on the concept of 'replacement value', rather that the current administratively registered "market" value.
- That displaced people should have some form of rights to a share in the benefits created by the project.
- That the interests of women must be better protected.
- And the recognition that genuine farmers should be compensated in the form of alternative agricultural land.

The Indian Land Acquisition Act was enacted in 1894 and amended in 1984. The legal process is time consuming, and involves several clearly laid down legal and administrative steps. The process, however, suffers from bureaucratic red tape,

---

[40]  W. Fernandes and V. Paranjpye, *Rehabilitation Policy and Law in India: A right to livelihood,* The Indian Social Institute, New Delhi, 1997, p. 6.

[41]  The states of Karnataka (1987), Madhya Pradesh (1985), Maharashtra (1976) have policies in the form of state laws, while several other states have issued Government Orders applicable to R&R in specific sectors or projects: Andhra Pradesh, Gujarat, Orissa, Punjab, Rajasthan, Tamil Nadu. The following state corporations have R&R policies: Coal India Ltd., Maharashtra State Electricity Board, and National Thermal Power Corporation.

problems with ownership records and data on actual property values, lack of transparency, and outright corruption and manipulation. In most land acquisition cases the project owner – the applicant – struggles not to lose time before getting access to the land, which invariably involves 'pleasing' and assisting the administration. The affected party, on its part, faces similar problems in getting his or her concerns addressed by the authorities, and poor people are mostly rendered helpless in this situation. Most observers agree that land acquisition is among the areas where corruption, and other forms of manipulation, is most rampant in India. Hence, there are numerous middlemen benefiting from the process, including also legal advisers and lawyers. The Indian courts are clogged with land cases. These are important factors in explaining why reforms are so slow to come about.

Another factor is the political ambitions of central and state governments to facilitate rapid industrialisation. While hydropower and irrigation schemes in India, such as Narmada, have hit international headlines, relatively less attention has been accorded another sector that has caused heavy displacement of people, namely coal mining. Most of the coal deposits in India are found in the highland areas of south and central India. This is at the same time India's tribal belt – the homeland of several ethnic minorities that have retained language, cultural practices, religion and economic adaptation, making them clearly distinct from the Indian mainstream society and caste system. Moreover, these tribal groups are recognised by the Indian constitution as Scheduled Tribes. The political rational of this classification, in the Gandhian tradition, was one of protecting the groups (e.g. through special land laws) and assisting their integration into the larger society through programmes of affirmative action. The vulnerability of these groups, however, has remained virtually unabated each time their lands and habitats have been the subject of greater economic interests, such as mining. The stories are many of impoverishment and social disintegration as a result of displacement.

The Indian coal sector represented by Coal India Limited (CIL) and its subsidiary companies, a parastatal that until recently enjoyed a monopoly on coal mining, has been receiving World Bank financing for many years. During preparations of the last and recently approved loan – the India Coal Sector Rehabilitation Project – two prominent social issues were put high on the agenda. First and foremost was the question of resettlement and rehabilitation, but looming in the background were also the social implications of the structural reforms of the sector that were formulated as conditions for granting the loan. One of the aims of these reforms is increased productivity through down-sizing of the workforce (CIL is 25 per cent overstaffed according to some Bank estimates) and reduction of labour costs (CIL pays at present government-approved wages that are 8-10 times the minimum wage rates).

The new loan would only finance investments in existing mines, through improvements and expansions. Although all land to be impacted by this has already been acquired by CIL in a legal sense, in some instances as much as twenty years back, large areas are still occupied and used by local farmers. The extent to which compensation, as per Indian law, has been paid in full varies. Some were paid ten years ago or more, but have continued using the land as long as the company did not require it for physical expansion. Others have received part payment or none yet. In any case, these compensation amounts are generally far below what it would take to buy equivalent replacement land in the same area. The way CIL have tried to keep the local land losers content, despite the harsh conditions of land expropriation, has been the offer of permanent employment in the mine. With the relatively high wage level of mine workers, this was considered by many a good deal, and at any rate, far better than what was given to people losing their land to other government projects. As a consequence, of course, CIL has to struggle with a problem of overstaffing.

In this situation, the World Bank, after considerable lobbying and pressure from NGO groups, agreed to initiate first a separate Environmental and Social Mitigation Project, and make a successful start of this project a condition for negotiating the main loan. It is in this connection that the problem of how to operationalise the OD 4.20 and 'the right to benefits from development' emerged.

Who have the rights to which benefits? Initially a controversy rose among social scientists in the Bank over the term 'indigenous', and the associated requirement of an Indigenous Peoples Development Plan. Some held the view that applying only the OD 4.30 on involuntary resettlement would suffice. Although scheduled tribes in most cases would qualify as indigenous, as per the definition of the Directive, the mine impact areas are also full of other vulnerable groups, such as scheduled castes. Moreover, surrounding these existing mines new settlements have developed of people primarily relying on incomes from the mine or activities supplying the mining community. These settlements are often socially and ethnically mixed and targeting special segments of the population would be very difficult. The Bank's management and legal division, however, ruled that OD 4.20 had to be invoked as well, necessitating the preparation of a special plan for indigenous and/or vulnerable people. The resulting Environmental and Social Mitigation Project ensured that the Bank could not be accused of by-passing its own directives, but conveniently, or one may well argue, realistically skipped over the issue of defining beneficiaries on the basis of ethnicity or vulnerability. Not surprisingly, the project has evolved into a broad-based social welfare programme, not significantly different from the kind of approach the CIL has sponsored for a long time already.

The main justification for the project, however, was not social welfare. It is intended to be a mechanism that ensures not only rehabilitation of displaced people, but also improvement in their living standard. The key to this is income generation. No longer being able to offer employment, and with generally no replacement land to offer, the approach of CIL, and the Bank, has been strategies of 'self-employment'. The chances of success are at best uncertain. "NGOs have learnt that it is simply not possible to take illiterate, unskilled people and overnight turn them into small entrepreneurs", critics say.[42] It remains to be seen whether the attempts by the CIL and the project to create an enabling environment for entrepreneurship will yield positive results for groups hitherto excluded from development benefits.

---

[42]   R. Bhengara., "Coal Mining Displacement", *Economic and Political Weekly*, March 16, 1996.

## CONCLUSION

In this paper we have attempted to build stronger links between two discourses that mostly are kept separate. In the discourse on economic, social and cultural rights the core problem appears to be the identification of violation. What are the minimum standards, as opposed to goals for incremental improvements that should not be trespassed by states that have ratified the covenant? As is the case with civil and political rights, it is necessary to move towards definitions of violation that make it possible to identify individual incidences of violation, not merely documenting aggregate negative trends. Likewise, it is necessary for practising rights as legal instruments to be able to identify the perpetrator and the victim of a violation of these rights.

It is our suggestion that focusing on the adverse consequences of planned development, it will be possible to advance at least one part of the ESCR discourse from the level of very general intentions and guidelines, phrased in the abstract language of international law, to more practical definitions of what constitutes an individual person's right and correspondingly a violation by a development agency to fulfil that right. The paper shows that the international discourse on social impacts, as part of forming standards for environmentally acceptable development, has much to contribute in this respect. Although the terminology of 'rights' is generally avoided in the operational policies of the World Bank (and other development agencies and financing institutions) on social impact, in the practical implementation of these policies a pressure for defining rights in order to protect interests of affected people soon emerges. By looking at concrete project policies for dealing with issues like resettlement, rehabilitation and vulnerable groups, human rights lawyers will be able to advance the 'violation approach' further. We would recommend that a study is launched which compiles project policies and experiences relating to the two types of 'rights' of affected people we have discussed – to rehabilitation and to development benefits – to compare concrete attempts at standard setting.

We would also argue, by way of conclusion, that the EA and social impact discourse stand to benefit from building bridges the other way. As reviews of resettlement operations and projects involving indigenous peoples have shown, implementation is the main bottleneck. The intentions and commitments enshrined in policies and plans do not get translated into satisfactory results on the ground. There are several reasons for this, such as weak institutional capacity, lack of involvement of affected people in decision-making, and getting started too late and ending too early. One overarching reason, however, is the fact that intentions and commitments are rarely properly translated into tangible entitlements. People do not know what their rights are. Unless projects for mitigating social impacts get backed by enforceable standards and rights, we will continue to witness the same gaps between plans and results. To bring social mitigation approaches from paternalism and handouts to individual rights and opportunities for self-fulfilment, a closer link-up with the human rights discourse will be necessary.

We have seen a move from hard-nosed compensation approaches to lofty strategies of community development in social mitigation. However, the latter approach might not serve the ends – rehabilitation and sharing of development benefits – unless institutions like the World Bank also develop a 'violation approach' to its policies. There is a need to define violations of the 'right to rehabilitation' and the 'right to project benefits', as much as violations of the rights in the Covenant on Economic, Social and Cultural Rights, and as we have tried to show, the two agendas ought to move closer.

# Dutch Official Development Aid to Guatemala: Are Human Rights Promoted?

*Hilde Hey and Carol Lasbrey*

In order to enable the population of the Third World to benefit from a real and meaningful enjoyment of human rights, development is a necessary pre-condition. This is the normative premise on which industrialised countries base their development aid policies.[1]

## INTRODUCTION[2]

That human rights have played a role in Dutch development co-operation, is beyond doubt. During the past twenty years the Dutch Minister for Foreign Affairs and the Minister for Development Co-operation[3] have published several policy papers concerning the place of human rights within their mandate. The first, published by the Minister for Foreign Affairs in 1979, sets out, amongst its other objectives, the basis for the relationship between Dutch development aid and human rights. Since then, the Minister for Development Co-operation has published two more policy papers which elaborate on the same theme. These policy papers emphasise the need for the protection of human rights, but say little about how human rights should be promoted through development co-operation.

The fact that Dutch development policy has concentrated on the protection of human rights is not surprising since, at an international level, the protection of human rights has also received more attention than the promotion of human rights. That is to say, international norms and mechanisms have been established to guarantee that States honour human rights. The focus on the protection rather than the promotion of human rights derives from the fact that internationally, human rights were established as a means of dealing with violations. In many cases these were violations of a gross and systematic nature. The consequence of this has, however, been that human rights have acquired a negative connotation. This means that human rights are mainly seen in terms of violations and little attention has been paid to the fact that resources are needed in order to prevent violations of human rights from taking place. Although development aid is used for the alleviation of poverty in general, it does not address human rights specifically. In other words, the need to promote human rights has been neglected. The time has now come to ensure that States not only refrain from violating human rights, but also use their available resources for the promotion of human rights. This applies not only to developing countries, but also to developed countries which, through

---

[1]   Authors' translation from: *De rechten van de mens in het buitenlands beleid* [Human Rights in Foreign Policy], TK 1978-79, 15571, nrs. 1-2, p. 106 in M.C. Castermans-Holleman, *Het Nederlandse Mensenrechtenbeleid in de Verenigde Naties*, [Dutch Human Rights Policy in the United Nations], The Hague: T.M.C. Asser Institute, 1992, p. 35.

[2]   The authors would like to thank Leandro Alvaro Coj, German Curichiche, Christina van Kooten, Oscar Perdomo, Walter Plomp and José Suasnavar for their willingness to be interviewed for this article. Peter Baehr, Marc Moquette, Jacqueline Smith and the editors are thanked for providing the authors with helpful comments on the article. The research for this article was completed by the autumn of 1998.

[3]   The Minister for Development Co-operation is a Minister without Portfolio, meaning that there is no separate ministry; instead, its administrative component forms part of the Ministry of Foreign Affairs. The elements of foreign policy which affect development co-operation and *vice versa* are determined by both ministers jointly.

69

the implementation of their development aid policy, should seek to achieve the advancement or promotion of human rights in the most effective way possible.

With the adoption of the Vienna Declaration in June 1993, the need to protect and promote all human rights was once again emphasised.[4] The fact that all human rights need to be protected and promoted arises from the internationally accepted notion that human rights are indivisible, interdependent and interrelated.[5] The concept that civil and political rights should be protected and social, economic and cultural rights promoted has become outdated. Instead, all human rights should now be approached on an equal footing. There is little dispute that development co-operation can contribute to the improvement of human rights. However, a coherent approach to development co-operation in terms of the protection and promotion of 'rights' remains to be developed. How effective are development aid projects actually in protecting and promoting human rights in developing countries? Presently, little can be said about whether support for one type of project is more effective for human rights than support for another. In this article we do not claim to provide answers to these questions. Rather, we hope to stimulate a discussion on the subject and provide some stepping stones for this discussion using Dutch development aid to Guatemala as an example.

The Dutch Official Development Aid (ODA) budget for Guatemala is small in comparison with Dutch ODA worldwide.[6] However, as a result of the signing of a series of Peace Agreements[7] between the Government of Guatemala and the *Unidad Revolucionaria Nacional Guatemalteca* (Guatemalan National Revolutionary Union; URNG), culminating in the Agreement on a Firm and Lasting Peace signed on 29 December 1996, the Minister for Development Co-operation decided in 1997 to double ODA[8] to Guatemala for an indefinite period. The signing of these Peace Agreements brought to an end an internal armed conflict which lasted for 36 years and sent a signal to the international community

---

4    "Vienna Declaration and Programme of Action", UN Doc. A/CONF.157/23, Part I, para. 4 reproduced in *Netherlands Quarterly of Human Rights*, Vol. 11, No. 3, 1993, pp. 346-368, p. 348.

5    "Vienna Declaration and Programme of Action", UN Doc. A/CONF.157/23, Part I, para. 5, *ibid.*, p. 348.

6    Dutch ODA world-wide in 1997 amounted to Hfl. 6,412.582 million. In 1997, the main recipient of Dutch ODA in Africa was Yemen, obtaining Hfl. 101,362 million; in Asia, India and Bangladesh were the main recipients, amounting to Hfl. 123,462 million and Hfl. 103,014 million respectively; in Latin America, Bolivia was the main recipient of Dutch ODA, receiving a total of Hfl. 87,586 million. Ministerie van Buitenlandse Zaken [Ministry for Foreign Affairs], *Jaarverslag Ontwikkelingssamenwerking 1997* [Annual Report Development Co-operation 1997], The Hague, July 1998.

7    The Peace Agreements include seven 'substantive' agreements in which both parties undertook a series of wide ranging commitments to the protection of human rights an undertaking to combat impunity, resettlement of displaced people, investigation into past human rights violations, demilitarisation, and the strengthening of civil society and civilian institutions, support for indigenous rights and the furtherance of economic and social development especially in rural areas. In addition, five 'operative' agreements relating to specific measures to be implemented - a cease-fire, a timetable for demobilisation and the reintegration of the guerrillas into civil society, constitutional reforms, the agreement on a firm and lasting peace and the programming of the implementation of the commitments contained in the substantive agreements.

8    Criteria as to what is considered ODA are determined by the OECD countries jointly.

that gross and systematic violations of human rights pertained to the past and that the Guatemalan Government, to the best of its ability, intended to uphold the rule of law and protect human rights. For the Dutch Government this implied a change in policy and an increasing emphasis on the improvement of human rights. Dutch development aid to Guatemala thus offers an interesting case study for considering ways by which human rights can be protected and promoted.

## HUMAN RIGHTS AND DUTCH DEVELOPMENT AID: A BACKGROUND

In the past twenty years, since the publication of the policy paper on human rights and Dutch foreign policy, the relationship between human rights and development has been reconsidered at various times. Initially, development co-operation was defined as contributing to the promotion and protection of human rights in general. That is to say, it was seen as promoting both social, economic and cultural rights, and civil and political rights. These two categories of rights were considered to be indivisible and interrelated. By 1984, a policy shift took place in that development co-operation was mainly seen as contributing to the promotion of social and economic rights, which as a consequence, would create an environment in which civil and political rights could thrive. For example, the funding of an improved basic education system would produce a more literate electorate which would be able to exercise its right to vote on the basis of more appropriate information and would be less subject to corruption or other forms of pressure. At the time, the promotion and protection of civil and political rights was not considered as a policy objective of development co-operation in and of itself.[9] By the early 1990s development aid policy had changed once again.[10] It was now believed that civil and political rights were imperative for the attainment of social and economic rights. For example, where the State, through the judicial system, upholds the right to freedom of association and the right to form and join trade unions, this will lead to improved working conditions and wage levels, and a higher standard of living. However, in practice, the bulk of development aid continued to be directed to poverty alleviation with some attention being paid to the strengthening of institutions vital to the protection of human rights. This included *inter alia* the training of judges and support for human rights organisations, especially non-

---

[9]  For a discussion on this see: M.C. Castermans-Holleman, *Het Nederlandse Mensenrechtenbeleid in de Verenigde Naties*, [Dutch Human Rights Policy in the United Nations], The Hague: T.M.C. Asser Institute, 1992, p. 35.

[10]  In 1990, the Minister for Development Co-operation published the Dutch version of the policy paper *A World of Difference: A New Framework for Development in the 1990s*, Ministry for Foreign Affairs, The Hague 1991; and in 1993 the Dutch version of the policy paper *A World in Dispute: A Survey of the Frontiers of Development Co-operation*, Ministry of Foreign Affairs, The Hague 1994. For an analysis of these policy papers see Oda van Cranenburgh, "Development Co-operation and Human Rights Linkage Policies in the Netherlands", in Peter Baehr, Hilde Hey, Jacqueline Smith & Theresa Swinehart (eds.), *Human Rights in Developing Countries: Yearbook 1995*, The Hague: Kluwer Law International, 1995, pp. 29-55. According to Cranenburgh the shift in policy was the result of an overall international shift in attention to domestic political factors which influence underdevelopment.

governmental organisations. This latter category, known as 'institutional strengthening', later came to be included under the wider rubric of 'Good Governance', which also included the strengthening of governmental accountability and the elimination of corruption in public administration with the objective of furthering democratisation.

The importance of civil and political rights as an integral part of development co-operation was emphasised again in 1997 with the re-organisation of the Ministry of Foreign Affairs. An important objective of the change at the Ministry of Foreign Affairs was that human rights should be considered as an integral part of foreign policy rather than a separate policy objective. As a result of this re-organisation the 'Division for Human Rights, Good Governance and Democratisation' was formed within the Ministry. This division, according to the Ministry, is "responsible for developing a consistent bilateral and multilateral policy in the field of human rights, good governance and democratisation."[11] Consequently, human rights considerations are regarded as an indispensable part of foreign policy including development co-operation and there is now a section of development aid specifically allotted to human rights, conflict management, democratisation and good governance. Apart from this category, aid is also allotted to the following categories: economy and employment,[12] agriculture and regional development,[13] environment,[14] social development,[15] education, research and culture,[16] humanitarian aid, macro-support and debt alleviation, aid for Suriname, the Netherlands Antilles and Aruba, multilateral programmes, and other programmes. Taken together, these categories of aid should contribute to the main objective of Dutch development co-operation, which is sustainable development and poverty alleviation. In 1997, Guatemala received aid under all of the first five categories mentioned above.

In 1997, the Dutch Government spent 0.81 per cent of its Gross National Product (GNP) on ODA, amounting to a total of Hfl. 6,082.663 million.[17] In

---

[11] Internet: www.minbuza.nl/English/f-sumabout14.html, August 1998.

[12] The idea behind this category is that: "If the productive sector of a country is stimulated in the right way this contributes to better employment and incomes." Authors' translation from: Ministerie van Buitenlandse Zaken [Ministry of Foreign Affairs], *Jaarverslag Ontwikkelings-samenwerking 1997* [Annual Report Development Co-operation 1997], The Hague, July 1998, p.15.

[13] The idea of this category is that agriculture is considered the most important sector generating employment in developing countries. Poverty is considered to diminish by means of rural development, thereby increasing productivity, food security and in the long-run enhancement of export income. Ministerie, *ibid.*, p. 18.

[14] It is considered that those who are poor degrade the environment, therefore the conservation of woodland is supported. Ministerie, *ibid.*, p. 22.

[15] This category aims at reducing absolute poverty by half by the year 2015. It includes primary education, primary health care, family planning, safe drinking water, sanitation and food intake. Ministerie, *ibid.*, p.26.

[16] The idea of this category is that people can participate and shape their society in the long run only if they possess certain skills. Ministerie, *ibid.*, p. 31.

[17] Ministerie, *ibid.*, p. 7. Two guilder equals about one US dollar.

compliance with international arrangements,[18] part of Dutch ODA is spent in the following ways: 20 per cent is spent on primary welfare;[19] four per cent on aid for reproductive health care (family planning); and 10 per cent on international nature and environmental policy. A minimum of Hfl. 50 million a year is also spent on preservation of tropical rain forest; and at least 0.25 per cent of GNP is spent on aid for the least developed countries.[20]

Presently, there is no fixed budget for human rights, conflict management, democratisation and good governance. In 1997, a total of Hfl. 102 million was spent in this category. For 1998, the budget has been reduced almost half to Hfl. 57 million.[21] It is estimated that of the total budget for human rights, conflict management, democratisation and good governance, 25 per cent is ODA.[22]

## DUTCH OFFICIAL DEVELOPMENT AID TO GUATEMALA

As stated in the introduction, Dutch development aid policy to Guatemala has recently changed. The main reason for this is that gross and systematic human rights violations have ceased. In the 1980s, under the regimes of General Lucas García, General Riós Montt and General Mejía Víctores, a 'scorched earth' policy was implemented, hundreds of indigenous communities were destroyed and thousands of people disappeared; these were the years in which the majority of massacres and disappearances took place. These human rights violations were the reason for the Dutch to channel development funds through Dutch co-financing organisations (*medefinancierings-organisaties*) to Guatemalan non-governmental organisations.[23] Although there was a gradual return to democracy with the election of a civilian President (Vinicio Cerezo), and the promulgation of a new and more democratic Constitution in 1985, human rights violations continued. For the Dutch this meant that aid was directed towards the protection of human rights. That is, money was made available to support human rights organisations, victims of human rights violations obtained support and money was made available for human rights education. At the time, aid was still mainly channelled through the co-financing organisations.

The signing of the Agreement on a Firm and Lasting Peace on 29 December 1996 between the Guatemalan Government and the URNG was cause for a change in Dutch development co-operation. After 36 years of internal armed conflict and

---

[18]  These arrangements are the outcome of the UN Conference on Environment and Development of 1992, the International Conference on Population and Development of 1994, the World Summit for Social Development of 1995 and the World Conference on Women of 1995.

[19]  Through primary welfare alimentation, healthcare and safe drinking water are provided for the poorest segments of society.

[20]  Ministerie van Buitenlandse Zaken [Ministry of Foreign Affairs], *Jaarverslag Ontwikkelings-samenwerking 1997* [Annual Report Development Co-operation 1997], The Hague, July 1998, p.10.

[21]  'Begroting 1999' [Budget 1999], *Internationale Samenwerking* [International Co-operation], No. 10, October 1998, p. 4.

[22]  Internet: www.minbuza.nl/English/f-sumabout14.html, August 1998.

[23]  At the time there were four co-financing organisations, namely: CEBEMO, ICCO, HIVOS and NOVIB.

gross and systematic violations of human rights, the Government of Guatemala and the URNG committed themselves to build a multi-ethnic and pluricultural society in which the development of the Guatemalan people would be central. For the Dutch Government the signing of the final peace agreement was an indication that the Guatemalan Government was committed to change. Consequently, in 1997 development aid was doubled for an indefinite period. In 1997, ODA amounted to Hfl. 19,570,000.[24] For 1998, the target budget was about Hfl. 25 million.[25] Of the 1997 budget almost 50 per cent was spent under the category of human rights, conflict management, democratisation and good governance, and close to 25 per cent was spent on agriculture and regional development. Although the total ODA budget allocated to Guatemala is insignificant compared with total Dutch ODA expenditure worldwide (0.3 per cent), the ODA allocated to Guatemala under the category of human rights, conflict management, democratisation and good governance constitutes a significant proportion of the total budget allocated under this heading worldwide (10 per cent). These data show that whilst Guatemala is not, on the whole, a major recipient of Dutch aid, financial support for human rights, conflict management, democratisation and good governance is considered vital in the current political context. For a breakdown of ODA according to the different categories see table below.

According to the Dutch Embassy in Guatemala, the priorities for development co-operation are: rural development, basic education and good governance.[26] The rubric of rural development includes all of the first four categories mentioned in the table and together makes up 45 per cent of all ODA to Guatemala. Under rural development, for example, funding is allocated to  support agricultural co-operatives and small businesses and aid is given for the development of safe drinking water facilities and reforestation. In 1997, rural development projects were concentrated mainly in two geographical areas: the Cuchamatanes, and the departments of Zacapa and Chiquimula. The Cuchumatanes is an area which takes its name from the mountain range covering the departments of El Quiche, Huehuetenango and Totonicapan. The majority of the population in these departments is indigenous[27] and the inhabitants were amongst those most severely affected by the violence during the years of conflict.[28] Prioritising aid to rural development projects in these departments has the effect of promoting the

---

[24]  Ministerie van Buitenlandse Zaken, *op. cit.*, p. 69.

[25]  Interview with  Walter Plomp, Dutch Embassy in Guatemala, 14 August 1998.

[26]  As above.

[27]  In El Quiche 83.4 per cent of the population is indigenous, in Huehuetenango 63.8 per cent, in Chiquimula 29.5 per cent and in Zacapa 4.4 per cent. In: *Guatemala: los contrastes del desarrollo humano* [Guatemala: the contrasts of human development], Guatemala City: PNUD/CEPAL, 1998, p. 220.

[28]  Of the 421 massacres, which took place between 1978 and 1985, 262 took place in El Quiche, 39 in Huehuetenango and 1 in Chiquimula. In: Summarised version of *Guatemala: Nunca Mas* [Guatemala: Never Again], the Report of the Interdiocesan Project for the *Recuperación de la Memoria Historica* (Recuperation of the Historical Memory; REHMI) published *by Oficina de Derechos Humanos del Arzobispado de Guatemala* (Office of the Human Rights of the Archbishop of Guatemala; ODHA), 6 June 1998, p. 34-38.

economic and social rights of the indigenous people in the area and indirectly addresses the issue of the marginalisation and discrimination suffered by the indigenous population in general. In contrast, the departments of Zacapa and Chiquimula were less affected by the violence in the 1980s and are inhabited mainly by *ladinos* (*ladinos* are Guatemalans of mixed descent who define themselves as 'non-indigenous'). This area was selected for support in the interests of 'balance', so that Dutch rural development aid would not be seen as favouring the indigenous population to the exclusion of the *ladinos*. In general, in both geographical areas the aim of these projects is to enhance sustainable development and encourage poverty alleviation.[29]

**Table 1**
**Total Dutch ODA to Guatemala in 1997[30]**

| Categories | | Total Expenditure in GuildersT | % of Total ODA |
|---|---|---|---|
| I. | Economy and Employment | 733,000 | 3.7 |
| II. | Agriculture and Regional Development | 4,681,000 | 24.0 |
| III. | Environment | 1,511,000 | 7.7 |
| IV. | Social Development | 1,829,000 | 9.3 |
| V. | Education, Research and Culture | 1,388,000 | 7.1 |
| VI. | Human Rights, Conflict Management, Democratisation and Good Governance | 9,428,000 | 48.2 |
| Total | | 19,570,000 | 100 |

In contrast to rural development aid, the Dutch Government supports basic education on a national rather than a regional basis. The Agreement on the Identity and Rights of Indigenous Peoples, signed in March 1995,[31] commits the Government to the introduction of bi-lingual and inter-cultural education at all levels. The State is also responsible for providing education according to international human rights norms. For Guatemala, a country with 22 Mayan indigenous languages and almost as many different ethnic groups, this implies a fundamental change in the State educational system. The Dutch Government is currently supporting Mayan educational non-governmental organisations which, together with the Guatemalan Ministry of Education, are preparing proposals for educational reform which will be introduced into the State system at the national level. Dutch aid for education will be discussed in more detail in one of the case studies below.

---

[29]  Interview with Walter Plomp, Dutch Embassy in Guatemala, 14 August 1998.
[30]  Ministerie van Buitenlandse Zaken, *op. cit.*, p. 69.
[31]  Although this agreement was signed in March 1995 it did not come into effect until the completion of the peace process in December 1996.

Support for good governance became a trend in development aid in the late 1980s after the World Bank announced that its support for economic development would be conditional on governments becoming more publicly accountable and transparent in their policy implementation.[32] In practice, this category has come to be used as a 'catch all' category which allows donor governments to channel aid to incipient democracies for projects which have an implicit human rights content (e.g. institution building, the strengthening of mechanisms for public participation, facilitating access to justice, improving the penal system) without explicitly stating that the promotion of human rights is their objective. When peace negotiations are in progress, there is normally a tendency for gross and systematic human rights violations to decrease (as in Guatemala). Once a peace agreement has been signed (as in Guatemala), this is regarded as a clear indication that the Government has undertaken a commitment to uphold the rule of law and protect human rights. To channel large amounts of development aid explicitly for human rights to a country where the Government had recently committed itself to uphold them, as in Guatemala, could be considered politically inopportune since support for human rights is normally taken to mean the protection of the individual against violations committed by the State. Providing aid for human rights is often still understood to mean that the Government is not fulfilling its post-conflict commitments. In an as yet precarious democracy, projects under the category 'good governance' which address the need to improve relations between the Government and the population by decentralising government institutions, modernising public administration and making it more accountable, or projects which support the setting up of participatory structures, do not bear the same negative connotations.

Nevertheless, the type of projects financed by the Dutch Government mentioned above and the specific projects listed below, which are defined as 'good governance', clearly involve activities for the promotion of human rights, both civil and political, and social, economic and cultural. Amongst these are: the right to take part in the conduct of public affairs, the right to organise, freedom of expression, freedom of association, the use of one's own language, the right to enjoy one's own culture and to practice one's own religion, the right to a fair trial and the right to education. Aid is not specified in terms of these rights or under the larger rubric of human rights. Rather these projects are defined under the ambiguous term of 'good governance'. The very ambiguity of the term, its lack of defining criteria and the fact that no international norms have been developed to determine whether Governments are complying with these criteria, mean that it is more difficult to hold governments accountable for non-compliance; a Government cannot, as such, be accused of violations of the principles of good governance. In contrast, human rights have an extensively developed norm system, which is internationally widely accepted and offers a mechanism by which Governments can be held to account for violations. It would be appropriate, where incipient democracies are receiving aid to improve their democratic structures and participatory mechanisms, for governments, both recipients and donors, to be held

---

[32]  World Bank, *Sub-Saharan Africa – From Crisis to Sustainable Growth*, Washington DC, 1989.

accountable for compliance with these objectives. If aid which is currently given under the rubric of 'good governance' were to be openly acknowledged as aid for the promotion and (in some cases) protection of human rights, this would be possible.

## The promotion of human rights through Dutch development aid

As shown above, the majority of aid to Guatemala falls within the category of human rights, conflict management, democratisation and good governance. Separate budgets exist for the different sub-categories.[33] In 1997, two projects in Guatemala received development aid within the sub-category of human rights. These support the work of the Human Rights Ombudsman and the Trust Fund of United Nations Mission in Guatemala (MINUGUA). The Hfl. 141,000 in aid for the Human Rights Ombudsman offices was in support of the Ombudsman's offices outside of the capital, which are poorly funded. These regional offices are essential for the rural population to have access to a national human rights institution to complain about violations. The money for the MINUGUA Trust Fund, Hfl. 186,000, was for the improvement of access to the judicial system in general. On the whole, the support for these projects contributes to the protection and promotion of human rights. Whether these projects achieve this in the most effective manner can only be evaluated by analysing them in detail and comparing them with other projects.

Under the sub-category of good governance a total of Hfl. 1,882,000 was spent on 14 different projects. Nearly 50 per cent of the money went to MINUGUA for the support of the following projects: a project to improve access to the justice system for indigenous people and to reduce discrimination in the legal system. This includes: the training of legal interpreters for work in the courts and the Public Prosecutor's Office; the education of lawyers, judges and legal officials to make them more aware of the principles of *derecho consuetudinario* (customary law);[34] a project for law centres offering free legal aid; support for the School of Legal Studies intended to improve the qualifications of judges and, as a result, their status in the judicial system; and one for strengthening the administration of justice in the department of El Quiche. The fund is also used to improve the penal system, for example improvement of prison conditions and the training of penitentiary personnel. Apart from MINIGUA allocation, other projects funded in the sub-category of good governance deal with such matters as the decentralisation of the Government and the strengthening of local authorities. Finally,, *the Comisión para el Esclarecimiento Histórico de las Violaciones a los Derechos Humanos y los hechos de violencia que han causado sufrimientos a la población Guatemalteca* (Commission for the Historical Clarification of the Human Rights

---

[33] The data for this section are taken from budget lists provided by the Ministry of Foreign Affairs and the Dutch Embassy in Guatemala.

[34] By customary law is meant the legal norms adhered to in the Mayan Communities.

Violations and Violent Acts which have caused suffering to the Guatemalan People; CEH)[35] is also supported under this sub-category.[36]

Amongst the small grants of less than Hfl. 150,000 which are administered directly by the Embassy there was a grant for the *Fundación de Antropologos Forenses de Guatemala* (Guatemalan Forensic Anthropology Foundation; FAFG) which, for the first time, received a grant for its work in support of the CEH. There was also a grant for an NGO whose objective is to encourage the participation of rural women in the affairs of their communities and in local government.

The criteria for funding a project from the sub-category human rights or good governance seems to be very fluid. So much so, that if money in one sub-category has been exhausted, funding for a project can be taken from the other sub-category. In terms of project funding this might not be a bad practice as funding seems to be more flexible. However, in terms of human rights policy development it should be questioned whether such a practice is advisable. On the one hand, it would seem to indicate that the sub-category of 'good governance' is inter-changeable with the sub-category of human rights and thus nothing other than a hidden human rights category. On the other hand, it avoids the necessity to define clear criteria for a 'rights' oriented development policy, making it difficult to hold either aid recipient or donor accountable for the promotion of human rights.

### Two case studies

To show how the projects supported contribute to the promotion and protection of human rights, two development aid projects have been analysed in depth, the first being an example of aid under the category of education and the second under good governance.[37] Under the first category *El Proyecto Mobilizador de Apoyo a la Educación Maya* (Mobilisation Project for the Support of Mayan Education; PROMEM) is analysed. This project is financed exclusively by the Dutch with funds channelled through UNESCO Maya. PROMEM supports Mayan educational non-governmental organisations which, in co-operation with the Guatemalan Ministry of Education, are currently engaged in preparing proposals for educational reforms which will introduce bi-lingual and inter-cultural education into the State system in accordance with the commitments undertaken in the Peace Accords. Under the sub-category of good governance a small grant, administered directly by the Dutch Embassy, was made to the FAFG specifically for the exhumation of a clandestine cemetery and a forensic report which is to be included in the report of the CEH.

---

[35] The CEH is the commission investigating human rights violations committed throughout the 36 years of internal conflict.

[36] The rest of the money in category VI was spent in the sub-categories of democratisation and conflict management.

[37] These projects were selected because of their accessibility for the purpose of gathering information. A project from the sub-category of human rights was not analysed because of its obvious contribution to the protection and promotion of human rights.

*Education*

In the case of Guatemala, basic education still needs much improvement. Illiteracy rates show that 37 per cent of the total Guatemalan population over 15 years of age cannot read or write; of these, 77 per cent live in rural areas.[38] In the department of Alta Verapaz, where 90 per cent of the population is indigenous, data show that 66 per cent of those over 15 years of age are illiterate. In rural areas the rate of illiteracy rises to 73 per cent. The illiteracy rate amongst women is even higher, reaching 86 per cent in 1996.[39] Promoting the right to education will not only improve literacy, but it will also provide people with better skills in general, allowing them to participate more actively in shaping their own society. In this way, support for the right to education contributes to the promotion of civil and political rights, and social, economic and cultural rights. Teaching people how to read and write will, for example, enable them to understand the legal terms contained in the title deeds which give them the right of possession of their small-holdings and will mean that they will no longer be subject to fraudulent take-overs which deprive them of their only source of subsistence. Furthermore, they will be better able to read instructions on how crop fertilizer should be used, thereby indirectly improving crop growth and food intake. With regard to the right to health, it will reduce the risk of health hazards because people will be able to read about the proper use of fertilizer and the health risks involved. It will also make people better equipped to organise and set up co-operatives which will improve their productivity and their ability to secure fair prices for their cash crops. On the whole, promoting the right to education enables people to be better informed about political decisions which affect them. In general, through education poor people's life expectancy, level of health and nutrition and standard of living will be improved. As the standard of living improves, civil and political rights will also be promoted. For example, a literate and prosperous rural population will be more likely to be able to take informed decisions in local and national elections as to which candidates will truly serve their interests, and less likely to be corrupted or deceived. They are more likely to be able to organise and lobby at the local and national level to further their social and economic interests, and more likely to be able and willing to participate in public life and exercise their civil and political rights. Consequently, development aid for increased educational coverage and improved levels of literacy promotes social, economic, cultural, civil and political rights.

Moreover, educational reform in Guatemala is essential, because the State education system has in the past discriminated against the indigenous population and indirectly supported State policies which have led to their social, economic and cultural marginalisation and to their being denied their civil and political

---

[38] UNDP/CEPAL, *Guatemala: los contrastes del desarrollo humano* [Guatemala: the contrasts of human development], Guatemala, 1998, pp. 38-39.

[39] Secretaria General del Consejo de Planificación Economico [General Secretary of the Planification and Economic Council], *Plan Marco para el Desarrollo del Departamento de Alta Verapaz* [Plan for the development of the Department of Alta Verapaz], Guatemala, 1996, p. 34.

79

rights. In the Agreement on the Identity and Rights of the Indigenous Peoples, the Government recognizes for the first time that Guatemala is a 'multi-ethnic, pluricultural and multi-lingual nation' and undertakes to reform the educational system accordingly and to recognize the indigenous languages as official languages on an equal footing with Spanish. These commitments are incorporated into the Agreement on a Firm and Lasting Peace, which re-affirms the necessity to recognise the rights and identity of the indigenous population.

The wide-ranging proposals for educational reform contained in the indigenous agreement commit the Government, amongst other things, to: decentralise the educational system and increase educational coverage, especially in indigenous areas; promote the use of indigenous languages in the State school system; and incorporate indigenous educational concepts and cultural content into the curriculum in a system of bi-lingual and inter-cultural education.

It is clear that any educational system plays a key role in instilling cultural and social values. In Guatemala a reformed education system in which the local indigenous language is taught as well as Spanish and which instills respect for indigenous cultural values and traditions can go a long way towards laying the basis for a truly multi-cultural society. In the long term it may contribute to the creation of a nation in which cultural diversity is respected and different ethnic groups can live together in mutual harmony exercising their democratic rights.

With regard to education, Dutch development policy is specifically interested in supporting education systems which are undergoing reforms.[40] This is especially true where reform will contribute to making the education system more accessible to groups which have been denied educational opportunities in the past. In general, through their development aid for education, the Dutch Government encourages governmental institutions and non-governmental organisations to co-operate and seek improvement in the education system and aims to enhance cultural identity and promote equality. In the Guatemalan case, development aid in support of educational reform is intended to contribute to re-affirming indigenous cultural identity, combating racial discrimination and creating the conditions necessary for a multi-ethnic participatory democracy.

The Dutch support educational reform in Guatemala through the funding of PROMEM, a UNESCO Maya project which provides assistance and promotes co-operation between the Government of Guatemala and UNESCO and whose objective is to support the Government, the organisations in the *Consejo Nacional de Educación Maya* (National Council of Mayan Education; CNEM) and other non-governmental organsations with a view to developing Mayan education.[41] Starting in 1996, PROMEM received Hfl. 3,600,000, for a period of three years, with the option of renewing their grant, and is entirely financed by Dutch development aid. This money is used partly to employ specialists to research aspects of Mayan culture which have been lost as a result of being consistently

---

[40]  Ministerie van Buitenlandse Zaken, *op. cit.*, pp. 31-32.
[41]  Manuel de Jesús Salazar Tetzagüic and Vicenta Telón Sajcabun, *Valores de la Filosofía Maya* [Values of the Mayan Philosophy], Guatemala: UNESCO / PROMEM, May 1998, p. 7.

undermined and undervalued in the educational system and the wider society. An example of one such study is an investigation into Mayan mathematics and the Mayan Calendar. PROMEM contributes its results to CNEM and other organisations involved in the formulation of proposals for the introduction of Mayan educational concepts and knowledge into the State education system, publishes text for use in schools and, together with the member organisations of CNEM, encourages initiatives to recover, revitalize and diffuse Mayan culture.

CNEM could be said to have a political role and a cultural role. It is currently the most important organisation involved in formulating proposals for educational reform and, in practice, acts as counterpart for the Ministry of Education. It co-ordinates more than 20 Mayan educational, research and cultural organisations, including associations of teachers and parents, all interested in educational reform. Amongst these is the *Associación de Escuelas Mayas* (Association of Mayan Schools), a group of private schools which have pioneered the introduction of Mayan educational concepts and content into the educational curriculum. It was set up in 1993, after the first National Congress on educational reform. Since then, it has been continuously involved in consultations with the Government on educational reform; it was represented on the *Comisión Paritaria* (Parity Commission: consisting of equal numbers of representatives of the Government and of Mayan organisations) set up under the Agreement on the Identity and Rights of Indigenous Peoples to make recommendations for educational reform and is currently represented on the *Comisión Consultiva sobre Reforma Educativa* (Consultative Commission on Educational Reform) together with representatives of the Ministry of Education. This group is  preparing practical proposals for changes in the curriculum of State schools on the basis of the recommendations of the Parity Commission.

Apart from contributing its expertise to CNEM, PROMEM has also financed it directly with a grant of Q2,000,000 (approximately Hfl. 570,000) for two years for the purposes of strengthening its organisational structure and administration.[42] This grant, which terminated at end of 1998, has been renewed. In the interests of balance, a smaller grant has been made directly to the *Dirección General de Educación Bi-lingue* (General Directorate of Bilingual and Inter-Cultural Education; DIGEBI) in the Guatemalan Ministry of Education responsible for supervising and developing bilingual and inter-cultural education in the State education system; the latter institution is also a member of CNEM. Thus, by supporting PROMEM, the Dutch government indirectly stimulates policy-making which will determine the nature of educational reforms which may change the face of Guatemalan society in the future and will certainly contribute to promoting the rights of the indigenous population.

In its cultural role CNEM benefits from the expertise of PROMEM and the experience of its own member organisations, promotes educational research and collects information and material which can be included in proposals for

---

[42]   Telephone conversation with German Curichiche, board member of CNEM, on 21 August 1998, Guatemala.

educational reform. In particular, it benefits from the practical experience of the Association of Mayan Schools, analysing their methods and drawing on the content of their educational curriculum for inclusion in its proposals for a reformed educational curriculum. The Mayan Schools, in their turn, benefit from their membership of CNEM to gain access to the latest research and ideas about Mayan education and have access to training courses provided on request by CNEM with funding from PROMEM.

One such Mayan School, which is used as a model by CNEM, is *Qawinaqel* (Our People in Poqomam), in Palin in the department of Escuintla.[43] *Qawinaqel* is the largest school in Palin (the capital of the municipality with a population of some 25,000, of whom 60 per cent are Poqomam), with over 400 students at primary and pre-primary level and 75 at secondary level taught by about 20 teachers. The school illustrates how bilingual and inter-cultural education could be put into practice taking into account the central aspects of Mayan educational philosophy. The pupils and teachers are all Poqomames. The children wear their traditional costume and all subjects are taught in Poqomam with the main concepts translated into Spanish. The school teaches the State curriculum but in addition it includes, for example, as part of literature, *Cuentos de los Abuelos* (Stories from our Grandfathers), and as part of history *La Palabra de Antes* (the Word from the Past), which are essentially orally transmitted traditional fables and history which have now been collected in written form. The school timetable is written according to the Mayan calendar on one side with Mayan numbers and according to the Gregorian calendar with Roman numerals on the other. The school has a football pitch and a science laboratory, but in addition it has a large plot of land for agricultural education and a central patio with a raised platform for Mayan religious ceremonies. All these features reflect the inter-cultural nature of the education and a respect for Mayan culture and values.

In accordance with Mayan ideas about the holistic or integral nature of education, as much importance is given to culture, music and dance and communication skills as to formal education. The school has a large and well-equipped theatre in which pupils and teachers together present dramatisations of the 'Stories from our Grandfathers', which essentially convey Mayan moral and ethical values and present performances of traditional dance and music. The school also has a radio transmitter which reaches the whole municipality. Teachers and pupils together present programmes in Spanish and Poqomam on such themes as the use of the Poqomam language, Mayan education, human rights and the Peace Accords. The Mayan view about the importance of the community is reflected in the fact that the school's facilities are open to the public. Community organisations can rent rooms for meetings, the community has free access to the library, which is the only one in Palin, members of the community attend the theatre in large numbers and the radio programme has a large local audience.

*Qawinaqel* is a private independent school recognised by the Ministry of Education, which initially received foreign funding for its construction. Until

---

[43]    Information about the school was gathered during a visit in August 1998.

1997, it was entirely financed by fees paid by parents of Q20 (Hfl. 6) per pupil per month.[44] In 1997, for the first time, it received a subsidy from the Ministry of Education of about Hfl. 2,600 per month for a period of 10 months in addition to the finance from parental contributions. The school is rather reluctant to become fully dependent on State funding because it fears that it might lose its independence and would have to adapt its curriculum to the State school system and lose its unique Mayan content.

In Guatemala there remains much scepticism amongst the *ladino* elite aboutMayan schools. Instead of regarding them as a way of promoting Mayan culture and inter-cultural understanding, they perceive them as a threat to their dominant *ladino* way of life.

However, it is clear that an indigenous population which is secure in its cultural identity and which benefits from improved social and economic conditions is more likely to have confidence in State authorities and public institutions and to take advantage of opportunities to participate in decision making which affect their lives. For instance, if indigenous organisations take advantage of the spaces for participation created in the Development Councils at municipal, departmental and regional level, they may be able to influence decisions about investment in rural development and in particular decisions about land use and conservation which are of vital importance culturally and economically to the indigenous population. Similarly, increased participation in politics at the national level will enable indigenous people to influence opinion and further their specific social and economic interests.

It is clear, as we have argued above, that increased access to basic education in the form of increased literacy will tend to promote human rights in general. From this it should follow that a reformed educational system in which the curriculum is taught in the indigenous languageand the cultural content and teaching methods respect and reinforce Mayan values and cultural concepts, is likely to promote human rights - both social, economic and cultural rights, and civil and political rights of the indigenous population in particular.

However, the proposals for educational reform have not yet been finalised and at present it is only possible to speculate on what the results of their implementation may be. A spokeswoman for the Consultative Commission on Educational Reform recently stated that the aim of educational reform was to eradicate the discrimination which Guatemala's indigenous population had suffered for more than 500 years.[45] An ex-member of the same Commission was of the opinion that the quality of the increased coverage in basic education provided up till now has not been sufficient to achieve any significant change amongst Guatemalans, that the social impact of the proposed educational reforms would not be measurable in less than ten years and that it would be premature to talk of

---

[44]    Taking into consideration that 70 per cent of the population in Guatemala lives in poverty, Hfl. 6 a month per child for education is a significant amount.

[45]    Eva Sazo de Mendez, spokeswoman of the Consultative Commission, in *Prensa Libre*, 11 January 1999, Guatemala.

immediate change since the educational reforms aimed to change the social structure of the country and that would take many years.[46]

Nevertheless, one can argue that Dutch support for PROMEM is even now contributing towards eradicating discrimination against the indigenous population since PROMEM seeks to encourage initiatives to recover, revitalise and diffuse Mayan culture. By spreading knowledge about the Mayan culture they will tend to reduce hostility towards it and diminish discrimination. PROMEM's financial support for CNEM has enabled it to strengthen its organisational structure and continue working with its member organisations to lobby the Government to achieve educational reform. The Dutch in this case are supporting not only institutional strengthening but also participation in the democratic process. In general, Dutch support for PROMEM and through it CNEM means that the Dutch have an input into educational reforms which, although their impact is not measurable at the moment, will in the long run certainly go a long way towards reducing discrimination. They are therefore directly promoting the right not to be discriminated against and with it, indigenous rights in general. Thus the Dutch, through their funding for educational reform in Guatemala are helping to lay the basis for a society in which cultural diversity is respected and in which different ethnic groups can live together in mutual harmony exercising their democratic rights. They are also, directly and indirectly, promoting a whole series of inter-linked human rights - civil, cultural, economic, political and social rights.

*Good governance*

In 1997, for the first time, the Guatemalan Forensic Anthropology Foundation (FAFG) received ODA funding from the Dutch Government.[47] At the request of CEH a grant of Hfl. 102,000 was made available specifically for the exhumation of a clandestine cemetery in Panzós, a town in Alta Verapaz where an estimated 100 Q'eqchi peasants were killed by the army in 1978. The CEH considered that the findings from this exhumation and three others (also carried out by the FAFG, but funded from other sources) would help to throw light on the motives and mechanisms of the violence in the 1980s and assist in the process of reconciliation. The United Nations Office for Project Services (UNOPS) which administers funds for the CEH had exhausted its allotted budget and approached the Dutch Embassy, which agreed to finance the project on condition that the findings would be for the use of the CEH and that the FAFG report would not be released for general publication without the prior authorisation of the CEH.[48]

---

[46] Dino Zaghi, ex-member of the Consultative Commission, in *Prensa Libre*, 11 January 1999, Guatemala.

[47] The information about FAFG was obtained through interviews with José Suasnavar, a forensic anthropologist working with FAFG, held between the end of August and the beginning of September 1998. One of the authors has been present at a number of the exhumations undertaken by FAFG in Guatemala. Furthermore, the interview held with Walter Plomp from the Dutch Embassy also provided information about the activities of FAFG.

[48] The CEH report was published on 25 February 1999.

The FAFG - originally known as the *Equipo de Antropologos Forenses de Guatemala* (Guatemalan Forensic Anthropology Team; EAFG) - was set up as a non-governmental organisation in 1992 and aimed, through publicising its findings, to make the public aware of the gross human rights violations which had occurred in the past. Working with human rights organisations, it considered itself to be part of the campaign to combat impunity. Since then, its objectives have evolved in line with the new political situation produced by the signing of the Peace Agreements and include support for the democratisation process and, through its reports, a contribution to the better understanding of the social and historical context of the events of the 1980s in order to promote the process of reconciliation. However, its main activities continue to be the exhumation of clandestine cemeteries and the campaign against impunity.

The organisation consists of a permanent staff of nine - amongst them archaeologists, social anthropologists and forensic anthropologists - and five support staff, including a photographer, a secretary, an accountant, a computer programmer and a laboratory assistant. Their overhead costs are currently covered by a grant from the Danish Government under their human rights programme[49] and the Soros Foundation.[50] Separate funds have to be raised to cover the specific costs of each exhumation which include contracts for international specialists, for example pathologists and radiographers. Some 53 exhumations have been undertaken in Guatemala to date, of which the FAFG has been responsible for 38. Their high technical standards and wide experience have brought them international recognition and their members are regularly invited to act as consultants for the UN in countries such as Bosnia-Hercegovina and Rwanda.

It can be argued that the work of the FAFG has contributed to human rights in Guatemala in different ways at different periods. In the period before the signing of the Peace Agreements, working as part of the human rights movement, they used their findings to expose the extra-judicial executions which had taken place in the 1980s and bring public attention to the effects of the counter-insurgency policy pursued at the time. Together with other organisations campaigning against impunity, the activities of the FAFG were directed toward the protection of human rights. In the changed political context produced by the Peace Agreements their activities continue to involve the protection of human rights, but also contribute to the promotion of human rights. In particular, its activities promote the right to association and participation. Since their findings can be used by the relatives of the victims seeking justice, their activities are also instrumental in protecting the right to an effective remedy.

In Panzós (a town of some 2,920 inhabitants) in the Valle Polochic in the department of Alta Verapaz on 29 May 1978, an army detachment, called in by the mayor and the local landowners, opened fire on 100 peasants demonstrating in

---

[49] *Programa para Derechos Humanos en Centro-America* (Central American Human Rights Programme; PRODECA).

[50] The Soros Foundation is a United States foundation supporting democratisation projects in Central America and Eastern Europe.

85

defence of their land rights outside the town hall; many died on the spot, others were wounded and died at home or in hospital. The unidentified bodies of 39 victims were interred in a mass grave on the outskirts of the town.

This was the forerunner of many other extra-judicial executions which were to take place all over the country. No charges were ever brought against the army commanders, the mayor or the landowners. Some of those responsible still live in the area side by side with the families of the victims. The perpetrators of the crime have enjoyed total impunity, while the peasants have continued to live in fear; as a result, no peasant organisations have been able to organise in the area until recently.[51] With the signing of the Peace Agreements, the arrival of MINUGUA and the gradual demilitarisation of the country, the pall of fear over the Valle Polochic began to lift. For the first time in 1996, the anniversary of the massacre in Panzós was publicly commemorated in the presence of national human rights NGOs and peasant organisations.

In 1996, a group of widows formed a Committee with the objectives firstly of securing a Christian burial for their relatives, secondly of opening legal proceedings against those they consider responsible and thirdly to obtain some form of indemnification for their sufferings. The first step was to obtain official authorisation for the Committee from the local mayor who, not surprisingly, placed obstacles in the way of its formation. Having overcome these obstacles and having heard about an exhumation carried out by the FAFG in a neighbouring department, the Committee asked the FAFG to do the exhumation in Panzós. The next requirement was for them to approach the Public Prosecutor's Office and officially denounce the existence of the clandestine cemetery and those whom they considered responsible for the crime. The Public Prosecutor's Office was then obliged to investigate and the Court authorised the FAFG to carry out the exhumation. This stage, too, was not without its difficulties, since prosecutors are often reluctant to proceed with exhumations for fear of reprisals and as a result judicial proceedings are often held up. However, in the case of Panzós, the *Familiares de los Desaparecidos de Guatemala* (Relatives of the Disappeared in Guatemala; FAMDEGUA), a national human rights NGO, became a party to the legal proceedings, offering legal advice and following through the judicial process.

Where an exhumation takes place in a town, as in the case of Panzós, the FAFG will organise public meetings to which the local authorities - the mayor, the justice of the peace, the police and community members - are invited and at which they explain their work and talk about the right to organise, about the right to seek an effective remedy and about how the judicial system works.

Generally, the physical work of excavation will be carried out by members of the extended family of the victims from several different communities working together voluntarily under the supervision of the FAFG while the widows and female relatives prepare food for the workers. At regular group meetings, attended also by a psychologist from the *Equipo de Estudios Comunitarios y Acción Psycho-Social* (Community Studies and Psycho-Social Action Team; ECAP) and

---

[51]  Interview with community members by the authors in the period 1995 through 1997.

the NGO which is supporting the relatives with legal advice (FAMDEGUA in the case of Panzós), the anthropologists explain what they are doing and give progress reports on their findings.

These meetings also offer an opportunity for those affected to voice their opinions and plan for the future. Members of one group, when asked 'What do you aim to achieve with this exhumation?', replied 'We want them to rest in peace' and 'We want the world and the Government to know that our relatives were not criminals but innocent victims' and 'We want the Government to believe that what we said is true' and from a woman whose husband and one son had been killed 'We want help from the Government because we had to bring up our children on our own' and from another 'We want tin roofing for our houses' and from another, 'We want money in compensation'. From these statements it becomes clear that justice is seen principally in terms of acknowledgement and reparation, but not in terms of retribution.[52]

An important part of the work of the anthropologists consists in interviews with survivors, witnesses and family members for the purposes of obtaining background information and identifying the victims. In these interviews, at which the psychologist from ECAP is present, people feel able to tell their stories without fear, often for the first time, and for the first time those listening hear the full history of what happened in their communities in the 1980s. For the first time too, they feel supported in their grief and bereavement.

The visits to Panzós of Christian Tomuschat, UN appointed Commissioner to the CEH, who had expressed interest in the exhumation and procured funding for it, and Julio Arango Escobar, the Human Rights Ombudsman, who had also supported it, gave a measure of public recognition to the achievements of the Widows Committee. The activities to mark the official interment of the bodies some months later organised by a Co-ordinating Committee of human rights, indigenous and peasant organisations including the Widows Committee, lasted two days and were reported extensively in the international media.

An analysis of this process of empowerment shows firstly how, in the context of an exhumation, a group of semi-literate indigenous women has learnt how to exercise their right to organise. The formation of a committee requires knowledge of administrative procedures and how to deal with local authorities. With the experience it has acquired this Committee, once it has achieved its original aims, may in the future widen its objectives and put pressure on the local authorities to finance rural development projects. In a similar case in Rabinal, Baja Verapaz, the Committee of Widows and Orphans converted itself into a Development Committee for the Victims of Violence and presented the municipality with

---

[52] Edgar Gutierrez pointed out that of more than 6,000 interviews not one person interviewed demanded vengeance. Public presentation by Edgar Gutierrez of *Guatemala: Nunca Más* [Guatemala: Never Again], the Report of the Interdiocesan Project for the *Recuperación de la Memoria Historica* (Recuperation of the Historic Memory; REHMI) published by *Oficina de Derechos Humanos del Arzobispado de Guatemala* (Office of the Human Rights of the Archbishop of Guatemala; ODHA), 6 June 1998 in Cobán, Guatemala, 5 September 1998.

proposals for the financing of safe drinking water and drainage systems in their community.

Secondly, members of the Widows Committee have lost their fear of the State and its agents, previously the principal violators of human rights, and have exercised their right to an effective remedy by making formal accusations against the perpetrators which the Public Prosecutor will be obliged to investigate. This is still a dangerous process and by so doing they expose themselves to the risk of intimidation and reprisals. In many cases this is the first time that members of a rural community have come into contact with State institutions and realise that these institutions can work in favour of their interests rather than against them.

Thirdly, the actual work of excavation unites peasants from various different isolated communities who may have relatives amongst the dead or who come to show solidarity with the families. This shared experience helps to restore the 'social fabric' of rural society, torn apart by years of militarisation and armed conflict. It also shows the participants that they are not alone in the struggle against impunity, and encourages them to denounce the existence of other clandestine cemeteries. For example, villagers from Canguacha participated in the exhumation at Panzós and thereafter decided to denounce the existence of the clandestine cemetery in Las Margaritas/Rubeltzul, where their relatives were buried. This clandestine cemetery was recently exhumed by the FAFG.

Most importantly, as a result of these exhumations the victims and their relatives have found a voice. For the first time they have been able to tell their stories, whose truth is irrefutably confirmed by the forensic evidence presented by the anthropologists. For the first time their suffering and grief has been acknowledged and 'dignified'.

Furthermore, during the exhumation process the widows and other community members came into contact, for the first time, with national and international human rights organisations which can provide them with a support network and help them achieve their objectives. In Panzós, the widows may have learned for the first time about the functions of the Human Rights Ombudsman and gave their testimonies to the CEH.

From the above, it is clear that the work of the FAFG has directly and indirectly contributed to the promotion of human rights. People have learnt to organise and to exercise their civil and political rights – once organised, they are likely also to demand their social and economic rights. They have learned how to use the judicial system and deal with public authorities. More than anything, they have learned how to participate in civil society and make their voice heard.

## CONCLUSION

During the years of conflict Dutch development aid to Guatemala was directed towards the protection of human rights. Human rights organisations were supported and victims of human rights violations were assisted. This type of development aid, given specifically for funding non-governmental organisations and channelled through co-financing organisations, may be seen as a form of silent protest on the part of the Dutch Government against the violations committed by the Guatemalan Governments at the time. The signing of the Peace Agreements however, was cause for the Dutch Government to change its development policy toward Guatemala. In 1997, aid was doubled and development funding shifted. Now that gross and systematic human rights violations belonged to the past and the Guatemalan Government itself had made a commitment to democratic principles and the protection and promotion of human rights, development aid for human rights was considered less necessary. Instead, aid was channelled to projects under the rubric of good governance.

This would seem to indicate that the Dutch Government does not consider it opportune to provide more than a minimal amount of aid specifically for human rights because support for human rights continues to be seen in terms of protection of the rights of the individual against violations by the State rather than the promotion of human rights, and would therefore have negative political implications. Thus, once violations of human rights are considered to have ceased, the allocation of development aid for human rights also diminishes.

This is not to say that human rights in Guatemala are not protected or promoted by means of Dutch development aid. On the contrary, the analysis of the two case studies shows that by supporting PROMEM the Dutch are not only promoting the right to education but also a wide range of social, economic and cultural rights, and civil and political rights. Dutch support for PROMEM will, in particular, help to combat discrimination against indigenous people in the education system and, in the long run, in society at large. It will therefore contribute to the promotion of the right not to be discriminated against. The analysis of the second case study, FAFG, shows that although the project was not funded as a human rights project, the work of FAFG clearly contributes to the promotion of civil and political rights. Specifically, the work of FAFG promotes the right to participation, freedom of association, and the right to an effective remedy for the victims.

These case studies show that development does promote human rights, although development aid does not address human needs in terms of 'rights'. It is somewhat surprising that Dutch development aid policy is not more specific about the rights it promotes, especially since it requires the recipient organisations to report on how the funds received have enhanced human rights. In the light of this, it would seem only appropriate for the Minister for Development Co-operation, in its annual report, to account for the ways in which its funds contribute to the protection and promotion of human rights. By engaging in a detailed analysis of the projects funded in terms of their contribution to human rights, the Minister for Development Co-operation would be able to identify the most effective ways of protecting and promoting human rights and clarify the policy objectives of development aid including, especially in the case of Guatemala, an open commitment to the promotion of human rights. This would mean that the recipient Government could also be subject to a greater measure of accountability in terms of human rights.

# Carrots and Sticks for Democratisation in Burma: Policies of the EU and the ASEAN

*Zaw Oo and Kai Grieg*

# INTRODUCTION

During the past decade, many developing countries have undergone great transformations – a phenomenon often referred to as 'the third wave of democratisation'. Being part of this international trend, the people of Burma demonstrated as early as in 1990 their desire to restore democracy and basic human rights by giving their mandate to the National League for Democracy (NLD) in the general elections. Thousands of Burmese have sacrificed their lives in pushing for a political opening towards a democratic transition, which the military regime has resisted at all cost by suppressing the implementation of the popular mandate.

Conventional wisdom, as expressed by various policy think-tanks and governments within the region, holds that a democratic Burma can effectively address the problems of both domestic and global concerns such as human rights, drugs and refugees, but that the international community can do nothing to make this outcome more likely. Conventional wisdom may be right on the first count, but probably wrong on the second. In Burma's struggle for democratic change, a propitious international environment could make a difference for victory in favour of the forces of change.

It is widely recognised that the current political situation in Burma is intolerable. UNICEF has aptly characterised it as 'a silent emergency' with serious implications for peace and stability in the region.[1] On the one hand, Burma's crisis is a fertile ground for a small group of foreign investors to do business with the ruling regime in extracting windfall profits from what economists call 'lootable resources'. On the other hand, the crisis imposes high costs on the population of neighbouring countries in terms of health, drug trafficking and abuse, human migration, security encroachment and heightened tension.

Domestically, the picture is similar. The beneficiaries of the political situation is the military elite and a handful of cronies who control the domestic end of business deals surrounding the exploiting the natural resource base, as well as extortion of the desperate population through money exchange, forced labour, forced procurement at below market prices, etc. This behaviour further complicates the prospects for economic reform as the ruling group benefits directly from a tightly controlled economy in terms of both personal wealth and political domination. Crony capitalism, therefore, thrives on a sizeable natural resource base as well as tax base (with a high share stemming from the primary sector). However, this state of total control fuels intense fear of repression in the population for their opposition to the regime. Correspondingly, the ruling group fears reprisals once it gives up the means of power. This has created a stalemate, which Nobel peace laureate Daw Aung San Suu Kyi has proposed to resolve through negotiation. In the meantime, the impasse causes 'a silent emergency' affecting the larger population. The majority of the population suffers individually from the deteriorating performance of the public sector, including lack of access to education, health services, economic opportunities and other human rights. Collectively, they are not accorded certain collective rights, including freedom of

---

[1] UNICEF, *A Situation Analysis of Myanmar's Children and Women,* Yangon, UNICEF, 1991.

association and self-determination. This situation is worse for the non-Burman ethnic population who are more severely effected individually by the non-performing state sector as well as by the lack of collective rights.[2] The population's desire for change is expressed through a highly organised democratic movement that has denounced violence as a means of power transfer.

Political change could reduce the current political and economic distortions, and give rise to greater opportunities on the individual level for a large number of people. The international community could play an important role in resolving the crisis by helping the Burmese overcome the deadly stalemate. The international community could assist not only by providing tangible resources, but also by reinforcing the legitimacy and credibility of political developments leading towards a comprehensive settlement, national reconciliation and long-term reconstruction. International stakeholders are agreed regarding this analysis as well as the need for change. However, for a number of reasons disagreement exists regarding the pathway of a process of change as well as the role of international stakeholders and the nature of external intervention. These disagreements stem from differing assessments of the effects of a specific policy instrument *per se*, as well as the parameters that drive the decision-making process among the stakeholders and their self-interest in a process of change. The significant potential for welfare improvement as a result of political change suggests that it is not a zero-sum game; win-win strategies can be successful.

## THE ARGUMENT

This article will present a preliminary examination of the issues appertaining to the international mechanisms employed in promoting democratic change in Burma. Particular attention will be given to the incentive and disincentive policies adopted by two regional organisations: the European Union (EU) and the Association for Southeast Asian Nations (ASEAN). The rationale of the different approaches will be scrutinised and the evidence weighed for and against them with reference to an analysis of their implications in Burma. Both the EU and the ASEAN deal with Burma for a variety of reasons, not all of them related to democratisation. Members of both these regional organisations have dealt with Burma in economic and diplomatic matters. This article deals specifically with those government actions taken collectively under broad regional institutional umbrellas – designed wholly, or to a significant extent, towards promoting change in Burma. Such actions are often referred to in general as 'incentive' and 'disincentive' policies, and are often portrayed in a dichotomous fashion as either sanctions or engagement.

The ASEAN is a regional institution whose stated mission is "promotion of regional peace and stability". The intense conflicts of the 1960s and 1970s that greatly undermined the stability of the whole region gave a major impetus for the ASEAN countries to establish a framework for regional order. Since its foundation, the ASEAN hopes eventually to include all Southeast Asian countries

---

[2] The term 'Burman' denotes the ethnic majority, whereas 'Burmese' refer to all inhabitants of Burma.

under its umbrella and has devised its own logic for integrating new members into the association. This drive for one Southeast Asia at the regional level is not frictionless, not least on the question of Burma becoming a member. It is in this context this article attempts to make a systematic analysis of the interactions between policies of the two regional institutions in attempting to bring meaningful change to Burma.

The role of the ASEAN in stimulating changes in Burma can be seen as a regional response to practical problems, whereas the EU policies are reflecting a more or less preferred strategy of the major international players, and providing a larger context that determine the outcome of regional approaches. In other words, Burma's problem cannot be treated as domestic or regional because its ramifications have already gone beyond the regional context, affecting sentiments and societies around the world. While a regional institution like the ASEAN can make an impact on Burma its actual contribution towards the objective of producing changes depends on how other institutions like the EU play their parts.

Against this international and local nexus, this article will look at the contrasts between regional organisations in their dealings with a country known for extensive human rights violations rather than looking at policies of individual European or Asian countries. In particular, the policy tools of incentives and disincentives – in the diplomatic and economic fields respectively – will be highlighted. The main purpose is to submit to critical review the conventional wisdom regarding incentive and disincentive policies adopted by various foreign governments and international organisations. The basic rationale, the underlying assumptions, tool selection, and supporting evidence will all be examined. Our argument is that conventional wisdom on the usefulness of disincentive policies has been seriously underestimated while the advantage of incentive policies are put forward without documenting any causal linkages with the desired goal, as if policy outcomes themselves become goals.

The second purpose is to develop an analytical framework for reassessing the effects of these policies on the targeted country, i.e. Burma. We argue that most observers who have commented on the debates between engagement and sanctions grossly neglected a proper assessment of the impact of these policy tools, particularly on the dynamics of political change. And finally, it is also our purpose to stimulate increased awareness of and thinking about the many forms of incentive and disincentive policy tools at the disposal of international players – organisations and governments alike. Also, the possibility of synergetic or confounding effects when combining these policies shall be examined carefully to test the benefit of greater co-ordination between various policy circles that are interested in formulating viable alternatives. In particular, the following questions will be addressed: what else could have been done, and could the outcome have been better from the point of view of the sender nations.

In order to examine these questions, this study will use the analytical framework used by David Baldwin. He adopts the notion of 'statecraft' in international politics, defined as "governmental influence attempts directed at other actors in the international system". Baldwin includes a whole range of psycho-social dynamics besides changes in the target's behaviour in the

95

'influence' process, through which policy-makers succeed in modifying behaviour in ways they would not have done on their own accord.[3] According to this definition, the influence attempts can be based on both incentives or disincentives, or any form of economic and non-economic tools being employed to influence or persuade other governments to change their behaviour or policies. These tools may have an order of increasing or decreasing severity and scope and can range from diplomatic persuasion, public appeals, official condemnation, non-economic sanctions, economic sanctions, tied aid including humanitarian assistance, and military action. They may be applied either unilaterally or multilaterally in conjunction with UN mechanisms or through other international organisations such as the World Bank and the IMF.

## PRINCIPAL ISSUES SHAPING APPROACHES TO BURMA

Against the backdrop of growing interdependence in the international system, eroding well-defined national borders of sovereign states, certain fundamental forces have influenced both the European Union and the ASEAN in shaping their policies towards Burma. Interactions in socio-cultural, economic, informational and technological spheres have expanded greatly, and nation-states have increasingly responded to these interactions in their governance structures. There are a number of consequences of this meta-trend of global interdependence on regional policy formulation.

In the economic sphere, both the EU and the ASEAN have given high priority to co-operation, and implemented various integrative measures such as a common currency – the Euro – and the ASEAN Free Trade Agreement to achieve their objectives. As a result of prevailing global and regional trends, previously isolated countries such as Burma and the Indochina states have to open up their economies to the world and become more pragmatic in their domestic economic and foreign policies in adjusting to globalisation pressures.

The impact of globalisation has been profound in the social and political spheres of societies tightly controlled by repressive regimes. In such societies, people have come to grasp with greater awareness the need to mobilise for fulfilment of fundamental human rights and meaningful participation in the decision-making processes that affect their daily lives. This is evident in Burma where people have increasingly become vocal about their right to democratic changes and their ground swell movement caught the attention of the international community. This led to greater expression of disapproval by the US, Europe and some Asian governments criticising the policies and behaviour of the Burmese military regime on human rights grounds.

The ASEAN has repeatedly referred to the non-interference principle as a cardinal rule for the association and adhered to it by admitting Burma as a member. This contrasts to action by the EU, which in June 1991 stated that "different ways of expressing concern about violations of rights, as well as requests designed to secure those rights cannot be considered as interference in the internal affairs of a state". However, developments within Burma were a major

---

[3]   David Baldwin, *Economic Statecraft*, Princeton, NJ: Princeton University Press, 1985.

source of concern for the governments of the region.[4] One of those concerns was Burma's rapid drift into the Chinese orbit of what was perceived as a geo-strategic penetration of mainland Southeast Asia. On the other hand, Thailand, a frontline state with a long border to Burma, has entertained concerns about the practical consequences of human rights violations and low-intensity conflicts of civil war across the border, which led to a devastating refugee crisis on the Thai side. Besides these sources of instability, regional governments are wary of potential spill-over effects from other sources of instability within Burma: rising production of narcotics and other stimulant drugs flowing into ASEAN destinations, constant migration of illegal labourers across borders, and the transnational spread of the AIDS epidemic.

Although the two regional organisations have viewed Burma from divergent ideological perspectives, there seems to be a common understanding of the complex nature of Burma's political, social and economic problems and the necessity to overcome them. Both organisations have stressed that Burma should be able to move ahead with new opportunities and strive for mutual benefits from co-operation and further integration into the regional and global family of nations.

As part of its Common Security and Foreign Policy (CSFP), the European Union in 1996 adopted a common position on Burma by calling on "the SLORC to enter into meaningful dialogue with pro-democracy groups with a view to bringing about national reconciliation".[5] With this objective in mind, the EU adopted a number of disincentive measures to promote democratisation in Burma.[6] The EU position was echoed in the Clinton administration's executive order to prohibit new investment in Burma. US Secretary of State, Madeleine Albright, explained the move: "we have used the prospect of new investment sanctions as a tool to encourage change. Specifically, we have urged the military authorities in Burma to begin a serious political dialogue with the National League for Democracy, led by Aung San Suu Kyi, and with the representatives of Burma's many ethnic minorities."[7]

Although the ASEAN has often cited the principle of non-intervention, the desire to see "peace and stability" was the central concern of the regional

---

[4] The ASEAN emphasis on the non-interference principle is questionable due to its inconsistent application. In 1990, when the military junta launched an ethnic cleansing operation against the Rohingya Muslims in the western border region, some ASEAN states not only condemned the action but also lent moral and humanitarian support to the Rohingya resistance groups in Burma.

[5] European Parliament, "Common Position Defined by the Council on the Basis of Article J.2 of the Treaty on European Union, on Burma/Myanmar", Press release, 28 October 1996. SLORC is the acronym for the State Law and Order Restoration Council – the ruling military bloc in Burma since 1988. It renamed itself SPDC (State Peace and Development Council) in November 1997.

[6] EU's disincentive measures included: expulsion of military attachés from Burmese missions in Europe; an embargo on arms, munitions and military equipment; suspension of non-humanitarian aid and development programmes; a visa ban on senior SLORC members, senior officials and their families; and suspension of high-level bilateral governmental visits to Burma. The common position has been renewed every six months since 29 October 1996 up to the present time. The original position has even been made more comprehensive; for instance, a ban on transit visas has been added.

[7] US Department of State, "Statement on US Sanctions Against Burma by Secretary of State Madeleine K. Albright", Press release by the Office of the Spokesman, US Department of State, Washington D.C., 22 April 1997.

association when bringing Burma into its fold. Malaysian Foreign Minister, Abdullah Badawi, summed up its rationale when stating: "We see the membership of Burma in the ASEAN from various angles – strategic and growth of regions. It should be brought into the regional organisation. (...) [W]e hope through our relations with Burma, we can bring changes to benefit its people."[8] Explaining the decision as a distinct 'ASEAN way' of moving the junta in the direction of political change and greater respect for human rights, Malaysian Prime Minister, Mahathir Mohammed, who was a prime mover behind Burma's entry into the association, stated that "[i]f it is outside, it is free to behave like a rogue or a pariah, while if it is inside, it would be subject to certain norms of behaviour."[9]

The ASEAN's concern over the Burmese political situation became more pronounced when the association's policy of 'constructive engagement' yielded no progress after several years, even after it became a member of the association. In response to the persistence of the junta's international pariah status, some ASEAN leaders began to consider alternative approaches. Malaysia's Deputy Prime Minister, Anwar Ibrahim, introduced the concept of 'constructive interventionism' and demanded that "Yangon should reciprocate by moving forward with its national reconciliation" after the ASEAN had given them a chance within the association.[10] His statement expressed frustration on the part of ASEAN young leaders over the old 'non-interference policy'. Instead, they subscribed to the regional consensus to strengthen civil society and the rule of law in the member countries.

To further Anwar's vision of a new humane ASEAN community, Thailand's young pair of Foreign Minister, Surin Pitsuwan, and his deputy, Sukhumbhand Paribatra, moved the 'constructive interventionism' proposition onto the informal agenda within ASEAN circles. They dubbed it 'flexible engagement' to make it palatable for the 31st ASEAN Ministerial Meeting (AMM) in line with a vision for the "ASEAN...[to] be more people-centred [and] more in tune with and responsive to the aspirations of its peoples."[11] Although their initiative 'to move the mountain' of status quo within the association did not win supporters overnight, the call broached a tacit shift in individual government stands towards the situation in Burma. The new thinking was evident in the ASEAN decision to meet Daw Aung San Suu Kyi, albeit informally. During 1998, the Malaysian Foreign Minister, Badawi and his Philippino counterpart, Siazon, met Daw Aung San Suu Kyi, and for the first time the ASEAN departed from its official line to keep the

---

[8] Agence France Presse, "Malaysia says Burma's entry into ASEAN promotes regional stability", 27 April 1997.

[9] Agence France Presse, "ASEAN stands firm on Burma's entry despite Western pressure", 1 May 1997.

[10] Anwar's response came right after Hun Sen's palace coup in Cambodia calling for the association to adopt this new framework for 'constructive interventionism' to prevent any spill-over from domestic economic, social and political upheavals within the region. See Anwar Ibrahim, "Rethinking ASEAN", *Newsweek,* 21 July 1997; and "ASEAN must take proactive approach, says Anwar", *Straits Times* (Singapore), 15 July 1997.

[11] See Kanjana Spindler, "Surin starts to move the mountain", *Bangkok Post,* 22 July 1998; and Ehito Kimura, "Thailand's coming challenge: Flexibility as the central plank in shaping our foreign policy", *Bangkok Post,* 7 August 1998.

dissident at a distance.[12] ASEAN Secretary General, Rodolfo Severino, also said: "a 'suggestion' to the regime to meet with the opposition should not be considered interference."[13] With different opinions within its ranks the ASEAN is at a crossroads in maintaining its profile in the wake of Asian financial crisis while overcoming its own diverging objectives on domestic affairs in nations with different ideologies and political systems. Thus, 'constructive interventionism', born out of frustration over developments in Burma, needs to capture both the reality in Burma and the *Realpolitik* of less progressive member states within the association, before it can test the actual usefulness of diplomacy in bringing peace to Burma.

Despite all the differences, there is a substantial degree of convergence between the two regional organisations with regard to how Burma should emerge from the current political stasis and start a dialogue between the junta and the NLD. The main difference lies in their application of policy instruments, one emphasising incentive policies and the other using disincentive policies to influence long-term changes. Since there are practical implications from the use of incentive and disincentive policies, it is important to analyse contextual variables and determinants of effectiveness in the use of each policy tool against actual developments in Burma.

## FRAMEWORK OF ANALYSIS: JUSTIFICATION AND RATIONALE

The analytical framework for assessing different policy tools of incentive and disincentive mechanisms will first make a review of available evidence to explain under which conditions and rationales these policies are presumed to produce the desired effects. It will analyse carefully whether the assumptions are reasonable or rational enough to justify the expectation of the desired outcome when implemented. The analysis will draw on international relations theory.

In international politics, governments make use of a number of policy instruments to achieve a wide range of goals. Thus, it makes sense to start the discussion of this framework of analysis by determining what is the overriding goal among multiple competing objectives. In the Burmese case, rewarding or punishing the military regime for progress towards or retreat away from democratisation is obviously the overriding goal for both regional organisations. With this point of departure it is relevant to distinguish between *means* and *ends*. The incentive and disincentive policies are the means to achieving the end of democratisation in Burma. In other words, rewards and punishments involved in incentive and disincentive policies are not the goals of these policies: they are the means designed to bend wills.

Baldwin makes a very clear distinction between means and ends of a given policy to analyse systematically its effectiveness, efficiency, or rationality. This distinction gives a useful analytical tool to clarify the goals (or ends) of an influence attempt and the scope (means) of the attempt. There may be different

---

12 See "Malaysian foreign minister met Suu Kyi in Myanmar", *Reuters,* 10 March 1998.
13 "It's About Time for ASEAN Members to Air Their Differences", *Asiaweek*, 10 July 1998.

levels of goals and their importance may vary, while the means being applied to achieve these different goals also carry different priority.

The economy of Burma against which economic sanctions have been applied may or may not be the primary target of the influence attempt. A common confusion of means and ends in an influence attempt is the assumption that economic means must have economic ends. Under such an assumption, the emphasis is put on the examination of 'economic capabilities' or 'economic leverage' of a sender state making an influence attempt on the targeted state whose 'economic vulnerability' is analysed strictly to evaluate the effectiveness or efficiency of the particular policies. Such a narrowly defined focus limits the analytical framework and misses the central question, that is, the efficiency of doing what? An illustration is provided in a study done by a well-known think-tank on US sanctions against Burma:[14]

> America's potential leverage over Burma has always been marginal at best. The United States is only the fifth largest foreign investor in Burma (Britain, France, Thailand, and Singapore lead the list), with total investment of 226 million. U.S. investment accounts for less than 10 percent of total foreign direct investment, and the share may be even smaller because of Burma's large black market economy. For example, 1993 total imports and exports reached nearly $ 2 billion, but the value of black-market trade with India and China was about $ 1 billion. In 1994 the United States accounted for about 1 percent of Burmese imports and took in about 7 percent of that country's exports. China, Singapore, and the rest of the Asian countries were the origin of about 90 percent of Burma's imports; and India, Singapore, and China were three main destinations for its exports.
>
> Those figures suggest that the U.S. economic stake in Burma is limited and that Burma therefore is not susceptible to U.S. economic pressure. Cutting U.S. economic ties with Burma will only reduce the already limited leverage the United States has on Rangoon. Consequently, the failure of U.S. unilateral sanctions to change the behaviour of Burma's rulers is inevitable.

Such a statement also underlies the dominant tendency in the study of economic statecraft to view disincentive policies as a simple chain of causal reasoning: economic value deprivation leads to economic disintegration, which in turn leads to political disintegration, which finally leads to compliance with the goal of the influence attempt.[15] Correspondingly, the same reasoning can be applied to incentive policies: economic input leads to economic growth, which in turn leads to political progress, which finally fulfils the objective of the policy. This 'general theory', which has become a standard for the study of economic statecraft, is championed by Johan Galtung and given an explicit interpretation by Losman: "for sanctions to be successful (...) the economic damage inflicted must be sufficient to unleash domestic political pressures that will either topple an

---

[14] Leon T. Hadar, *U.S. Sanctions against Burma: A Failure on All Fronts,* Washington D.C.: Cato Institute, Trade Policy Analysis No. 1, 26 March 1998.

[15] Johan Galtung, "On the Effects of International Economic Sanctions with Examples from the Case of Rhodesia", *World Politics,* Vol. 19, No. 3, 1967.

intransigent regime or bring about the adoption of new policies more in accord with the norms of boycotting nations."[16]

This simple causal logic imposes a rather narrow standard of analysis on the effects of economic statecraft. Since behaviour modification is the purpose of economic sanctions, policy makers will normally consider it a success when the target state concedes to the coercer's demands; if not, the policy will be judged a failure.

On the other hand, those who favour incentive policies often overestimate the linkage between economics and politics, by taking for granted that politics will improve following economic growth. Advocating engagement with Burma, John Imle, president of UNOCAL oil corporation that has invested in a $ 1 billion-worth natural gas pipeline project, subscribes to a kind of analysis overestimating US businesses' ability to positively influence the manner in which development occurs.[17]

> If Washington wants to influence the future of Myanmar, it must make it possible for U.S. companies to increase their investment, not reduce it. That would strengthen American influence by speeding up transfer of U.S. business principles, fair labour practices, health and safety and environmental standards and technologies. (...) Foreign policy and international trade experts call this 'engagement'. We call it common sense. American companies like UNOCAL will continue to lead by example, investing in quality projects that lead to higher living standards in the region.

Significantly, the linkage between economic growth and democracy has become a questionable premise in the wake of East Asian crisis. Not only has the financial troubles of Asian economies meant less investment in Burma, it has also reduced the possibility of Asian firms substituting Western companies withdrawing or not investing in Burma. As the possibility of 'substitution' wanes, the potential effects of US and EU sanctions, combining both investment bans and vetoes on multilateral aid, have become more than mere expressions of concern, but rather bearing real pressures on the capability of the target regime.

The deterrence effect of a policy to discourage the target state from taking certain actions which the sender states do not like can be equally important as the effect to comply with the demands. Elizabeth Rogers have pointed out that conventional wisdom has emphasised the deterrence part of the influence attempt while neglecting the deterrence functions of a particular policy.[18] Rogers considers the difficulty of documenting the effectiveness of particular statecraft because target states may never openly admit to having been deterred from taking specific actions. Successful deterrence can result in a non-event, which hardly serves as evidence to prove causality.

However, the deterrence mechanism seems important in the case of Burma, particularly regarding human rights violations. The regime's propensity to use

---

[16]    Donald L. Losman, *International Economic Sanctions: The Cases of Cuba, Israel and Rhodesia,* Albuquerque: University of New Mexico Press, 1979.

[17]    John Imle. "Keep Door Open in Myanmar", *Journal of Commerce,* 28 February 1997.

[18]    Elizabeth Rogers, "Economic Sanctions and Internal Conflict", in Michael E. Brown (ed.), *The International Dimensions of Internal Conflict,* Cambridge, MA: MIT Press, 1996.

harsh measures against the civilian opposition can be effectively checked by international mechanisms to reward or punish a particular course of action. Evidence of this deterrence effect is a major student demonstration that effectively paralysed government functions in December 1996 but ended with minimal use of force by the government. Riot control by using water cannons and baton-equipped police contrasts sharply with the use of armed soldiers, as was the case during the events of 1988 and 1989. Since both the EU and the US have constantly monitored the human rights situation in Burma the regime took extra care in using limited force against the student demonstrators, given the prospects of more pressure from the West.

Another important consideration in the usefulness of economic statecraft is the humanitarian effects of applying incentive and disincentive policies. Humanitarian concerns are frequently cited in the critique of disincentive policies. Ernest Preeg has pointedly criticised US sanctions against Burma for causing unintended economic hardship for the poorest people.[19] John Imle of UNOCAL also contrasts negative impact of US sanctions (on poor people) with the positive spill-over of his investment project by citing social welfare benefits from employment creation and other projects such as three-year $ 6 million rural development schemes benefiting 35,000 people living in the pipeline area.[20] The importance of humanitarian consequences from disincentive policy tools was emphasised by Pope John Paul II in his speech to the Vatican diplomatic corps in 1995:[21]

> The embargo in particular, clearly defined by law, is an instrument that needs to be used with great discernment, and it must be subjected to strict legal and ethical criteria. It is a means of exerting pressure on governments, which have violated the international code of good conduct and of causing them to reconsider their choices. But in a sense it is also an act of force and, as certain cases of the present moment demonstrate, it inflicts grave hardships upon the people of the countries at which it is aimed (...) Before imposing such measures, it is always imperative to foresee the humanitarian consequences of sanctions, without failing to respect the just proportion that such measures should have in relation to the very evil which they are meant to remedy.

However, the humanitarian costs (or benefits) of a particular policy has to be examined thoroughly to understand precisely what is the cost, how it is generated, and which social groups are likely to bear the burden. In the case of Burma, disincentive policies have impacted on the ruling government without causing much adverse humanitarian damage. Foreign investment has plummeted, particularly in the petroleum sector and in hotel and tourism operations, which

---

[19] Ernest H. Preeg, "Unilateral Economic Sanctions in Asia", Testimony before the Senate Foreign Relations Committee, Sub-committee on East Asian and Pacific Affairs, *Federal News Service,* 26 February 1998.

[20] See Imle, *op.cit.,*1997. However, the employment creation argument is questionable for capital intensive and highly sophisticated investment project like natural gas production. Besides, several human rights groups have charged that the rural development project is a showcase to cover up the severe impact of forced relocations in the pipeline construction area.

[21] Robert A. Sirico. "Free Trade and Human Rights: The Moral Case for Engagement", Washington D.C.: Cato Institute, Trade Policy Briefing Paper No. 2, 17 July 1998.

account for nearly three-fourths of all foreign direct investment. Typically, investments in the petroleum sector (accounting for in excess of 40 per cent of total foreign direct investment) are capital-intensive and generate little employment. The hotel and tourism business, on the other hand, would be expected to generate employment and have linkage effects to the domestic economy. However, much of the investment in hotels and tourism is purely speculative with a view to reaping windfall profits in the land market. Besides, the majority of hotel businesses have never become operational due to the Asian crisis. Moreover, investments are rather vehicles for laundering illegal drug money. As a result, the reduction in foreign direct investment has produced insignificant adverse secondary knock-on effects on the population at large. However, deriving substantial income from these sectors the government has seen a significant revenue shortfall resulting from dwindling foreign investment.

## HISTORICAL BACKGROUND

Historically, Burma has been an active player in regional politics. During her brief parliamentary period of fourteen years immediately after independence, Burma championed a "policy of positive neutrality" whose "faithful pursuance best serves both Burma and the world".[22] The late Prime Minister, U Nu, personally assumed a role of international activist "to bridge the gulf between the two opposing blocs with a view to promoting world peace" while the capital, Rangoon, became a major regional centre for international meetings and a transit point for foreign dignitaries.[23] On the regional level, Burma was one of the original signatories to the Bandung Resolution in 1955, which became the cornerstone of the Bangkok Declaration that formed the basis of the creation of the ASEAN in 1967.

Much of the responsive elements of Burma's foreign policy vanished quickly after the military took power in 1962. The outward-looking posture of the country was abruptly turned inward in pursuance of 'negative neutralism'. The latter stemmed from lack of legitimacy and the self-serving isolationist tendency to insulate society from contact with the outside world. The Burmese way to socialism added an ideological cover for the inward-looking policies that essentially cut off the country from the rest of the world.[24]

In the early 1980s, Burma's economy suffered from a prolonged period of isolation, compounded by serious mismanagement. The dire economic situation compelled the incumbent regime to negotiate agreements with multilateral agencies while actively seeking official aid, albeit in a gradual manner. The

---

[22] William C. Johnston, *Burma Foreign Policy*, Cambridge, MA: Harvard University Press, 1963.

[23] Chi-shad Liang, *Burma's Foreign Relations: Neutralism in Theory and Practice,* New York: Praeger, 1990.

[24] For a detailed scenario of the foreign policy shift in the early 1960s, see Maung Maung Gyi, "Foreign Policy of Burma since 1962: Negative Neutralism for Group Survival", in F.K. Lehman (ed.), *Military Rule in Burma since 1962,* Singapore: Maruzen Asia, 1981. Gyi refers to 'negative neutralism' as a policy that (a) is inward-looking, xenophobic, and immature in its *Weltanschauung,* (b) fails to infuse dynamism into the nation's economy, and (c) lacks courage to pursue an active and leading role in regional matters. Burma went even deeper into isolation when it decided to withdraw from the Non-aligned Movement in 1979.

substantial inflow of ODA, 75 per cent coming from Japan alone, did not help revive the economy but worsened the country's external debt position. Economic discontent was a major cause of the popular uprising in 1988, which led to brutal suppression and violent killings of unarmed civilian protestors.[25] These gross human rights violations prompted the international community to suspend all official aid to Burma, in addition to diplomatic condemnation.

Thailand was the first country to break the diplomatic isolation of the Burmese military regime following the massacres in 1988. The Thai army commander-in-chief, General Chavalit Yongchaiyudth, visited Rangoon in December 1988. During his visit, the cordial and close relationship between the two armies was established, including agreement on concessions for Thai companies to exploit Burma's rich natural resources. The official policy of Chatichai's administration to turn the battlefields into markets facilitated further rapprochement between two neighbours, and business dealings with Thai companies, particularly concessions on timber, minerals, and fishing rights, expanded on a massive scale.

However, at the regional level the ASEAN began to consider Burma's problems seriously when the dialogue partners from the EU, the US, Australia, Canada, and New Zealand raised the issue of human rights violations and the political stalemate in the country during the ASEAN post-ministerial meeting in July 1991.

During the meeting, the Thai Foreign Minister, Arsa Sarasin, laid down the official Thai position towards Burma. It was here that the first reference was made to 'constructive engagement' and Thailand was given a special role as a spokesman for the association.

At that time, the ASEAN did not have any common or co-ordinated stand on Burma and the Thai position was not readily accepted by other ASEAN members who interpreted the 'constructive engagement' policy differently to suit their perceptions and preferences. Both Malaysia and Indonesia voiced strong concerns over the human rights violations and the subsequent ethnic cleansing activities of the Burmese military vis-à-vis the Muslim minorities, better known as the Rohingyas populations in the western part of Burma.

The ASEAN attempted to solve the matter by sending the Philippines' Foreign Minister, Raul Manglapus, as a special envoy. The ASEAN initiative was flatly rejected by the SLORC, which later accepted Manglapus' visit only in his private capacity. Meanwhile, Burma remained an issue in heated debates during the ASEAN dialogue partner meetings. During the 1993 ASEAN meeting, the preoccupation with the establishment of a new regional security framework, the ASEAN Regional Forum (ARF), pushed the debates on Burma into the background, despite the escalation of human rights violations in the country.

In 1994, the position of the SLORC suddenly improved when Thailand made a controversial decision to invite the Burmese Foreign Minister, U Ohn Gyaw, as a guest of Thailand to attend the ASEAN meeting for the first time. The Thai recognition of the SLORC as a serious partner in regional co-operation was driven by the worsening security relations between the two countries following the successful SLORC offensives against several ethnic insurgent bases along the

---

[25]   David I. Steinberg, *Crisis in Burma: Stasis and Change in a Political Economy in Turmoil*, Institute of Security and International Studies, Bangkok: Chulalongkorn University Press, 1990.

Thai-Burma border. Many lucrative business concessions extended to Thai firms were abruptly terminated by the SLORC in late 1993 and the Thai government, under various pressures, opted to appease the Burmese junta.

The SLORC seized the opportunity at the Bangkok meeting and launched a diplomatic offensive in the ASEAN capitals to express its interest to accede to the Treaty of Amity and Co-operation (TAC), and to become an observer in the regional association. To the surprise of many international observers, Burma's pro-democracy leader Daw Aung San Suu Kyi was released just before the ASEAN foreign ministers' meeting in Bandar Seri Begawan in July 1995. With the precedent from Bangkok, Brunei again invited U Ohn Gyaw as a special guest to attend the meeting. With the quieting down of the Rohingya situation in western Burma, the SLORC gained critical support from both Malaysia and Indonesia for its bid for ASEAN membership.

In 1996, Burma became an observer of the ASEAN and a member of the ARF with strong support from Indonesia. Contrary to an earlier understanding to consider Burma's admission only after Cambodia and Laos had been admitted, the Jakarta informal summit introduced the principle to "establish an ASEAN comprising all countries in Southeast Asia" and that all three potential new members be considered together. Meanwhile, Malaysian Prime Minister, Mahathir Mohammed, actively promoted the early admission of Burma along with Cambodia and Laos (buy two, get one free formula). Mahathir's strong personal support for Burma's admission was also timed with Kuala Lumpur's hosting of the ASEAN's 30th anniversary. To many in ASEAN circles, the admission of Burma, the last odd man out in the region together with Laos and Cambodia, amounted to fulfilling the thirty-year old dream of uniting the region as envisaged by the founding fathers.

While Burma's entry into the regional association remained a contentious issue between the West and the ASEAN members, the Clinton administration decided to impose sanctions against the Burmese regime in April 1997. Although the executive order to ban new investments in Burma was made to pre-empt more comprehensive congressional measures introduced by Senator McConnel, the American action was interpreted by some ASEAN states as too intrusive over a matter of regional concern. When the Europeans followed suit by taking limited measures such as withdrawal of GSP privileges and a visa ban against SLORC officials, the issue was depicted as a struggle between a 'Western approach' and an 'Asian way' of resolving Burma's problems. To polarise the issue further, the US Department of State issued a statement of concern over Burma's membership and made a public remark against Burma's membership. This public statement touched ASEAN's raw nerve and pushed the association further into negating the impression of kowtowing to Western pressures.

In response, with the intention of demonstrating its independence from any Western influence, the ASEAN swiftly made the decision to admit Burma as a member during the meeting in May 1997 after the ASEAN secretariat had completed the formal assessment of membership preparation by Rangoon. Meanwhile, the palace coup and the subsequent violent clashes in Phnom Penh disqualified Cambodia for admission. Ironically, the pariah status of Rangoon was not a thorny issue when the ASEAN justified its refusal to admit Cambodia on the basis of a strictly domestic political situation. This led Cambodia's strongman, Hun Sen, to burst out bitterly that the regime in Rangoon was less gentle than his government.

## POLICY OF ENGAGEMENT AND THE ASEAN RATIONALE

### Effectiveness of quiet diplomacy

The intended objective of constructive engagement was defined thus by an editorial of the *Straits Times*, a government-leaning Singapore newspaper: "[c]onstructive engagement means gentle persuasion and quiet diplomacy to prod the regime [the SLORC] into political liberalisation. This means keeping the dialogue with the SLORC leaders." Indonesian Foreign Minister, Ali Alatas, publicly defended the policy by saying it was better "quietly talking them out of their shell and asking them to see the benefits of being open".

With this rationale, the ASEAN officials maintained that the constructive engagement policy had produced some improvements in the human rights situation in Burma, citing the release of Daw Aung San Suu Kyi and other political prisoners, thus taking credit for their quiet diplomacy.[26] This led to the following response from Daw Aung San Suu Kyi herself:

> The question is for whom has it been constructive? Was it constructive for the forces of democracy? Was it constructive for the Burmese people in general? Was it constructive for a limited business community? Or was it constructive for SLORC?

In the light of Daw Aung San Suu Kyi's criticism, it is important to assess the merits of 'constructive engagement' as an ASEAN approach to improving the human rights situation in Burma. The key question to ask is whether it actually promotes engagement or quiet persuasion in changing the regime's policy towards respecting international norms including human rights and in accelerating a political reform process to install some sort of government with acceptable legitimacy and legality. In other words, the real qualification has to be made with regard to the 'constructive' part of the engagement policy by examining how 'constructive' is interpreted and practised in the actual engagement with the regime.

In this respect, it may be pointed out that the ASEAN policy of 'constructive engagement' lacked the essence of what the US had practised when attaching the same label to its policy towards South Africa in transforming the *apartheid* regime. The US policy featured direct high level contacts and painstaking multilateral negotiations with the South African government. It produced progress towards domestic political liberalisation, including a negotiated settlement of Namibia's independence as well as the ending of the regional conflict in Angola. By contrast, the ASEAN diplomatic engagement with the SLORC was limited, at least in the public arena. It also lacked, as Australia's Foreign Minister, Gareth

---

[26] "ASEAN stand on Burma draws flak", *The Nation* (Bangkok), 25 July 1992.

Evans, observed: "the kind of energy that it demonstrated for so long in seeking to resolve the Cambodian problem."

Not only was there a lack of political will on the part of the ASEAN to involve itself in Burmese affairs, but also in Burma's disdain for diplomatic niceties. The weak point of the 'quiet diplomacy' argument, therefore, is history. Burma had no history of dealing with the association since its foundation in 1967. Worse still, the association was viewed historically as 'lackeys' of Western powers and Burma's attitude towards the ASEAN frontline state, Thailand, was never relaxed. The shift to an open-door economic policy and the granting of business deals to ASEAN firms seem to be driven by survival and business considerations rather than an embrace of the ASEAN's role in Burmese politics.

In addition, the ASEAN claims about spill-over benefits from good behaviour through involvement in webs of institutional links and official engagement was somewhat limited by the strict principle of 'non-interference' guiding the official conduct within the association. That is why the progressive members of the ASEAN had tried to modify the principle to be able to take advantage of 'quiet moments' to discuss with and influence their Burmese counterpart to change course.

## Economic integration and growth-led gradual 'abertura'

Another rationale underlying 'constructive engagement' was promotion of economic reform in Burma, which presumably would lead to prosperity, peace, and gradual development of a middle-class-led democratic transition. With this justification, the policy allowed ASEAN countries to conduct business with the SLORC. Prime Minister Mahathir of Malaysia advocated such links as a means of promoting economic reform introduced by the SLORC:

> Poor neighbours are no asset to anyone. The problems of the poor are likely to spill over in the form of refugees, smuggling, black markets, etc. ... Helping neighbours to become prosperous is therefore mutually beneficial.[27]

Mahathir's assertion was further elaborated by his deputy, Anwar Ibrahim, who suggested that the ASEAN could serve as a conduit for foreign direct investment into Indochina, arguing that the wealthy nations of Southeast Asia have a moral obligation to help those that are less wealthy to prosper and develop. Such assistance would bring more than just economic benefits to the states of origin: "there is more prosperity and greater benefits to be derived from neighbours who are equally prosperous. Prosperous neighbours will have a stake in ensuring that peace and stability prevail in the entire neighbourhood."[28]

In this regard, the need for regional equalisation between the rich ASEAN and poor Indochina countries plus isolationist Burma was put forward in conjunction with the internal need for economic development in Burma. The main objective of this strategy context was "to prevent the division of Southeast Asia into two parts,

---

[27] "Myanmar Monsters", *The Economist,* 15 March 1992.
[28] Ashraf Abdullah, "Anwar: Rich Southeast Asian Nations Must Help", *New Straits Times,* 1 June 1996.

one rich (ASEAN), and one poor (CLM [Cambodia, Laos, Myanmar] countries). Such a division will be the surest source of future instabilities in the region, which could be exploited by outside powers."[29] Thailand's National Security Council Chief, Geernal Charan Kullavanijaya, whose country's GDP per capita is twice that of the combined total of Vietnam, Cambodia, Laos, and Myanmar, echoed this view, and observed that "brothers in the same region should develop together so people of this region enjoy well-being. Differences in development will eventually become dangers."[30]

Despite its ambitious plan to help the backward Southeast Asian states to catch up with the affluent members, the ASEAN way of 'economic integration' is rather limited in both 'breadth and depth'.[31] Unlike European integration, the ASEAN process deals only with trade liberalisation under the ASEAN Free Trade Agreement (AFTA). In terms of depth, the fulfilment of the AFTA depends on the political will of the national governments to implement the Common Effective Preferential Tariff (CEPT) scheme, the core mechanism in AFTA, within a time frame of ten years. In addition, the respective countries can still maintain their list of national exemptions while the procedures to tackle non-tariff barriers and investment opportunities remain less clear.[32]

### Strategic imperative: containing China

Another reason for engaging and eventually integrating Burma into the ASEAN is the security objective to contain the Chinese expansionary threat to mainland Southeast Asia by uniting all states of the region. ASEAN diplomats have aired concerns over Rangoon's leaning towards Beijing and its reliance on Chinese military assistance. Many reports have documented Rangoon's dependence on Chinese arms and ammunition. ASEAN officials were alarmed when learning that heavy investment was being made by official Chinese development assistance in transport lines through the Yunnan border to the Martaban seashore.[33] Persistent

[29] Jusuf Wanandi, "ASEAN Summit produces major results", *ASEAN Update*, Vol 1, January-February 1996.

[30] Anuraj Maihbhandu, "Regional Unity under ASEAN a Necessity", *Bangkok Post,* 15 December 1995.

[31] Dato Ajit Singh, "Towards one Southeast Asia", *ASEAN Economic Bulletin,* Singapore: Institute of Southeast Asian Studies, November 1997. Singh was Secretary-General of the ASEAN and undertook an evaluation on the preparedness of Burma for admission to the association. Three criteria were examined: tariff reduction, political stability, and an English-speaking bureaucracy. Burma was praised for being better prepared than the other two candidates, Cambodia and Laos. Also see, "Myanmar more prepared than Cambodia and Laos to enter ASEAN", *Xinhua News Agency,* 1 December 1996.

[32] The debate on the ASEAN achievements in economic co-operation remains heated. For instance, John Ravenhill has seriously questioned the official rosy picture. See John Ravenhill, "Economic co-operation in Southeast Asia", *Asian Survey,* Vol. 25, No. 9, September 1995.

[33] In early May 1997, Beijing formally announced the beginning of the Irrawaddy Corridor Project on the basis of a new agreement, which, according to the Yunnan Province authorities, covers "the joint development of the Irrawaddy River, a major inland river of Myanmar, to open a new, short channel to the Indian Ocean." En Clare, "Beijing consolidates its hold on Myanmar", *Defense & Foreign Affairs' Strategic Policy*, International Media Corporation, July 1997.

intelligence reports point to Chinese involvement in building of naval base and signal outposts in the Bay of Bengal.[34]

Security issues have increasingly taken centre stage in ASEAN meetings as leaders have become more apprehensive about China's growing economic and military power. Chinese occupation of Mischief Reef in 1995, which is claimed by the Philippines, and the subsequent adoption of maritime baselines following ratification of the UN Convention on the Law of the Sea (UNCLOS), caused serious concern in some ASEAN circles. Given the unilateral stance by China with regard to disputes over Spartlys islands in the South China Sea, the ASEAN has taken strategic considerations seriously by accelerating the admission of Burma.

On the Western front, the Chinese influence over the Burmese army has already alarmed New Delhi. Burma had become a potential flash point for the China-India nexus as Paul Dibb observed: "the most likely intersection of future Indian and Chinese military interests – other than along their common border – is in Southeast Asia, where India has forward bases in the Andaman and Nicobar islands and China has a growing interest in Myanmar."[35] It is reported that China has already been seeking access to two islands for listening intelligence.[36]

Despite ASEAN wishes, China's economic and political leverage over Rangoon is much greater than the ASEAN can counter, and Chinese influence is gaining ground in the wake of ASEAN decline and economic crisis. From a Burmese perspective, having a powerful ally with a permanent member status in the UN Security Council guarantees its protection from any potential multilateral action against the regime, while much-needed military hardware can be obtained at a friendly price, particularly in the wake of the EU arms embargo. Since the ASEAN cannot substitute this 'protection', Burma is unlikely "to play the role of an independent or pivotal player in regional security affairs".[37]

**Rhetoric of Asian values**

As international criticism has mounted regarding Burma's admission to the association, the ASEAN needs to repair its image and to maintain an international status of respectability commensurate with its impressive records in economic development and regional peace-making efforts. Since the main source of criticism lies in the association's handling of the human rights violations perpetrated by the Burmese military regime, the ASEAN has insisted on 'the ASEAN way' to improve Burma's human rights record through quiet persuasion towards political liberalisation.

The ASEAN has justified its own way by citing different conceptions of human rights while rejecting the Western notion of individual rights and freedoms. It challenged the view that human rights are universal and emphasised the

---

[34] William Ashton, "Chinese Bases in Burma – Fact or Fiction?" *Jane's Intelligence Review*, Vol. 7, No. 2, 1 February 1995.

[35] Paul Dibb, *Towards a New Balance of Power in Asia*, Adelphi Paper No. 295, International Institute of Strategic Studies, Oxford: Oxford University Press, 1995.

[36] *Far Eastern Economic Review*, 4 August 1994.

[37] Mohan Malik, "Burma's role in regional security – Pawn or Pivot?" in Robert I. Rotberg (ed.), *Burma: Prospects for a Democratic Future*, Washington D.C.: Brookings Institution Press, 1998.

significance of regional and national particularities and various historical, cultural and religious backgrounds. The Bangkok Declaration on Human Rights in April 1993 asserted the notion of 'Asian values' and contended that economic and social rights are far more important than political rights and freedoms. It was argued that Asian states give priority to the community and family rather than the individual as they strive for consensus, harmony and political stability rather than diversity and choice.

One extension of the 'Asian value' thesis is the implicit claim that economic and social development has to be achieved *before* full political and civil rights can be realised. In terms of this philosophy, a 'strong state' and a 'benevolent authoritarian' style of governance is justified, conveniently fitting the Asian cultural predisposition. Accordingly, economic development first, democracy later has become a standard recommendation in the ASEAN approach towards Burma. It is worth examining this logic of growth-led political liberalisation from the very beginning. A query is warranted whether Asian values have anything to do with economic growth, even before linking them with democratic development. There appears to be no intrinsic value of economic efficacy in authoritarian regime types. When the economy is rising, it tends to rise more rapidly than others. On the other hand, when the economy is down, as is evident in the recent economic crisis in Asia, these governments tend to perform worse than more democratic governments.

How the government will respond under conditions of resource scarcity and economic contraction is particularly relevant for Burma in the present situation. Nobel laureate Amartya Sen has argued that "[t]he governmental response to acute suffering often depends on the pressure that is put on it, and this is where the exercise of political rights (voting, criticising, protesting, and so on) can make a real difference."[38]

## POLICY OF DISINCENTIVE MECHANISMS AND EU'S RATIONALE

Promotion of human rights and democracy has become an increasingly important objective for European states. Since the 1980s, the donor community has stressed that human rights and democracy are main goals in development co-operation, and made it clear that sustained aid flows is contingent upon an acceptable human rights record and democratisation in the recipient countries.[39] In order to pursue a common purpose, European states have developed an institutional capacity to advance human rights and democracy in developing countries. The pillar of such a capacity is the Maastricht Treaty, signed in 1992, and giving more attention to democracy and respect for human rights as principal aims of the development aid of the European Community (article 130U, section two). In connection with the revision of the Lomé arrangement in 1995, the condition of respect for human

---

[38] Amartya Sen, "Human rights and Asian values", *New Republic* (Washington D.C.), 14-21 July, 1997.

[39] Hilde Selbervik, *Aid as a tool for promotion of human rights and democracy: What can Norway do?*, Oslo: Ministry of Foreign Affairs, Evaluation Report 7.97, October 1997.

rights and democracy was included in the new agreement covering the period 1995-2000. Thus, article five of the revised Lomé IV Convention states:[40]

> Respect for human rights, democratic principles and the rule of law, which underpins relations between the ACP States and the Community and all provisions of the Convention, and governs the domestic and international policies of the contracting parties, shall constitute an essential element of this Convention.

EU interest in human rights and democratisation reflects the concerns of the larger international community. The Organisation for Economic Co-operation and Development (OECD), where the EU constitutes a core membership, has emphasised the importance of human rights and democracy in its guidelines for disbursement of aid. It stressed that there is a "vital connection between open, democratic, and accountable systems of governance and respect for human rights, and the ability to achieve sustained economic and social development".[41] EU promotion of human rights and democracy is linked with the increasing recognition of good governance by the multilateral aid agencies. The annual meeting of the IMF in September 1996 adopted a 'Declaration on Partnership for Sustainable Growth', which states that "promoting good governance in all its aspects, including ensuring the rule of law, improving the efficiency and accountability of the public sector, and tackling corruption" is an essential element of an environment in which countries achieve sustainable growth.[42] With this emphasis on governance issues, the EU and other donors have increasingly used development assistance as a lever to effect political changes in developing countries.

In the execution of linkage policies, the EU Council, however, preferred an incentive or positive approach that stimulates human rights observance and encourages democracy. However, disincentive policies or negative sanctions can also be considered in cases of grave and persistent violations of human rights or serious interruption of democratic processes. In sanctions scenarios, the EU has pledged to try and avoid penalising the population and make efforts to continue helping the more vulnerable parts of the population through the intermediary of non-governmental or informal channels while at the same time keeping a distance from the government concerned. The EU's current position on Burma, however, is bent on maintaining *ex ante* conditionality, requiring the recipient regime to document progress in the democratisation and human rights arena as a condition for maintaining an aid relationship.

Under the Common Foreign and Security Policy (CFSP), the EU can impose economic sanctions on a third country. Any interruption or reduction of economic

---

[40] Council of the European Communities, Commission of the European Communities, *Treaty on European Union*, Luxembourg: Office for Official Publications of the European Communities, 1995.

[41] Development Assistance Committee, "Participatory Development and Good Governance", OECD, Paris, 1995.

[42] Michel Camdessus, "Good governance has become essential in promoting growth and stability", Address to Transparency International on 21 January 1998, *IMF Survey*, Vol. 27, No. 3, 9 February 1998.

sanctions with third states under Article 228a, requires a prior CFSP decision in the form of a common position or joint action. The Community has on a number of occasions resorted to sanctions for reasons of human rights concerns. In the case of Haiti, Iraq, Libya, Serbia and Montenegro the sanctions in the form of different Council regulations were imposed pursuant to mandatory UN Security Council resolutions. The EU has also imposed sanctions on its own against Sudan and Nigeria, without prior UN Security Council authorisation but through 'joint actions'. Although the EU has not reached a level of imposing sanctions on Burma, it has developed a joint position to undertake a series of disincentive actions against the military regime.[43] The EU's joint actions are indications of priority, leading to binding foreign policy actions – clearly a big step forward towards closer foreign policy co-ordination within the European Community. In this regard, the joint action towards Burma certainly signalled continued strong commitment by the EU to human rights and democratisation, while reaffirming European confidence in the achievement of those goals.

### Evolution of EU actions

In executing joint actions, the EU has imposed a number of disincentive measures incrementally and tightened them gradually. These disincentive measures are employed as instruments of a larger diplomatic repertoire, including declarations, demarches and condemnations of the regime. They are used as pressure mechanisms accompanying diplomatic actions either through the UN or regional fora such as ASEAN-EU meetings. The disincentive mechanisms the EU used initially included: 1) expulsion of all military personnel attached to the diplomatic missions of Burma in member states of the European Union; 2) withdrawal of all military personnel attached to diplomatic mission of the member states of the European Union in Burma; 3) an embargo on arms, munitions and military equipment; and 4) suspension of non-humanitarian aid or development programmes.

Typically, enforcement of these measures are based on monitoring of domestic events in Burma. Therefore, the common positions are renewed every six months, subject to a review of the target situation. Major initiatives for reviews and reiteration of common positions come mainly from the European Parliament. On 24 March 1997 the Council adopted, as suggested by Messrs. Kinnock and Jensen of the European Parliament, a regulation denying access to generalised tariff preferences for Burma in the industrial and agricultural sectors in view of the country's forced labour practices. When President Clinton imposed economic sanctions by prohibiting new US investments in Burma, the European Parliament also took an initiative by requesting the EU commission to implement full economic sanctions against the SLORC.

The EU has imposed disincentive measures in a calibrated manner by consistently demanding that they be reponded to in an observable fashion. It has called on the SLORC to enter into meaningful dialogue with pro-democracy

---

[43]    European Union, Common Position 96/635/CFSP defined by the Council on the basis of Article J.2 of the Treaty on European Union, Official Journal No. L. 287, Vol. 8, No. 11, 28 October 1996.

groups with a view to bringing about national reconciliation. The European Council, which is responsible for monitoring developments in Burma, has to make a careful periodic assessment of the overall situation to make decisions on suspension or escalation of disincentive measures. However, the situation in Burma has not improved since the inception of EU's joint actions. Therefore, new disincentives have been added to the existing list. For instance, a ban on temporary visas was recently imposed against senior members of the SLORC and their families, thus prohibiting transit through European cities to other destinations.

### Influencing frontline states: the EU-ASEAN dialogue mechanism

In order to maximize its influence, the EU has acted through its institutional links with the ASEAN to raise concerns about conditions in Burma. With the deepening political dialogue between the two regional associations, the EU has adopted a linkage diplomacy approach by raising issues on Burma in the ASEAN-EU dialogue process to remind the ASEAN that it should not be complacent about its obligations to promote changes in Burma. President of the EU Council, Jacques F. Poos, stressed this point at the ASEAN post-ministerial conference on the day after Burma was formally admitted to the ASEAN in 1997. Trying to avoid embarrassing the hosts he quoted the aspirations of the founding fathers of ASEAN "to integrate all South East Asian States in a community of ten, in a joint effort to promote economic cooperation and the welfare of the people in the region". He continued by saying: "The EU expects that the accession in particular of Burma/Myanmar to ASEAN will contribute to an improvement of the internal situation in this country."

At the same meeting, Jacques Poos told his ASEAN counterparts that the EU would not change its position on Burma unless five conditions were met:[44]

- Release of all political prisoner;
- An end to the arrest of political dissidents;
- The restoration of political dialogue with pro-democracy leaders;
- A new democratic general election at the earliest opportunity;
- A guarantee of freedom of speech and movement.

Continuing this benchmark policy the German Foreign Minister, Klaus Kinkel, suggested in late October 1997 that contact should be established between Burma and the EU. At the same time Kinkel put forward four areas where the EU wanted to see change: Release of all political prisoners; an end to military rule; granting democratic parties in Burma access to "political life"; and promulgation of a democratic constitution. This marked a shift in words compared to those used by Jacques Poos only three months before. The move was seen as a way to meet the ASEAN half way and set a precedent for the burgeoning friendship between the ASEAN and the EU, which later led to the Asia-Europe Meeting (ASEM).[45]

---

[44] Kulachada Chaipipat, "EU sets conditions for Rangoon", *The Nation* (Bangkok), 29 July 1997.
[45] Kavi Chongkittavorn, "EU, ASEAN risking it all over Burma", *The Nation* (Bangkok), 13 November 1997.

At the same time the Thai Foreign Ministry announced that the EU would, in a Thai-brokered arrangement, let Burma participate at the upcoming meeting between the two regional groups. This started a long dispute that continued into 1999 over Burma's role at these meetings. These meetings are called "ASEAN-EU Joint Co-operation Conference" (JCC). The first such meeting was scheduled for November 1997. The conflict as reported in the media was about the role of Burma at these meetings. On the one hand, the ASEAN insisted that Burma be included as any other ASEAN member. The EU, on the other hand, referring to the common policy to cut off of all high-level ties with Burma after the slaughter of demonstrators in 1988, insisted that Burma be barred from participating.

What followed was a long exercise in the art of diplomacy. Still believing the obstacle could be overcome the ASEAN suggested that Burma and Laos be allowed to attend the meeting as observers: "They will sit with us as observers with their countries' flags hoisted. However, we will mention their status as observers in a press statement" said the permanent secretary in the Thai Foreign Ministry, Saroj Chavanviraj.[46] At the same time a letter from the EU was leaked to the press, in which the EU stressed that Burma was not party to the 1980 co-operation agreement signed between the two blocs. Consequently, Burma could not participate in the JCC meeting in any capacity, as it would require the explicit agreement of all participating members. The newspaper, obviously in possession of a copy of the letter, claimed that: "in an effort to find a path that is mutually acceptable to both sides, ... the EU has suggested that Burma's presence at the meeting could be arranged (...) by allowing Burma to attend the meeting in an 'informal and passive' manner, which would mean a different seating arrangement and that it not display its flag."[47] This suggestion was turned down by the ASEAN bloc and the EU then cancelled the meeting. Referring to the ASEAN's arrangement for the meeting, an EU spokesman said: "the ASEAN is asking us to do the impossible. Legally, we are bound to say no." The meeting in Bangkok was expected to pave the way for stronger trade and customs co-operation and to signal heightened political interest in forging closer relations. One observer suggested that the ASEAN was hoping that the Burmese junta would demonstrate some goodwill towards opposition leader Aung San Suu Kyi by initiating a dialogue for national reconciliation. Such a positive sign could have made more palatable the compromise of the Burmese observer presence at the meeting, with or without flags.[48] That the conflict came out into the open made one Luxembourg diplomat say: "It chills our relationship and shows we are not capable of handling political issues in a mature and discreet way."[49]

In December 1997, Burma expressed interest in joining the Asia-Europe Meeting (ASEM), thereby challenging EU's visa ban on Burmese officials. The ruling junta had at that time changed the name from the Orwellian 'SLORC' (State Law and Order Restoration Council) to 'SPDC' (State Peace and Development

---

[46] "ASEAN Steps up Pressure on EU", *The Nation* (Bangkok), 12 November 1997.

[47] Kavi Chongkittavorn, "EU, ASEAN risking it all over Burma", *The Nation* (Bangkok), 13 November 1997

[48] *Ibid.*

[49] "EU-ASEAN ties set to remain chilly", *The Nation* (Bangkok), 15 November 1997.

Council). The EU bluntly rebuffed Burma's overture with reference to the visa ban. The ASEM 2 meeting was held at the beginning of April 1998 in London. Later in April, the UN Human Rights Commission was meeting in Geneva. Interestingly enough, none of the other ASEAN countries assisted Burma in advocating a weaker text when a strongly worded resolution was tabled.

In May 1998, Britain, which at that time held the EU Presidency, suggested that Burma could attend the EU-ASEAN meeting scheduled for 22 June if it maintained a "passive presence". That meant no talking, no handshaking and no seat at the main negotiating table. The meeting was later postponed. The German Deputy Foreign Minister, Helmut Schaefer, met on 5 June 1998 with the Prime Minister in the Burmese government in Exile, Sein Win. Schaefer assured the Burmese opposition that the German government would put the Burma issue on the agenda of top-level political consultations between the EU and the ASEAN, which were to take place in Manila on 28-29 July.

The EU diplomats thought they had struck a deal on an "informal and passive" Burmese presence at the talks. But Rangoon persisted in arguing that it be given full observer status, including a seat at the negotiating table. According to the *Far Eastern Economic Review* Burma's stance was a source of irritation to the EU and other ASEAN governments who wanted to put the long-standing EU-ASEAN relationship back on track as quickly as possible.[50] Then again, the ASEAN put forward a new proposal for the EU to consider, to the effect that Burma be admitted into the two groupings' co-operative framework during the meeting in Manila at the end of July 1998. During the autumn, the EU proposed to send a mission of senior officials to Burma for talks with the government and Aung San Suu Kyi. The proposal was rejected by the SPDC.

**Tightening the screw**

Meanwhile, the political situation inside Burma had deteriorated as NLD stepped up its political campaign to convene parliament by the deadline of 21 August 1998. This prompted the SPDC to arrest several hundred MPs. On 16 September NLD annonced the formation of the Committee Representing the People's Parliament (CRPP), consisting of 10 persons and headed by U Aung Shwe. On 19 September 1998 the European Parliament criticised the increased repression of NLD by SPDC, and stated: "Calls on the Council to respond to Aung San Suu Kyi's request for EU economic sanctions against the SPDC by ending all links between the European Union and Burma based on trade, tourism and investment in Burma by European companies; as a first step, calls on the Council to expand the measures taken in the common position be ending trade promotion and expanding the ban on entry visas."

Not long thereafter, the British tried to sharpen the existing disincentive policies by putting additional restrictions on the role of European tour operators' drive to promote tourism in Burma. The British move followed the SPDC rejection of an EU mission as had been suggested by the EU. The EU foreign ministers warned on 5 October 1998 that they were considering tougher measures against the Myanmar

---

[50]    "Blowing Hot and Cold", *Far Eastern Economic Review*, 2 July 1998.

leadership in view of the deteriorating human rights situation. The meeting at the end of October was also postponed.

Thailand's Foreign Minister, Surin Pitsuwan, had managed to convince his ASEAN colleagues in July 1998 that they drop earlier calls for Rangoon to be given observer status. Instead, in a move the EU welcomed, Surin suggested that Burma not be given the right to speak at the meeting and that the only flags allowed in the room would be the EU and ASEAN banners. "The idea was to make Burmese representatives more or less invisible," said an EU diplomat. Burma's recent crackdown on the opposition had, however, complicated the emerging compromise. At least three EU governments were adamant that there be no contact with the military regime. Britain's Foreign Office Minister, Derek Fatchett, had written to his counterparts suggesting that in addition to the current ban on military co-operation and the granting of visas for Burmese military personnel, the EU should consider asking travel operators not to offer tours to Burma and to stop any government-sponsored promotion of trade with the country.[51]

At a ministerial meeting in London in mid-October 1998 Fatchett demanded that the International Labour Organisation (ILO) take action against Burma. He said Britain would call for Myanmar's suspension from the UN agency if it failed to meet its obligations as a member within three months. The Dutch Ministry of Foreign Affairs wrote a letter in October 1998, arguing for tougher sanctions against Burma: "the lighter sanctions have had no effects". France did not support tougher sanctions. The French Development Co-operation Minister, Charles Josselin, said before the meeting that France "has always expressed a position of reserve vis-à-vis embargoes [...] on the observation [that] it is almost always the civilian population, the weakest people, who are the first victims of such economic sanctions, without their attaining the political objective."[52]

At the EU Council meeting on 26 October 1998 it was decided to extend the visa ban to include transit visas, applicable to tourism officials as well. "The Common Position also echoes the view, expressed by Daw Aung San Suu Kyi, that, in the present situation, it is inappropriate for tourists to visit Burma" it stated.[53] At the same time the EU acceepted Burma's presence at the next JCC meeting, albeit on certain conditions. Thai newspapers welcomed this move, citing Thai Foreign Ministry sources commending the EU. Burma was also commended by Thai officials for showing flexibility, sacrifice and understanding by offering to refrain from speaking at the meeting, "if not necessary". The ASEAN and EU flags would be used to represent the two sides at the meeting, dropping an earlier arrangement whereby national flags were to be used.

At the end of January 1999 it was clear that the JCC would be postponed again because of "EU member countries' refusal to sit at the same table with Myanmar officials", according to the Singapore press. The Thai press reported that the postponement was due to the EU's two other conditions that Myanmar and Laos be seated separately, and for the JCC to display the ASEAN and EU flags rather

---

[51]   "Doors slam on Burma", *Far Eastern Economic Review*, 8 October 1998.

[52]   "French minister not keen on santions on Burma", *Bangkok Post*, 22 October 1998.

[53]   EU Press Release: Luxembourg (26 October 1998) – No. 12274/98 (Presse 351).

than national flags, and to label the tables with the plaque 'non-members'. Thailand suggested then that the table be labelled 'non-signatories.'

The third meeting was the ASEAN-EU Ministerial Meeting (AEMM) scheduled for Berlin in late March 1999 in conjunction with the ASEM meeting, to discuss implementation of a number of joint programmes of EU technical assistance to the region worth several million dollars. The meeting was postponed after EU decided it would not lift the visa ban for SPDC members, thus making it impossible for the Burmese Foreign Minister to attend the meeting. The nine-member ASEAN insisted that all of its foreign ministers be allowed to attend.

EU diplomats said they were unwilling to issue a visa for the Burmese Foreign Minister, Win Aung, to be able to attend the scheduled meeting unless the junta made some type of 'humanitarian' gesture. The regime immediately released two high-profile political prisoners. The EU made a new suggestion: under the adopted proposal, the talks would go ahead but instead of all 15 member states being present, the EU would be represented by a troika of Austria, Germany and Finland. "There are hardline opinions on both sides. The ASEAN will not compromise on Myanmar's participation and the EU will not compromise its stance on human rights. It's a stalemate," said John Avila, political economist at Manila's Centre for Research and Communications.[54]

An important aspect of the international mechanisms of incentive and disincentive policies is its impact on the internal dynamics within the target state. Domestic conditions favouring or hampering the successful operation of international mechanisms in the target state are critically important considerations for policy-makers in both associations. The existence of a favourable domestic coalition behind the international mechanism makes a real difference in orchestrating broader domestic support for either incentive or disincentive policies. International mechanisms can create partners in the target state who favour execution of a particular policy and exert pressure, therefore, on the recipient state for the desired political changes.[55]

In Burma, the ruling junta has tried to mobilise popular sentiments against EU actions by appealing to national pride and survival. This populist approach might have achieved some results if there were no domestic coalition that could explain and educate the public about the real nature of EU actions. Daw Aung San Suu Kyi and her party, NLD, had made public announcement in support of EU's actions and even called for stronger measures. Since the EU and the US maintain limited trade relations with Burma, the cronies of the regime need to make little effort to manipulate black market trade to capture some of the economic rent generated by the sanctions.[56] Arguably, ASEAN's constructive engagement, which

---

[54]  "Analysis: ASEAN-EU ties tested by Myanmar", *Reuters*, 17 March 1999.

[55]  William J. Long, "Trade and Technology Incentives and Bilateral Co-operation", in David Cortright (ed.), *The Price for Peace: Incentives and International Conflict Prevention*, New York: Rowman & Littlefield, 1997.

[56]  David Rowe, "The Domestic Political Economy of International Economic Sanctions: The Case of Rhodesia." Paper presented to the Annual Meeting of the International Studies Association, Washington D.C., 1999. The paper explains how the target government can manipulate the sanctions by shifting economic rents to the favoured group in return for political resistance to the sanctions. Cases in point include Haiti, Castro's Cuba, and Hussein's Iraq.

tended to engage selectively with the government and its preferred groups of business friends, has unwittingly brought the public image of crony capitalism of the regime into sharper focus and reinforced public support for the EU call for human rights and justice in the country.

An important dimension of the internal dynamics of the sender countries is the number of vibrant Burma support groups in Europe, such as trade unions and NGOs. They mobilise critical awareness about human rights conditions and draw the attention of their respective governments to violations. Grassroots campaigns are being organised on a global scale, similar to the anti-*apartheid* movement from the early 1960s to the beginning of the 1990s. More importantly, the mass media and the NGO community in the ASEAN countries have strongly criticised the 'constructive engagement' policy and pointed out the moral bankruptcy of the ASEAN approach. All these networks of second-track or citizen diplomacy have given international legitimacy to the pressures that are brought to bear on the Burmese regime by official policies.

### The junta's response and underlying motives

In the wake of the cessation of aid from both multilateral and bilateral donors following the massacres in Rangoon, the SLORC had no option but to open up the country and invite foreign investors, especially from the resource-poor neighbouring countries, to exploit its rich natural resources. The desire to improve its international image and regain political recognition was the main motive for the SLORC to seek admission into the regional association. This desire was expressed by the chief of Burma's ruling junta, Senior General Than Shwe, who declared that associating with the regional grouping would not only uplift the stature of the ASEAN to rival other regional blocs, especially those of the West, but also enable it to "withstand the storm in unity".[57] However, such intentions were refuted by the Indonesian Foreign Minister, Ali Alatas, who did not "believe Burma is trying to use the ASEAN to ward off attacks by the international community".[58]

Nonetheless, the influence of the ASEAN in boosting the image of the Burmese regime was quite substantial. It had already influenced the way in which other countries outside the region approached the regime, considering the ASEAN position as a stamp of approval. For instance, South African President Nelson Mandela, despite his similar experience in confronting the oppressive *apartheid* regime, at a press conference in Bangkok refused to be drawn into a public condemnation of the SLORC and support for fellow freedom fighter Daw Aung San Suu Kyi. Instead, he maintained that "whatever contribution we want to make [towards democratisation in Burma] we will make in the region through the ASEAN."[59]

The inner life of the Rangoon regime is the subject of much speculation. The main sources for information about the views and the politics of the regime come from its own statements and rare interviews. The strictly controlled and censored

---

[57] "Than Shwe boasts ASEAN to rival Western bloc", *The Nation* (Bangkok), 31 July 1997.
[58] "Altas defends Burma's membership of ASEAN", *Bangkok Post*, 14 December 1995.
[59] Aung Shwe Oo and Peter Janssen, "Burmese Regime Looks Forward to Legitimacy Boost from ASEAN", *Thailand Times*, 23 July 1997.

newspapers in Rangoon run 'news commentaries', believed to be written by senior military personnel. Burma has for many years been one of the most secluded countries in the world. In recent years the military regime has followed a policy promoting a 'free-marked-economy' while at the same time strictly controlling all political activity and access to information. Most commentaries written by the regime or its allies give the impression that the regime is following its own political course. However, there is evidence that that the regime is sensitive to voting in the United Nations on the human rights situation in Burma. The regime has been orchestrating public relations activities before the sessions of the UN Commission on Human Rights in Geneva and the General Assembly in New York.[60] Recent changes in the military government, such as the autumn 1998 reshuffle of ministerial posts where Ohn Gyaw was replaced by Win Aung as Foreign Minister could be seen as an indication that the regime wanted to change its international image. In recent years, more comments have been provided by regime representatives, and more 'information sheets' have been made available on the Internet. The logic of these comments is hard to unravel but some features will be apparent from the examples below.

After the EU withdrew GSP trade benefits in March 1997 the official Burmese newspaper said that the EU "would think Myanmars (the regime's reference to the Burmese) would become bewildered and wide-eyed and some kneeling down and be subservient. However, Myanmar felt nothing about it and did not care less and even did not blink eyes."[61]

In October 1997, Klaus Kinkel, the Foreign Minister of Germany, suggested that contacts between the EU and Burma be boosted and at the same time spoke about the need for political changes. In response, a military official said Burma welcomed the offer but on the condition that Europe refrained from interfering in Burma's internal affairs.

In 1998 the tone of the statements became sharper. After the EU Foreign Ministers put more restrictions on travels by regime leaders to Europe the statements sounded thus: "They believe that slowing Myanmar's economic development through sanctions and boycotts will hasten the transition to democracy [...] However, history compels us to be more realistic."[62] The military seems to believe that the US somehow directs the policy of the EU. A letter written by the Burmese Ambassador to the US, Tin Winn, addressed to the British Foreign Office Minister, Derek Fatchett, stated: "If the British Government decides to impose sanctions on Myanmar, it will merely be following [...] the Americans." Fatchett had suggested that Burma be expelled from the ILO for its practice of forced labour. Tin Winn's letter continues: "In the circumstances, your threat to dislodge Myanmar from the ILO simply rings hollow [...] If you should decide to single out Myanmar and carry out the threat, I am confident that those who stand for justice and human rights will not allow such tyranny to prevail." In the UN General Assembly in March 1998 Burma's Foreign Minister, Ohn Gyaw,

---

[60] Stefan Collignon, "The Burmese Economy and the Withdrawal of European Trade Preferences", *EIAS Briefing Paper*, No 97/02, April 1997, p. 10.
[61] *Europe* (News service of the EU), No. 6948, 5 April 1997.
[62] *Bangkok Post*, 7 October 1998.

said that the world, including the UN, had no right to interfere in his country's internal affairs.

The SPDC decided in November 1998 that officials from Britain and Denmark would not be allowed to visit Burma. The move was interpreted as an 'accolade' by British Foreign Office Minister Derek Fatchett.[63] In a rare interview, Senior General Than Shwe, chairman of the State Peace and Development Council, suggests that removing the sanctions and "having international assistance and support will greatly facilitate our economic and political endeavours and will also help us build a democratic system more quickly by facilitating the handing over of state power back to the people."[64]

In an interview with *Japan Times,* Brig. Gen. Kyaw Win, gave his view on the policy of sanctions on Burma by US and European countries: "We see their policy as not very practical. Actually, if you do not have a strong economy – if you do not have a strong basic infrastructure – transformation from one political system into another, especially from a one-party socialist system into a multiparty political system, will not be possible. So we think their policy is not very practical, not realistic."[65]

The Burmese Embassy in Washington issued a press release about sanctions at the end of December 1998:

> The growing use of economic sanctions to promote foreign policy objectives is deplorable not only because it is unconstitutional but because it does more harm than good. Sanctions have always fallen short of their stated purposes. Unilateral sanctions are clearly ineffective. Despite sanctions, countries like Iran, Cuba, Libya, Iraq and Myanmar remain strong and resilient. The reason is not hard to fathom. Today we live in a global village and in a global economy unilateral sanctions are blunt weapons at best. Any slack created by the withdrawal of US companies is taken up by competitors. Unilateral sanctions invariably impose greater costs for US companies than on the target countries. Where it hurts is that sanctions, more often than not, produce undesirable results. For example those severely affected by the US sanctions in Iraq are the infants and the elderly, not least the sick and the infirm among them.
>
> In the case of Myanmar sanctions are ill-advised. All that they have accomplished is to take away jobs from workers employed in the garment and tourist-related industries. The people of Myanmar have lived under self-imposed isolation for 26 years and are conditioned to severe shortages of consumer goods and other luxury items. They understand the hardship boycotts entail and fully appreciate what the government has done in the past decade to strengthen the fabric of the nation, to open up the economy and to ensure an orderly transformation to a democracy. Now that peace reigns in the country they are looking forward to a more prosperous future in an open-market economy. They have begun turning faltering steps into firm strides and resent those who put obstacles in their way. In the circumstance, the people are wary of the antics of Aung San Suu Kyi and her supporters in the West who call for

---

[63] According to *Reuters*, 1 December 1998, his statement to parliament was as follows: "I have been told today that the Burmese authorities will not allow me to visit Burma, and I see that probably as an accolade for the work that we have done and the fight we have made for democracy and human rights in Burma."

[64] *Leaders Magazine*, vol. 21, no. 2, January 1999, (at www3.itu.int/MISSIONS/Myanmar/shwe. htm).

[65] "Sanctions failing to sway Myanmar", *The Japan Times,* 5 February 1999.

sanctions and attempt to rock the boat. As a result she is anathema to Myanmar. So much so that her own supporters are quitting the party in droves and the remaining members no longer dare to strut about in their uniforms as they once did.

At the beginning of January 1999 the new Burmese Foreign Minister, Win Aung, a career diplomat with a service record from Britain said he hoped that "friendship and co-operation with the EU and its members and the US could be regained as in previous years".[66] He also told reporters that "[o]ur mentality is not to succumb to any pressure. If there is pressure put upon us, we become more resistant to this pressure ...They [the EU] are saying the ball is in my court now. These remarks make it difficult for both of us. I don't want to say the ball is in their court, but we need to reach some understanding."

## Domestic partnership for international mechanisms

Since both the EU and the ASEAN seek to shape the process of political change in Burma, their policies must be able to influence the preferences and actions of important actors within the country. The junta is resisting external influence of any sort, be it by coercion or persuasion, while the NLD and its leadership favour the reforms sought by the external actors. Moreover, the NLD is willing and able to mobilise domestic constituencies in support of sanctions, thus incorporating external pressures into the domestic political dynamics when bargaining with the regime. Daw Aung San Suu Kyi explains the importance of sanctions in these words:

> We continue to believe in sanctions, because they provide a psychological boost to the democracy movement and keep foreign investors and policymakers focused on the situation in Burma.[67]

Mobilising popular sentiment in support of external policies such as sanctions is very sensitive. However, the public education and awareness campaign led by Daw Aung San Suu Kyi has been successful in harnessing domestic support for international action. Beyond its moral justification, this support was obtained more fundamentally because the economic benefits from foreign investments and trade have very little 'trickle-down' effects on the general population. Rather than hurting ordinary people, the exclusiveness of foreign economic relations makes a sanctions policy impact directly on the regime with negligible humanitarian side effects as Daw Aung San Suu Kyi has pointed out:

> I can say with absolute confidence that the general public of Burma would be very little affected, if at all, by sanctions. So far, the kind of investments that have come in have benefited the public very little indeed. If you have been in Burma long enough, you will be aware of the fact that a small elite has developed that is extremely wealthy.

---

[66] He said this to diplomats according to a state-run newspaper, *The New Lights of Myanmar*, 3 January 1999.

[67] "Diehard Optimist", *Far Eastern Economic Review*, 7 May 1998.

Perhaps they would be affected, but my concern is not with them but with the general public. Because of rampant inflation, living standards have been dropping for the great majority of the population. The people are poorer because standards of health and education have fallen. And conditions in the rural areas are worse off than they have ever been. So, you cannot equate the so-called open-market economy adopted by the SLORC with any real development that benefits people. Of course, there is a trickle-down effect but the trickle is a very, very small trickle. And it's dissipated very easily.

It is essential to institute a legal framework that would ensure justice and improve the quality of life in Burma immediately, because the greatest suffering among the people at the moment is caused by lack of justice and lack of the rule of law.[68]

Conversely, the incentive policies – due to the seclusion of quiet diplomacy and elitist business deals – have failed to mobilise widespread political support. Consequently, ASEAN policies ended up as being perceived as 'appeasement' of the corrupt generals – a scenario which Daw Aung San Suu Kyi and the NLD had warned against:

When the ASEAN was considering Burma as a permanent member a couple of years ago, we made two points. One was that admitting Burma as a member would make the regime more repressive, because they would think that their policies have been endorsed. They would see it as a seal of approval. Or, at least, if it was not a seal of approval it was a sign that the ASEAN countries didn't mind about the human rights record of the military regime. And the second thing we said was that Burma under this military regime was not going to be an asset to the organisation. And I think we can claim that both these views have been vindicated.[69]

The ASEAN could help Burma by using its institutional leverage to nudge the country towards democratisation. Since the Asian crisis has deprived many Southeast Asian countries of investment capital and trade opportunities, the ASEAN should not overestimate its collective economic strength to offer incentives to the regime. Despite its economic weakness, however, the ASEAN has no shortage of means and capabilities to induce changes in Burma in fundamental ways. The ASEAN capability in settling political disputes was evident in the Cambodian peace process. By setting a comparable objective for itself in Burma, the ASEAN could contribute to facilitating the transition in Burma. The immediate challenge for the ASEAN is not finding the right modalities but appreciating the complexity of the Burmese problem, and willingness to work with all parties to foster a national dialogue that can end the crisis. The NLD has already appealed to the Association in this regard:

We believe that support from the ASEAN – which comprises Thailand, Malaysia, Indonesia, Philippines, Singapore, Brunei, Laos and Vietnam and which Burma recently joined – is crucial to our quest for democracy. If the ASEAN can persuade or

---

[68]  Leslie Kean and Dennis Bernstein, "Aung San Suu Kyi", *Progressive* (Madison,WI), March 1997.
[69]  Roger Mitton, "Interview with Daw Aung San Suu Kyi", *Asiaweek*, Special Online Edition, 11 June 1999 (http://www.pathfinder.com/asiaweek/current/issue/nat 4-8.html).

put pressure on the present regime to convene the Parliament that was elected by the people, this could be the first step towards democratisation.[70]

## Policies and practice: conventional wisdom reconsidered

Although the ASEAN intended its engagement policy to influence the behaviour of the SLORC towards easing state suppression of the political opposition, the human rights situation in Burma has not improved. Violations of all kinds, both at the local level and on a national scale, have been on the increase despite Burma's entry into the regional organisation.

UN human rights reports from 1997 onwards have been highly critical of the government's persistent human rights violations. During the last two years, the military regime has taken severely repressive measures against the NLD. The crackdown included detention of about 150 elected people's representatives and 400 other members of the NLD; sentencing to long prison terms NLD members and student activists who organised support for the NLD call to convene the people's parliament; constant harassment of NLD MPs to make them give up their candidacy; and closure of NLD offices in several townships.[71]

The government has stopped co-operating with the International Committee of the Red Cross, which used to inspect prisons. Following this denial of access for independent human rights monitoring missions, there have been rumours about poor prison conditions and mistreatment of prisoners. A strong testimony was disclosed by a group of Thai fishermen who were arrested for illegal fishing in Burmese territorial waters and later released after bilateral negotiations. The fishermen related their ordeal and incarceration under poor prison conditions that affected their health and mental well-being. They also reported various kinds of ill treatment. Additional evidence was provided by former prisoners who had gone through very painful experiences while surviving in notorious detention centres such as the Insein prisons.

The cumulative effect of severe repression provoked a strong reaction by the strongest resistance group of the democratic movement: the students. A series of student protests erupted at the Rangoon Institute of Technology in August 1998 as hundreds of students staged the largest anti-government rally since 1988 in commemorating the historic 8 August 1988 uprising ten years previously. The students mobilised support for Daw Aung San Suu Kyi's call for parliament. The regime used massive security personnel to suppress the demonstrations, albeit with constrained use of force, and detained dozens of student leaders. All universities and colleges were immediately shut down and students sent home.

Foreign investment that has steadily flowed into the country under the official guise of 'constructive engagement' has not been able to change the regime's record on human rights violations. Worse still, some types of investment, particularly in infrastructure and capital-intensive projects like oil exploration, are

---

[70] Daw Aung San Suu Kyi, "Nudge Burma Towards Democracy", *The Nation* (Bangkok), 13 July 1999.

[71] UN Human Rights Special Rapporteur, Rajsoomer Lajlah, said in his latest reports that human rights conditions continued to deteriorate in Burma. See *Reuters*, 15 March 1999.

"harming and not helping the people".[72] The projects are "being implemented in a system, which lacks any semblance of the rule of law" and local people who suffer physical and environmental damage as a result of these projects have no legal avenue for relief. One such example is the multi-billion Yadana gas pipeline project that will export gas to Thailand in 1999, where the state petroleum company, the Petroleum Authority of Thailand, is both an investor in the project and the importer of the gas. Since the feasibility studies were completed and construction started, the project has drawn international criticism for the scale of its human rights violations in forced relocation of people and use of forced labour. It led to a refugee exodus to neighbouring Thailand from the project area.

Recently, the Philippino Foreign Minister, Domingo Siazon, broke the ASEAN customary mode of diplomacy and commented that the Burmese people should learn more from the Philippine's experience (people's power) of democratic changes. In support of Siazon's approach, giving unsolicited advice to the democrats in Burma, Thai Foreign Minister, Surin Pitsuwan, called on members to abandon their longstanding reluctance to criticise one another when politics or economics in one country affected another.

As one of the most democratic states within the Association and, more importantly, the only country that shares a border with Burma, Thailand has made a bold statement in redefining what policy the ASEAN should pursue vis-à-vis Burma:

> Thailand will continue to follow the situation in Burma very closely. We will continue to encourage all our friends in that country to engage in a sustained process of dialogue without any preconditions, with a view towards bringing about lasting national reconciliation, for such a development will surely benefit everyone in the region.
>
> We will continue to encourage new initiatives, such as the ones taken by the UN Secretary-General last October and the European Union a few days ago. As a close neighbour, we will not hesitate to express our concerns and to make constructive suggestions, if and when questions arise which affect the region's and Thailand's security and well-being.[73]

As the effects of globalisation are increasingly being felt in the ASEAN region, with increasing attention on issues such as transparency, accountability and good governance by multilateral institutions, donors, international media, NGOs and corporate entities, all ASEAN countries will need to make appropriate adjustments. Global dynamics forge linkages between domestic and international issues, such as the need for Burma to make progress on democratisation as a step towards reintegration into the international community. Against this reality, the

---

[72]    Earth Rights International and Southeast Asian Information Network, *Total Denial: The Report on the Yadana Pipeline Project in Burma,* Bangkok, July 1996. The report can be obtained on-line at http://metalab.unc.edu/freeburma/docs/totaldenial/td.html.

[73]    M.R. Sukhumbhand Paribatra, "Burma, ASEAN, Democracy, Dreams and Realities", *The Nation* (Bangkok) 16 July 1999. The author is the Deputy Foreign Minister of Thailand and presented his own perspective on Burma in response to Burmese Nobel Peace Laureate Daw Aung San Suu Kyi's article, "Nudge Burma Towards Democracy", which appeared in the 'Voicing my thoughts' column of *The Nation* (Bangkok) on 13 July 1999.

ASEAN can ill afford to remain the last bastion defending a dictatorial regime against global forces at the expense of its long-standing integrity and image. Thailand's Deputy Foreign Minister, M.R. Sukhumbhand Paribatra, recently outlined his view of the way in which the ASEAN ought to modify its principles in tune with changing realities in the environment:

> All principles can of course be modified through changing time and circumstances. Today, with rapidly growing global and regional interdependence, the dividing line between purely domestic issues, on the one hand, and domestic issues with international, regional or transnational implications, on the other, is becoming difficult to discern, as the recent financial crises, environmental disasters, and problems of drugs, diseases and illegal migration demonstrate.[74]

The rationale on the part of the ASEAN for an adaptation of its stance on Burma is already in place. What is still lacking is the political will to design an appropriate roadmap and to find the right modalities of implementation. Only then can the Association's relevance in international diplomacy be maintained.

The ASEAN objective of discouraging Burma from forging closer ties with China is yet to see any impact. The opposite appears to have occurred. Chief of general staff of the People's Liberation Army, Fu Quanyou, stated that the relations between the armies of China and Burma is an important part of the Sino-Burma relations and that constant visits have strengthened their friendship.[75]

Despite ASEAN wishes, China's economic and political leverage over Rangoon is much greater than the ASEAN can counter, and the Chinese influence has increased in the wake of ASEAN decline after the economic crisis. An expression of this influence is the rapid transformation of Burma's second city, Mandalay, which is replete with high-rise buildings, modern shops, and brand-new villas owned by Chinese and Yunnanese merchants and immigrants who have acquired Burmese citizenship through bribery.[76]

A realistic assessment of China's strategic and economic needs and Burma's predicament shows that Beijing is unlikely to easily give up what it has already gained. Past experiences suggest that Beijing never provide diplomatic protection, arms, aid and finance to Third World states on generous terms. The SLORC can hardly expect to be an exception to this past practice.[77] The only *quid pro quo* Burma can offer to Beijing is letting the Chinese use Burma as a gateway to South and Southeast Asia.

Since China adopted an 'open door' economic policy, it has always looked for a gateway to South and Southeast Asia, particularly for its landlocked regions in the Southwest. One of the shortest and possibly the cheapest access to the sea routes is through Burma. With the cash-strapped junta in Rangoon, this strategic plan became feasible. In March 1997, Beijing and Yangon (Rangoon) embarked on a new major project – the Irrawaddy Corridor Project – which, once completed, would enable China to quickly transfer large forces to the coast of the Bay of

---

[74]   *Ibid.*
[75]   *Xinhua News Agency,* 16 October 1998.
[76]   Stephen Mansfield, "Myanmar's Chinese Connection", *The Japan Times,* 12 May 1999.
[77]   Mohan Malik, "Burma slides under China's Shadow", *Jane's Intelligence Review,* 1 July 1997.

Bengal, on the Indian Ocean. The proposed plan consists of land transport routes linking Dehong Dai-Jingpo Autonomous Prefecture in Yunnan to the river ports of Bhamo and Myitkyina in Northeast Myanmar, and from there on the Irrawaddy all the way to Yangon.[78] With such a large-scale infrastructure project under way, it is unlikely that the Burmese junta will be able to withstand Beijing's pressures.

There is little hope that the ASEAN can influence its Burmese member to seriously address the upward trends in heroin production and rising addiction in the border areas along the major trafficking routes all over the region. International observers have estimated that income from illegal drug exports has exceeded by far the country's income from official exports.[79] In effect, Burma's economy has become more and more dependent upon the shadow drug economy to the extent that the junta can hardly resist the temptation to turn a blind eye to the problems.

Therefore, the official complicity in the drug economy continues. Military intelligence forces, under the leadership of General Khin Nyunt, has been identified as the kingpin in protecting drug traffickers, including fugitives wanted by Thailand.[80] The cease-fire agreement between major ethnic armies and the regime has provided a stable environment in which drug trade may thrive without interruption. One ethnic resistance leader, who has close contacts with former colleagues now doing business under the agreement, openly commented that Burma will do nothing to stem the flow of Golden Triangle heroin because the government protects the trade.[81]

According to a US State Department report, drug seizures account for less than one per cent of Burma's total opium output, and Burma remains the world largest source of heroin.[82] A more alarming situation is the introduction of a new, cheap stimulant drug, amphetamine, by Burma's drug lords and their trafficking networks to the regional markets of the relatively affluent ASEAN capitals. According to Thailand's Narcotics Control Board, amphetamine addiction among teenagers has surged in the past five years and Burma accounts for more than 100 million pills smuggled into Thailand annually.[83]

Burma has acceded to the ASEAN Free Trade Agreement (AFTA). However, the continuous improvement of co-operative elements and the specific policies for region-wide economic integration will remain shallow in the foreseeable future. Unlike other free trade areas, the ASEAN does not compel Burma to liberalise other sectors of the economy as a precondition for joining the association. Nor is it necessary to adjust domestic policies to the regulatory framework of the dominant partners (for example subsidies and non-trade barriers). It can be concluded,

---

[78] En Claire, "Beijing Consolidates Its Hold on Myanmar", *Defense & Foreign Affairs' Strategic Policy*, July, 1997

[79] Bertil Lintner, *Burma in Revolt: Opium and Insurgency since 1948,* Boulder, CO: Westview Press, 1994.

[80] *The Nation* (Bangkok), 14 January 1999.

[81] *Reuters,* 22 February 1999. Shan State Army leader, Col. Yod Suk, commented to reporters at an Interpol meeting in Rangoon.

[82] U.S. Department of State, *International Narcotics Control Strategy Report,* Washington D.C: U.S. DOS, 1997.

[83] *Bangkok Post*, 9 November 1997. It has been estimated that 8 million amphetamine tablets are smuggled each month from Burma.

therefore, that there is very little prospect that ASEAN membership would benefit Burma through economic integration.

## The impact of the Asian financial crisis

The current headlines on the Asian economic problems rarely feature Burma. A top general, responsible for running the Burmese economy, senselessly asserted that the 'Asian flu' has not reached his country. The remark missed the point. The economic woes of Burma are home-made rather than due to exogenous factors. Still, the generals' optimism that Burma does not suffer from capital flight is under challenge. Considering the non-existence of an equity market in Burma, talk about sudden reversal of capital flows is irrelevant. What is relevant is the contagious effect of the sick Asia that is likely to exacerbate the already stagnating economy.

The impact of the Asian financial crisis has already taken a big toll in Burma. First, Asian firms, accounting for 70 per cent of foreign direct investment in Burma, have either reduced or postponed putting money into Burmese operations and projects following the credit squeeze on their home fronts. Some even wanted to divest altogether but the generals banned any repatriation of capital. The immediate flight of capital would be so damaging that the regime would risk its credibility and set a bad precedent for future investors. Second, over half of Burmese exports went to Asia and many imports come from that part of the world. The cash-strapped Asians would be reluctant to buy non-essential though major exports from Burma such as teak and gems while attempting to dump their own exports as part of a global strategy out of the financial crisis. Surely, Burma will also face tough competition from her neighbours in selling its low-quality agricultural produce. Moreover, the pressures on the weak Burmese currency were felt in 1998 as speculative attacks caused a 150 per cent depreciation at the height of Asian flu. Finally, in the short run, Burma's hope of benefiting from the spill-over from ASEAN dynamism is now dashed since every ASEAN country has its own priorities for survival.

In economics, crises often come in series. Unfortunately, the forces of nature do not seem to have blessed Burma recently. Massive floods of 1998 caused severe damage to the country's agriculture. For instance, the government can export only 20,000 ton of rice in 1999 — a fraction of previous year's volume, not to speak of the 1 million ton exported in 1995. This will reduce the government revenue, likely to precipitate a crisis in the balance of payment. In turn, this has prompted speculative attacks on the already weakened *kyat*.

## Where is the trickle-down effect?

Long before the Asian crisis, Burma had experienced a silent emergency. Take the example of rice production. Being the backbone of the country's economy, accounting for 50 per cent of GDP and 65 per cent of the total labour force, the rice economy has lost its efficiency. The sector has lost its optimal structure of relative prices and, consequently, productivity has been reduced given a poor supply response. The main reason is lack of market incentives. Agricultural prices have been strictly controlled under the urban-bias policy of the regime, whose stability depends on the acquiescence of urban residents. Through the monopolistic mechanism of 'marketing boards' and export controls, the government secured huge revenues by buying rice from the farmers at a very low procurement price and selling it on the world market for a much higher price. This implicit tax was not returned in the form of greater investment in the rice sector; it was instead used to finance the government's political projects including an ambitious defence force of half a million.

The proponents of 'Asian models' contend that the negative effects of such micro-distorted economies could be a positive trade-off if the government would benevolently adopt a 'big push' strategy and allocate resources for investment in the sectors with a higher social rate of return. The authoritarian advantage theory tells us that 'strong' states, less dependent of electoral cycles, have greater capacities to implement policies. However, the key underlying assumption is the implementation of 'right policies' under 'right fundamentals'. The military regimes in Burma have wronged on both policies and fundamentals with a disastrous outcome. The obstinate practice of self-reliance that favoured import-substitution industrialisation and isolationism cost the socialist economy dearly. Nor did the market opening under the present regime result in viable policies to revive the economy plagued by dirigisme, rent-seeking, and stop-and-go cycles. Meanwhile, unchecked public spending made the whole macro-economic environment unstable and not conducive for capital accumulation and growth.

Fiscal crises, associated with soaring inflation and an extreme current account imbalance, are recurrent features of the military regimes in Burma. The economy has suffered from a chronic budget deficit since the SLORC came to power in 1988. To a great extent, the growth of the public sector accounted for these deficits. The government's expenditures mushroomed and the fiscal deficit reached nearly eight per cent of GDP after ten years of SLORC rule, which had started with a near balanced budget.

The government also lost the useful source of external public financing of budget deficits after the donors decided to terminate ODA flows following the political riot suppression in 1988. Since then, it has relied on domestic financing, leading to a sizeable expansion of the money supply. The result was not only accelerating inflation but also depreciation of the *kyat*. The government's die-hard adherence to the unrealistic fixed exchange rate made economic matters worse, hurting especially the country's potential exporters further by shrinking the revenue base and aggravating the resource gap. In such an inflationary environment, it would not come as a surprise that Burma scores the lowest among the Southeast Asian countries in terms of investment rate: 12 per cent.

**The failure of a growth-led development strategy**

When the SLORC came to power in 1988, the opening of the country to foreign investment was adopted as a way of regaining government control of the fiscal accounts and the economy. The windfall income generated from the sale of natural resources and a number of signatory rights from oil exploration enabled the regime to defer essential economic liberalisation. Far from a trickle-down effect of FDI, the inflow of foreign capital bred a 'new class', exclusively tied to the top

128

generals, which drained substantial amounts of the newly found wealth into unproductive investments such as real estate. Since the inflow of external resources temporarily secured internal equilibria, the government reallocated the resources according to their political priorities. This reliance on foreign financing of the domestic resource gap made the regime highly vulnerable to the 'Asian flu'.

As the situation deteriorated, the government attempts to reverse the negative trends. However, the policy tools with which the government was trying to remedy the economic ills were non-economic. The government sent agents to the foreign exchange counters and arrested any trader who made transactions outside the range the government has set for them. The trade licenses the regime had created in the first place to profit from rent-seeking activities were temporarily suspended. Military troops were sent to seal off the border to stop cross-border trade. Given the total halt in external trade, the exchange rate recovered marginally. The government then hailed their action by claiming that they had effectively constrained demand and tamed consumption. The unthinkable was happening: Burma was returning to autarky!

These policies may sound irrational to outsiders. For the generals, they were deemed necessary. How does irrational behaviours become rational in Burma? The answer may be found in the political economy of the authoritarian disadvantage. In this model, the generals are bounded by various interests groups and can only take selective measures. The fundamental interest is, of course, to maintain the military in power. It is possible that the military think that the development goals of the state can only be fulfilled by the military, and that, as a corollary, usurping power is imperative and justified. In any case, the means to attain this end involves the evolution of what development economists term a 'predatory' state, i.e. self-seeking extraction of resources for the maintenance of power and for rewarding the supporters of the regime. The rationale is not promotion of economic growth but rather regime stability. The government appears prepared to use every resource to fulfil this goal.

The under-performance of the Burmese military regime can be explained with reference to a number of factors. First, the sale of the country's rich natural resources conferred monopoly rents on the business groups while yielding quick revenue to the state. In these resource-based investments, the foreign firms have been forced to make joint ventures either with state enterprises or companies set up by the regime's associates. This Dutch disease phenomenon led the regime to postpone essential reforms. Second, in order to stabilise the urban food prices and to sustain revenues from the government monopoly in rice export, the government continued to squeeze the rice sector. Price controls are essential to appease the restive urban population. In fact, some observers use the rice price as a political risk barometer in Burma. Third, the government allowed a steady rise of luxury imports to satisfy the taste of the *nouveaux riches*, who also benefited from the rents of import licensing. The overvalued exchange rate was defended partly due to concerns about social unrest among the urban populations and partly to satisfy the new rentier class. Fourth, lacking political capital and legitimacy the regime had to spend money on political monuments and to pay for political patronage. Symbolic rather than substantive development has been favoured. For instance, sports festivals for the youth are organised while universities are continually closed. Electrical power is distributed for touristic 'Visit-Myanmar-Year' type promotion rather than for manufacturing industries.

### Military spending kills economic potential

A particularly worrying decision by the regime is to expand the size of the army to half a million, following the collapse of the socialist machine when the government lost all 'control' structures. At the height of the 1988 uprising, the socialist party members resigned, some defected to the opposition while many party cadres denouncing the 'guardian-cum-captains of the Titanic'. This was damaging to the generals and prompted them to fall back on the military structures they knew and had always trusted.

Not bothering to nurture the army-party again, the generals embarked on building the army by allocating most of the budgetary resources for military purposes. Despite fiscal constraints, the Burmese army mounted a parallel programme of modernisation and numerical force expansion at the same time. Senior army officers have been given high positions in the state as the primary vehicle for accumulation of wealth, status, and power. Thus, the Frankenstein bureaucracy took over statecraft, further draining the state coffers, with less efficiency and more corruption. Meanwhile, the share of military spending in the state budget was maintained at a high level at the expense of education and health. By 1993, the share of military spending in the total state budget had reached a peak of 42 per cent, and has remained at that level ever since.

That military expansion and other politically motivated expenditures did a lot of damage to reform efforts became very clear by the end of a decade of military rule. On paper, the decline of the economy was concealed by reports of a steady GDP growth rate, which at one point reached a double-digit figure (disputable in view of the official underestimation of the inflation rate). However, the country's social indicators have been showing a dangerously declining trend over the years. The use of inflationary tax measures and the concomitant decline in social expenditure led to rising levels of poverty. The rates of malnutrition, under-five mortality, school drop-out, and maternal mortality have risen sharply. Inequality is clearly visible in the city where the cronies of the military live in villas and drive Mercedes, while the rest are forcibly relocated to shantytowns with poor infrastructures and an over-crowded public transport system. Having built a large army for societal control purposes, the generals think they can crush any social dissent and political opposition with brute force.

### CONCLUSION: TOWARDS A FRAMEWORK FOR EFFECTIVE INTERNATIONAL POLICIES

By the end of 1998, the economic crisis in Burma had become acute. Hardest hit was foreign direct investment which saw a mere US$ 11.2 million for the five-month period from April to August – a shocking drop from US$ 339.6 million in the same period of the previous year.[84] Popular investments in the hotel and

---

[84] Economist Intelligence Unit, *Myanmar: EIU Country Report 1st Quarter 1999*, London, 1999.

tourism sector virtually dried up after the end of the Visit-Myanmar-Year – a promotion campaign designed by the government to entice visitors. The ASEAN engagement rationale had been undermined by the unforeseen impacts of the Asian crisis. The policy of 'constructive engagement' was designed to work under vastly different circumstances. As the flows of ASEAN investment into Burma virtually stopped and existing projects were either postponed or withdrawn, the prospects for economic integration and its associated dynamics had hit rôck bottom.

With its overriding preoccupation with political survival, the regime has still not given any satisfactory answers in dealing with deep-seated economic problems. Instead, the generals are concerned with control of a shrinking productive base while being evasive on serious reform and restructuring. The doomsday scenario of fiscal collapse and violent changes, reminiscent of ten years ago, could be repeated. At this point, the relevant question is whether the incentives – either resumption of foreign aid or removal of US sanctions – might alleviate the Burmese crisis. It depends on the conditions under which such incentives would be offered. Since the political determinants of economic decision-making are so pervasive, for any economic reform programme to be successful and sustainable the political structures must be changed first. In other words, economic reform requires a transition to democracy because cronyism, nepotism, and stop-and-go policy cycles, as evident in Indonesia, could derail the reform process.

At this juncture, a strong argument can be made that the national task of economic revival is more likely to succeed under a democratic political framework. First, for any austerity measures to produce results, the government needs to restrain expenditure and increase revenue. Democratisation can facilitate stabilisation because a democratic regime may help reduce the economic burden of unproductive spending and limit the scope "for *ad hoc* decision-making, for rent-seeking, for undesirable preferential treatment of individuals or organisations".[85] Second, the implementation of economic reforms must be underpinned by the credibility and trust that only a democratic regime can provide. Tough stabilisation measures and economic reforms incur social costs and only a regime enjoying the confidence of its citizens stand a chance of sustaining the process. Third, mobilising domestic and foreign private capital is a critical component of economic recovery. Sustaining the private capital flows and creating a climate conducive to investment requires the rule of law, transparency in public administration, and above all, political stability. Moreover, the lessons learned in the past should also guide decisions about incentive strategies.

It must be recognised that earlier ASEAN efforts to use incentives to induce desired political changes in Burma have proved insufficient. First, the ASEAN has been shy in identifying and addressing the root causes of the current crisis in Burma. The fundamental need of Burma is to resolve the political stalemate

---

[85] Executive Board of the International Monetary Fund issued new instructions on aid conditionality, stressing its concern for governance. For details, see Harold James, "From Grandmotherliness to Governance: The Evolution of IMF Conditionality", *Finance and Development*, Washington D.C.: IMF, December 1998.

between the military authorities and elected civilian representatives. Second, the ASEAN incentive package to induce the regime in Burma to change its behaviour or policies contained too few material benefits. The military in Burma are looking for the kind and volume of resource that can make a fundamental difference in putting the economy on a take-off course. In essence, the regime wants to see the resumption of ODA and structural adjustment loans without changing the political equation. Only the Western donors and Japan, not the ASEAN, have the means to deliver what the junta wants. Third, the most damaging outcome of the ASEAN policy was the appearance of rewarding an evil regime in Burma. It can be concluded with a fair amount of evidence that the ASEAN co-operative gestures have been taken as a sign of weakness or as an act of appeasement. Since the policy was adopted, the regime has not only failed to improve its domestic behaviour, but rather committed acts of aggression against a fellow member within the association, i.e. Thailand.[86]

On the other hand, the EU policy seems to have exerted much more influence than expected on regional dynamics and Burmese politics. Again, an important factor in this dynamics is timing. Unexpected events in the regional environment has brought additional pressures to bear on the junta in ways that make it more difficult to compensate for a democratic deficit through economic benefits to the public. The junta's grip on power has been severely undermined by lack of resources while the danger of renewed conflict with both the civilian opposition and armed ethnic groups has created a political deadlock which is hurting the junta. Under such circumstances, the need to resolve the political crisis has been acknowledged in diplomatic circles. In other words, the EU's firm policy on Burma, combined with that of the US, has sharpened international opinion – a significant step forward towards a unified international approach to the crisis in Burma.

The question of the efficacy of EU policy cannot be measured on the sole criterion of impact on the target regime's policies. Although EU's policy apparently did not produce dramatic policy changes in the target country, it has affected significantly the capability of the military junta to consolidate its power position. This capability must be measured in relational terms. The efficacy of external policies must be judged against how they affect the relative power of the military junta vis-à-vis the democratic opposition. EU policies need not necessarily inflict economic damages on the target regime to be effective. Contrary to conventional wisdom, EU's disincentive policies work on Burma through non-economic mechanisms.

In analysing both ASEAN and EU policies, the nature of objectives sought is one of the most important variables affecting their potential effectiveness. The clearer the focus and objective, the better the chances of success. In the case of the ASEAN, shifting interests and purposes have often led to confusion and undermined the clarity of the message delivered to the regime. An example of

---

[86] The persistence of unlawful trespassing and attack on refugee camps within Thailand by Rangoon's militia caused security nightmares for Thailand. This and other factors forced Thai foreign policy analysts to reconsider the value of being an ASEAN member. See "To Stay, or Not to Stay", *Asiaweek,* Intelligence Section, 23 April 1999, p. 12.

competing goals is when ASEAN governments wanted to reap economic benefits from associating with the regime while at the same time seeking Rangoon's co-operation in changing its political behaviour. Although the EU policy has had a consistent objective in demanding a move towards democratic change, the exact mechanism for attaining these goals is less clear. The questions of human rights, democracy and dialogue are clearly enunciated in EU's position but such abstract goals need to be operationalised. In other words, the EU position may have needed to be more oriented towards facilitation than just signalling moral disapproval. By moving towards a facilitating role, EU's position could articulate specific but feasible objectives or benchmarks.

With the shortcomings and limited leverage of either approach, it may be appropriate for the two regional institutions to co-ordinate their efforts. The indispensability of joint action arises from the recent row between the two regional organisations over the inclusion of Burma in the ASEM process. Neither regional organisation should let the Burma question obstruct important co-operation on investment and aid. Instead, they may need to consult adequately to ensure that they understand, accept, and share their respective objectives. Since Burma as an ASEAN member state can thwart such co-ordination, a possible venue for consultation might be the good offices of the United Nations, where both EU and ASEAN diplomacy have played a critical role in shaping a multilateral framework for resolving Burma's problems.

In fact, a multilateral modality for such concerted efforts already exists. The UN General Assembly in November 1998 authorised the Secretary-General to facilitate a process that might induce "the Government of Myanmar to urgently expand and intensify its contacts with the National League for Democracy with a view to engaging in a substantive political dialogue with the General Secretary of the League, Aung San Suu Kyi, and other political leaders, including representatives of ethnic and other groups, as the best means of promoting national reconciliation and the full and early restoration of democracy".[87] Dialogue is emphasised, including a novel approach by multilateral aid agencies, such as the World Bank and the UNDP to extend offers of 'aid-for-talk'.[88] The UN also has established an informal consultative body comprising some EU and ASEAN members to buttress the UN's role in Burma.[89] By enlisting the UN Secretary-General as a mediator in Burma, the EU and the ASEAN would complement their policies towards achieving common goals.

At any rate, a dialogue process will have to commence in Burma before sanctions are lifted and aid resumed, either in a preliminary form of talks between the junta and the NLD, or in a broad sense of a UN-sanctioned tri-partite process involving representatives from the armed forces, democratic organisations and ethnic groups. The intervention of a neutral mediator will be crucial in such

---

[87] United Nations General Assembly, "Situation of human rights in Myanmar", Fifty-third session, Third Committee Agenda item 110 (c), 13 November 1998.

[88] "Myanmar aid-for-talks dialogue to resume this year", Agence France Presse, 2 June 1999.

[89] Several EU and ASEAN diplomats participated in the 12-23 October informal, closed-door meeting at Chilston Park in the southeastern town of Kent in England to map out strategies for UN mediation in Burma. See Suthichai Yoon, "Carrot from Chilston to Rangoon", *The Nation* (Bangkok), 3 December, 1998.

dialogue, given the lack of experiences of all parties and the difficulty inherent in negotiations over power arrangements. Such mediation efforts cannot be sustained without serious international involvement. As long as both the ASEAN and the EU are serious and determined to achieve their goals, they may adopt different approaches to co-ordination with each other and with the lead external player, the UN Secretary-General. Such a strategy has already been endorsed by Aung San Suu Kyi: "It is not that either sanction or engagement is a more effective policy over the other, but, what we need is a concerted effort from the international community to synergise both strategies to have maximum influence on the changes in Burma."[90]

## CHRONOLOGY OF EVENTS 1996-98

- 28 October 1996: EU's Common Position established with effect from the following day.
- March 1997: EU withdrew GSP trade benefits with respect to Burma's agricultural and industrial products.
- April 1997: US banned all new investment in Burma.
- 1 June 1997: ASEAN announces that it will admit Burma as member in July, considerably earlier than expected.
- 11 June 1997: EU informs Thailand that new members of the EU or of the ASEAN would not be accorded automatic rights to join ASEM in London, April, 1998.
- 24 July 1997: ASEAN formally admits Burma in Kuala Lumpur.
- 25 July 1997: ASEAN Secretary General, Ajit Singh, admits to problems with the EU and the US over Burma.
- 28 July 1997: EU Foreign Ministers inform ASEAN that the EU will not allow Burma to join the ASEAN-EU meetings held in Europe.
- 1 September 1997: The Malaysian Prime Minister, Mahathir Mohammed, announces that he would treat any move by the EU to discriminate against Burma as discrimination against ASEAN.
- 20 October 1997: EU extended Common Position on Burma.
- 10 November 1997: Bulgaria, Cyprus, the Czech Republic, Estonia, Hungary, Iceland, Latvia, Lithuania, Norway, Romania, Slovakia and Slovenia declared their national policies to conform to EU Common Position on Burma as extended on 20 October 1997.
- 13 November 1997: ASEAN-EU Joint Co-operation Council scheduled for 17-19 November 1997 in Bangkok postponed indefinitely by the EU after Thailand invited Burma as a "full observer" for the meeting.
- 1 January 1997: Burma attends an ASEAN-EU working group meeting in the Philippines.
- 19 February 1997: European Parliament Resolution calls for EU economic sanctions against Burma.

---

[90] Quoted from Aung San Suu Kyi's address to the international conference, *Burma at the Crossroads,* held in New York, 23 October 1996 with the sponsorship of the Friedrich Ebert Stiftung.

- April 1998: Most ASEAN countries and EU members meet at the second ASEM (Asia Europe Meeting) held in London. Burma did not attend due to a visa ban for Burmese officials by EU.
- 27 April 1998: EU extends common position for another six months without amendment.
- 14 May 1998: US denies SPDC visas for ASEAN-US talks. Venue changed to Manila. European Parliament resolution calls on Commission and Council to implement economic sanctions against Burma.
- 28-29 July 1998: German Federal Government would put the Burma issue on the agenda of top-level political consultations between the EU and the ASEAN to take place in Manila on 28-29 July.
- 1 August 1998: EU proposes to send a mission of senior officials to Burma for talks with the government and Aung San Suu Kyi. The proposal was rejected by SPDC. A Thai-brokered arrangement to allow Burma to attend the JCC meeting without the right to speak was of no consequence because some EU countries asked for "signs of positive development" in Burma.
- 14 August 1998: SPDC rejects proposal by UN General Secretary, Kofi Annan, to dispatch an envoy for urgent talks.
- September 1998: SPDC begins arresting members of NLD and members of Parliament.
- 4 September 1998: World Bank announces cut in financial ties with SPDC for failure to repay past loans.
- 16 September 1998: NLD forms "Committee Representing the People's Parliament" (CRPP), consisting of 10 persons.
- 30 September 1998: NLD reports that 961 party members, including 202 members of Parliament are under detention.
- 28 October 1998: EU steps up sanctions against Burma, including a ban on transit visas for military personnel and a ban on visas for tourism officials. At the same time it becomes known that the deadlock between the EU and the ASEAN is resolved as Burma will be allowed to join the next JCC meeting, but "will not speak unless necessary".

## SUGGESTIONS FOR FURTHER READING

ALTSEAN, *Report Card: SLORC's progress as a member of ASEAN*, Bangkok, Alternative ASEAN Network, November 1997.

Badgley, John, "The Burmese Way to Capitalism", *Southeast Asian Affairs 1990*, Singapore, Institute of Southeast Asian Studies, 1990.

Bray, John, *Burma: The Politics of Constructive Engagement*, Royal Institute of International Affairs, London 1995.

Cook, Paul and M. Minogue, "Economic Reform and Political Change in Myanmar (Burma)", *World Development*, Vol. 21, No. 7, 1993.

Dapice, David O., *Policies to Increase and Sustain Agricultural Output in Myanmar*, Cambridge, MA: Harvard Institute of International Development, unpublished monograph, 1996.

Guyot, James F., "Burma in 1988: Perestroika with a Military Face", *Southeast Asian Affairs 1989*, Singapore, Institute of Southeast Asian Studies, 1989.

Khin Maung Kyi, "Will Forever Flow the Irrawaddy?", *Southeast Asians Affairs 1994*, Singapore, Institute of Southeast Asian Studies, 1994.

Lintner, Bertil, *Outrage: Burma's Struggle for Democracy*, Bangkok, White Lotus, 1990.

Mya Maung, *Burma Road to Poverty*, New York, Praeger, 1991.

Mya Maung, "Damage to Human Capital and the Future of Burma", *The Fletcher Forum*, Winter, 1992.

Mya Maung, *Totalitarianism in Burma: Prospects for Economic Development*, New York: Paragon House, 1992.

Mya Than and Joseph L. H. Tan, *Myanmar Dilemmas and Options: The Challenge of Economic Transition in the 1990s*, Singapore, Institute of Southeast Asian Studies, 1990.

Steinberg, David I., *Crisis in Burma: Stasis and Change in a Political Economy in Turmoil*, ISIS Paper no. 5, Bangkok, Institute of Security and International Studies, Chulalongkorn University, 1989.

Steinberg, David I.,"Burma Under the Military: Towards a Chronology", *Contemporary Southeast Asia*, Vol. 3, No. 3, 1981.

Steinberg, David I., "Economic Growth with Equity? The Burmese Experience", *Contemporary Southeast Asia*, Vol. 4, No. 2, 1982.

Steinberg, David I., "Japanese Economic Assistance to Burma: Aid in the 'Tarenagashi' Manner?", *Crossroads*, Vol. 5, No. 2, 1990.

World Bank, "Myanmar: Strategies for Sustaining Economic Reforms", Washington D.C.: World Bank, 1995.

# From Norm to Action: Standard-setting and Technical Co-operation in the Field of Child Labour

*Hugo Stokke*

# INTRODUCTION

This article is concerned with criteria for assessing organisational functions and with the expectations of members, customers, and clients. A key question is whether the expectations from various quarters are in any sense consistent and thus provide the organisation with clear and unambiguous criteria for such an assessment. The International Labour Organisation (ILO) has the distinction of setting standards within its domain of competence and has, in the course of 80 years, accumulated a large number of international labour standards in the form of Conventions and Recommendations. This standard-setting authority illustrates the *normative* function of the organisation as it attempts to regulate by legal means the world of work within and across societies. While the normative function has been part of the organisation from its establishment in 1919 with the League of Nations, the *technical* function is of a comparatively more recent date and expanded rapidly with the rising membership of developing nations. The technical function is defined as the delivery of advisory and other services through the design and execution of development projects made possible with funds provided by the developed nations, primarily to the benefit of developing nations. The normative function rests on a concept of regulation which may be described as ways of constraining and regularising behaviour,[1] whereas the technical function rests on a concept of developmentalism wherein concerted action is undertaken in order to reach a desired goal or end-state. The goal may be the one stipulated by the rule or regulation or it may be altogether more diffuse. The typical objective is to improve upon the state affairs and to achieve a measure of progress by concerted action. The question this article attempts to address is whether these two functions operate in concert or in conflict, whether the overlap of functions is large, small or non-existent.

I shall approach this question in two steps. First, I shall discuss some concepts from organisation theory that may help explain the nature of relations between organisations and their environments. Two key concepts in this regard are those of *technical* and *institutional* environments, which, I will argue, fit the topic under review. In the former environment, developmentalism predominates whereas in the latter, regulation is more important. A great deal of research is currently being done on this interrelationship, in Scandinavia and elsewhere, but very little, unfortunately, on *international* organisations. The attention has so far been directed mostly to national and sectoral organisations within the public sphere, although research is more and more branching out to include private organisations as well, be they of a profit or non-profit making type.

Secondly, I shall suggest an area of ILO competence in which the normative and technical functions collide head on: the case of child labour. The problem of child labour and how to overcome it fully or partially can be tackled both normatively by drafting legal instruments and technically by designing effective development projects. The ILO has been pursuing both functions in handling this

---

[1]  See W. Richard Scott, *Institutions and Organizations*, London, Sage Publications, 1995, pp. 35ff.

problem. On the normative side, the process of drafting a legal instrument was started in 1996/97 with the preparation of a law and practice report, and a questionnaire. Given the standard ILO procedure of two years for drafting and approving an instrument, the Convention (with its accompanying Recommendation) was eventually adopted by the International Labour Conference at its June 1999 session. The discussions and negotiations on the drafting of an international Convention depicts in typical form the institutional environment of the ILO as government, employer and worker members sit together to draft a new Convention.

Thirdly, on the technical side the ILO has been operating its International Programme to Eliminate Child Labour (IPEC) since 1992 and progressively expanding its coverage as more donors have joined the programme in recent years. In this article, a brief look at activities in South Asia region, with a special focus on Nepal and Bangladesh, will illustrate the workings of the technical environment as implementing agencies of different sorts try to achieve the objectives set by the standards and improve upon the material conditions of the target groups.

## INSTITUTIONAL AND TECHNICAL ENVIRONMENTS

In this section, I shall introduce some concepts from organisation theory and argue why they can be applied to the study of international organisations. At the outset it should be clarified what is meant by organisation and environment, respectively. Defining an organisation might be considered a fairly straightforward task, but when browsing the organisational studies literature it soon emerges that definitions are not independent of theoretical positions. However, one widely held school of thought would have it that "organisations are collectivities oriented to the pursuit of relatively specific goals and exhibiting relatively highly formalised social structures."[2] This *rational* definition of organisations has been undermined on both of their purported features, viz. organisations need not be highly formalised to be defined as organisations and they may have no overarching goals other than securing their own survival. Any goal of effecting change in the external world is hence only instrumental for securing the survival of the organisation itself, according to this alternative definition of an organisation as a *natural* system. While these two theoretical positions diverge on definitions regarding formalisation and goals setting, they share a common shortcoming in bracketing the environment of the organisation. Accordingly, a third contending definition would argue that "organisations may be systems of interdependent activities linking shifting coalitions of participants; the systems are embedded in – dependent on continuing exchanges with and constituted by – the environments in which they operate." This definition, and particularly its latter part, suggests that organisations are not only dependent on, but also constituted by their respective

---

[2] For this and subsequent definitions, see Richard W. Scott, *Organizations: Rational, Natural and Open Systems,* Englewood Cliffs, Prentice Hall, 1992, pp. 22-26.

environments. What does this mean and why is it of particular relevance to international organisations?

The third definition is based on the view that organisation studies have hitherto been too preoccupied with the internal workings of organisations under the presumption that their environment is predictable and relatively uniform. This *closed systems model* has more and more come to be replaced by an *open systems model,* which considers that environments are neither predictable nor uniform. Hence, shifting coalitions of participants, interdependent activities and continuous exchanges with the environment are the order of the day in organisations.

For the purposes of this paper, I shall define the organisation under scrutiny as the International Labour Organisation and the environment as whomever and whatever the ILO interacts with – in the literature defined as the *organisational set*.[3] The set is the various partners with which the organisation interacts, depending on its role and the expectations of the partners. The environment would then in this sense be the members of the organisation and secondly, the customers and clients of the organisation. It may perhaps be odd that the members of an organisation are defined as belonging to its environment, but it must be kept in mind that the members are in this instance not the employees of the organisation, but its employers or owners. They provide funding through their contributions to enable the Organisation carry out the work assigned to it by the members. The members are also the Organisation's customers and clients, indicating their double role as overseers and monitors, on the one hand, and users of services, on the other. This alludes to another key concept, as there may be diverging opinions about what constitutes *the organisational domain*, i.e. the claims the organisation makes as to its area and range of operations.[4]

The question was put above why this definition should be of special relevance to international organisations. This type of organisation views itself very much at the service of its members, having been constituted for that purpose. Secondly, the members are in most instances, though not for the tri-partite ILO, solely the governments of member countries, and thus presumably having considerably more clout than if the members were individuals. Thirdly, if members pay their contributions according to economic ability, large contributors have more clout than smaller ones, even if they both hold one vote. Considering these points, it is reasonable to assume that international organisations are more dependent on their environment than most other organisations, even if there may be considerable latitude for manoeuvring by the leadership. This dependence extends to recruitment policies, which follow national quotas in proportion to contributions rather than merit as the only relevant consideration.

The above *open systems* definition indicates that environments are not uniform or hold uniform expectations of what the organisation should do or how it should

---

[3]    On organisational sets, see Peter M.Blau and W. Richard Scott, *Formal Organizations,* San Francisco, Chandler, 1962.

[4]    On organisational domains, see James D. Thompson, *Organizations in Action,* New York, McGraw-Hill, 1967.

141

be evaluated. In other words, different environments apply divergent criteria for evaluating performance. The environment of customers and clients, the users of the services of the organisation, shows that the organisation is faced with a task environment. The task environment, also called the *technical environment*, is one in which organisations "produce a product or a service that is exchanged in a market such that they are rewarded for effective and efficient performance". The organisation is conceptualised here as a business whose survival is dependent on there being enough customers and clients to keep operations afloat and hopefully expanding. Businesses, whether in manufacturing or in services, operate in this type of environment. My argument is that international organisations do so, too. But it is not the only environment in which they operate.

The environment of members, is, as it shall be argued, an *institutional environment* "characterised by the elaboration of rules and requirements to which organisations must conform in order to receive legitimacy and support." In this type of environment, "organisations are rewarded for utilising correct structures and processes, not for the quantity and quality of outputs."[5] Typical examples of the latter type are schools and mental hospitals, whereas banks and general hospitals are examples of organisations in which both environments are important in evaluating legitimacy and effectiveness. Members are more concerned with the overall goals of the organisation, its procedures and questions of domain than are customers whose only concern is whether the organisations can provide the product or service they desire.

International organisations are facing both types of environments and research has come up with different answers on how to capture the interaction between organisations and their various environments. *Contingency theory*, a term coined by Lawrence and Lorsch, posits that different environments place different demands on organisations and that their mode of response varies depending on whether environments are uncertain and rapidly changing, or predictable and stable.[6] The former case would require more differentiation and flexibility, and less hierarchy and integration than the latter. Any movement in favour of one or the other would, however, solve one problem by aggravating the other. The organisations analysed by Lawrence and Lorsch are typically operating in a technical environment whereas international organisations, as argued above, are operating in both. The organisational response favoured by Thompson, in a book which came out at the same time as that of Lawrence and Lorsch, is to seal off the technical level from outside interference to the extent possible while keeping the institutional level open to outside influence.[7] Organisations should pretend to be technically rational even if they are not, and this balancing act falls to the managers, the middle level in its three-tiered hierarchy. Weick similarly allows for flexibility and stability, and in his influential book the focus is on information

---

[5]   Scott (1992), *op.cit.*, p. 132.
[6]   Paul R. Lawrence and Jay W. Lorsch, *Organization and Environment: Managing Differentiation and Integration,* Boston, Graduate School of Business Administration, Harvard University, 1966.
[7]   Thompson, *op.cit.*.

processing and selective retention of information and the adaptation of the organisation to the environment by trial and error as much as by rational design.[8] In his view environments are enacted rather than reacted to and action often precedes goals and purposes rather than the other way around as rational theories posit. This approach emphasises the cognitive and interpretative capabilities of the participants in their exchanges across the boundaries of organisations and their environments.

Meyer and Rowan argue, following on from Thompson and Weick, that "organisations in institutional environments will be inclined to selectively decouple their formal structures from the activities carried on in their technical core. The rationalised myths that provide meaning and legitimacy to the formal structure do not provide clear guidelines for technical activities. The result is that the organisation conforms closely to the ritually defined meanings supplied by the environment but does not attempt seriously to implement them at the operational level."[9] On this account, there is no connection between what the organisation says it does and what it actually does, but the connection is still 'virtually' necessary for purposes of legitimacy.

A common feature of these various theories is that environments matter and that they impose divergent and potentially conflicting demands on the organisation. Organisations can therefore not be rational in the usual sense of high formalisation and unitary goal structure, but they may still have a variety of mechanisms with which to cope. As shall be seen below, this heterogeneity of expectations has implications for how to assess organisational functions. In what follows, it will be shown that what takes place with the technical and institutional environments involves different actors, procedures, presumptions and priorities and that they are only weakly correlated.

## ILO FUNCTIONS

It was argued above that the ILO is facing an institutional as well as a technical environment, its members as well as its customers and clients. The ILO considers itself a universal organisation, not only by virtue of its membership, but also its body of international labour standards, Conventions and Recommendations, and its activities. Its values and services need to be relevant to the rapidly changing global conditions, requiring a process of continuous adaptation. This might, however, lead to inconsistencies and possible trade-offs such as working for full employment, on the one hand, and stressing the quality of jobs on offer, on the

---

[8]   Karl E. Weick, *The Social Psychology of Organizing,* 2nd edition, Reading, Mass., Addison-Wesley, 1979. Weick's emphasis on information processing, attention and learning is also found in more recent writings by James G. March and Johan P Olsen. See, *inter alia,* James G. March and Johan P. Olsen, *Ambiguity and Choice in Organizations,* Bergen, Universitetsforlaget, 1976.

[9]   Scott (1992), *op.cit.,* p. 279. The argument was originally formulated in John W. Meyer and Brian Rowan, "Institutionalized Organizations: Formal Structure as Myth and Ceremony", *American Journal of Sociology,* vol. 83, no. 2, 1977, pp. 340-363.

other. Consistency must also apply to the drafting of standards so as to promote the twin objectives of growth and equity.

The chief means at the disposal of the ILO towards achieving its objective of social justice is the principle of *tripartism*. This has been the distinguishing feature of the Organisation, setting it apart from practically all other international organisations. Since representatives of employers' and workers' organisations are members of the governance structure, in addition to governments, the ILO has never been an inter-governmental organisation in contrast to the other UN specialised agencies. While tripartism is a principle, it is also an instrument that has to be evaluated in terms of its effectiveness. As the international system of organisations is built on the state as its pillar, tripartism may be a disadvantage if it is not found in other organisations deciding on issues affecting the three partners. Trade, finance and aid have their organisational outlets in which tripartism is conspicuously absent.

The main instrument for promoting the ILO values is its set of international labour standards. While these instruments reinforced the values of the West in the Cold War period of ideological competition, the post-Cold War period presents a different scenario where not only communist regulation has been defeated, but arguments against Western welfare state regulations have been made as well. In a climate where attracting foreign investment and raising production and exports are paramount concerns, domestic regulation may put states at a competitive disadvantage.

Furthermore, the promotion of basic social rights runs up against limitations because the ILO possesses no authority to enforce compliance unless the ratifying state recognises it as a legal (and political) authority. The question of sanctions was raised with regard to international trade when the ILO was established, but hastily dropped because it might discourage  membership of the Organisation and ratification of Conventions. The normal approach is to adopt a legal instrument on a voluntary basis, allowing for inspection to verify whether unfair competition practices are, in fact, taking place.

The above issues, related to the role of the ILO in policy and standard-setting, are at play in the institutional environment. They relate to cognitive and normative matters, to interpretations of the changing world around the organisation, to responses to urgent issues and longer-term trends, and to drafting of legal instruments to regulate work and labour in consonance with the ideational foundation of the Organisation. However, as argued above, the organisation is also faced with an environment in which its services are requested and performance evaluated. These are particularly related to the ILO's role as a partner in technical co-operation.

Technical co-operation has its institutional roots in the initial advisory work on social security and labour administration in the 1930s, expanding with the rise of UN involvement in economic and social development in the 1950s. This environment is technical as expectations converge on the concentration of activities in fields wherein organisations have a clear competence and a definite comparative advantage and can exercise their true role: providing technical guidance and policy advice within their own core mandate.

The ILO response has been to launch an 'active partnership' policy where its constituents are more closely drawn into the ILO technical co-operation programme and its other means of action and to stress the linkage between labour standards and technical co-operation. In this manner, standard-setting and tripartism, on the one hand, and technical co-operation, on the other, were expected to proceed in tandem. While the linkage is not to be construed as imposing conditions on recipients to ratify standards, it does have certain other implications. First, the ILO should not engage in any activity that would be in breach of its own standards. Second, the Organisation should not consider whether the reciprocity inherent in a partnership calls for reviewing or reorienting its technical co-operation programme in countries of persistent violation of basic ILO standards. In this sense, the 'active partnership' policy is not unlike bilateral aid donors espousing human rights as a condition (among others) for selecting and reviewing countries.

The brief overview above has set out some of the general challenges facing the ILO in its relationship with what has been called the institutional environment as well as the more specific challenges in its relationship with the technical environment. The institutional environment has to do with cognitive and normative matters and the technical environment with the services the organisation renders and their relevance, timeliness and effectiveness in relation to customer needs. The issue of *comparative advantage* is an issue in the technical environment, while the *core mandate* is an issue in the institutional environment. They may, however, be linked in the following way: a focus on the organisational core mandate, assuming it is significantly distinct from that of other organisations, would yield a comparative advantage in selling services or products to customers, assuming that the services are demanded by them. Below, the field of child labour will be investigated as a field in which the ILO has an undisputed legal mandate, but presumably also a comparative advantage as donors have provided large amounts of funding for ILO's efforts to combat this problem.

## THE CASE OF CHILD LABOUR

Child labour is a subject matter that covers the range of standard-setting and technical co-operation. It is a subject matter on which the ILO has a mandate for legislative and operative action alike. It is thus a subject matter of some importance in both the institutional and technical environments and create the task of assessing the expectations of these two environments on ILO performance in the field of child labour. One possible hypothesis may be that if a subject matter or issue is strongly favoured by the institutional environment, then effectiveness and efficiency in the technical environment matter less. Conversely, if a subject matter is considered peripheral in the institutional environment, e.g. the issue is perceived to be outside the core mandate, then effectiveness and efficiency matter comparatively more. In the organisation studies literature, an argument has been

145

made that organisations persistently failing to be productive and profitable in the attainment of their official goals may still survive because the stakeholders are more interested in maintaining the organisation than measuring organisational performance.[10] The stakeholders, to follow the adopted line of reasoning, would be actors in the institutional environment. However, this is an argument where other types of rationality, for example that of politics, come to outweigh the technical or instrumental type of rationality.

There is agreement in the literature that measuring and explaining effectiveness are more complex than commonly appreciated. Two dimensions are essential for measuring effectiveness: *standards of desirability* and *cause-effect relationships*.[11] Three tests can be undertaken on the basis of these two dimensions. First, if standards are clear and cause-effect relationships are known, an *efficiency* test can be undertaken. If standards are clear, but cause-effect relationships are unknown, an *instrumental* test can be done to evaluate whether the expected outputs were attained, regardless of the relative amount of resources expended. If standards are ambiguous and cause-effect relationships are not known, a *social* test can be done in which validation is by consensus and authority. Effectiveness is achieved if a sufficient number of constituents or important constituents find it to be so. This latter test would be applied to organisations for which the institutional environment matters most.

Similar difficulties obtain in selecting indicators of effectiveness. In the literature, indicators can be sought for measuring outcomes, processes and structures.[12] Indicators on *outcomes*, or effect or impact, attempt to measure the change in the state of the object due to the intervention of the organisation concerned. While this is regarded as the quintessential indicator of effectiveness, it is not without problems similar to those of efficiency tests. These problems relate to the presumption of knowledge about cause-effect relationships and to the possibility of isolating organisational inputs and outputs from other factors that may have an effect on the object under study. If none of these presumptions hold, then outcome indicators are of less value in evaluating organisational effectiveness.

Therefore, many evaluations instead employ *process* indicators, which are indicators of effort rather than of effect. The assumption is that if the amount of efforts is proportional to the task at hand with due consideration given to quality checks thorough-out, the organisation will perform effectively. Many evaluations take this line of approach and assume thereby that the design of the programme or project is basically correct and the task is essentially to investigate the extent to which implementation followed the plans and procedures laid out in the programme or project document. Again, this presumption may not hold. Similar to the social tests mentioned above, this type of reification might apply specifically to

---

[10]   See Marshall W. Meyer and Lynne Zucker, *Permanently Failing Organizations,* Newbury Park, Sage, 1989.
[11]   See Thompson, *op.cit.*, pp. 84-87.
[12]   Scott (1992), *op.cit.*, pp. 353-57.

146

"the case of organisations in the institutionalised environments, in which, to a large extent, process is substance. In these organisations, conformity to ritually defined procedures produces a successful outcome, by definition."[13]

The third possibility are *structural* indicators, which are still a further step removed from outcomes. These indicators measure neither effects nor efforts, but capacity to undertake a task or organisational inputs as a substitute or proxy for outputs. The assumption, weak as it may appear to be, is that an organisation will perform a task effectively if it has the capacity to do so.

These considerations may be kept in mind while attempting to come to terms with ILO action in the field of child labour. But it should also be kept in mind that responses to child labour may take various forms with differential degrees of effectiveness. There is the regulative option, advocating legislation combined with trade sanctions by governments and consumers against purchasing products made by the offending party. Alternatively, there is the developmentalist option, advising against punitive sanctions and rather advocating compensatory measures or courses of action that will make child labour progressively superfluous.[14] The ILO may be said to combine legislative action with operational activities of a developmental kind. In the field of child labour, both regulative and developmental means have been employed and in the remaining parts of the article, both types shall be explored in detail.

### Negotiating a new convention on child labour

The typical legislative ILO action in the field of child labour is the drafting of international instruments. This process is procedurally initiated with the production of a so-called law and practice report,[15] based on information collected from member countries and other sources, and a questionnaire, setting out some initial suggestions on the form and content of the instrument(s), for members to reply to. Following the double-discussion procedure, these documents and the replies to the questionnaire and the initial draft of the instrument(s) were made available to the 1998 session of the Conference. The deliberations resulted in a draft version submitted for final discussion at the June 1999 session at which the Convention and its accompanying Recommendation were adopted. As the ILO imposes a time constraint on the process of standard-setting, it avoids the disadvantage that the drafting process drags on indefinitely. Nonetheless, an early indication of where the instruments were headed was given in Question 7 of the questionnaire which members are required to answer:[16]

---

[13] *Ibid.*, p. 356.

[14] For a general and applied discussion of the normative and developmental options, see Arne Wiig, *Trade and Labour Standards: Child Labour* (in Norwegian), Bergen, Chr. Michelsen Institute, Report R 1996:4.

[15] International Labour Office, *Child Labour. Targeting the Impossible,* Geneva, ILO, 1996.

[16] International Labour Office, *Report VI(1): Questionnaire. Child Labour,* International Labour Conference, 86th Session 1998, Geneva, ILO, 1996.

Should the Convention provide that each ratifying Member should suppress immediately all extreme forms of child labour including:

a. all forms of slavery or practices similar to slavery, sale and trafficking of children, forced or compulsory labour including debt bondage and serfdom;
b. the use, engagement or offering of a child for prostitution, production of pornography or pornographic performances, production or trafficking in drugs or other illegal activities;
c. the use and engagement of children in any type of work which, by its nature or the circumstances in which it is carried out, is likely to jeopardise their health, safety or morals.

The response from the ILO member governments and employers' and workers' organisations was overwhelmingly in favour of immediately eliminating extreme forms of child labour. While child labour of a less extreme form might be progressively abolished, by means of compulsory primary education or long-term poverty alleviation, the extreme forms called for immediate suppression. The forms described under (a) and (b) were considered by most respondents to be criminal offences requiring a more serious response than would 'mere' breaches of labour standards. The reactions to (c) called for more specificity in describing the types of hazardous work likely to have such debilitating effects on health, safety and morals. Some respondents wanted to add lack of education to the adverse effects. But if all types of work likely to jeopardise education were to be regarded as extreme child labour, the scope of the proposed instrument would be considerably widened and put an obstacle in the path of ratification, according to the ILO drafters. Other respondents wanted to specify that health should be defined as meaning both physical and mental heath, to which the ILO drafters concurred. While respondents generally prefer a greater degree of specificity, the standard mode of drafting has been to keep the Convention brief and to the point, while leaving the specificities to the accompanying Recommendation which, however, is not legally binding on ratifying States.[17] Such specificities were listed in Question 14, following from Question 7(c) on types of hazardous work, comprising underground and under-water work or work at great height, unhealthy environments with exposure to hazardous substances or extreme temperature and noise levels, dangerous machinery or heavy loads or inconvenient working hours. The responses ranged from those wanting to transfer greater detail into the provisions of the proposed Convention to those finding that too much detail in the proposed Recommendation would underestimate the difficulties encountered under differing national conditions. The mean opinion on this point maintained that the listing of criteria of hazardous work be appropriate for a Recommendation.

A similar concern arose in relation to Question 20 asking whether national law should consider the types of child labour listed under 7(a) and (b) as criminal

---

[17] International Labour Office, *Report VI (2)*. *Child Labour,* International Labour Conference, 86th Session 1988, Geneva, ILO, 1998.

offences. Some respondents wanted this to come under the Convention which would create specific penalties for specific violations as a means for states to suppress extreme forms of child labour. Similarly, Question 21 asks whether criminal penalties might also be attached to the serious and persistent violations of the type listed under 7(c). Some respondents questioned whether making a distinction between the three different types listed in Question 7 was warranted, arguing that all three should be regarded as criminal offences. On the subject of redress to the victims of child labour, the main conclusion was that this was an area for national law to decide and also for any legal sanctions against establishments employing children under extreme working conditions.

In summary, the points under Question 7 were worded as follows in para 9 of the Proposed Conclusions:

For the purposes of the Convention, the expression "extreme forms of child labour" should comprise:

a. all forms of slavery or practices similar to slavery, such as the sale and trafficking of children, forced or compulsory labour, debt bondage and serfdom;
b. the use, engagement and offering of a child in illegal activities, for prostitution, production of pornography or pornographic performances;
c. any other type of work or activity which, by its nature or the circumstances by which it is carried out, is likely to jeopardise the health, safety or morals of children, so that they should not be used or engaged in such activity under any circumstances.

The answers to the set of questions in the ILO questionnaire are summarised in the Proposed Conclusions which provide the raw material for the drafting of international legal instruments. The next step in the process in the drafting of an instrument is the discussion in the Committee of Child Labour of the International Labour Conference. As the ILO has established a double discussion procedure, the Proposed Conclusions is put before the Committee in its first round of discussions. In 1998 the Committee considered the ILO draft at the 86th session of the Conference.[18] One change adopted by the Committee was to alter the wording of the preamble of the Proposed Conclusions from stating that the instruments should be adopted for "the immediate suppression of extreme forms of child labour" to "the prohibition and immediate elimination of the worst forms of child labour". This amendment served to make a distinction between legal action, viz. to prohibit an activity, and to act on it, viz. to immediately eliminate the activity. The amendment to substitute "worst forms" for "extreme forms" was also thought to be more in line with proper terminology. The amendment to emphasise immediate elimination was opposed by some representatives of developing countries, but failed to garner enough support. Their suggestion to include an amendment

---

[18] International Labour Office, *Report of the Committee on Child Labour,* International Labour Conference, 86th session, Geneva, 1988.

referring to extreme forms of child labour being caused by poverty also failed to muster adequate support.

As to the contents of para. 9 of the Proposed Conclusions, some members thought that illegal activities should not be conflated with prostitution and pornography. Therefore, another point was added, i.e. concerning "the use, procuring or offering of a child in illegal activities, in particular in production and trafficking of narcotic drugs and psychotropic substances as defined in relevant international treaties". A second addition was proposed by the government member of Italy, referring to "all forms of activity which involve the use of violence, including all forms of military activity". However, some members felt that the subject was being dealt with in the work of the Human Rights Commission on a proposed Optional Protocol to the Convention on the Rights of the Child. After a vote, the Committee decided that it was competent to deal with the issue, but, due to internal dissension, decided also to defer the issue to the second round of discussion in 1999.

The discussion regarding 9(c) turned to the necessity of retaining the last part of the sentence which some members felt to be redundant. Some members desired the phrase "the health, safety and morals of children" to be replaced by the "health and safety of children or to harm their physical, mental spiritual, moral or social development", but this proposal was not widely supported. Similarly, a suggestion to substitute "physical and psychological well-being and emotional development" for "morals" was also defeated. The workers members wanted to replace "morals" by "access to basic education". A number of members argued, however, that lack of access to education should not be included in a definition of what constitutes the worst forms of child labour, such as para. 9(c), even though education might be an essential part of rehabilitation efforts.

The Committee discussion did not only review the definitions of what constitute the worst forms of labour, but also the implementation mechanisms for removal of these forms, comprising points 10-12 of the Proposed Conclusions. The workers members wanted an exhaustive list of types of hazardous work to be included in the Convention, but this amendment fell because of the perceived need to keep Conventions brief and not too detailed in order to secure as many ratifications as possible. However, the workers and employers combined their efforts to defeat an amendment proposed by the government members to include "other concerned groups" as participants in the consultation procedures. They were wont to emphasise the exclusivity of the tripartite arrangements, but the government members signalled their intention to bring it up again at the second round of discussion.

However, some more specific language did manage to work its way into the draft text, against the protest of the employers members who felt that such language would make the Convention unratifiable and accomplish little by way of removing the problem:

Each Member which ratifies the Convention should, taking into account the importance of education in eliminating child labour, take effective and time-bound measures to:

(a) prevent children from engaging in the worst forms of child labour;
(b) provide the necessary and appropriate direct assistance for their removal from work, rehabilitation and social reintegration through, *inter alia*, access to free basic education; and
(c) identify and reach out to children at special risk and to take account of the special situation of girls.[19]

The important inclusions were the references to free basic education as well as the special situation of girls. Further amendments from the workers members to include references to inspection systems, public awareness campaigns and information and complaints procedures with protection against reprisals of the complainants did not receive support.

After the first round of discussion of the Conference Committee, the ILO drafts the texts of the proposed Convention and Recommendation, which are again sent out to members for comments and suggestions for revision. The drafts are then revised depending on the ILO's assessment of the comments received. If comments do not point in any specific direction, as is often the case, the matter is referred to the Conference Committee for its second and final round of discussion. A vexing issue was child soldiers. In the ILO summary, a variety of options on how to handle this subject was laid out, including favouring an explicit reference in a separate subparagraph; preferring that the issue be dealt with in relation to the ongoing negotiations in the United Nations on a draft optional Protocol to the Convention on the Rights of the Child on involvement of children in armed conflict; arguing that it should only be explicitly mentioned in a provision that remains within the focus of the new Convention – the worst situations – and refer to the situation of young children who are forcibly recruited and involved in combat or arguing for inclusion of the use of children who are recruited, whether forcibly or not, into the armed forces for whatever purpose.[20]

As this was to be taken up at the second round of discussion of the Conference Committee, the options were referred to the Committee for their consideration and final decision. Another issue referred to the Committee was that of basic education. As the ILO drafters felt that the focus should be kept on the worst forms of child labour and as Convention 138 on the Minimum Age for Employment already had a reference to basic education, there was no need to insert a reference as part of the definition of what constitutes the worst forms. Yet another topic referred to the Committee was whether consultations should reach wider than the employers' and workers' organisations and include NGOs with expertise on child labour issues.

---

[19] *Ibid.*, para. 215.
[20] International Labour Office, *Report IV (2). Child Labour*, International Labour Conference, 87th session, Geneva, 1999.

The last step in the drafting process is the second and last round of discussion of the Committee on Child Labour of the International Labour Conference, which met from 1 to 17 June 1999. It is the task of the Committee to negotiate the final text of the legal documents and since the standard-setting process is time-bound, agreement has to be reached at the second round of discussion if there is to be an international legal treaty at all. The first task is to agree on a title. The ILO had suggested 'Convention concerning the prohibition and immediate elimination of the worst forms of child labour'. However, some members felt that immediate elimination would be beyond their capacities and wanted either to delete 'immediate' or to have it replaced by 'effective'. The workers members insisted on retaining 'immediate' in some form in the title, arguing the urgency of action. Ultimately, a compromise was struck by adopting the rather cumbersome phrase of 'prohibition and immediate action for the elimination of the worst forms of child labour'.[21] As is standard practice, a shorter title was selected for inclusion in lists and catalogues and the 'Worst Forms of Child Labour Convention' became the abbreviated version.

The issue of children in armed conflict was raised anew in relation to Article 3(a) of the proposed Convention. In the opening round of presentations, the government representative of the United States had said that "(r)ecalling the debate on the age of eligibility for military service, he thought it inadvisable to add unnecessary obstacles to ratification. The intention of the Convention was not to limit traditional national military training and voluntary service consistent with current international law. International legal obligations set an age limit of 15 years, which admittedly was low; but in trying to address these issues it would be prudent not to establish a norm that would prove unworkable or counter-productive. The emphasis should be on the coerced or criminal imposition of military activity."[22] This viewpoint was reiterated by the government representative in the discussion on Article 3(a) in which the reference would be to 'forced or compulsory recruitment of children for use in armed conflict" and not to lawful recruitment of 17-year olds on a voluntary basis which may entail service during armed conflict. Moreover, voluntary service should not be covered under Article 3(d) definitions of 'hazardous work'. This restriction on the definition of children in armed conflict met with disappointment from some other government representatives, including the representative from Norway, who "argued that a restrictive formulation introduced the question of how to determine whether participation is truly voluntary or involuntary and how to protect the children involved. She expressed disappointment and deep regret for the impossibility of providing a basic level of protection to this group of children."[23] Several members hoped that the formulation would not bar progress on a more comprehensive

---

21  International Labour Office, *Report of the Committee on Child Labour,* International Labour Conference, 87th session, Geneva, 1999, paras. 61-72.

22  *Ibid.*, para. 41.

23  *Ibid.*, para. 154. See also 'World Panel Adopts Treaty to Restrict Child Labour', *New York Times* (Internet Edition), 18 June 1999.

prohibition of children in armed conflict related to the work on an Optional Protocol to the UN Rights of the Child Convention.

Another remaining issue was whether the denial of access to basic education would be part of the definition of types of worst forms of child labour. An amendment to insert a new paragraph after 3(d) was introduced by a group of industrialised countries to read as follows: "work which systematically deprives children of access to education in accordance with applicable compulsory education requirements as established by national laws or regulations or by the competent authority".[24] As it did not garner the support of the developing countries and met with strong protest from the government of India, it was subsequently withdrawn. Another concern of a number of industrialised countries was to include 'other groups in civil society' beyond the government and the employers' and workers' organisations in the determination of hazardous work. NGOs working for children should in their view also be a part of the determination process. However, in order to reach consensus, the amendment was withdrawn and Article 4 consequently refers only to the social partners. Some government members and the workers members proposed an amendment to Article 7(c) to add 'including those in hidden work situations' to the formulation 'identify and reach out to children at special risk', referring to children in domestic service.[25] However, some government members and the employers members felt the term was not clear enough to be included in a legal treaty and the amendment was withdrawn.

While developing countries tend to be reticent about inserting too strong obligations in instruments like the one discussed, they are less reticent about accepting international assistance to promote the goals of the instruments. The proposed Article 8 of the Convention spoke of 'enhanced international co-operation and assistance including support for social and economic development, poverty eradication programmes and universal education. In questions of funding, the industrialised countries are the reticent party, not inclined to provide assistance as an obligation deriving from an international legal treaty. As a compromise, the workers members suggested that 'and' be replaced by 'and/or' so that co-operation may or may not be accompanied by assistance of a financial nature. As the government representative of Hungary acutely observed, 'and/or' effectively means 'or' – an inference disputed by the government representative of India who reaffirmed his understanding that there was an obligation under the Convention for members to assist each other.

With the adoption of Article 8, the substantive part of the Convention was effectively adopted. For reasons of brevity, the negotiations on the final text of the accompanying Recommendation shall be left out here. In summing up, the Committee members had the opportunity to congratulate themselves on their efforts to reach a final text and several noted that not once was there a need to decide by formal voting, every decision having been taken by consensus. However, any compromise text is less than ideal and the members pointed to

---

[24] *Ibid.*, para. 178.
[25] Article 7(d) of the final Convention text.

specific provisions where more might have been achieved. In particular, there was general disappointment that not more had been accomplished in prohibiting children from taking part in armed conflict. As stated poignantly by Mr. Steyne, workers' advisor, United Kingdom: "There is little logic in saying that we wish – quite rightly – to ban all sex work for children under 18, even if they are over the age of consent, but want to permit children of 16 and 17 to volunteer as combatants in war".[26] Other shortcomings mentioned by speakers again pointed to domestic child labour and the absence of a listing of hazardous work in the text of the Convention.

However, the drafting of a new instrument does not mean that extant instruments do not apply to varying degrees. Convention no. 138 on Minimum Age and Recommendation no. 146 on Minimum Age are instruments relevant to addressing child labour as is Convention no. 29 on Forced Labour, as well as Convention no. 105 on Abolition of Forced Labour for particularly egregious forms of child labour. As the two latter Conventions are ratified widely, the ILO supervisory bodies have been given an opportunity to address this issue effectively. The UN Convention on the Rights of the Child has also been ratified widely.

The above discussion has demonstrated the highly procedural nature of standard-setting whereby governments, employers' and workers' representatives negotiate among themselves in order to reach a final legal text which can be approved by the Conference in plenary. The key word is regulation, i.e. fashioning institutions with a view to constraining behaviour deemed unacceptable. In the world of technical co-operation, constraints may not be immediately imposed, priorities may differ and only approximations sought. Developmentalism is incremental, not categorical.

### Enforcing standards or promoting development: implementing the International Programme to Eliminate Child Labour (IPEC)

The following sections shall look at how the problem is addressed in operational terms, i.e. in terms of technical co-operation. The ILO International Programme for the Elimination of Child Labour (IPEC) was set up in 1992. Initially funded almost exclusively by Germany, it has since been joined by 10 other donors. Germany is still the dominant donor, having pledged a total of USD 65 million for the 10-year life span of the programme. Spain is the second largest donor, with a pledge of USD 12.5 million, followed by the United States as the third largest with USD 3.6 million. The initial group of target countries comprised Brazil, India, Indonesia, Kenya, Thailand and Turkey. They were joined in 1994-95 by Bangladesh, Nepal, Pakistan, the Philippines and the United Republic of Tanzania. In 1995-96 the programme expanded further to include a number of countries in

---

[26]  International Labour Office, *Report of the Committee of Child Labour. Submission, Discussion and Adoption,* International Labour Conference, 87th Session, Geneva, June 1999.

Latin America, and by the end of September 1995 a total of 31 governments had each signed a Memorandum of Understanding with the ILO, committing them to start a country programme against child labour.

The *aims* of the IPEC include:
- to support, rather than supplant, national efforts to combat child labour;
- to give priority to the eradication of the most abusive and exploitative types of child labour;
- to put the emphasis on preventive measures; and
- to build sustainability into all demonstration programmes from the start and assess their potential for integrating them into the regular programmes of the partner countries.[27]

The *priority target groups* of the IPEC include:
- children working under forced labour conditions and in bondage;
- children in hazardous working conditions and in occupations;
- children who are particularly vulnerable, i.e. very young working children (under 12 years of age) and working girls.

The *strategy* of the IPEC is to assist governments in their co-operation with employers' and workers' organisations, NGOs and other parties to adopt measures which aim at:
- *preventing* child labour;
- *withdrawing* children from exploitative and hazardous work and *providing alternatives*; and
- *improving working conditions* as a transitional measure towards the elimination of child labour.[28]

This strategy can be decomposed into a phased, multi-pronged strategy, which consists of the following steps:
- *motivating* ILO constituencies and other relevant partners to engage in a dialogue on child labour and to create alliances to overcome the problem. This culminates in a formal commitment by the government to co-operate with ILO-IPEC, expressed in a Memorandum of Understanding between the government and the ILO;
- carrying out a *situation analysis* to find out the nature and magnitude of child labour problems in a given country;
- assisting the concerned parties within a country in devising *national policies and plans of action* to address specific child labour problems;

---

[27] International Labour Office, International Programme on the Elimination of Child Labour, *Implementation Report. Review of IPEC Experiences 1992-95,* Geneva, ILO/IPEC, 1995, p. 5.
[28] International Labour Office, International Programme on the Elimination of Child Labour, *ILO-IPEC Highlights of 1996-97 and Guidelines for Future Action,* Geneva, ILO/IPEC, 1996, p. 7.

- *strengthening* the existing organisations and setting up institutional mechanisms in order to achieve national "ownership" of the Programme. A National Steering Committee is established, consisting of the concerned ministries, workers' and employers' organisations and NGOs, to advice on policy implementation;
- creating *awareness* of the problem of child labour nation-wide, in the community and at the workplace;
- promoting the development and application of protective legislation;
- supporting *direct action* with (potential) child workers and their environment to demonstrate that it is possible to prevent children at risk from entering the workforce prematurely and to withdraw children from exploitative and hazardous work;
- *reproducing* and *expanding* successful projects in order to integrate their strong points into the regular programmes and budgets of the social partners; and
- *integrating* child labour issues systematically into social and economic development policies, programmes and budgets.[29]

As may be surmised from the above, many of the strategy components have to do with the institutional environment of the programme. Only one component speaks of direct action specifically, whereas most deal with the institutional prerequisites for direct action to succeed. It was argued above that the more the institutional environment matters, the more *social tests* will be employed to assess the attainments of the programme. Most of the strategy components can be evaluated by employing *structural* indicators, indicators that measure capacity to solve a problem. But inputs are no substitute for outputs. Since the necessary conditions may not exist to undertake *efficiency tests* by employing *outcome* indicators, *instrumental* tests using *process* indicators may be a weaker alternative in assessing the adequacy of efforts in reaching the objectives of the programme. But there are no hard benchmarks for assessing adequacy of efforts. In fact, an internal review of the IPEC Programme in India noted the weaknesses of the programme over the 1992-95 period. There was lack of a structured procedure for selection of projects; lack of clear expectations; short contractual period; small supporting staff at ILO; an elaborate system of reporting; limited network and interaction between NGOs; lack of effective monitoring; and lack of background information on target groups.[30] These shortcomings, identified by the national programme co-ordinator, mainly dealing with managerial problems, illustrate that estimates of effort may not at all provide the basic data needed for assessing adequacy. Similarly, only two of the nine identified successes of the programme concerned efforts that involved direct action for the benefit of children. These included education initiatives and sensitisation and rehabilitation of working children. Other successes included flexibility of programme approach, direct funding pattern, strength in numbers of

---

[29]  *Ibid*, p. 7.
[30]  International Labour Office, International Programme on the Elimination of Child Labour, *IPEC in India 1992-95: Looking Back*, New Delhi, ILO/IPEC, 1996, pp. 44-6.

NGOs, involvement of trade unions and employers' organisations, introduction of child labour components into institutes dealing with labour and related issues, development of sectoral strategies, and awareness generation.[31]

On account of the above, an evaluation of the institutional environment of the programme would be feasible. The normative framework of the proposed legal instrument on child labour as well as IPEC specifically addresses the urgency of suppressing the most exploitative forms of child labour immediately. Efforts towards that end must be evaluated and the data needed and the monitoring required must be in place to do so successfully. As argued above, a technical co-operation project has technical in addition to institutional aspects. The mix, however, may vary from one project to another, depending on their objectives.

To assess efforts technically, it is an advantage that the institutional environment is supportive. This would include the institutional components mentioned specifically above as parts of the programme strategy, including the conduct of research and surveys to estimate the nature and magnitude of the problem. With these data in hand, estimates of efforts needed to reduce or eliminate the problem can proceed. The key problem is arriving at reasonable estimates of the population of child labourers. This can be made easier if there is a clear demarcation of the target population, for example the number of children working within a specific industrial sector.

### The IPEC in South Asia

The magnitude of child labour in Bangladesh, following the 1989 Labour Force Survey, is estimated at about 15 million, i.e. classified as economically active in the 5-14 age category.[32] Of these, 82 per cent are in the agricultural sector and seven per cent in manufacturing and transport sectors, of which 22.5 per cent are in urban areas. The figures show that child labour in Bangladesh is overwhelmingly a rural phenomenon. Estimates for the ready-made garments (RMG) industry, for which no reliable data are available, range between 10-70,000 child workers. The survey found that the children aged 10-14 years in the RMG industry were mostly females, rural migrants and concentrated in a small segment of the industry. They were by and large engaged as sewing and finishing helpers – often working in the same factory as a senior member of their family, and earning considerably less.

Attention to this issue came first and foremost from the United States by the introduction of legislation, viz. the Child Labour Deterrence Act of 1993, and by the lobbying efforts of NGOs advocating consumer boycotts of products thought to involve child labour. The response of the Bangladesh Garment Manufacturers & Exporters Association (BGMEA) in considering the likelihood of a consumer boycott was to start setting up schools in co-operation with the ILO, UNICEF and

---

[31] *Ibid.*, pp. 42-3.
[32] Information in this section is drawn from Debapriya Bhattacharya, *International Trade, Social Labelling and Developing Countries: The Case of Bangladesh's Garments Export and Use of Child Labour*, Dhaka, Bangladesh Institute of Development Studies, 1996, mimeo.

the Ministry of Labour. One such school/clinic was inaugurated in Dhaka in July 1994. On the same date, the BGMEA announced that the factory would be rid of child workers by the end of October. The possibility of large-scale retrenchment without adequate safeguards for the affected children led to expressions of concern by local NGOs and international agencies. A round of negotiations ensued between the BGMEA and US officials and the first Memorandum of Understanding (MOU) was signed in early 1995. However, the MOU was rejected by the general meeting of the BGMEA due to the provision allowing for factory inspections by NGOs. A second round of negotiations followed, now with the ILO and UNICEF present as the BGMEA members were more comfortable with them than with the NGOs. The deliberations resulted in the conclusion of a MOU in August 1995, signed by BGMEA, ILO and UNICEF. The terms of the MOU may be worth quoting *in extenso*:

(i) Child workers below 14 years of age will be removed from the garment factories by October 31, 1995; but no termination will take place without placement of the child workers in an education program.

(ii) UNICEF will initially contribute $ 175,000 towards the envisaged education program. The BGMEA will contribute $ 50,000 per year to UNICEF sponsored school program. It is expected that ILO-IPEC funds will also be made available for the purpose. The program will be made in consultation with the Government of Bangladesh.

(iii) The children under the education program will receive a monthly stipend of Tk. 300 with a view to offsetting, at least partially, the income loss. The BGMEA will contribute 50 percent of the costs of such stipends for three years.

(iv) The ILO will, in collaboration with the GOB, help devise a system to monitor the phased child labour elimination program. The process of monitoring the RMG units with ILO assistance will continue for two years, thus, verifying in a professional manner the implementation of the program.

(v) BGMEA will offer employment to qualified family members of the under-aged workers whose employment will be terminated under the program.

(vi) The survey or rapid assessment of all children working in Bangladesh garment factories will be conducted by 25 survey teams of UNICEF and BGMEA. No child worker will be terminated before the survey is completed.

(vii) Efforts will be made to arrange food supplementation program for terminated workers to be placed in schools.

(viii)UNICEF and ILO will work towards creating other income generation opportunities after school for the retrenched child workers to occupy their time productively and prevent an income loss.[33]

---

[33] *Ibid.*, p. 16.

In this case, the institutional environment was hardly supportive. The initial reaction on the part of the government and the manufacturers was to play down the existence of child labour. Many domestic NGOs were also sceptical in a different sense; while not denying child labour, they were seeing the proposed legislation and the lobbying as manifestations of protectionism. It was the likelihood of a boycott that made urgent action necessary and got the parties around the negotiating table for a MOU. A supportive environment was in this instance not necessary for initiating action. However, it does not invalidate the argument above that a supportive environment would still have to be in place, with government leaders, employers, NGOs and trade unions participating in consort with the development agencies, for purposeful action to ensue. Due to the specifics of this particular case, a measurement of efforts using process indictors is part of the terms of the agreement. An evaluation of IPEC would, as already stated, also have to take into account to which extent the structural preconditions are there for all concerned parties to take direct action voluntarily.It should be borne in mind that this project, although having attracted a great deal of political and media attention, is but one in a multitude of projects in the South Asian region. IPEC operates in all the major countries in the region; Pakistan, India, Nepal, Bangladesh and Sri Lanka. Table 1 sets out the magnitude of the programme divided by country and including some activities that are regional in scope.

**Table 1**
**Programme and budget 1998-99 for the South Asian region (in USD 1000)**

|  | Bangladesh | India | Nepal | Pakistan | Sri Lanka | Regional |
|---|---|---|---|---|---|---|
| Institutional and policy development | 142 | 165 | 220 | 375 | 40 | 115 |
| Programme development | 25 | 60 | 50 | 25 | 110 | 50 |
| Awareness raising | 19 | 125 | 45 | 35 | 75 |  |
| Direct action | 431 | 155 | 320 | 3193 | 100 | 35 |
| Total | 617 | 505 | 635 | 3628 | 325 | 200 |

Source: ILO Office in Kathmandu, Nepal

As the table shows, the average biennial IPEC country programme hovers around the USD 500,000 mark and may contain anything from four activities (Sri Lanka) to about 25 (Nepal). The anomalous country on the list is Pakistan, but the brunt of the expenditure is borne by two projects only, accounting for well over USD 3 million. One is a project with a budget of about USD 1.2 million, funded by the United States, to eliminate child labour in the football industry in Sialkot district. The project is clearly a response to media exposure in the West of children being engaged in football manufacturing and the aspersion thereby cast upon Western football associations. The other is a project to combat abusive child labour through prevention, withdrawal and rehabilitation. Funded by the EU (USD 1.2 million) and the Government of Pakistan (USD 0.6 million), the project targets bonded and child labour through concerted action by both government and non-governmental agencies. The project appears to be in response to the long-term concern of the ILO Committee of Experts about the existence of forced labour in certain industries in Pakistan and in view of the new Worst Forms of Child Labour Convention, to respond to its priority-setting agenda.

The table also reveals that activities in most countries are fairly evenly divided between indirect activities, comprising institutional, policy and programme development and awareness creation, on the one hand, and direct activities, on the other, comprising activities directly targeted at children and their living environment. However, projects of the magnitude of the two in Pakistan invariably have built-in institutional components. This fact goes to underscore that the institutional environment of these and other activities are part and parcel of any assessment of project achievements.

**Addressing child labour in Nepal**

The following section will look more closely at one of the countries in the region, namely Nepal. This country has a diverse and large programme in terms of activities if not of funding, and is the poorest country of the lot. The project portfolio is distributed evenly between indirect, institutional activities and direct activities targeting specific types of work and categories of child labourers. The institutional environment is favourable, with government, employers' and workers' organisations as well as a welter of NGOs being actively involved in the programme. Moreover, all activities under the programme have been generated from inside Nepal and not, as with the two large projects in Pakistan, in response to outside concerns. Space does not allow for a detailed investigation of each and every project; only a few salient features will be highlighted.

Estimates of the prevalence of child labour in Nepal are based on the 1991 Population Census which found 532,000 economically active children 10-14 years of age, 23 per cent of the total of the age category. There are also economically active children below the age of 10. Most of the children are working in agriculture, animal husbandry and trades and occupations as well as helping out with domestic chores. With industrialisation and urbanisation, more children are engaged in the manufacture of carpets, in brick kilns and stone quarries and in urban hotels and restaurants. Nepal was in 1997 the first country in the South Asian region to ratify Convention No. 138 on the Minimum Age for Employment and has had an IPEC programme in operation since 1995.

Structurally, the IPEC programme in Nepal is headed by a National Steering Committee chaired by the Minister for Labour. The Committee comprises representatives of other ministries concerned such as education, industry and ommerce, the major employers' and workers' organisations, NGOs as well as advisory members such as ILO, UNICEF and GTZ – the German agency for international development. The latter is the main funding source of the IPEC programme. The Committee serves as a vetting mechanism for project proposals from both the government side and private associations, which are, subject to approval, forwarded to IPEC for funding.

A national workshop held in Kathmandu in August 1995 made a number of recommendations for a national action plan with four major components:

(i)    Formulation of appropriate policies and programmes by governmental and non-governmental organisations;
(ii)   Review of legislation and enforcement machinery;
(iii)  Programmes for direct intervention with child workers;
(iv)   Awareness raising and community mobilisation.

As the objectives suggest, a large part of the effort is indirect in nature, i.e. defining policies and programmes, reviewing capacity to undertake action and changing the popular mindset against the use of child labourers. Returning to the four-fold division of activity types in Table 1, the same categories may be employed to show the composition of the IPEC project portfolio in Nepal. The portfolio is a mixture of activities carried over from previous years and proposed activities for the current biennium.

*Programme area and activities 1998-99 for IPEC in Nepal*[34]
(a) Institutional and Policy Development
• Strengthening the capacity of the Ministry of Labour to formulate and implement policies and programmes and enforce legislation on child labour;
• Social education in schools;
• Inclusion of child labour component in training of senior police officers;
• Development of a package on child rights and child labour for inclusion in the Bachelor of education;
• Management training of IPEC's partners and potential partners;
• Establishment of a National Information Centre on child labour;
• Strengthening the networking of governmental and non-governmental organisations;
• Setting national strategies for the elimination of girl trafficking and commercial sexual exploitation of children in Nepal and funding governmental and non-governmental organisations to implement Action Programmes.

(b) Programme Development
• A situation analysis on hazardous and abusive forms of child labour;
• An Action Programme to combat child labour in Bidi factories;[35]
• Rehabilitation of children working in construction;
• Review of IPEC action programmes.

---

[34]   Documents obtained from the ILO Office in Kathmandu, Nepal.
[35]   Bidis are locally made cigarettes, popular in the region as they are quite cheap compared to foreign imports.

(c) Awareness raising
- Raising awareness on child rights and child labour through training and development of local drama groups;
- A video film on domestic girl child labour;
- A video film on effective interventions against child labour in Nepal;
- Sensitisation programmes for parliamentarians and District Development Committee chairpersons on child labour, child trafficking and children in bondage.

(d) Direct action
- Rehabilitation of children of bonded labourers in Bardia district in Western Nepal;
- Rehabilitation, including education programmes for children of the local bonded labourers, the 'kamaiyas' in Kailali district, Western Nepal;
- Support programme for the children working as domestic servants;
- A programme to sensitise employers in the industrial sector on child labour;
- Phasing out child labour in the carpet industry of Nepal;
- Non-formal education for child labourers of the sweeper community;
- The elimination of child labour in communities engaged in informal sector at Janakpur;
- Prevention of migration of children for the purpose of employment;
- Combating child labour and rehabilitating children working in factories manufacturing biscuits and match boxes in Biratnagar industrial area;
- Improving the conditions of children working as rag-pickers;
- Combating child labour in the tea estates;
- Towards child labour free area in Baglung municipality.

The above list shows that the range of activities is indeed wide, but also that it does not evolve from a master plan, establishing clear priorities among more serious and less serious forms of child labour. The selection process by the National Steering Committee appears to be more reactive than proactive in the sense that it is more supply- than demand-driven. The Committee may be more concerned with accommodating the range of interested parties than with selecting projects on the basis of its own priorities. With the adoption of the Worst Forms of Child Labour Convention and its listing of what constitutes the worst forms, action programmes would have a standard for assessing what should be targeted first, given limited resources.

Among the proposed programmes for the 1998-99 biennium is one targeting girl trafficking and commercial sexual exploitation of children. Corresponding to one type of the worst forms of child labour, the project may receive support from the US Ministry of Labour. Objectives include awareness-raising among government officials and members of the public, and in a second phase, the setting-up of prevention and interception camps along the India-Nepal border. The government counterpart is the Ministry of Women and Social Welfare.[36]

This is the largest of the proposed projects in terms of funding, but still minuscule compared to the amounts targeted at football manufacturing in Pakistan. Not only may allocations be scant, an added bureaucratic constraint is that IPEC funding is confined to the biennial budget period. However, a number of projects frequently enter into a second or third phase corresponding to successive budget periods. Thus, momentum may not only be lost in the hiatus between project phases, and the possibility of entering into longer-term partnerships with organisations may be squandered as well.

The importance of long-term partnerships was brought up by Child Workers in Nepal Concerned Centre (CWIN). Established in 1987, but informally dating back to the late 1970s, CWIN is the oldest NGO in Nepal in the field of child labour. It is represented on the IPEC National Steering Committee, but has not implemented any IPEC action programme since its start-up in 1994-95. A chief reason may be that CWIN has a long-term partnership with the Norwegian NGO Redd Barna, which has provided support since the beginning as have a number of international NGOs as well as UNICEF.[37] As CWIN has had an established partnership of long standing with a foreign counterpart, it may be less dependent on intermittent funding from IPEC.[38] CWIN has lately started publishing an annual report on the state of the rights of the child in Nepal, again with support from Redd Barna.[39]

The partnership question was also mentioned by the Women's Rehabilitation Centre (WOREC).[40] The Centre received funding under IPEC to provide children working as domestic servants with non-formal education (10 classes with 30 children in each) and skill training for half of those selected. WOREC's request for bridging funds from IPEC was rejected as confirmation was needed from headquarters for money to be released. The plan is to continue with another batch of 600 children, and to have about 200 from the first batch admitted to regular or vocational schools. Domestic servants in middle class households were found to be treated worse than expected. Horror stories of beatings, brandings and rape have necessitated setting up a legal unit, though experience with legal action is limited. WOREC has also been engaged in surveying child street prostitution which is on the rise in Kathmandu. A cross-border network has been established not only for monitoring of girl child trafficking, but for domestic servants as well. Demands have been directed to the Mayor of Kathmandu that domestic servants be registered. WOREC's work in Kathmandu shows that documentation and action on 'hidden work situations' is progressing, even though it was not included in the Convention, despite efforts to that end by the industrialised countries.

---

[36]  Some interviewees expressed doubt as to whether this Ministry is the appropriate counterpart for an undertaking of this magnitude.

[37]  Redd Barna is the Norwegian branch of the Save the Children Fund.

[38]  Interview with Gauri Pradhan, CWIN, Kathmandu, May 1998.

[39]  Child Workers in Nepal Concerned Centre (CWIN), *State of the Rights of the Child in Nepal 1998*, Kathmandu, CWIN, 1998.

[40]  Interview with Renu Rajbhandari, WOREC, Kathmandu, May 1998.

With regard to IPEC, WOREC felt that it should be less bureaucratic, emphasise programmes rather than projects, encourage flexibility in project implementation, forge long-term partnerships, develop baseline data as well as qualitative indicators on progress towards achieving the objectives, and finally, to assume a stronger role in both advocacy, and monitoring of abuse cases.[41]

Bonded labour was identified as a worst form of child labour in the new Convention. In Nepal, two NGOs have been funded under IPEC to undertake action programmes among the Kamaiya with a view to preventing child labour bondage. The Informal Sector Service Centre (INSEC) works, among others, in the Kailali district of Southwest Nepal, whereas Rural Reconstruction Movement Nepal (RRN) works in the adjoining Bardia district. Both projects provide non-formal education to children. In phase I RRN covered altogether 80 children, evenly split between regular schooling and skills training.Phase II will extend the coverage to include 240 children, again evenly divided between basic skills and vocational skills. INSEC has similarly provided non-formal education through a nine-month course to 450 children during phase I as a prelude to formal schooling, adding another 90 during phase II, plus follow-up of those who entered school (about 500) and vocational training for another 100 during phase III. Inter-linked with this educational effort in favour of children is an attempt to change the overall system of bondage, which involves both advocacy through the Kamaiya Conscience Group to free labourers and to provide opportunities for those freed, including loans, land and housing. IPEC is thus able to provide some funding support for work among bonded labourers, but the problem obviously extends beyond the children solely, with estimates ranging from 17,000 (govt. figure) to 40,000 (INSEC), depending on whether individuals or families are counted. Both individual and family bondage is practised in the affected districts. The system is apparently expanding beyond the original local communities.

Other NGOs work with urban-based children. Concern for Children and the Environment (CONCERN), established in 1993, work with children from carpet factories and squatter communities in order to prevent them from becoming street children. With funding from Western NGOs and UNICEF, children are given education and regular health check-ups at the CONCERN compound and four external centres. In this way, 150 children have been reached and the cost of sending them to regular schools is borne 60-40 per cent by CONCERN and the parents. Under IPEC funding, CONCERN has targeted child porters.[42] Activities comprise simple vocational training, for instance bicycle repair and flowerpot making, and access to a small, mobile health clinic with a full-time nurse and a part-time doctor. In addition, family reconciliation and home village visits are included in the action programme, as many are migrants from rural areas. Child Protection Centre (CPC), on the other hand, has worked with children in a quartz

---

[41]   Many of the same points were echoed by Gauri Pradhan at CWIN who underlined conceptual clarification of objectives, training and the establishment of measuring rods.

[42]   Concern for Children and Environment, *Burden on Childhood. Child Porters in the Kathmandu Valley,* Kathmandu, CONCERN, 1997.

mine in an inaccessible area in Eastern Nepal. Fifty children have been reached, of which two-thirds have been given basic education, the remaining being put in day-care centres. Both of these targeted types of work arguably come under worst forms of child labour in the sense that they are hazardous to the health, safety and morals of children.

All of the above examples attest to the crucial role of civil society organisations in addressing issues raised by the Worst Forms of Child Labour Convention. However, they have not been given any formal role in determining what types of hazardous work come under the Convention, which monitoring mechanisms should be put in place and which action programmes are to be designed, though their views may be taken into consideration on the last point.[43] Although the involvement of these organisations was pushed by several of government members of the industrialised countries, it was ultimately not included in the Convention, which remained focused on the tripartite consultations of government, employers and workers. This fact indicates that the institutional environment of the ILO is at odds with its technical environment in which funders and implementing agencies have other channels and sources to pursue. Nepali NGOs may have direct funding from Western governments or sister NGOs or have established better working relations with UNICEF than with the ILO despite the undisputed mandate of the ILO in the field of child labour.

The preceding paragraph should not be construed to suggest that the tripartite partners have a marginal role to play in IPEC, although they are certainly not dominating the action programmes. The Nepali Trade Union Congress (NTUC) is running 20 schools, eight of which funded by IPEC, targeting working or out-of-school children in the 8-12 age bracket, the objective being to induce them to re-enter school at the third grade. Morning and evening classes are run with three hours of teaching in each session over a period of nine months. Altogether 3,000 children are planned to be covered in this manner. Selection is through NTUC members in industrial towns and rural areas. The NTUC felt that although the IPEC monetary contribution is very small, it did create an impression and an atmosphere.

The General Federation of Nepalese Trade Unions (GEFONT) has undertaken a survey of children on tea estates, though no funding for follow-up activities had materialised at the time of the author's visit to Nepal (May 1998). GEFONT has also worked with the garbage cleaners' community in Kathmandu and provided non-formal education to children of sweepers, 400 in total under 12 years of age, of whom half have received formal education, as well as providing day-care centre placement for the youngest. Initially concentrated in Kathmandu, activities are envisaged to spread out to Lalitpur and Bhaktapur in the second phase. Regarding IPEC, the GEFONT representative felt that resources were spread on too many implementing agencies and that more attention should be given to the rural areas where the majority of working children reside – approximately 2 million, of whom 1.5 million are in service and organised sectors.

---

[43]    See articles 4-6 of the Convention in the Appendix below.

On the part of the employers, the Federation of Nepalese Chambers of Commerce & Industry – Employers' Council (FNCCI) has an advocacy role in relation to their members. Regional workshops have been held for all employers, studies related to specific sectors (tea, brick kiln, leather, rice mill) have been commissioned, and members have been encouraged to contribute to a permanent fund under the Ministry of Labour. Apart from a contribution from the Ministry, the Central Carpet Industries Association and the Wool Development Board have contributed funding, though the Fund is still far from the required projected volume; a little less than half remains to be committed. The intention of the FNCCI is to induce employers to contribute to a sustainable institution consisting of a training centre with infrastructure, land, trainers and a rehabilitation centre. The latter has been implemented by the National Society for the Protection of Environment and Children (NASPEC), which has accommodated 700 children below 14 years of age in a rehabilitation centre, accounting for an estimated 5 per cent of the total working child population of 15,000 in the carpet industry. About 200 have received vocational training while more than 1700 have been through non-formal education courses. Implementation problems were encountered, such as fake birth certificates, compensatory pay demands for loss of working when attending non-formal education classes, and frequent shifts from one factory to another. Sustainability is not assured as funding continues to be sought for rehabilitated children attending school. NASPEC is an NGO which, while receiving support from government and employers, also co-operates with other NGOs, notably CWIN. Finally, the Ministry of Labour has also received funding to enhance its capacity to undertake action against child labour. In particular, budget and manpower is needed for inspection tasks, which at present do not match the requirements. Furthermore, the Ministry is also engaged at the local level through Village Development Councils to seek out child labour prone families, and to provide training in local skills and marketing skills.

The above has given snapshots of IPEC activities in the field of child labour. Is it possible on the basis of the evidence to fashion criteria for evaluation? It has been argued above that a social test might be the most appropriate one for a multi-dimensional programme such as IPEC. Efficiency tests cannot be employed nor can instrumental tests. In the latter type of test, standards are clear-cut, but cause-effect relationships are hard to establish in order to assess which are the most effective means to reach a goal. It is not at all clear whether process indicators may be used to measure the effort needed to find a solution to the problem. In the case of Nepal, capacity has to be built as a first step, before energy can be expended in resolving the problem subsequently. For activities involving unclear standards and cause-effect relationships, social tests can be performed through consensual validation. For an organisation in which the institutional environment matters most, social tests would be the most appropriate validation method.

However, the social environment of standard-setting and technical co-operation differs in critical respects. In the framework of standard-setting, the established and tested procedures are well suited to the task. However, if applied in the world

166

of technical co-operation, the same procedures may not measure up to the task. In particular, the tripartite framework, which has served standard-setting well, may appear too confining for technical co-operation in the field of child labour. While NGOs have an obvious part to play as implementing agencies, only employers' and workers' organisations have a recognised role as stakeholders to be consulted in policy-making process relevant for implementing the provisions of the Convention, even though the IPEC objectives are more open-ended on this point. Secondly, the centralised administrative structure of the ILO may not be conducive to establishing the long-term partnerships that may be necessary to achieve results over the long haul. These partnerships are often sought by NGOs, but the ILO may not be in the best position to respond, given its administrative and budgetary inflexibilities. Thirdly, the available funding, although large by ILO standards, may not at all be adequate to come to grips with the magnitude of the problem. Efforts appear too diverse to allow for a clear ordering of priorities, given scant resources.

However, dispersed allocation of funds may further underline the importance of the social environment of the programme. It may be an objective in itself that most constituents feel they have a share in the programme; strict prioritisation means selectivity in the choice of implementing agencies. For focused action to be effective, resources in the amount channelled to the football manufacturing sector in Pakistan are probably necessary, but it is doubtful whether priority-setting on the basis of the worst kinds of child labour would put this on top of the list.

In sum, whereas the ILO has a core mandate to set standards on child labour, it is not certain that this mandate will translate into a distinct technical co-operation advantage in the field.

## CONCLUSION

In this article, the International Labour Organisation has been analysed as an organisation combining regulative with developmental functions. It has a mandate for standard-setting as well as for technical co-operation. These functions correspond to different environments with their different expectations. The question is to what extent they overlap or diverge. While the institutional environment relationship revolves around organisational outlook, prioritisation and task setting, the technical environment relationship stresses the relevance and quality of services. Thus, the article has presented the negotiations for a new Convention on the worst forms of child labour as an example of the workings of the institutional environment, and the ILO's IPEC programme as an illustration of the modes of operation of a technical environment.

This admixture of expectations also reappears in programme and project implementation and has repercussions on how performance is evaluated. The case of child labour has been used to illustrate how the institutional and technical environments differ in fashioning criteria for assessing performance. The article has argued that for a programme with multiple objectives, some aiming at governmental capacity-building and awareness creation and others directly targeting action for the benefit of children, a social test will be the most appropriate method of evaluation. Furthermore, in an organisation where the institutional environment matters, the appropriateness of a social test may be reinforced as a means to assess achievements.

However, the article has also argued that the social environment differs across arenas. Whereas the tripartite framework is tested and found well suited for purposes of standard-setting, a much wider constituency framework is needed for technical co-operation in the field. Whereas the administrative structure is well suited for tasks of a centralised kind, it appears constraining in the field.

In the final analysis, while a strong institutional environment may have its shortcomings in circumstances that demands flexibility and decentralised management, it may ultimately be decisive in securing organisational survival.

# APPENDIX[44]

## Convention 182

## CONVENTION CONCERNING THE PROHIBITION AND IMMEDIATE ACTION FOR THE ELIMINATION OF THE WORST FORMS OF CHILD LABOUR

The General Conference of the International Labour Organization,

Having been convened at Geneva by the Governing Body of the International Labour Office, and having met in its 87th Session on 1 June 1999, and

Considering the need to adopt new instruments for the prohibition and elimination of the worst forms of child labour, as the main priority for national and international action, including international cooperation and assistance, to complement the Convention and the Recommendation concerning Minimum Age for Admission to Employment, 1973, which remain fundamental instruments on child labour, and

Considering that the effective elimination of the worst forms of child labour requires immediate and comprehensive action, taking into account the importance of free basic education and the need to remove the children concerned from all such work and to provide for their rehabilitation and social integration while addressing the needs of their families, and

Recalling the resolution concerning the elimination of child labour adopted by the International Labour Conference at its 83rd Session in 1996, and

Recognizing that child labour is to a great extent caused by poverty and that the long-term solution lies in sustained economic growth leading to social progress, in particular poverty alleviation and universal education, and

Recalling the Convention on the Rights of the Child adopted by the United Nations General Assembly on 20 November 1989, and

Recalling the ILO Declaration on Fundamental Principles and Rights at Work and its Follow-up, adopted by the International Labour Conference at its 86th Session in 1998, and

Recalling that some of the worst forms of child labour are covered by other international instruments, in particular the Forced Labour Convention, 1930, and the United Nations Supplementary Convention on the Abolition of Slavery, the Slave Trade, and Institutions and Practices Similar to Slavery, 1956, and

Having decided upon the adoption of certain proposals with regard to child labour, which is the fourth item on the agenda of the session, and

Having determined that these proposals shall take the form of an international Convention;

adopts this seventeenth day of June of the year one thousand nine hundred and ninety-nine the following Convention, which may be cited as the Worst Forms of Child Labour Convention, 1999.

---

[44]  The appendix reproduces the substantive provisions of both instruments. The formal provisions are not included.

## Article 1

Each Member which ratifies this Convention shall take immediate and effective measures to secure the prohibition and elimination of the worst forms of child labour as a matter of urgency.

## Article 2

For the purposes of this Convention, the term "child" shall apply to all persons under the age of 18.

## Article 3

For the purposes of this Convention, the term "the worst forms of child labour" comprises:

(a) all forms of slavery or practices similar to slavery, such as the sale and trafficking of children, debt bondage and serfdom and forced or compulsory labour, including forced or compulsory recruitment of children for use in armed conflict;

(b) the use, procuring or offering of a child for prostitution, for the production of pornography or for pornographic performances;

(c) the use, procuring or offering of a child for illicit activities, in particular for the production and trafficking of drugs as defined in the relevant international treaties;

(d) work which, by its nature or the circumstances in which it is carried out, is likely to harm the health, safety or morals of children.

## Article 4

1. The types of work referred to under Article 3(d) shall be determined by national laws or regulations or by the competent authority, after consultation with the organizations of employers and workers concerned, taking into consideration relevant international standards, in particular Paragraphs 3 and 4 of the Worst Forms of Child Labour Recommendation, 1999.

2. The competent authority, after consultation with the organizations of employers and workers concerned, shall identify where the types of work so determined exist.

3. The list of the types of work determined under paragraph 1 of this Article shall be periodically examined and revised as necessary, in consultation with the organizations of employers and workers concerned.

## Article 5

Each Member shall, after consultation with employers' and workers' organizations, establish or designate appropriate mechanisms to monitor the implementation of the provisions giving effect to this Convention.

## Article 6

1. Each Member shall design and implement programmes of action to eliminate as a priority the worst forms of child labour.

2. Such programmes of action shall be designed and implemented in consultation with relevant government institutions and employers' and workers' organizations, taking into consideration the views of other concerned groups as appropriate.

## Article 7

1. Each Member shall take all necessary measures to ensure the effective implementation and enforcement of the provisions giving effect to this Convention including the provision and application of penal sanctions or, as appropriate, other sanctions.

2. Each Member shall, taking into account the importance of education in eliminating child labour, take effective and time-bound measures to:

(a) prevent the engagement of children in the worst forms of child labour;

(b) provide the necessary and appropriate direct assistance for the removal of children from the worst forms of child labour and for their rehabilitation and social integration;

(c) ensure access to free basic education, and, wherever possible and appropriate, vocational training, for all children removed from the worst forms of child labour;

(d) identify and reach out to children at special risk; and

(e) take account of the special situation of girls.

3. Each Member shall designate the competent authority responsible for the implementation of the provisions giving effect to this Convention.

## Article 8

Members shall take appropriate steps to assist one another in giving effect to the provisions of this Convention through enhanced international cooperation and/or assistance including support for social and economic development, poverty eradication programmes and universal education.

Recommendation 190

RECOMMENDATION CONCERNING THE PROHIBITION
AND IMMEDIATE ACTION FOR THE ELIMINATION
OF THE WORST FORMS OF CHILD LABOUR

The General Conference of the International Labour Organization,

Having been convened at Geneva by the Governing Body of the International Labour Office, and having met in its 87th Session on 1 June 1999, and

Having adopted the Worst Forms of Child Labour Convention, 1999, and

Having decided upon the adoption of certain proposals with regard to child labour, which is the fourth item on the agenda of the session, and

Having determined that these proposals shall take the form of a Recommendation supplementing the Worst Forms of Child Labour Convention, 1999;

adopts this seventeenth day of June of the year one thousand nine hundred and ninety-nine the following Recommendation, which may be cited as the Worst Forms of Child Labour Recommendation, 1999.

1. The provisions of this Recommendation supplement those of the Worst Forms of Child Labour Convention, 1999 (hereafter referred to as "the Convention"), and should be applied in conjunction with them.

## I. Programmes of action

2. The programmes of action referred to in Article 6 of the Convention should be designed and implemented as a matter of urgency, in consultation with relevant government institutions and employers' and workers' organizations, taking into consideration the views of the children directly affected by the worst forms of child labour, their families and, as appropriate, other concerned groups committed to the aims of the Convention and this Recommendation. Such programmes should aim at, inter alia:

(a) identifying and denouncing the worst forms of child labour;

(b) preventing the engagement of children in or removing them from the worst forms of child labour, protecting them from reprisals and providing for their rehabilitation and social integration through measures which address their educational, physical and psychological needs;

(c) giving special attention to:

    (i)  younger children;

    (ii) the girl child;

    (iii) the problem of hidden work situations, in which girls are at special risk;

    (iv) other groups of children with special vulnerabilities or needs;

(d) identifying, reaching out to and working with communities where children are at special risk;

(e) informing, sensitizing and mobilizing public opinion and concerned groups, including children and their families.

## II. Hazardous work

3. In determining the types of work referred to under Article 3(d) of the Convention, and in identifying where they exist, consideration should be given, inter alia, to:

(a) work which exposes children to physical, psychological or sexual abuse;

(b) work underground, under water, at dangerous heights or in confined spaces;

172

(c) work with dangerous machinery, equipment and tools, or which involves the manual handling or transport of heavy loads;

(d) work in an unhealthy environment which may, for example, expose children to hazardous substances, agents or processes, or to temperatures, noise levels, or vibrations damaging to their health;

(e) work under particularly difficult conditions such as work for long hours or during the night or work where the child is unreasonably confined to the premises of the employer.

4. For the types of work referred to under Article 3(d) of the Convention and Paragraph 3 above, national laws or regulations or the competent authority could, after consultation with the workers' and employers' organizations concerned, authorize employment or work as from the age of 16 on condition that the health, safety and morals of the children concerned are fully protected, and that the children have received adequate specific instruction or vocational training in the relevant branch of activity.

### III. Implementation

5. (1) Detailed information and statistical data on the nature and extent of child labour should be compiled and kept up to date to serve as a basis for determining priorities for national action for the abolition of child labour, in particular for the prohibition and elimination of its worst forms as a matter of urgency.

(2) As far as possible, such information and statistical data should include data disaggregated by sex, age group, occupation, branch of economic activity, status in employment, school attendance and geographical location. The importance of an effective system of birth registration, including the issuing of birth certificates, should be taken into account.

(3) Relevant data concerning violations of national provisions for the prohibition and elimination of the worst forms of child labour should be compiled and kept up to date.

6. The compilation and processing of the information and data referred to in Paragraph 5 above should be carried out with due regard for the right to privacy.

7. The information compiled under Paragraph 5 above should be communicated to the International Labour Office on a regular basis.

8. Members should establish or designate appropriate national mechanisms to monitor the implementation of national provisions for the prohibition and elimination of the worst forms of child labour, after consultation with employers' and workers' organizations.

9. Members should ensure that the competent authorities which have responsibilities for implementing national provisions for the prohibition and elimination of the worst forms of child labour cooperate with each other and coordinate their activities.

10. National laws or regulations or the competent authority should determine the persons to be held responsible in the event of non-compliance with national provisions for the prohibition and elimination of the worst forms of child labour.

11. Members should, in so far as it is compatible with national law, cooperate with international efforts aimed at the prohibition and elimination of the worst forms of child labour as a matter of urgency by:

(a) gathering and exchanging information concerning criminal offences, including those involving international networks;

(b) detecting and prosecuting those involved in the sale and trafficking of children, or in the use, procuring or offering of children for illicit activities, for prostitution, for the production of pornography or for pornographic performances;

(c) registering perpetrators of such offences.

12. Members should provide that the following worst forms of child labour are criminal offences:

(a) all forms of slavery or practices similar to slavery, such as the sale and trafficking of children, debt bondage and serfdom and forced or compulsory labour, including forced or compulsory recruitment of children for use in armed conflict;

(b) the use, procuring or offering of a child for prostitution, for the production of pornography or for pornographic performances; and

(c) the use, procuring or offering of a child for illicit activities, in particular for the production and trafficking of drugs as defined in the relevant international treaties, or for activities which involve the unlawful carrying or use of firearms or other weapons.

13. Members should ensure that penalties including, where appropriate, criminal penalties are applied for violations of the national provisions for the prohibition and elimination of any type of work referred to in Article 3(d) of the Convention.

14. Members should also provide as a matter of urgency for other criminal, civil or administrative remedies, where appropriate, to ensure the effective enforcement of national provisions for the prohibition and elimination of the worst forms of child labour, such as special supervision of enterprises which have used the worst forms of child labour, and, in cases of persistent violation, consideration of temporary or permanent revoking of permits to operate.

15. Other measures aimed at the prohibition and elimination of the worst forms of child labour might include the following:

(a) informing, sensitizing and mobilizing the general public, including national and local political leaders, parliamentarians and the judiciary;

(b) involving and training employers' and workers' organizations and civic organizations;

(c) providing appropriate training for the government officials concerned, especially inspectors and law enforcement officials, and for other relevant professionals;

(d) providing for the prosecution in their own country of the Member's nationals who commit offences under its national provisions for the prohibition and immediate elimination of the worst forms of child labour even when these offences are committed in another country;

(e) simplifying legal and administrative procedures and ensuring that they are appropriate and prompt;

(f) encouraging the development of policies by undertakings to promote the aims of the Convention;

(g) monitoring and giving publicity to best practices on the elimination of child labour;

(h) giving publicity to legal or other provisions on child labour in the different languages or dialects;

(i) establishing special complaints procedures and making provisions to protect from discrimination and reprisals those who legitimately expose violations of the provisions of the Convention, as well as establishing helplines or points of contact and ombudspersons;

(j) adopting appropriate measures to improve the educational infrastructure and the training of teachers to meet the needs of boys and girls;

(k) as far as possible, taking into account in national programmes of action:

(i) the need for job creation and vocational training for the parents and adults in the families of children working in the conditions covered by the Convention; and

(ii) the need for sensitizing parents to the problem of children working in such conditions.

16. Enhanced international cooperation and/or assistance among Members for the prohibition and effective elimination of the worst forms of child labour should complement national efforts and may, as appropriate, be developed and implemented in consultation with employers' and workers' organizations. Such international cooperation and/or assistance should include:

(a) mobilizing resources for national or international programmes;

(b) mutual legal assistance;

(c) technical assistance including the exchange of information;

(d) support for social and economic development, poverty eradication programmes and universal education.

# Caught between the State and the Community: Lessons from Civil Wars in El Salvador, Guatemala and Peru from 1970 to 1990

*Stener Ekern*

## PRESENTATION

### Preliminaries

By ushering in a wave of insurgencies and counterinsurgency warfare, the anti-authoritarian student rebellion that marked the end of the post-war reconstruction period of the Western world in 1968 took a far more violent turn in South and Central America than in Europe and North America, reaching civil wars proportions in countries like Peru, Guatemala, and El Salvador. Here, in the 1980s, left-wing guerrilla groups were able to control parts of the national territory and the local population living there, and engage national armies in fighting that, at least in El Salvador, approximated real warfare, that is, a situation with regular fighters battling each other along fixed geographical fronts. But, in the main, the warring parties fought each other all across the respective national territories in a highly irregular manner. Insurgents built politico-military organisations in order to enlist the masses in an attempt to conquer the state. They established secret groups that raised money through kidnappings and executed persons considered to be enemies of the people. On the other side, the armed forces usurped government in the name of national security and applied brutal counter-insurgency strategies that included indiscriminate killings of real and suspected rebels, often closely allied with vigilante groups of the extreme political right known as death squads. In their most intense phases the irregular or 'dirty' wars claimed substantially more lives than the regular fighting between the armies and the guerrillas. Moreover, the victims were often unarmed civilians.

Parallel to the development of these civil wars, and perhaps as an answer to the images they produced among citizens at home and abroad, since the mid 1980s human rights have become increasingly important as a standard for evaluating political and military action all over the world. Possibly precisely for this reason the stories from the Guatemalan, Salvadoran and Peruvian wars that were presented by news media and academic analysts increasingly became narratives of human rights violations. Today, as civilian government appears to be taking hold in the three countries in question, and as truth commissions investigate the terrible events of the past, it has become common knowledge that national governments and armies were responsible for gross human rights violations during the wars. It is tempting to believe that human rights reports and human rights workers have been instrumental in the current peace processes by making the world aware of the atrocities and by holding up a vision of civilised rule that can unite everyone.

### Limitations on human rights reporting

Seen from afar, such an affirmation might hold true. However, the statement 'human rights reporting helps build peace' is, at best, a simplification. In contemporary nation-states, the stories in which people participate invariably unfold at both the local and the national level. Any human rights reporter will be familiar with cases where events have different meanings in different settings: The victim is both a political activist and a member of a family that has unsettled accounts, the killer both an ideologue and a clansman. Where the great narratives of student rebellions, brutal armies, human rights and civilian governments take place on the national political scene, this article will focus on the little narratives in which local people also do politics and perpetrate violence. The first objective of the present article is to explore limitations on human rights reporting by examining the above-mentioned conflicts as a set of social processes in selected communities in El Salvador, Peru, and Guatemala. I will use the local community as an entry point and relate chains of events in which social actors are informed by, and act within, both local and national contexts.

I will argue that because human rights are so closely tied to the existence of modern nation-states, and hence to the state as an agent for negotiating loyalties, human rights reporting tends to miss local and non-state political allegiances and agency, downplay the distinctness of the different communities involved, and underestimate the challenges of integrating traditional polities into a modern state. If human rights reports are to promote respect for human rights, they need to situate violations also in local contexts in order to communicate better with the locals. It becomes necessary both to explain local history and to discuss the status of local community-based rights and obligations versus human rights and state obligations.

In a recent anthology, an English anthropologist Richard Wilson makes a similar argument and suggests that the role of anthropology is "to restore to accounts of political violence both the surrounding social relations and an associated range of subjective meanings".[1]: Thereby he situates himself in an on-going debate within human rights organisations between "legalists, who advocate the narrow circumscribing of information to that which is relevant for the prosecution ... and the contextualists, who argue for the inherent value of including a wider scope of social and contextual meanings". The present article takes the same position.

## Human rights between the local and the national

The second objective is to examine how interpretations of cause, effect and agency vary with context. When a victim is victim because of both family connection and ideological affinity, this person is, as it were, victimised simultaneously in different communities. In less integrated nation-states like the three we have chosen here, the first, usually termed 'the local community', will characteristically be dominated by face-to-face-interaction and family-based social relations, and will also show limited institutional specialisation. The other community is the national community in which the local community has the civil rights of its members defined.

---

[1]     Richard A. Wilson, "Representing Human Rights Violations: Social Contexts and Subjectivities", in Richard A. Wilson (ed.): *Human Rights, Culture and Context. Anthropological Perspectives*, London: Pluto Press, 1997, p. 335.

In South and Central America, the national community is, by definition, the modern, Christian, citizen-based nation-state, modelled on the French and American Revolutions of the 18th century. Indeed, the states here have always been actively engaged in the construction of the international human rights system. However, many countries in the region remain weakly integrated in the sense that large sectors of the population are peasants that participate only marginally in the national state and market. In Peru and Guatemala the local community is frequently also an indigenous community in which the international human rights system ensures Andean and Mayan peasants the right to keep their identities as members of separate communities. In El Salvador, the peasants may not be indigenous in the sense that they practise different social rules, but still the situation is very different from that of a highly integrated society in which the political divisions of a local community directly mirror those of the national community.

Separate communities may have different ideas about good governance and about how rights and obligations ought to be distributed. However, no society is without rules and norms and thus without tensions between the individual and the collective. Moreover, the production of a collective identity seems to be a prerequisite for the formation of a community. Communities are thus moral communities (or 'cultures'). In a recent study, the Indian anthropologist Veena Das examines the complex relationship between the community, the state and human rights.[2] She traces the wounds that individuals receive as both the community and the state impose their rules, and defines culture as 'the distribution of pain'. Her discussion of the similarities of the often violent social mechanisms that discipline individuals and produce identities and loyalties, both in the little community and the big community, provides a way of overcoming the dualism between the local and the national. I agree with Das in holding that human rights as a standard for civilised human interaction should apply not only on the level of the state. The community frequently inflicts as much pain and suffering as the state. However, I also insist that the national community should accommodate local rules as long as they do not violate human rights standards. My overriding concern is that human rights reports ought to communicate with people where they live.

**The material**

The three cases are presented with different types of material: human rights testimonies from El Salvador, historical narratives from Peru and anthropological analysis from Guatemala. In order to understand how, for instance, Guatemalan Maya-speaking peasants may read a human rights report, the presentations of the respective local contexts are rather extensive. The point is not to investigate the three social processes as such, but to illuminate problems that human rights

---

[2]    Veena Das, *Critical Events. An Anthropological Perspective on Contemporary India*, New Delhi: Oxford University Press, 1993.

181

analysts are confronted with as they try to construct reports that reflect multiple contexts and to communicate their findings to members of different communities.

The material from El Salvador is taken from testimonies that I myself collected when I was engaged as a consultant to the Truth Commission of that country in 1992.[3] Close to 40 per cent of the events described in the testimonies that the Commission received were parts of processes in which communities were purged or 'ideologically cleansed'. According to the informants, the purges were executed by masked, armed civilians referred to as death squads, often in cooperation with units from regular police or army forces, particularly the local civil defence. Selected testimonies give first-hand accounts of fateful moments, but limited visions of the war. By examining this testimony-based image of the Salvadoran war, it will be shown that more context is needed in order to understand the events and eventually enter into a meaningful dialogue with local victims and perpetrators.

The war between the Shining Path division of the Communist Party of Peru and the Peruvian government is discussed in The Peasant Militias and the Defeat of the Shining Path, edited by Peruvian anthropologist Carlos Iván Degregori. The book gives a rich ethnographic account of how this Maoist-inspired guerrilla movement lost the battle for the hearts and minds of the oppressed masses precisely in the most marginalised of all Peruvian communities, that of the iquichanos of the highest cultivable zones of the Andes. This happened when the rebel politico-military organisation laid the foundations of a new order by literally eliminating the old, methodically killing off the leaders of the civic-religious hierarchies that traditionally organise iquichano communities. The revolutionary action provoked what the contributors to the book call 'the rebellion of the chorus'.[4] Up to then the peasants had been treated as passive subjects by both the government and the rebels, but by forming militias or committees for civil defence in collaboration with the army, they took the lead in the counter-insurgency offensive that eventually won the day. Now many impoverished Andean peasants think of themselves as the real winners of the war, and are about to take the step from the chorus up to the stage, as political protagonists in their own right also on the national scene.

In his account of the war between the Guerrilla Army of the Poor (EGP) of Guatemala and the Guatemalan army in the territories of the Ixil Mayas of Guatemala, North American anthropologist David Stoll makes a similar argument about how a local indigenous people caught between two contenders for far-away state power were able to use "[the army-imposed patrols for civil defence],

---

[3]   My work for the commission also included an investigation of death squads. One of the commissioners, Dr. Reynaldo Figueredo, later encouraged me to continue my investigations, and kindly permitted me to use material collected by the Commission in order to combat the phenomenon. Cf. Stener. Ekern, "Dødsskvadroner i El Salvador: Hvordan ble de til? Kan fenomenet bekjempes gjennom et rettsoppgjør?", in Bård-Anders Andreassen og Elin Skår, *Rettferdighet eller forsoning? Om beskyttelse av menneskerettigheter gjennom sannhetskommisjoner og rettstribunaler.* Oslo: Cappelen, 1998.

[4]   The expression is taken from the book of the same title by the Argentine philosopher José Nun.

religious congregations, and other seemingly subordinate, conformist institutions to reconstruct civil society, that is, political space to make their own decisions".[5] And in a thesis about the history and the functions of the civil patrols in another Mayan community, North American sociologist Paul Kobrak confirms Stoll's argument. The rebellion of the chorus may appear as a surprising result of the violent clashes that many human rights reports described as civil wars between right-wing dictatorships and liberating forces. However, by focussing on the local community, and following its interaction with national forces that compete for its loyalties, such an outcome is seen in fact to be logical.

## The local community and civil society

Stoll and others that report about locals who feel caught between two armies have been attacked because it is felt that their reports unjustly put a brutal army in the same category as the people themselves and their defenders.[6] Kobrak points out that if one is to write the history of a counter-insurgency, one cannot leave the insurgency out. The absence of the guerrilla in many (if not most) human-rights accounts of the wars we are to discuss is indeed striking, and cannot only be explained by human rights-dictated needs to put narratives in a de-contextualised reporting format.[7] As Stoll remarks, the reason is that many human rights reports not only limit their coveragereach to the state and its obligations, but also adopt the 'solidarity perspective' too easily. In a country with severe human rights violations, both human rights reporters and solidarity activists mostly stay in contact with opposition forces. But whereas the first group does so out of principle, the latter simply shares the political views of the opposition. It is my view that these overlapping agendas should be separated more clearly.

Here the concept of civil society may help us as it identifies an extremely important aspect of the relationship between the state and the local community. By labelling locally based organisations and militias or defence patrols 'civil', the above analysts also say that local politics has an important role to play in a democratic society. By participating in civil society locals learn to become citizens. In this perspective those who feel that the first task of the human rights reporter is to defend the people should recognise the importance of the narratives about how peasants made the civil patrols their own. But they should also avoid romanticising the local community: traditional civil-religious hierarchies are not necessarily up to human rights standards. Human rights may, after all, indicate better ways of constructing communities.

---

[5]   David Stoll, *Between Two Armies in the Ixil Towns of Guatemala*, New York, Columbia University Press, 1993, p. xiv.

[6]   Charles R. Hale, "Consciousness, Violence and the Politics of Memory in Guatemala", in *Current Anthropology*, vol. 38, no. 5, 1997: Forum on Anthropology in Public.

[7]   Beatriz Manz, *Refugees of a Hidden War. The Aftermath of Counterinsurgency in Guatemala*. New York: State University of New York Press, 1988; IDHUCA (Instituto de Derechos Humanos de la Universidad Centroamericana), "1997: Buscando entre cenizas", in *Estudios Centroamericanos* (ECA) 589-590, Nov.—Dec. 1997, pp. 1115 – 1156.

## CASE ONE: EL SALVADOR

### Interpreting testimonies of human rights violations

When the United Nations began to negotiate between the government and the FMLN (Frente Farabundo Martí para la Liberación Nacional) rebel force of El Salvador, the first thing the parties agreed to was accepting human rights as a common yardstick for future action. This agreement, later known as the San José Accord, also included a clause in which the parties named a Truth Commission mandated to investigate "grave acts of violence whose imprints in society urgently demand that truth become publicly known", and to produce a report because "events of this character ... should be subject to exemplary processing by the system of justice". The Truth Commission had very limited resources (twelve consultants and six months to go), so their report did little more than confirm existing knowledge about a brutal war. Anyway, five days after its presentation, El Salvador's legislative assembly ratified an amnesty law that blocked the judicial investigation that the report called for.

Six years later, the governing ARENA (Alianza Republicana Nacionalista) right-wing party of El Salvador maintains that the levels of violence used by the government and the army were necessary, rarely unlawful, and justified by the threat posed by the insurgents. On the other side, FMLN leaders who advocate accepting responsibility for crimes committed during the war meet with little sympathy within the party and among voters. Very probably the exemplary justice called for in the San José Accord has limited popular appeal. The most likely reason for this is the complexity of the issue of guilt in a civil war.

In addition to the investigation of a selection of causes célèbres (the killing of Archbishop Romero in 1980, etc.), the Truth Commission decided to open its doors and receive individual complaints from Salvadoran citizens. During ten weeks about 1,200 people presented their testimonies to the consultants. Another 800 were collected by distributing forms where 'self-declarations' could be filled in during visits to areas that had been held by rebel forces during the war. The resulting 2,000 reports obtained from 'direct sources' were processed statistically, but not checked or compared with other evidence, for instance the 24,000 complaints that the commission received from different Salvadoran NGOs, as well as the army.

During the interviews at the commission, the informants were always asked to specify their relationship to and names of victims, date and place of violation, type of violation, and, if possible, to indicate the perpetrator. This practice followed a standard format for human rights reporting that apparently takes for granted that such context-less bits of information are sufficient to establish the truth. From the beginning I felt that such a denuded story left me with more questions than answers. This was often the case with the informants, too. Many of them wanted to share their reflections on the tragedies they had seen. Through discussions with informants, the consultants gained an increasingly comprehensive picture of how the war had unfolded in urban and rural El Salvador that, in turn, informed the next interviews.

Another for me unsatisfactory aspect of the reporting work of the Truth Commission was the lack of any attempt at situating the informant, as a witness, in a political or historical context. Whereas many urbanites arrived alone at one of the commission's offices, the overwhelming majority of the many people of rural extraction arrived in groups transported by NGOs that worked in their home area. The resulting problems with representativity, referred to as 'the filters' by the other UN missions to El Salvador, was not addressed by the Truth Commission. In general terms, the informants almost always were first degree relatives of the victims, who came to denounce the killing or disappearance of their loved ones, claim innocence about or deny any relation between the victim and a warring party, and give credence to the version of the war given by 'their' NGO. The fact that other neighbours had also died was frequently only mentioned after making inquiries about the context.

The work of listening to and writing down tales of torture, pain and human evil is taxing. As the weeks passed, I found that my way of coping was by entering a kind of 'watching a movie' attitude, that is, to treat the events as stories. I suspect this is how many survivors deal with the events, too. By asking questions and making comparisons, the informant and the consultant constructed a meaningful narrative about a past event that had taken place in both a local and a national context. The event became both a history of the victim and his or her family, and of "we the Salvadorans during the war" and the process of taking the testimony became a kind of joint undertaking. The consultant, as a foreign researcher, gained access to intimate and important information (and, in the case of the causes célèbres, a golden opportunity of furthering his or her own career). The informant used the opportunity to write history in an important book and confirm a particular narrative. The construction of the testimony was also a way of honouring the dead and of making sense of the brutal departures of loved ones. As the work of the commission neared its end, and the consultants realised that nothing further would be done with the material they collected, their consolation was the cathartic effect that could be observed when the informants signed their statements with a thumbprint.

The narratives that were constructed in the Truth Commission were thus produced in a situation akin to that of social science fieldwork. In an article, the Dutch anthropologist Antonius Robben relates his experiences from fieldwork in Buenos Aires among victims and violators of the 'dirty war' in Argentina in the 1970s, and examines what he calls 'ethnographic seduction. He writes that only after months of interviewing did he learn to "distinguish seduction from good rapport", and goes on to observe that "seduction can be intentional but also unconscious and can be compared to the ways in which filmmakers, stage directors, artists, or writers succeed in totally absorbing the attention of their audiences".[8] Robben concludes that "seduction as a dimension of fieldwork (…) is

---

[8]   Antonius C.G.M. Robben, "The Politics of Truth and Emotion among Victims and Perpetrators of Violence", in Carolyn Nordstrom and Antonius C.G.M. Robben (eds.), *Fieldwork under Fire. Contemporary Studies of Violence and Survival*, University of California Press, 1995, p. 83.

185

especially prominent in research on violent political conflict because the interlocutors have great personal and political stakes in making the ethnographer adopt their interpretations".[9] Seduction happens in subtle ways: The courteous and well-educated army officer who gently reminds the inquisitive European about the rules and the realities of war, the nameless pain of the father who presents the details of the cruelties committed against his beloved son, and the sophisticated social scientist-cum-guerrilla leader with whom your own days of student politics are so easily recaptured during long conversations about the political structure of Argentine society at a bourgeois café. Who dares break the rapport and forfeit the possibility of receiving more stories in such a situation?

Of these three types of seductive challenges it is the second that most often confronts human rights reporters in poor and overwhelmingly rural El Salvador, Guatemala and Andean Peru. It takes courage to penetrate what Robben calls the 'emotional shroud' that surrounds the victim "with questions that might be easily misperceived as apologetic, uncaring, cold, callous, and hurtful"[10]. Having received scores of Salvadorans in similar close encounters, I can subscribe to Robben's conclusion: "The more emotional the reaction, the greater (the) personal inhibition to discuss these issues further." The point I wish to make is that in receiving testimonies about human rights violations, the sympathy for the victim that is often the decisive factor in calling the attention of human rights reporters in the first place, can also be a main source of error. Moreover, the aspect of the violation that is most easily retold incompletely or even erroneously is the historical context, which is precisely where questions of agency and guilt are determined. On several occasions I had to stop taking a testimony because as I asked for more details, it turned out that the victim had been armed, too, and actively participating in the events that led to his death.

## War stories

Whatever the status of the testimonies received, the conversations I had with 176 witnesses enabled me to collect short narratives of 231 events involving grave cases of violence during the Salvadoran civil war. Adding another 93 incidents collected by a colleague, I have analysed a total of 324 cases that together account for approximately 15 per cent of the testimonies that the commission received. Of these cases, 305 involved extra-judicial killings or disappearances; the rest were mainly cases of illegal detention of trade union leaders. In no less than 146 cases, or 47,9 per cent, the perpetrators were described by the witnesses as 'death squads' (i.e. armed civilians acting anonymously by hiding or painting their faces), 'men acting as members of death squads', or 'mixed groups' consisting of both uniformed men from the armed forces or one of the country's three police corps, and death squads. FMLN fighters, also hiding their identities, were held

---

[9]   Robben, *ibid.*, p. 86.
[10]  Robben, *ibid.*, p. 92.

responsible in 23 incidents (7,5 per cent). In the remaining cases, the army acted alone or the violator couldn't be identified.

These percentages are not very different from the ones that were calculated from the entire universe of primary source material collected by the Truth Commission, but here the category of 'death squad' was reserved for the urban variety of armed civilians.[11] The rural and the 'mixed group' varieties were classified as 'paramilitary' because these men usually belonged to the Civil Defence forces, or, before the establishment of the Civil Defence in 1980, to its precursor, the right-wing peasant organisation ORDEN (Organización Democrática Nacionalista). ORDEN was affiliated to the military-dominated PCN (Partido de Conciliación Nacional) party that governed during the 1960s and 1970s. (Few informants cared to distinguish the Civil Defence from ORDEN anyway.) This way of classifying all non-uniformed killers as death squads follows the local logic and has the merit of allowing for a discussion of the war from a local point of view. More often than not the death squads would consist of people from local or neighbouring civil defence groups and frequently the perpetrators would be known to the witnesses. The following narrative is typical of the 106 stories involving rural death squads:

(...) on 13 June, 1980, approximately 150 soldiers from the National Marine [base at] Puerto La Libertad, in co-operation with approximately 150 elements from the local divisions of the ORDEN organisation of the cantons[12] of La Loma, Buenos Aires, Macehual and others (...) entered La Loma and killed 14 peasants with bullets and machete blows.

Already since 1977 extensive organisational work had developed in La Loma, through the Catholic Church. A base community had been formed around the reading of the Bible and pamphlets distributed by the Fathers. From there also politics entered the game, and for that reason they began to persecute the families that participated in the organisational work. In this epoch, with the militaristic government and its policies, death squads were formed between ORDEN and the Marines of the port. It was dangerous to sleep at home, and as the entire community was organised, precautions were taken, for instance, by preparing caves as refuges around the canton. The families that belonged to ORDEN – around 3 of the total of 60 – realised what was happening, and with that began the repression. The soldiers and the

---

[11]  The final report of the Truth Commission arrived at a figure of 7,470 extra-judicial killings, of which the categories 'paramilitaries' and 'death squads' were responsible for respectively 1,931 and 699, or 35.2 per cent combined. FMLN was held responsible for 221 deaths, or 2.9 per cent of the total number of victims. Cf. Comisión de la Verdad para El Salvador (CV), *De la locura a la esperanza. La guerra de 12 años en El Salvador,* San Salvador, New York, Las Naciones Unidas, 1992 , Appendices, volume II, table 10. Interestingly, in a universe of 7,200 extra-judicial killings from the period 1975-1994 (the Truth Commission worked with the period 1980-1991) reported in 40,000 (?) testimonies received by four important left-leaning Salvadoran NGOs and later cross-referenced by the Human Rights Centre (IDHUCA) at the Central American University (UCA) in San Salvador, 'paramilitary groups' account for 2,812 and 'unknowns' – i.e. death squads – for 1,359, which gives a combined total of 57.9 per cent, whereas 'insurgent forces' were accountable for 297 (5.3 per cent) of the reports filed by these NGOs. Cf. IDHUCA, *op.cit.*, p. 1122)

[12]  The canton is the smallest administrative unit in El Salvador, and may comprise one or several hamlets.

187

paramilitaries surrounded the canton at around six o'clock in the morning, and at eight the bullet rains began. Everybody fled; however, seven people were killed in the community and another seven on footpaths as they fled. (The testimony continues with the names of the victims, and ends with the information that to this day, none of the refugees have returned and that many have emigrated to the United States.)

This story of what I propose to call 'ideological cleansing' of communities was repeated time after time during hundreds of testimonies. A common detail apparently omitted by this informant was how local ORDEN people did indicate or 'put the bad finger at' the people that were to be killed as subversives. The unusual thing about this peasant's story is the broad drama that unfolds as he sets out to present the history of his community as such, and his willingness to acknowledge local divisions and the close relationship between the Christian base community and unknown persons who start defensive preparations. The typical informant would mention that the victim was killed during an *operativo* or a *limpieza* (cleansing), but omit or deny any reference to an earlier phase of organisational work. However, this peasant leader too declined to enter into details about the pre-war sequences of the story.

The leader of another Catholic group had more critical distance to certain types of organisational work and provided the commission with the following narrative:

(...) on 9 April, 1980, in the village of Monte San Juán ... members of the FPL (Fuerzas Populares de Liberación, the biggest single fraction of the FMLN) executed the following four people (their names are given) ... At six o'clock in the morning, between the canton of Candelaria and Monte San Juán village, a FPL group met. They hid their faces with handkerchiefs where the letters 'FPL' were written. Some of their victims the FPL people encountered in the streets of the village, and these were killed instantaneously, except for EH and AV. The former was brought to the hamlet of Soledad, where he was executed. His body was tied up when they found him. NP was executed and accused of being a member of ORDEN. PF was killed to prevent him from reporting what he had seen. AV was killed because he was a member of the militias.

By 'militias' the informant referred to a group of voluntary police reinforcements associated with the National Guard. The Guard was responsible for policing El Salvador's rural areas until 1992, and co-operated closely with ORDEN and the Civil Defence during the war. The testimony continues to relate more FPL executions, then proceeds with the second part of the drama:

As a consequence of these events there were organised more militias and civil defence groups. All the members of the patrols armed themselves with revolvers and ammunition that they received precisely by forming a patrol. As militias they had only used sticks and sickles, but now the National Guard provided them with firearms. The local commander, who at that time was Sergeant CFR, asked for arms to the civil defence groups from the headquarters in [the provincial capital of] Cojutepeque. Here Major OA was in command. ... He gave instructions to the civil defence and drilled them at the town square. He said that he gave them arms because they were to fight against the guerrillas. And that everyone who heard about their movements had to give reports. The spies, who were from ORDEN, reported that guerrilla fighters had a meeting. But when the patrols arrived, they only found good men who didn't carry any weapons. ... During one of these actions, members of the Civil Defence, together with agents from the National Guard, killed SH. SH was the leader of the guerrillas in Monte San Juán.

Before this happened, the patrols used to arrest people and bring them [to the National Guard headquarters in Cojutepeque]. But because they were unable to find evidence, they had to set them free. When they killed SH the patrols took courage, for at last they had killed a guerrilla combatant. From then on the National Guard gave the patrols permission to kill those they suspected of being guerrillas. From then on the patrols had no problems in killing people. Patrols from different communities united and cleansed their areas of subversives. When all were expelled, the guerrillas left for the neighbouring town of Tenancingo (about 15 km to the north). But as the subversion ended, the patrols began to take their own reprisals. They formed different groups ... and no longer did they fight subversives, rather they used their arms to back up their own will and make victims of their neighbours.

Other testimonies from the same area tell how peasants associated with ORDEN met in private homes, painted their faces, worked themselves up into a rage against the destructive forces of the reds, and then proceeded to unite on hilltops, meet with guardsmen or regular army units, descend upon a selected canton and expel or kill everyone associated with base communities, peasant leagues or other FMLN-related organisations. Moreover, the establishment of this local death squad network very likely took place in close co-operation with the intelligence sections of the National Guard and the Army, within a loosely organised nationwide network that responded to repeated calls for a total war against the 'red menace' from the right-wing politician Roberto D'Aubuisson who also was instrumental in the founding of ARENA. This party grew rapidly during the war and since 1989 it has enjoyed the presidency and a majority in the country's legislative assembly.

The testimony was given by a local leader in the Christian Democratic Party (PDC), who insisted in giving a context-rich account of how a war initiated and sustained by two extremes had torn his community apart. For him the war was a tale of polarisation and degeneration, a conclusion that was echoed in many testimonies and also in the final report of the Truth Commission itself. Together, the two narratives give a clear picture of how a line between 'us and them' was drawn. On the other side of this line between the two contenders for state power, events similar to those told in the following story were not atypical:

(...) on 24 June, 1985, a group of guerrillas from the FPL captured the young demobilised soldier JAM from his home in the canton of Los Enríquez ... took him away and later killed him (...) JAM was tired of life in the military and didn't want to serve more. For this reason he didn't want to renew his service card. In this area, controlled by the FPL during these days, it was common knowledge that those who wanted to renew the service card would be executed by the FPL. It was also expected that demobilised soldiers give information to the FPL.

IEA, from the village centre of the canton, was the one in charge of finding such information in the area where JAM lived (...) Probably for some personal reason, or because he wasn't content with JAM, IEA denounced JAM. On the day of the crime, the house of JAM's family was surrounded by uniformed elements of the FPL. They called out to JAM that he couldn't run, because if he did, they would gun him down. The entire family was at home, already gone to bed. Two of the fighters entered the house, and one of them was recognised by the parents as 'Neto', and he accused JAM of wanting to renew the service card. [When he denied this] they insisted that someone had denounced him, and then they tied him up and took him away.

(...) two or three days later, through a friend of a lady who cooked in the FPL camp in the canton of Quipure, close to the Honduran frontier, they learnt that JAM had been tortured and killed on a hillside close to the camp. The torture had consisted in hanging him close to the fire in order to suffocate him. Later, he was forced to prepare his own grave (...) The following year, a former FPL fighter or deserter from that force ... told relatives of JAM that the story the cooking lady had told was true.

Other testimonies from FMLN-controlled areas tell about expulsions of people who didn't collaborate (Adventists or other Protestant groups who refused to carry arms) and who were suspected of collaborating with or spying for the armed forces, or give telling glimpses of how the revolutionaries cleansed areas of ORDEN elements as they established their control by selective killings. In FMLN areas the chains of command were often more obscure than on the government's side, and except for the occasional International Red Cross office, there were no neutral or alternative institutions to go to. Thus we see that the control mechanisms established by the belligerent parties were similar in their brutal simplicity. Moreover, by plotting the testimonies onto a map of the movements of the war fronts, it can be shown that the areas that suffered the big cleansing operations usually lay where the FMLN tried to establish liberated zones, and where the army decided to open free-fire zones. This observation is corroborated by the fact that a full 80 per cent of all the killings and disappearances during the war took place between 1980 and 1982, that is, before geographically defined fronts crystallised.

On the other hand, there is little reason to doubt that in the main, the rebels fought a cleaner war than the government. The FMLN probably never massacred entire hamlets just on suspicion, and their fighters didn't exterminate whole families just because a son or a daughter had been active in a government-affiliated organisation. But our main point here is that both parties unlawfully killed civilians, and that neither party showed much respect for civilian institutions. Just as the FMLN, as a Marxist-Leninist-inspired politico-military organisation, denied the very possibility of an independent judiciary (considered to be, at best, a bourgeois illusion), its adversaries among the founders of the ARENA party concluded that the Salvadoran judiciary simply didn't function because it was unable to contain revolutionary action. Therefore it was necessary to form anti-communist command groups, that is, death squads, and 'disappear' the subversives. A telling detail is that both parties justified this by referring to patriotism, albeit within different vectors: FMLN talked about the need to build a new nation because an oligarchic landowning class had misused it and sold it to

U.S. imperialism. ARENA spoke of the need to defend the existing nation from the attacks of world communism. In both cases, the local community paid a terrible price before it could be integrated in the respective national project.

### War rhetoric

For the average Salvadoran, embedded in never-ending sequences of violence and counter-violence, human rights talk was – and still is – catalogued as a discourse typical of the left. This is because human rights rhetoric was introduced in El Salvador by the left, as a way of framing criticism of the government. The following conclusion to a discussion of the human rights violations during the war in a recent Salvadoran report is typical:

> The dictatorial military regimes, imposed through coup d'états or electoral fraud, in indissoluble alliance with enormous economic interests, progressively developed a politics of militaristic authoritarianism and social submission, in which the democratic aspirations of vast national sectors were frustrated and relegated. The fights for social rights and improved conditions of living were stigmatised as subversive and repressed (...) The effect of the closure of spaces for democratic participation and the oppression carried out by those powerful economic sectors began to be seen with the rise of organised social forces and armed insurgent groups that called for democratic changes in the reigning structure.[13]

In the first place, the authors of this passage presume an almost mechanical relationship between 'powerful economic sectors' and the practices of the army, oblivious to the profound paternalistic political traditions of the country and its low level of integration. Secondly, a series of fundamental political decisions (e.g. the use of violence and the type of organisation to build) and a long history of clandestine organising are conflated into a kind of spontaneous and natural rebellion. Consequently, otherwise important human rights reports are easily dismissed by the Salvadoran national political centre and right as partial and insufficient. Moreover, international reports often limit themselves to a simple recounting of rights violations and denunciations of alleged perpetrators and omit the preceding spiral of violence and disintegration. Thus they unwittingly adopt the conflated solidarity perspective and fail to catch a public beyond those who see the war from an international perspective or who stand to profit politically from the fact that the government always receives the lion's share of the bad press.

In his discussion of the shortcomings of context-free human rights reports, Wilson notes that "like the discourse of development, the human rights literature draws upon Manichean dualisms (violated/violator, powerless/powerful) to construct its subjects as innocent victims (...) Human rights organisations draw a great deal of their rhetorical power from how they represent themselves as

---

[13]   IDHUCA, *op.cit.*, p. 1155.

campaigning on behalf of weak innocents against powerful and violent governments in the pursuit of justice, truth and the rule of law".[14]

Ironically, Manichean dualism is the language of war, too. Wars are best justified by framing them as defensive and this also holds true for rebellions. The first line of defence is to define the attacks as legitimate responses to aggression. In answer to criticism of brutality and a Peruvian bishop's call for peace, Abimael Guzmán, leader of the Shining Path guerrilla movement, observed: "In Peru, because of the malicious dominant system annually 60,000 children under one year die (...) compare this to the official figures of casualties (...) in ten years of popular war a third of the total of minors that die in a single year have died. Who kills children in the cradle? [President] Fujimori and the old, reactionary state".[15]

Under certain conditions Guzmán's argument is correct, and indeed it is an argument that has moved thousands of human right reporters, researchers and aid workers into action, as well as solidarity people and armed rebels. However, just as the Salvadoran human rights analysts cited above conflate a complicated 'rise of organised social forces' into a natural event, Guzmán's argument presupposes the existence of an integrated national community where the state is present in every remote corner, from cradle to grave. This is simply not the case in Peru (if anywhere at all), and even Peruvians highly critical of their own government may feel estranged by foreign human rights reports that compare Peruvian statistics to an ideal born in a highly integrated welfare society.

Peruvians feel even more estranged by foreigners who explain and understand Shining Path by general references to the prevailing levels of poverty. In contrast to e.g. FMLN of El Salvador, Shining Path didn't hesitate to commit mass murders, nor did the movement ever seek to build fronts or alliances with other groups on the left (on the contrary, they were declared to be enemies, and executed). For this reason it became difficult to build an international solidarity movement romanticising the armed fight against the Peruvian government. Nevertheless, from a human rights point of view, the difference between FMLN in the days when the different factions of this alliance advocated the building of a liberated nation and called on the masses to take up arms and fight in the trench indicated by the vanguard, and Shining Path, is one of degree rather than of order. When Lenin, regarded by both these revolutionary parties as a founding father, called for war against the bourgeois state, he did this by turning Clausewitz upside down. When politics is nothing but the prolongation of war, everything is justified, including the elimination of political adversaries.

---

[14]  Wilson, *op.cit.*, p. 142.

[15]  Carlos Iván Degregori, "Cosechando tempestades: Las rondas campesinas y la derrota de Sendero Luminoso en Ayacucho", in Carlos Iván Degregori (ed.), *Las rondas campesinas y la derrota de Sendero Luminoso,* Lima, IEP, 1996, p. 202.

## CASE TWO: PERU

### Nation and community in the Andes

"Seen from the capital, the peasants of Ayacucho tend to appear as a homogeneous social group. Nothing could be more untrue." Thus Peruvian anthropologist José Coronel opens his account of the rebellion started by Shining Path and the ensuing counterinsurgency war in the province of Huanta in the Ayacucho.[16] His central observation is that the war was won by the Committees for Civil Defence (CDC) and that even though the creation of CDCs was part of the counterinsurgency strategy of the armed forces, the will of the peasants themselves was decisive in their formation. This conclusion is reached by closely tracing events in three selected communities and comparing the data with developments in other provinces and at the national level. All data, except for those that deal with events on the national level, were collected during fieldwork and extended visits to the affected communities. Hundreds of peasants have been systematically interviewed, often collectively, in open community meetings. Another article in the same volume analyses the strategies of the Maoist insurgents. Sources include interviews with former rebels and soldiers.

In this Peruvian drama, the turning point comes when Shining Path, after celebrating its second national conference in 1982, decides to carry out the last stage of the First Phase of the Prolonged People's War strategy, baptised 'Whipping in Order to Advance Towards the Bases of Support.'[17] In the high mountain communities of Huanta, this whipping meant the killing of traditional authorities and the installation of Popular Committees. However, the replacement of the *varayoc*, or 'staff-holders', with young Shining Path cadres didn't only go against current political arrangements, but also against an entire morality.

A defining characteristic of the Andean world is verticality. Different communities are situated at different heights along the deep valleys that cut the high mountain massifs. By belonging to different ecological zones, different communities have become differently connected to regional and central authorities in Ayacucho and Lima. In valley bottoms, irrigation and comparatively favourable temperatures permit intensive agriculture and urbanisation at centres like the town of Huanta. Further up, conditions for agriculture grow worse. At the top, the lands are suited for little but pasture and the growing of potatoes. Until the agrarian reform of the late 1960s, a majority of the peasants in the lower zones worked as serfs on big, private estates. Above this colonial world, *iquichanos*, though still subject to work obligations, were allowed a marginal existence in communities governed by traditional authorities. Here, all heads of family had to participate in a hierarchical system of civil-religious positions of authority.. The production cycle was regulated by a series of communal fiestas and work efforts. Communitarian

---

[16]  José Coronel, "Violencia política y respuestas campesinas en Huanta", in: Degregori (ed.), *ibid.*, p. 29.

[17]  Mao divided the Prolonged People's War into three phases: Defensive (establishing the bases), Strategic Equilibrium, and Offensive. Shining Path opened Phase II in 1988.

life put a premium on 'good conduct', defined as dedication to the community and by clearly prescribed roles. The *varayoc* always had to be consulted. In cases of transgression, they had the customary legitimate power to persuade or punish in order to correct improper behaviour and repair the damage. The national judicial system was rarely, if ever consulted. As for school and church, the two big nation-building institutions, few pupils advanced beyond the third year and few priests bothered to climb the mountainsides. In 1979, 95 per cent of *iquichanos* only spoke their native Quechua.

Starting in 1968, left-leaning military governments of Peru expropriated the estates and attempted to build a co-operative, socialised agriculture. However, in general the peasants were more interested in establishing themselves as private farmers. As the government disregarded local authority patterns when naming the people who were to lead the collectives, by the late 1970s the co-operatives had disintegrated and the family had become the most important social unit in the lower areas. There, the *varayoc* system of the higher zones had fallen out of use long ago and was anyway stigmatised as backward by the residents of the valleys. To a certain extent, the national political parties, the peasant leagues that had been organised to carry out the agrarian reform, and the national police replaced the authority of the old estates, but in the main, valley communities found themselves in a power vacuum when Shining Path cadres started their work around 1976. The favoured recruiting ground was the school system that was far more extensive and accepted here than up in the mountains. In 1979, 70 per cent of the population in the valley was bilingual in Spanish and Quechua.

The contrasts between the two zones of the Andes were thus profound. Moreover, they mirrored the deep national cleavage between urban, modern, Spanish-speaking, rich and powerful Lima and a rural, backward, Indian, Quechua-speaking, poor and powerless countryside. For the peasants down in the valleys, the *iquichanos* symbolised a past they aspired to get out of. Agrarian reform and the national school system had exposed them to what Degregori calls 'the myth of progress', and by 1980, a substantial part of the young generation attended secondary schools and even university courses in Ayacucho. But in Huanta, and even more in Ayacucho, the students were strongly confronted with the same contempt that they themselves felt for the *iquichanos*. For many, the simple economistic interpretations and the rapid and action-oriented solutions offered by Shining Path became the answer.

**The revolution enters an Andean community**

At that time, Abimael Guzmán taught philosophy at the Huamanga University in Ayacucho and if nothing else he was a master of the art of simplifying the message of Marxism-Leninism.[18] On the other hand, he never bothered to analyse local contradictions. For his pupils and party cadres, the complexities of the Andean social landscape were resolved in a sea of 'semi-feudal masses' whose 'archaic'

---

[18]  This image of Guzmán was given to me by a former teacher at the Huamanga University.

ideas had to be overcome. Unfortunately for the masses in question, this most likely had to be done violently. In May, 1981, Guzmán warned his militants that they should prepare to cross 'the river of blood of the Revolution'.[19] Shining Path built an armed movement based on absolute loyalty to the great leader. Cadres always stressed that 'the thinking of President Gonzalo' (Guzmán's *nom-de-guerre*) was the party's most powerful weapon. The movement boasted of its coercive powers. The use of violence probably functioned as a kind of rite of passage.

With its simplified analysis of the evils of the present system, a disciplined and authoritarian approach, and promises of victory by 1985, young Shining Path cadres succeeded in expelling the weak police force and establishing a presence in the provinces around Ayacucho during 1981 and 1982. In Culluchaca, an *iquichano* community 1,000 metres above Huanta, residents remember them as 'the students' because of their youth and their triumphalist discourse: They would "take the city and all the authorities and the rich would disappear and then there will be no more contempt for the peasants of the heights".[20] But apart from the reference to discrimination the guerrillas had little to offer. The agrarian reform had done away with all work obligations and guaranteed their collective land titles. Shining Path entered not as an ally, but as a power, punishing adultery and cattle raiding.

In late 1982, the scene was set for the whipping of the bases. Resistance against the popular committees was interpreted as 'feudal-fatalist' thought. Shortly afterwards, as part of a strategy to 'strangle the cities' (disregarding the very complex and often kin-based trading patterns between town and countryside), the party decided to ban local markets. In November, representatives from Culluchaca and neighbouring *iquichano* communities secretly met and decided to co-ordinate action against the new power. In January, 1983, responding to the campaign against police stations and other government officesin Ayacucho, the government sent the Peruvian Marine Corps to battle the insurgents. In the Culluchaca area, the Marines and surviving *varayoc* quickly agreed to establish civil defence committees to keep Shining Path out. Residents of outlying areas had to move into multi-communal settlements close to army bases. In retaliation, Shining Path attacked the new settlements. During 1984, the guerrillas massacred 22 and 51 people in two such attacks. The Marines killed twelve in a Culluchaca hamlet where people preferred to stay behind. In the end, most people fled the violence and around 60 per cent of the population sought refuge in Huanta, Ayacucho or even Lima.

In 1986, after the Army replaced the Marines and during an apparent lull in Shining Path activity, a group of families decided to test the waters and return to Culluchaca. In 1989, Shining Path entered again and forcibly recruited seven youngsters. The second exile began and now the entire remaining population moved to a place halfway down to the valley. Here they were exposed to NGOs

---

[19]   Degregori, *op.cit.*, p. 198.
[20]   Coronel, *ibid.*, p. 70.

and government relief work and development programmes. As the danger of war faded, the CDC became involved in these activities, too. The *varayoc* system had disappeared, but now it reappeared in the CDC as this institution consciously involved everyone by rotating tasks and regularly appointed respected elders as leaders. In December, 1993, 120 of the original 350 families of Culluchaca returned to their original lands.

### Cycles of revolution and repression or dual violence

Geographically just above Huanta town, but culturally midway between traditional Culluchaca and the comparatively modern communities at the valley bottom, lies the community of Ocana. Since the expropriation of the estate to which Ocana belonged ten years earlier, no new authority had managed to crystallise. Shining Path was active already by 1976, quietly recruiting young students and slowly succeeding in building a kind of passive support network that gave food to passing Shining Path columns. Then, in 1983, the Marines entered. Three people were killed in Ocana and seven in neighbouring Pampa for presumed collaboration with the guerrillas. Neighbours knew this to be untrue, but recognised a message of collective punishment. In July 1984, Shining Path demonstrated their punitive powers, too. They killed several members of two particular families for allegedly providing the Marines with information about guerrilla activity. The two families in question were both among the slightly better off, but were also closely related to a majority of the other families.

The Marines didn't bother to check the suspects. Among the different branches of Peru's armed forces, the Marines are commonly known as the most urban and racist. For the officers and soldiers from the Pacific coast, Ayacucho was Indian, backward and completely infected with guerrillas. Their counterinsurgency campaign was indiscriminate and brutal, aiming at terrorising people away from the revolution. However, in spite of the terror, the people of Ocana and most neighbouring communities refused to collaborate with the Marines in setting up CDCs. In 1985, after much criticism from Peruvian and international human rights groups abroad, and as Alan García and his Social Democratic APRA replaced the conservative Fernando Belaúnde government, the Marines were pulled out and replaced with army units.

In 1990, Ocana residents finally agreed to set up a CDC in co-operation with the army. The important posts, however, were staffed with younger men who tended to abuse their office, for instance by threatening to take the lands of villagers in exile. So most families still tried to appear neutral in the struggle between the army and the guerrillas. They didn't report passing guerrilla columns and in CDC service they dragged their feet. By 1995, the community still suffered a lack of internal cohesion. Reconstruction and development work was performed with visibly less enthusiasm than in e.g. Culluchaca.

400 metres below Huanta town lies Cangari, one of 24 settlements with irrigated lands on the valley bottom. With 100 families and a comparatively well-educated population, and situated at an important crossroads, Cangari received

special attention both from Shining Path and the Marines. Apart from an irrigation board, the community had not had any recognised authority since the fall of the estate system and there were many unresolved conflicts. Shining Path entered early, recruiting students and offering their services as day labourers to prosperous farmers. The revolutionaries ignored the peasant leagues. They probably succeeded in establishing widespread, passive support, but when Shining Path forbade people to go to the markets, the order was simply ignored in Cangari. Then came the Marines. In August and October, 1983, the area suffered two massacres with six and 49 victims. In Cangari 15 people were killed during the reign of Marines, most of them belonging to four specific families. Cangari refused to establish a CDC. Communities that did were attacked by Shining Path. These were years of dual violence and studied neutrality.

The army that replaced the Marines in 1985 increasingly used dialogue in their relations with the local population. In 1995, the army base in Huanta even allowed local boys to do their service locally. Extra-judicial killings still took place, but much more selectively. For their part, Shining Path killed a local, highly esteemed peasant league leader and this produced much resentment. In 1988, the stage was set for 'Strategic Equilibrium', but now the inhabitants of Cangari refused to collaborate with the guerrillas. In ten years, Shining Path had delivered nothing but blood and hardship. The army proposed to set up a CDC and now Cangari accepted. In September, 1990, Shining Path retaliated. 70 guerrilla soldiers engaged the CDC in a four-hour battle. On the Cangari side, everyone participated, men and women. People knew that those who acted individually would be avenged either by the army or by the guerrillas. The Cangari CDC won, and without casualties. A year later, in October, 1991, Shining Path attacked again, with 120 fighters. The Cangari CDC asked for help from the army base. All they received were grenades and ammunition, but once more they beat the guerrillas and suffered only one killed. The following year the Cangari CDC even attacked a passing Shining Path column and turned 'the young lads' (*¡eran tan muchachos!*) over to the army.

Thus the people of Cangari come out of the war as more united and more proud than before. The peasants who had been maltreated by the marines and considered 'masses' by the guerrillas now exercise local autonomy through a CDC that dedicates itself to communal mobilisations and development projects. Together with another 17 peasants from the area, a Cangari civil defence leader participates on the election ticket of an independent civic union that beats the traditional parties and takes municipal power in Huanta. It is also worthy of note that Andean culture, understood as the more 'authentic' musical and artistic traditions of the *iquichanos*, emerged from the war with a much higher status than before. Coronel interprets this as another effect of the increased respect that *iquichanos* earned in the valley and elsewhere as the first group to resist and beat Shining Path, but also as a sign of increased peasant autonomy vis-à-vis the urbanites of Huanta and Ayacucho.

## Six conclusions about local history

From the wartime histories of Culluchaca, Ocana and Cangari, José Coronel draws a series of conclusions that are worth repeating. The first has regard to the relative power vacuum in the province after the agrarian reform that allowed for the establishment of alternative authorities, particularly in divided communities like Ocana. The second focuses on the exclusivist and triumphalist attitude of Shining Path. The lack of interest in building alliances and lack of medium-term planning meant that they had nothing to offer in a sustained war and against an army that learned to apply dialogue. Third comes the total disregard for local history. By applying an outside paradigm focusing solely on material conditions and a single, national context, they ended up reproducing colonial attitudes against the backward peasant masses.

The fourth is the fact that in spite of the terror, the Marines didn't succeed in setting up CDCs and that those which were eventually set up at the insistence of the army performed badly in divided communities. CDCs function best when they include elements of traditional authority patterns and thus may be said to express the will of the community. In these cases they become new, civil institutions that engage in communal development. Moreover, they do not automatically militarise community life, as is often assumed in human rights reports. Fifth, far from strangling parasitic cities and liberating rural hinterlands, the war accelerated modernisation. Never before has the state had a greater presence in the Huanta region and never before have iquichanos and valley dwellers so eagerly and optimistically sought connections with national institutions. Finally, peasants participate in politics as never before, but in a locally based party with a locally determined agenda. They distrust traditional political discourse and concentrate on practical development.

## Lessons for the human rights reporter

Comparing the Peruvian material with the case of the Salvadoran Truth Commission above, the isolated testimony as a reporting format can be said to produce a series of photo slides where Coronel and Degregori tape video films. Further, by limiting the focus to the illegitimate behaviour of the armed forces of the countries in question, as most human rights reports do, the slide series necessarily produce images of helpless victims and irresponsible governments. It is against such a background that the rebellion of the chorus appears as a surprising outcome.

An extended reporting format, for instance that which was used in the country reports of previous editions of *Human Rights in Developing Countries Yearbook*, which includes sections on social, economic and cultural rights, may allow the reader to glimpse the underlying socio-economic problems and structural tensions. Detailed sections on political and civil rights can describe the limitations of the rule of law and hence indicate eventual power vacuums. In keeping with the film metaphor used above, such an extended format could be compared with a silent movie of stylised action – e.g. army abuse, official silence and cover-ups – set in a continually changing landscape, but always containing identical features – e.g. prison cells, instruments and methods of torture, etc. What happens when we watch such films is that we fill in the dialogue and the plot with our own, locally constructed conjectures about what is really happening. In Northern Europe, the film will frequently invoke memories of e.g. fascist dictatorships and the persecution of the great social movements produced by industrialism. Thus a well-intended lack of context produces a wrong context.

But if we fill in the blanks in the Salvadoran slide series with the character masks, the visions and the meanings characteristic of a society closer to El Salvador than Northern Europe, for instance those that we attributed above to the Peruvian actors, we learn new details of the Salvadoran war. Particularly helpful is the reconstruction of Shining Path's early clandestine work and the discussion of how Shining Path and the Marines thought about the war and the civilian population they tried to control. The descriptions of traditional and changing authority patterns is also an important feature of Coronel's and Degregori's narratives. The result is that we see a film that gives a credible but also moving drama with its own dangers of seduction: how can we know that Coronel's and Degregori's reconstruction isn't their own dramatisation of the material that they collected? We cannot know for certain, but at least we can falsify the less likely reconstructions. In this case, it would seem that by relying on a similar example from a similar society, we can understand more about the Salvadoran war than by extrapolating from European or North American experiences with political unrest.

To its credit, the 1990 report on Peru in the *Human Rights in Developing Countries Yearbook* makes it very clear that "the ruthless method of the insurgent movements, in particular the Shining Path, have seriously disrupted the democratic process".[21] About Shining Path the report says that "it seems safe to conclude that the organisation does not share even the basic values and principles expressed in human rights and humanitarian law instruments".[22] But the report also concludes that "while the political violence to a large extent must be attributed to the insurgents (...) it is beyond doubt that Government forces, too, have been guilty of extra-judicial executions, disappearances (...) on a scale which shows a clear pattern rather than constituting individual violations. Those responsible do not face trial (...) The outgoing García Government (1985-90) initially made some pledges to respect human rights and curb the activities of the military and police. These pledges have largely been left unheeded (...) and the government and leading politicians have increasingly resorted to the policy known from the Belaúnde Government (1980-85) of attributing the human rights violations to the actions of the insurgent movements and to exaggerations and distortions presented by 'outsiders' such as the international press and Amnesty International".[23]

---

[21] Allan Rosas, "Peru", in Bård-Anders Andreassen and Theresa Swinehart, *Human Rights in Developing Countries. 1990 Yearbook,* Kehl, N.P.Engel, Publisher, p. 304.
[22] Rosas, *ibid.,* p. 313.
[23] Rosas, *ibid.,* p. 305.

## Towards a transformation of the local into the civil?

Whereas Coronel and Degregori give a narrative of the war, and try to understand historical developments, as a human rights report the Yearbook text is normative. This means that it automatically becomes a judgement of the Peruvian government, even if the author of the 1990 report does his best to inform the reader about the problems that face Peruvian authorities. What is more fundamental, however, is that the ideal against which the Peruvian government is judged to a large degree is alien to the Andean political communities in which the war was actually fought. As Wilson notes, "accusations of state violence rest upon a clear distinction between the state and civil society which is not the way that either society or violence are organised".[24] In Culluchaca, neither Shining Path nor the Marines killed civilians per se; they killed 'Indians' or 'masses' that served the enemy. Moreover, to a certain extent, both parties performed within an Andean pattern of legitimate authority. In its role as a new ruler, Shining Path (and later, the Marines) could be hard and inflexible, particularly in the process of replacing an old, unjust and abusive ruler.

However, a new ruler must also operate within the logic of the local law. Degregori says that the fundamental of Andean common law is "persuasion, conviction, to reach the restitution of the group".[25] In this terrain Shining Path failed completely. The revolutionaries didn't protect their clients, they ordered women to work, they prohibited the fairs, they killed instead of applying corrective punishment, and, perhaps most importantly, they named young and inexperienced 'students' as leaders. The following testimony from a former rebel and schoolteacher reveals this dynamic: "The worst that Shining Path did was to have confided in very young people in each community, with very little experience (…) They immediately distorted totally the plans for government of Shining Path, and adopted vengeful and quarrelsome attitudes. Suddenly a father had a fight with another father because of some question of boundaries between fields, or because of animals, of theft, of losses, of quarrels with spouses or with women; as Shining Path had given them the responsibility for the community, they began taking their own reprisals, that is when the massacres start, that is where the harmony breaks up".[26]

In short, they broke with a local morality, and indeed Shining Path rebels were frequently portrayed as demons or the much feared pishtaqos, beings that kill solitary wanderers and suck the fat out of their victims. In contrast stand the Marines and the army, that certainly killed, but didn't try to impose a new order. In popular imagery, they were understood more as foreign mercenaries, possibly from Argentina. Compared with the rebels, the armed forces negotiated a deal with the existing community, about its outward defence. In other aspects of life, the peasants were generally left alone. Unlike the popular committees, the CDCs were allowed to fit local authority patterns and even to transform themselves into a kind

---

24     Wilson, *op.cit.*, p. 140.
25     Degregori, *op.cit.*, p. 202.
26     Degregori, *ibid.*, p. 196.

of stronger and more autochthonous civil society. Here lie the roots of Degregori's and Coronel's optimistic conclusion, too. They see the chorus of locals enter the scene and take up an independent role in politics at the national level.

It is difficult to see that this emancipating development could have been caught by human rights reporters. It might be argued that the human rights reports that condemned the Marines contributed to its replacement by a more dialogue-minded army. But it might also be argued that the reports in question just made the armed forces close ranks against the outsiders and convince practical military men about the impracticality of idealistic human rights reporters.

## CASE THREE: GUATEMALA

### Conflict lines at the national level

The counterinsurgency campaign that the Guatemalan army carried out against various guerrilla factions from 1981 to 1983 was executed with such brutality that it has become a sort of paradigmatic example of the cruelty of right-wing dictatorships in human rights and solidarity literature. The conventional analysis of the bloodbath usually comprises the same issues as those that were discussed by IDHUCA for the Salvadoran case: an army at the service of the rich quenches the democratic aspirations of an impoverished people. Under a kind of army-controlled dictatorship since 1954, in Guatemala the oligarchy had been guaranteed that the poor, and the Mayas of the highlands in particular, would serve as cheap labour on big plantations and that no government would ever initiate agrarian reforms. When popular organisations challenged this state of affairs in the 1970s, and tried to democratise society, the army reacted with repression and terror. With all roads towards peaceful change closed, guerrilla groups formed. After years of war, international pressure, and long negotiations, a peace agreement was reached in 1996. Perhaps the most sinister part of the counterinsurgency warfare was the creation of Patrols for Civil Defence (Patrullas de Autodefensa Civil), PACs, in which all adult males had to serve the army in a paramilitary system and carry out surveillance against community neighbours. To the army massacres of the early 80s were added the abuses of the patrols.[27]

There is no doubt that Guatemala's government and army were responsible for gross human rights violations during the 1980s. Nor is there any doubt that forced participation in the civil defence patrols was a violation of human rights as well as Guatemala's own 1985 constitution that guarantees freedom of assembly. But for many Guatemalans, and particularly the Mayas of the highlands, community law takes precedence before state law and individual human rights. In many communities the patrols therefore became a community institution. And whereas most human rights reports focus on the coercive aspects of patrol service, after prolonged fieldwork in heavily affected areas, Stoll and Kobrak find that for the peasants, the obligation to defend the community was the supreme value.

---

[27]  See Manz, *op.cit.;* Americas Watch, *Guatemala: A Nation of Prisoners,* New York, 1984; Americas Watch, *Persecuting Human Rights Monitors: The CERJ in Guatemala,* New York, 1989.

Moreover, they report that a clear majority of the population in the areas they investigated thought of the war as a conflict initiated by outsiders.[28]

In this perspective, the PAC gave thousands of Mayan peasants an opportunity to play an active role in the calamities that engulfed them, albeit by accepting an alliance with one of the two armed powers. In 1982, when the institution was introduced, people had to choose sides. In the areas where the EGP guerrilla (Ejército Guerrillero de los Pobres) sought control, the alternative was to join an EGP column or become 'organised masses' in an 'irregular fighting force' or FIL (Fuerzas Irregulares de Lucha).[29] As a movement that subscribed to the thesis that the Revolution would be achieved through a Prolonged People's War, EGP did not differentiate between civilians and fighters. On the other side stood the army, threatening to eliminate the entire community if it were suspected of EGP collaboration. But the sides they had to choose between locally were not necessarily the national left and the right of the conventional human rights-cum-solidarity text outlined above. Nor was the individual the agent that had to choose. By focussing on local social change, too, Stoll and Kobrak are able to offer a much more powerful analysis of the war and the civil patrols.

## Conflict lines at the local level

A whole array of anthropological and historical studies of Maya-speaking communities in Guatemala and Mexico during the last 50 years underline the importance of the community as a social unit. The classic picture is that of the 'closed corporate community painted by Eric Wolf, which in many ways was a self-governing unit encapsulated in the respective national states.[30] Self-rule was upheld through the maintenance of a civil-religious hierarchy (cofradía and/or municipalidad indígena), in which men performed the duties that were necessary to keep the world in balance. On top sat the elders or principals (principales), supreme interpreters of the laws of the gods and the ancestors. In such a system, the authority of fathers over sons, land inheritance and religious loyalties become connected and supremely important issues. The great challenge in hundreds of Mayan communities since the 1950s has been how to accommodate a rapidly growing population and deal with external pressures such as work migration, Catholic and Protestant missionary activities, a national school system, and the 'myth of progress' within the old order. This was impossible, and conflicts between costumbristas who defend custom, and modernisers, most frequently in the form of the catequistas of reforming Catholicism, have been long and bitter and occasionally violent. Still, as scholars like Paul and Demarest and Ebel show, the result has often been a fairly open competitive political system that in many

---

[28]   David Stoll, *op.cit.;* Paul Hans Robert Kobrak, *Village Troubles: The Civil Patrols in Aguacatán, Guatemala,* Ph.D. Dissertation (Sociology), University of Michigan. 1996.

[29]   Later also known as FGL (*Fuerzas Guerrilleras Locales*).

[30]   Eric Wolf, *Sons of the Shaking Earth,* University of Chicago Press, 1959.

ways have been more responsive to community tension than has been the case on the national level.[31]

In a comprehensive study of the war between the guerrillas and the government, which mostly took place in Mayan lands, French sociologist Yvon Le Bot observes that there was little or no articulation between these great changes in the Mayan world and the left-right cleavages of the national community that sent soldiers into local communities. He sees the young, modernising Mayas as carriers of a social movement that introduce new productive and organisational techniques into isolated Mayan worlds. Peasant leagues, co-operatives and a virtual small-scale industrial revolution were transforming the social landscape. For Le Bot the armed conflict was a "rupture with the social movement" rather than "its derivative".[32] This point is further illustrated when he analyses events in a trade union movement that concentrated more on revolutionary positioning vis-à-vis the state than on collective action: "The behaviour of the oligarchy (...) habituated to see a subversive threat in any social demand, and the behaviour of the revolutionaries, who interpret every social struggle as a stage and a promise in the perspective of a radical political rupture (...) reinforce each other and prevent the constitution of a social movement".[33] Moreover, the militaristic strategy of the two contenders for state power also obstructs and delays a transformation of local communities into a national, civil society.

## Cycles of revolution and repression or dual violence

Aguacatán in the department of Huehuetenango is one Mayan community where the changes in the Mayan world and the social movement that preceded the war are unusually well documented by scholars.[34] The town lies in a valley where strong natural springs give favourable conditions for intensive agriculture. Above rises the Cuchumatanes mountain range, along which runs the border with the Ixil-speaking municipality of Nebaj to the north. To the east, down the valley, lie the lands of the K'iche' Maya, like Nebaj belonging to the province of El Quiché. In addition to the urban centre and the surrounding irrigated lands, Aguacatán comprises some 40 outlying communities. Up on the mountain, the population is mainly K'iche', immigrants who settled in this remote area around 1900 because they refused to send their children to government schools. After three generations, they were still considered 'visitors' by the Awakatekos, along with the Spanish-speaking ladinos who used to dominate local politics and monopolise relations with the wider world.

---

[31] Benjamin D. Paul and William J. Demarest, "The Operation of a Death Squad in San Pedro la Laguna" and Roland H. Ebel, "When Indians Take Power: Conflict and Consensus in San Juan Ostuncalco", in Robert Carmack (ed.), *Harvest of Violence. The Mayan Indians and the Guatemalan Crisis*, University of Oklahoma Press, 1988.

[32] Yvon Le Bot, *La guerra en tierras mayas. Comunidad, violencia y modernidad en Guatemala(1970-1992)*, México D.F.: Fondo de Cultura Económica, 1995, p. 26

[33] Le Bot, *ibid.*, p. 158.

[34] Douglas Brintnall, *Revolt Against the Dead: The Modernization of a Maya Community in the Highlands of Guatemala*, New York: Gordon and Breach, 1979; Kobrak, *op.cit.*

Up to the late 1950s, Awakateko society was tightly controlled by the principals, who maintained cultural autonomy by allowing local ladinos to recruit labour to the plantations on the coast and the army to recruit soldiers through a system of local military commissioners. Then came modernisation in the form of reform-minded Catholic priests and missionaries who introduced new agricultural techniques that made it possible for sons to become economically independent of their fathers and even refuse to do service in the traditional hierarchy. A Catholic Father's defence of a young and ambitious Awakateko who refused to serve the elders paved the way for the fall of the system. Since then, Awakatekos have moved into new positions everywhere, replacing 'the law of tradition' with 'the law of the school'. Eventually, in 1970, Aguacatán elected its first Mayan mayor, a Christian Democrat. Now the municipality and electoral politics have replaced the civil-religious hierarchy as the focus of local loyalties. Up on the mountain, however, there had not been any corresponding emancipation and local K'iche's were often still dependent on patronage from urban ladinos. Moreover, these K'iche's were often in conflict over land with the Awakatekos down in the valley, and sometimes also among themselves.

For the EGP guerrillas, Aguacatán was a zone of possible expansion from their strongholds across the mountains, in Ixil Maya territory. There may have been clandestine guerrilla organising in Aguacatán, but Kobrak finds little evidence of this. Instead, the guerrilla movement appears by way of a one-day occupation of the town centre and an armed propaganda meeting, and the ambush of an army truck that left 30 soldiers dead near the outlying community of Llano Coyote in March, 1981. Up on the mountain, during 1980 and 1981, EGP established a network in communities like Chex, Pajuíl Chex and Las Majadas, storing weapons, ammunition and food. As Stoll shows was the case for the neighbouring Ixil-speaking municipalities, the Mayans who were willing to explore contacts with the guerrillas belonged to factions that for one reason or another were dissatisfied with the status quo and on the lookout for possible allies. In the case of Chex, a community already sorely divided, the possibility of enlisting armed allies was to prove fatal.

The army launched its great offensive in late 1981. The armed forces first secured the Pan-American highway that crosses the Maya-speaking highlands through southern El Quiché, and from there pressed northwards to the Ixil country. During the offensive villages suspected of EGP collaboration were eliminated. In March, 1982, the army arrived in Aguacatán. Llano Coyote and Pajuíl Chex were burned and respectively 37 and 53 people were massacred, possibly as a revenge in the case of Llano Coyote and most likely as part of a general strategy to sow terror all across the mountain communities in the latter case. That same month there was a coup in Guatemala City and Army General and charismatic Protestant Efraín Ríos Montt was named president. He offered a general amnesty and started to organise the civilian population into civil patrols, possibly inspired by the irregular battalions of the EGP. Shortly afterwards, people from the communities up on the mountain met to discuss recent events. The decision was not whether the community was to organise, but with whom. As a K'iche' agricultural promoter explained to Kobrak: ".. we were between two laws. Finally we accepted the army and the guerrilla got mad".[35] In most communities, this meant that EGP contacts were either allowed to leave quietly or 'amnestied' by way of serving in the patrol. In Las Majadas, it meant the end of a divided community as some families left for EGP territory and another group moved to Chex. In Chex itself it meant that the faction that controlled the civil patrol turned 27 men over to the army. The 27 were never seen again. The following month EGP descended on Chex and 22 people were massacred in an action that locals understand as a punishment for the decision to join the army.

In this manner 300 to 450 people were killed during the war in Aguacatán, in at least 11 massacres in seven communities. The EGP was responsible for four. In the town centre five or six 'suspects' disappeared; the rest of the war was ten years of patient patrolling in order to keep the EGP away and assuage the army. This is the situation described as being 'between two fires' and that Stoll defines as follows: "In Ixil country, village massacres began in 1980, following EGP ambushes that killed soldiers. The army presumed that nearby civilians knew about the impending attack and failed to warn it; [Ixils] argue that, since the guerrillas warned members of their network to leave the area before an ambush, the bystanders whom the army killed were the innocents." In such desperate straits, the honourable course of action for a Mayan peasant was to unite with his community and fight for its collective survival. In retrospect, the K'iche's on the mountain ridge were satisfied with their decision: "Because we accepted the law of [the military base], we are on our land, with our families. If we had accepted the guerrillas, who knows where we would be know. Perhaps in the jungle"[36]

## Human rights reporting caught between the local and the national

Against this background we understand how a statement like "we have sinned greatly" can be a meaningful explanation of the war. In the traditional system, the greatest obligation was to preserve the heritage of the ancestors. Guatemalan anthropologist Claudia Dary and a team of 126 Mayas have interviewed hundreds of war victims from five different language groups in eight municipalities about the causes of the war.[37] Divine punishment (disobedience), dual violence and poverty (or inequality) were given as the most common explanations. Richard Wilson writes about the war in Q'eqchi' territory (far more traditional than Aguacatán) and shows how local narratives about the war place it within a world where the laws of the ancestors have been disregarded, thus inviting punishment. The leader of a large educational programme in Q'eqchi' territory confirmed the

---

[35] Kobrak, *ibid.*, p. 142.

[36] The informant here probably refers to the so-called Resistance Communities or CPR (*Comunidades de Población en Resitencia*) formed under EGP control during the war, and that possibly underwent a similar emancipatory process vis-à-vis its armed protector. See Kobrak, *ibid.*

[37] Claudia Dary, *El derecho internacional humanitario y el orden jurídico maya. Una perspectiva histórico cultural,* Guatemala, FLACSO y CICR, 1996.

importance of the religious idiom during a visit I made there in 1997. He added that his congregation, when explaining the workings of the capitalist market, always accompanied the new visions of a national political scene with the idea of negotiation and dialogue. He claimed that the war had taken fewer lives in 'his' areas than in areas where other congregations had put more stress on the fight for liberation.[38]

Militarily, the Guatemalan guerrillas had lost the war by 1984. The areas that had been hardest hit were the areas where the insurgents established their bases, far away from the modernised areas where the social movement described by Le Bot was and is strongest. And within these areas, it was the divided communities that suffered the worst massacres. It was also in such communities that the war continued to take lives even as the fighting subsided and both the army and the guerrillas mostly stayed in their bases. In Llano Coyote in Aguacatán, where insurgents probably received logistical support and the army committed a massacre in 1982, the civil patrol was never able to overcome local divisions. In 1993, a group of eleven presented a complaint against the PAC to the Huehuetenango office of the government human rights procurator. They complained about harassment and insisted on their right not to patrol. The next day an official delegation from the procurator arrived to investigate. An angry crowd of more that 200 villagers surrounded the government jeep. Patrollers rounded up the resisters and "roughed up the ombudsman when he tried to intervene. ... Just then the military commissioner in Aguacatán arrived and angrily ordered the patrollers to desist. After four hours of forced detention the armed patrollers finally allowed the government officials to leave".[39]

Similar episodes took place repeatedly in Guatemala in the early 1990s. In one case, patrollers opened fire against a human rights demonstration led by a popular organisation closely connected with the EGP. Such incidents show how the patrol system eventually contributed to a kind of freezing of Guatemalan politics, forcing an incipient local democracy into the sterile confrontations of national politics. As in El Salvador, the focus on government responsibility also situated human rights discourse in the camp of the national left. But the episode in Llano Coyote also demonstrates the strength of what Kobrak, following local idiom, has termed 'local law': when the municipal judge arrived the day after and insisted on speaking with the patrol leaders, the crowd answered: "Take us all, because we are all responsible".[40] A few days later, a young health promoter and patrol enthusiast explained the limits of Guatemala's freedom of assembly to Kobrak in the following terms: "Yes, there it's voluntary ... here there is another system. It is the national law that makes the patrols voluntary. But there is also a local law. And here we have decided that all must continue to patrol".[41]

---

[38]  Richard A. Wilson, *Maya resurgence in Guatemala. Q'eqchi' Experiences,* University of Oklahoma Press, 1995.

[39]  Kobrak, *op.cit.,* p. 237.

[40]  Kobrak, *ibid.,* p. 237.

[41]  Kobrak, *ibid.,* p. 240.

# CONCLUSIONS

## Interpretative frames

Yvon Le Bot opens his book by affirming that "Of all the characteristics of the Guatemalan war, those that follow from its regional and continental inscriptions are the less original and the easiest to capture".[42] To this might well be added David Stoll's conclusion about how human rights and solidarity narratives about the same war have been constructed within non-local frames: "What seems clear consequences of national and international developments to cosmopolitan observers are, for local people, wrapped in all the ambiguity of local life".[43] Here both Le Bot and Stoll point to an important limitation of human rights reporting, which is the question of interpretative frames.

Events acquire meaning through their inscriptions in narratives, either as we live them ourselves, or through an act of interpretation. In the first case, the event will form part of a local history in which the individual also participates. In the second case, the meaning will be determined by comparisons to events experienced or known by the listener – events that may belong to totally different contexts. Thus judgements about the meaning of events will be quite different, at least in the case of a human rights reporter and a victim or a perpetrator. Moreover, as we noticed when we discussed the dangers of ethnographic seduction, the assignment of a meaning to a past event will also be determined by what is at stake in the present. There is no easy solution to this problem of translation. For the human rights reporter, the challenge is to be aware of the situation and strive to create increasingly more congruent narratives that enable meaningful dialogue. This is what Kobrak and Stoll do by informing the reader about what they believe are the contexts that shape local events and the narratives through which Mayans interpret events and decide what action to take. This is also what Degregori and Coronel do for the Peruvian war.

Another way to deal with the problem is to define a fixed format into which different narratives may be translated. In our case, one could, for instance, compare what Mayan 'local law' has to say about relations between rulers and ruled with the corresponding human rights government law, and delimit overlapping zones of sanctionable behaviour. This solution has many advantages and it also has the merit of taking locals seriously. Claudia Dary's examination of Mayan history and Mayan custom pertaining to warfare, norms for the exercise of authority and the treatment of war victims is a good example. In effect she recognises that a Mayan variety of humanitarian law might be constructed from the historical record of the conquest and a normalisation of current custom.[44] But this solution has its problems, too.

The first is that Mayan local law is, in fact, illegal. The law of the lands of the Mayans is the national republican law of Guatemala. True, by ratifying the

---

[42]  Le Bot, *op.cit.*, p. 18.
[43]  Stoll, *op.cit.*, p. 259.
[44]  Dary, *op.cit.*

Convention on the Rights of Indigenous and Tribal Peoples, Guatemala accepts the validity of customary law (Mayan local law) in conflicts within the Mayan cultural community. Interestingly, Kobrak notes that the local human rights prosecutor often asked Mayan individuals who complained about being forced to perform community duties to take their share of village labour, even if such a community obligation was contrary to the country's constitution. On the other hand, a high-ranking official at the prosecutor's central office told Kobrak that "local law" was a "pre-modern vestige", a "product of rural norms", and argued that "(...) we cannot extend to a group of civilians control and authority over their community if corresponding state institutions exist".[45] This point brings us back to the difficult position of the community between the state and the individual, and also the problems of communicating with people who are engaged with creating an integrated, modern society out of a mosaic of local communities.

The second is that human rights law is a law that presupposes the existence of states and citizens, concepts that may be incomprehensible in a traditional community. At a deeper level, this may be where much resistance towards human rights discourse in Latin America is located. It is felt that human rights are too idealistic in their complex, divided societies. More fundamentally, it might be argued that a mechanical application of human rights puts the local community in an unfairly disadvantageous position. Not because this is to measure local norms against an ideal, universal standard, but because the universal standard in question was formed in a much bigger and more sophisticated society in terms of institutional specialisation and available narratives. Very often the human rights reporter will belong to that society, too. This problem becomes clear when we compare the comparatively context-rich human rights texts about the Guatemalan civil patrols that Americas Watch has published. In a report called *Guatemala: A Nation of Prisoners* we read the following:

> As far as the community is concerned, the creation of the civil patrol system reporting to the local military commander effectively displaces traditional forms of self-government and maintenance of order ... It represents a complete disregard for community elders and elected leaders, and for judicial settlement of disputes ... Militarising the rural population, indeed, requires replacing civilian and indigenous values with new ones.[46]

This quotation contains many valid points, but it disregards the collective nature and the negotiated quality of the patrols that Stoll and Kobrak have demonstrated at least in some areas. The reasons are, I believe, firstly that the authors of the Americas Watch reports have missed the communitarian logic that impels patrollers to behave as they do (e.g. they believe they punish free-riders when Americas Watch say they persecute people who think differently). Secondly, the authors also seem to presume that patrollers are one class of community members,

---

[45]  Kobrak, *op.cit.*, p. 251.
[46]  Americas Watch, *op.cit.*, p. 82.

whereas resisters (or human rights activists) constitute another, victimised class of citizens. Thirdly, the community that Americas Watch portrays is an ideal form that doesn't exist or at best is a local replica of the national community that one finds in highly integrated societies, and where national and local conflict lines are almost identical. As the revolt against the dead in Aguacatán demonstrated, young Awakatekos might have found little civility in the indigenous norms that they fought against. But on the other hand, the portrait of the ideal community that Americas Watch paints may show the way to a future local civil society.

## Local and national norms

At this point, Veena Das's comparisons of the state and the local community as similar communities or zones of collective human action may be helpful. Conventionally, she says, the local community has been thought of as a sphere of intimate, face-to-face interaction, whereas the state is an imagined community demanding allegiance to distant, bureaucratic institutions. The hidden assumption seems to be that it is better to be disciplined by a known face than by an anonymous agent. Such a contrast ignores the occurrence of local violence. In our case it is worth noting that Kobrak and Stoll do not romanticise the rule of the elders. Das suspects that the two forms of community in question really are opposite poles of a conceptual axis that stretches from tradition to modernity and she sees a lack of realism in current discussions about cultural rights where the local community tends to serve as a "resonance for re-moralising areas of life denuded of moral meaning by bureaucratic and impersonal rationality".[47] Possibly this is what Americas Watch had in mind when their report suggested that the patrols threatened 'civilian and indigenous values'. It is, in fact, not unreasonable to believe that the indigenous civil-religious hierarchy of the Mayans is the historical outcome of a Spanish imperial colonisation no less brutal than the war of the 1980s, a fusion of Catholic brotherhoods and a clan.

The observation made by the former Shining Path cadre about how young Andean peasants began to 'take their own reprisals' when they became leaders of the popular committees, and the allegation from the Salvadoran peasant that members of the local civil defence patrols began to 'take their own reprisals', confirm Das's scepticism. Consider also the following observation about the introduction of the national school system and the war from a Q'eqchi' elder:

> The child that knows how to read and write at once says he may know anything and everything, he won't ask for support or advice from the ancients, for what would he want the advice of the great if they don't know anything? True? So, that's where the error lies.[48]

Local law, too, may provoke rebellions. Applying this perspective on what it means to be young in the world of the *iquichanos*, it would seem that the Peruvian

---

[47] Das, *op. cit.*, p. 51.
[48] Dary, *op.cit.*, p. 266.

anthropologists tend to paint an uncomplicated picture of the traditional Andean community.

Veena Das' characterisation of culture as 'the distribution of pain' also fits the cases that we have discussed. Particularly in El Salvador and in Guatemala, the front line that eventually crystallised between the army and the rebels consisted of repeated drawings of bloody lines between and inside of local communities forced to choose sides. Those that aligned themselves with the national ally that lost local territorial control were expelled or simply eliminated. In order to survive, the community was cleansed – and perhaps it cleansed itself, too.

Das's discussion of human rights and community obligations also contains another valuable lesson for this study. She first asks whether the state is "the only possible organisation of collectivities that can be bestowed with legal personality in the matter of rights".[49] Then she observes that the identities and meanings that we construct through social interaction (the 'culture' of the community in question in everyday parlance) rarely are 'finished' and immediately 'shareable'. Rather, they are "achieved and won" and thus they constitute a "hegemonic set of identifiable ideas".[50] She then defines culture as "both a system of shared meanings which defines the individual's collective life, as well as a system for the formulation of judgements which are used to exclude alterities, and which thus keep the individual strictly within the bounds defined by society".[51]

By applying these insights to our discussion of state and community rights and obligations, we realise how close is the relationship between the two political entities that compete for loyalties and identities in less integrated nations. Both want to organise our experiences, monopolise our memories and generally serve as conduits for our individual experiences. Both may be "crucial for the development of legal structures within which the collective dimension of human existence takes shape".[52] Das concludes that a solution to this conflict "can occur only if the state ceases to demand full ideological allegiance from the various collectivities which constitute it; and if communities, instead of demanding complete surrender from individual members on the pretext of preserving their culture, recognise the paradoxical links of confirmation and antagonism from its members. An individual's capacity to make sense of the world (…) presupposes the existence of collective traditions, but individuals must be able to experiment with these collective traditions by being allowed to live at their limits".[53]

**Human rights at the local level**

This brings us back to the discussion about the validity of human rights at the level of the local, and, in the cases of Peru and Guatemala, also indigenous, community. Given that human rights are fundamentally a systematisation of Western ideas

---

[49]  Das, *op.cit.*, p. 89.
[50]  Das, *ibid.*, p. 90.
[51]  Das, *ibid.*, p. 91-92.
[52]  Das, *ibid.*, p. 89.
[53]  Das, *ibid.*, p. 116.

about 'just rule' that give legitimacy to the state, there is no reason that non-state local authorities should not comply with a similar minimum standard for how to rule its members. It follows that political violence cannot be tolerated more on the local level than on the state level. From Das's observation about the need for individual freedom to keep a culture alive, it would even seem that human rights are a prerogative for positive social development. Indeed many young Mayans in Guatemala refer to the rule of the principals as gerontocratic.

The premise that events only acquire meaning when they are inscribed in narratives has important consequences not only for the interpretation of events, but also for their re-telling. Above, as we applied the slides and film metaphors to illustrate the shortcomings of different reporting formats, it was suggested that the most likely trap is the uncritical inscription of reported incidents into well-known and general narratives, often resulting in a mixing up with the context in which the observers themselves live. Our discussion of the art of taking testimonies indicated another subtle source of error. The seductive powers of sympathy easily obscure the border between human rights reporting and solidarity literature. An apparently easy way of combating this is to leave out as much detail as possible in order to appear neutral. This is the context-free approach. Some of the weaknesses of this solution have already been touched upon. Meaningful communication with victims and perpetrators becomes difficult and the resulting text is easily misused by the parties to the conflict as political ammunition because it tends to be constructed around Manichean opposites. Moreover, the normative thrust tends to polarise the situation instead of bringing people together – as was vividly demonstrated when civil patrols and human rights demonstrators fought each other in Guatemala.

From a human rights point of view, it is clear that the governments of El Salvador, Guatemala, and Peru gravely violated their own republican ideals, human rights and humanitarian law during the years of armed conflict. Still, it is important to note that the actual fighting was initiated by politico-military organisations representing a political project that disregarded fundamental democratic arrangements. This is most easily seen in the case of Peru, where the mechanical application of Maoist dogma by Shining Path also revealed the shortcomings of the theory of Prolonged People's War. In Guatemala, the EGP guerrilla movement in particular applied the same tactics when it started to organise the Mayan masses into irregular battalions. The leaders knew that this would provoke army retaliation, as had happened in the eastern part of the country in the 1960s. Other Guatemalan guerrilla forces did not rely on these tactics, and the result was a much cleaner war in their areas. The Salvadoran FMLN also occasionally created martyrs in order to increase recruitment, but in general they fought a cleaner war than their colleagues in Guatemala. Before the war, however, FMLN was responsible for a wave of politically motivated kidnappings and killings in order to collect money and maximise a social and political crisis that eventually led to civil war.[54]

---

[54] Jorge G. Castañeda, *La utopía desarmada. Intrigas, dilemas y promesa de la izquierda en América Latina.* Buenos Aires, Ariel, 1993.

Returning to the armies, our examinations of war stories from the three countries seem to put a particularly heavy responsibility on the Salvadoran army for its reliance on a Civil Defence organisation that from its inception was built on a party network. In Peru and in Guatemala, the army presented locals with a brutal ultimatum, but in effect accepted an alliance with local authorities. The Peruvian army (but not the Marines) appears to have done this quite consciously towards the end of the war, even allowing locals to serve in local units. In Guatemala, the picture is mixed. In some areas of the El Quiché department the patrols may perhaps be likened to El Salvador's rightwing Civil Defence by solely responding to one faction of the local K'iche' community. But in the lands immediately to the north, the Ixil Mayas little by little managed to conquer a space for independent action.

The state- and individual-oriented focus of human rights reporting tends to obscure both the responsibilities of the armed rebels and the response of the local community. The result has been an obscuring of the differences between the human rights and the solidarity agenda, and the consequent reading of human rights groups as a kind of eternal, and therefore irresponsible opposition. It is only in the 1990s that human rights reporters have started to focus on the non-governmental forces too, accepting, perhaps, an argument about political violence formulated by Pedro Nikken, former UN independent expert to El Salvador:

> The insurgent armed groups, that … in general terms, exercise a de facto authority over other people, possess an embryonic public power, that obliges them, just like the regular government, to keep within the limits set by human rights.[55]

The same demand could be laid at the door of community elders. The quest for giving protection to the community and different cultural traditions often blind us to the violence exercised by locals. This is where the concept of civil society enters, for this is the space where the local community must be permitted to live after integration. Not only that: according to democratic theory, the existence of a local space for voluntary forms of association may be crucial for the growth of a citizen-based polity because this is where individuals can "live at their limits". In the light of this wisdom, the transformation of the rule of the ancestors into a pluralistic Mayan municipality and the rebellion of the Andean chorus are positive events that may be guided also by informed human rights reporting.

---

[55]  IDHUCA, *op.cit.*, p. 1119.

# Constitutional Reform and Ethnicity in Kenya - Multiple Identities and State-Region Relations

*Bård-Anders Andreassen*

# INTRODUCTION

African countries in transition towards competitive, multiparty politics have one transitional challenge in common: The need for establishing or redefining constitutional legitimacy, and for constructing legitimate democratic institutions. In many countries of Sub-Saharan Africa this has been the main subject of 'transitional politics'. At stake is the formulation or reformulation of the 'basic law' of the land and the design of key political institutions for the exercise and control of state power. However, apart from concerns with constitutional documents, attention is being paid to the dynamic process of constitution-making. One dimension of this process concerns the creation of civic commitment and adherence to the principles of the constitution, or constitutionalism. Constitutionalism refers to the principles of constitutional authority, and adherence to these principles by the ruling elites. A key component of constitutionalism is the constraints put on both the legislative and executive branches of government, and the protection of the rights of minorities. This implies, for instance, that majoritarian democracy has to respect minority rights. Constitutional government is limited.[1] In Africa, however, this principle became seriously impaired in the years following independence. Soon after independence, the principle of limited government embodied in many of the independence constitutions in Africa was replaced by the practice of absolute government, which concentrated state power in the hands of the president. The constitutional practice that emerged was one of "constitutions without constitutionalism".[2]

Constitutional development operates within social and cultural contexts. In culturally divided societies the establishment of constitutional legitimacy involves striking a balance between the protection of a wide array of minority interests and the power of a central state authority. In the recent wave of constitutional reforms in African countries finding this balance has become a source of contention, but it is not new to African constitutional history. It is argued in this article that the formative experiences during the process of decolonisation have a bearing on the current search for a viable constitutional solution in countries undergoing constitutional reform processes. In other words, the struggle for constitutional reform raises a number of questions that bind the present to the past, and asks what lessons history has to offer. How was the independence constitution established and how well has it served the polity? Why have so many African countries experienced constitutional decay? Did the decay of constitutional practice that emerged shortly after independence influence the development towards authoritarian rule in the decades to follow? What sort of constitutional reform is likely to secure and enhance the transition to democracy in divided societies? In this article these questions are being addressed in light of constitutional

---

[1]   See Jon Elster and Rune Slagstad, *Constitutionalism and Democracy,* Cambridge: Cambridge University Press, 1988; Welshman Ncube, "Constitutionalism and Human Rights: Challenges of Democracy", in Pearson Nherere and Marina D'Engelbronner-Kolff, *The Institutionalisation of Human Rights in Southern Africa,* Oslo: Nordic Human Rights Publications, 1993; J.B. Ojwang, *Constitutional Development in Kenya. Institutional Adaptation and Social Change,* Nairobi: Acts Press, 1990.

[2]   Ncube, 1993, *op. cit.*, p. 11.

215

experiences in Kenya. Several theoretical perspectives are drawn upon, which may help understand the unfolding process. The basic premise is that constitutions result from bargaining between a variety of actors, and that in democratic transitions constitutional legitimacy requires popular involvement and participation.

## Constitution and conflict

The main objective of a constitution is to establish and ensure (a) state coherence and sovereignty; and (b) principles and institutions for constitutional government. The former represents the legal-territorial dimension of constitutions, that is, assertion of the right to self-determination and the preservation of the territorial integrity of the state. The constitution provides the state with formal jurisdiction over a particular territory and a government apparatus to exercise authority within that territory. The latter dimension is legal-political and defines the structures for civil and political communities, and the protection of the rights of minorities and individuals. These structures are designed to provide political stability, and rest, in principle, on common values and goals. If successfully constructed, the constitution produces regime legitimacy. In societies composed of several distinct socio-cultural or ethnic groups, the interrelationship of these two dimensions of constitutions represents a particular challenge.

Constitutions define the basic rules of the political game. In times of political transition, these rules are redefined, and if democratically pursued, the outcome is contingent on negotiations between so-called 'stakeholders', or in sociological terms, interest groups, including civic organisations and political parties. In many instances these represent conflicting interests. This is what constitution-making is all about: Constitutions are 'negotiated packages' of normative and legal standards for the formal structuring and functioning of power. It follows that constitutions are political compromises. Functional constitutions are, in addition, open to future adaptation and adjustment through amendment. However, the amendment procedures should be made in ways that hinder easy, manipulative change.[3]

In transitions from authoritarian rule to formal democracy constitution-making may represent a significant step towards democratic consolidation. In plural societies the process of constitution-making is at the same time an important, yet insufficient, mechanism for securing a modicum of national identity – or 'togetherness' – as well as for enhancing social and inter-cultural trust. This requires recognition of the fact that citizens of divided societies embody multiple identities, and that the notion of national identity provides 'space' for their co-existence. The labelling of the South African nation as a 'rainbow nation'

---

[3] On a comparative note, the Norwegian constitution can only be amended according to a procedure, which requires that a general election be held between the tabling of a bill and its ultimate adoption. The bill shall be tabled in the first, second or third year of the four-year parliament term, and shall be publicly announced in printed form. "But it shall be left to the first, second or third [session of the] *Storting* [the name of the Norwegian parliament] after the following general election to decide whether or not the proposed amendment shall be adopted." (Article 112). Such amendment, however, shall not contradict the principles embodied in the constitution, nor alter the spirit of it. (One parliamentary session lasts from October until June the following year).

illustrates this point. In one way or another, the recognition of multiple identities needs institutional and, in some cases, constitutional protection.

A bargain-theoretic approach to constitutional analysis views constitutions as compromises reached through negotiation between competing interests, ideologies and world-views.[4] The study of constitution-making, moreover, should cover factors that may secure popular legitimacy of the end product. Although popular support of a constitution depends on a series of factors (e.g. the ability of the new political dispensation to operate effectively, and to deliver political output and material results), current constitutional thinking in Africa assumes that the making of constitutions involves genuine popular participation, securing the legitimacy of the final document. The case of South Africa may offer support to this assumption, although the long-term effects of the fairly inclusive South African process are difficult to predict. Yet, surveys of the South Africa experience indicate that almost half of the population had a feeling of being part of the process, although submissions on the formulation of the new constitution from individual citizens were few. A participatory approach to constitution-making, however, encounters a number of difficulties. In Kenya, the failure of the initiative in 1995-97 by the National Convention Assembly (and its executive arm, the National Convention Executive Council) to create a 'national constitution-making project' through a process of inclusion and dialogue on a broad-based popular platform, illustrates the difficulty of bringing together actors of different persuasions and interests in one constitution-making project.[5] Still, the constitutional review process launched by the Constitution of Kenya Review Commission (Amendment) Bill of 1998 builds to a large degree on a similar model of popular involvement. Moreover, the Kenyan experience demonstrates amply the difficulty of creating a national inter-cultural process. It also illustrates that the process of constitution-making is confronting class interests and differences: "Constitution-making as experienced in Kenya between 1992 and 1997 is therefore depicted as a project of the political and economic citizens – i.e. the middle class. This is so because the process of constitution-making in Kenya has been about relations of power – in which the 'subject' has little power. Had the question focused on the question of resource use and allocation, the subject might have had a stake in the whole process of constitutional reformation." [6]

In severely divided societies, the legitimacy of a constitution is likely to depend on how the constitutional compromise is able to secure and accommodate 'sub-cultural pluralism' including ethnic, religious or regional sub-cultures. If any segment or substantial group in society feels that its way of life, identity, values or basic interests are threatened by another segment of the population, it "creates a

---

[4]  This approach resembles Adam Przeworski's view that transition to democracy is the contingent outcome of conflict. Cf Adam Przeworski, 'Democracy as a contingent outcome of conflicts' in Jon Elster and Rune Slagstad, 1988, *op. cit.*

[5]  Cf. Willy Mutunga, *Constitution-Making From the Middle. Civil Society and Transition Politics in Kenya, 1992-1997*, Nairobi, SAREAT, 1999.

[6]  Cf. Mutahi Ngunyi, "Comparative Constitution-Making in Africa: A Critique of the Kenyan Process from Seven Countries", in Mutunga, 1999, *op.cit.*, p. 264.

217

crisis in a competitive system".[7] What is at stake is the accommodation of not just sub-cultural identities and interests, but *multiple* identities, that is, the general competence and feeling of belonging to a national as well as one (or several) sub-cultural identities. In severely divided societies this is a necessary condition for state coherence and stability.

## The quest for constitutional reform and the Kenyan transition

One of the principal demands of civic organisations and the political opposition in Kenya since the democratic opening in 1990, has been a constitutional review or a 'comprehensive constitutional overhaul'. The government has responded with piecemeal concessions. Most significant was the repeal of Section 2a in December 1991, which led to the re-introduction of multiparty democracy after 22 years of *de facto* one-party, authoritarian rule. Unable to halt the democratic tide, the government opted for a strategy through which it tried to control the reform process, and hence to protect the position and interests of the ruling political elite.

The reluctance of the regime to enter into genuine political and constitutional dialogue with the key actors in the reform process produced a political stalemate after the first transitional elections in 1992. This coincided, however, with a process of political fragmentation within the political opposition, which had begun before the elections. Fragmentation and factionalism weakened the opposition dramatically and continued during the interlude between the 1992 and 1997 elections, in the so-called *second cycle* of the transition.[8] The democracy that emerged has been dubbed a *hobbled democracy*.[9] This denotes a type of democracy in which the past authoritarian power apparatus remains largely intact – despite piecemeal and minimal concessions to the demands for reform – yet unable to thwart the process. In a hobbled democracy, the chief function of incumbency is to direct or obstruct the democratic process in order to steer its direction. Although competitive and formal democratic institutions were introduced, including new autonomous organisations, the incumbent government was able to impede the conclusion of a democratic compromise that might have facilitated democratic expansion. Instead, the Kenyan transition in the period from the first to the second transitional elections (1992-97) proceeded very slowly and in an intermittent manner, although the overall direction was positive.[10] Despite the expansion of democratic space, the incumbent regime continued to behave as if the one-party state remained in place. The dismantling of authoritarianism has proved to be a slow and intermittent process.

---

7    Dahl, Robert, *Polyarchy. Participation and Opposition*, New Haven: Yale University Press, 1971, p. 105.

8    The notion of transitional cycle has been suggested in Mutahi Ngunyi, "Civil Society and Two Transition Cycles in Kenya", *SAREAT Working Paper* 11, Nairobi, 1998.

9    Cf. Bård-Anders Andreassen, Gisela Geisler and Arne Tostensen, *A Hobbled Democracy. The Kenya General Elections 1992*, Report R 1993:5, Bergen: Chr. Michelsen Institute, 1993. See also Arne Tostensen, Bård-Anders Andreassen and Kjetil Tronvoll, *Kenya's Hobbled Democracy Revisited. The 1997 General Elections in Retrospect and Prospect*, Human Rights Report No. 2, Oslo: Norwegian Institute of Human Rights, 1998.

10   For further details, cf. Tostensen et al., 1998, *op.cit.*

How did this political regime evolve? Where does the patrimonial and authoritarian state stem from? In what sense does the unsteady process of 'hobbled' democratic development originate in the constitution adopted at independence? These questions guide the analytical orientation of this article.

In the first part of the article, the constitutional legacy of Kenya is addressed in the context of decolonisation and post-independence political developments. The role of ethnicity and the process of constitutional decay are of particular interest. The 're-creation' of a patrimonial state is examined, and is seen in part as resulting from the failure to reach a genuine and legitimate constitutional compromise at independence.[11] The second part addresses the constitutional issue in the period of multiparty politics in the 1990s. The third part discusses two key dimensions of constitutional conflict-reducing techniques in severely divided societies, i.e. devolution of central powers to regional and local representative bodies, and electoral reforms. A central concern in this context is the restructuring of the relationship between the state and ethno-regional groups.[12]

## PART I: THE CONSTITUTIONAL LEGACY: FROM INDEPENDENCE TO THE PRESENT

The present constitutional debacle in Kenya originates in the process of decolonisation, and the evolving pattern of constitutional decay in the decades following independence. Politically, this evolution reflected a trend of growing authoritarian control by the ruling elite throughout the 1980s, with antecedents in the 1960s and 1970s.[13] Throughout this period, the determining factor in constitutional change was the consolidation of elite economic interests, which occurred in a context of ethnicisation of politics and policy-making.[14]

### The independence constitution

Kenya became independent in December 1963 after a process of constitutional negotiation at Lancaster House in London. Between 1960 and 1963 three constitutional conferences were held. The most consequential was held from 14 February until the first week of April 1962 when the main structure of the constitution was worked out. The 1963 constitution contained a complex set of institutions. It provided, *inter alia*, for a semi-federal (*Majimbo*) system of government consisting of seven regions, each with regional assemblies and public services; a bi-cameral legislature at the national level; several national staff commissions for different branches of the civil service; and a parliamentary

---

[11] The patrimonial state as it evolved in Africa, is a 're-creation' of the colonial legacy with 'centralising administrative states with organic-statist orientation'. Cf. Thomas M. Callaghy, "Politics and Vision in Africa", in Patrick Chabal (ed.), *Political Domination in Africa,* Cambridge: Cambridge University Press, 1986, p. 32.

[12] Cf. Herb Feith and Alan Smith, "Self-determination in the 1990s: Equipping the UN to Resolve Ethno-Nationalist Conflicts", in Kumar Rupesinghe et al. (eds.), *Conflict Transformation,* Basingstoke: St. Martin Press, 1995.

[13] Cf. Joel Barkan, "The Rise and Fall of the Governance Realm in Kenya", in Goran Hyden and Michael Bratton, Boulder, CO: Lynne Rienner, 1992.

[14] Musambayi Katumanga, "The Political Economy of Constitutional Amendments in Kenya 1895-97", *SAREAT Working paper/IPAR Collaborative Paper* 005/98, Nairobi, 1998.

219

system, in which a government would be formed by the majority party in parliament, or the alliance of parties with majority support.[15]

The most important political issue on the independence agenda was land. This was one of the most important issues underlying the constitutional struggle as well. The main political forces to emerge out of the process of decolonisation were two competing 'parties': Kenya African National Union (KANU) and Kenya African Democratic Union (KADU). Both 'parties' were formed in preparation for the 1961 elections, the first general elections under universal suffrage. The term 'party' is placed in inverted commas because both KANU and KADU basically built on "an amalgamation of pre-existing district organisations, grouped around individual personalities."[16]

In the pre-independence elections held in March 1961, KANU won 61 per cent of the votes and 19 seats in Parliament. In addition to garnering support among the Kikuyu, Embu and Meru and Luo, KANU also enjoyed widespread support among other major groups, including the Kamba and the Kiisi. KADU won 16 per cent of the votes and 11 seats. In addition, Europeans and Asians were guaranteed a few seats.[17] Despite winning a landslide victory, KANU refused to form a government before the release of Jomo Kenyatta, who remained in detention. The colonial administration, therefore, called upon KADU to form the government. KADU had the active, and possibly financial support of the settler community, yet was seen as the party of the 'small', the 'have-nots' and the 'immobilised', with support from district organisations located in relatively remote and economically underdeveloped areas.

There were few real political differences between the two parties. They differed, however, on a principal constitutional issue. While KANU strongly favoured a unitary form of government, KADU insisted with equal vigour on a federal arrangement, referred to as '*Majimboism*'.[18] The support of the settler community for KADU was an attempt to secure regional interests in land and commercial farming in the Rift Valley highlands. Central to the issue of regionalism was the smaller ethnic communities' fear of being dominated by the largest communities, and of losing control over land. According to Gary Wasserman:[19]

---

[15] *Constitution of Kenya*, Kenya Gazette Supplement No. 105, 10 December 1963, Ch. VI, Parts 1-6 (articles 91-117).

[16] Githu Muigai, "Ethnicity and the Renewal of Competitive Politics in Kenya", in Harvey Glickman (ed.), *Ethnic Conflict and Democratisation in Africa*, Atlanta: African Studies Association Press, 1995, p. 166.

[17] Institute for Education in Democracy. *National Election Data Handbook. Kenya 1963-97*, Nairobi. IED, 1997, p. 17.

[18] *Majimbo* is the plural form of the Kiswahili term 'jimbo', which means 'region'.

[19] Gary Wassermann, "The Independence Bargain: Kenya Europeans and the Land Issue", in *Journal of Commonwealth Political Studies*, Vol. XI, 1973, p.113. In general, the independence constitution was a mixture of a Westminster-type political system and various components from other constitutional systems, e.g. the Indian federal system. It contained numerous checks and balances on the exercise of power, and sought to avoid the highly repressive legal machinery of the colonial power. It included a Bill of Rights, inspired by the European Convention on Human Rights and Freedoms.

Regionalism (the policy of devolving many of the central government's functions to four or five regional governments which would have control over land) was a method seen by the [European] liberals and KADU Africans as affording protection against the Kikuyu-Luo-militant nationalist domination of the central government which they feared. It reflected an appreciation that KADU would probably not be able to control the post-independence government.

Colonial bureaucrats with their tradition of strong central control were generally opposed to regionalism as liable to lead to administrative chaos and resurgent tribalism, and unlikely to continue once the British left. Farmers and officials connected with land also opposed regionalism on the grounds that it would make land transfers difficult, confuse the question of ownership, complicate the lending procedures of the World Bank (who would only loan to a central authority) and undercut an independent Central Land Board which the farmers still held as their 'only hope for the future'.

The settler economy depended on massive migration of primarily Kikuyu to the White Highlands of the Rift Valley to work on settler farms.[20] Generally, the Highlands were located in areas traditionally inhabited by Kalenjin and Maasai communities. During the colonial period, however, other 'immigrant' communities, in particular Kikuyu from Central Province, and to some extent Luo from Nyanza Province, had been able to establish themselves as squatters on the fringes of the settler economy. These population groups, KANU claimed, would become victims of land evictions under a regional, *Majimbo* form of government. In particular the Kikuyu had become increasingly integrated into the settler economy. Not least due to their proximity to the expanding economy of the rapidly growing capital city of Nairobi, they had been able to accumulate wealth to be used for land acquisition outside their own 'homeland' in Central Province, where land had already become scarce. This was possible as land transactions were based on a free land market (willing seller, willing buyer principle). The KANU constituency, however, feared that this principle would be jeopardised by the setting up of regional authorities with control in matters of land.

### Failure of constitutional compromise: adopting and abandoning the 'Majii..bo' constitution

In June 1963, KANU won the parliamentary and local elections and formed a government, whose immediate task was to prepare for independence. Before that, however, the constitutional negotiations had to be concluded at Lancaster House in the final constitutional talks set for October 1963. In these negotiations, the KADU representatives succeeded in making *Majimboism* a basic principle of the government structure. This reflected the critical issue at Lancaster House, that is, the issue about how to accommodate the competing interests of the various ethnic communities within the boundaries of a territorial state. While the federalists,

---

[20] According to Frank Furedi, there were three main reasons why Kikuyu emigrated to the Rift Valley in the 1920s: landlessness, a desire to avoid military service with carrier corps, and a desire to escape the "despotic rule of the chiefs and their agents", cf. Frank Furedi, 'The Kikuyu squatters in the Rift Valley: 1918-1929, paper presented at the Annual Conference of the Historical Association of Kenya, 1972.

fighting for a *Majimbo* constitution, feared that a unitary state would endanger their regional interests, the unitarists saw their powers curtailed by devolution of state power to regional assemblies. They also genuinely feared mass expulsion of their kin from the Rift Valley.

During the last phase of constitutional talks, the *Majimbo* issue nearly brought the negotiations to a complete halt. In October 1963, a KADU leaders' meeting in Nakuru, "held under the chairmanship of Daniel arap Moi, the then President of the Rift Valley Regional Assembly and chairman of KADU", sent a cable to the party's delegation in London, saying: "forget *Majimbo* and demand partition immediately."[21] A tense situation ensued, but secession was avoided by the adoption of a federal constitution – against the wishes of the party in power, KANU, and key nationalist leaders like Jomo Kenyatta and Oginga Odinga.

The most important immediate goal of the KANU elite, however, was independence. Having achieved this goal, the freedom to amend the constitution "would be added on". The KANU leaders knew they would run the government after independence due to the overwhelming numerical strength of their respective communities.

Therefore, the federalists' apparent victory in the final stages of the constitutional talks proved to be short-lived. One year after the final Lancaster House negotiations, the KANU-dominated parliament amended the constitution and scrapped its federal character. In other words, it was the unitary preference, championed by the KANU nationalist elite that won ultimately. The thrust of their nationalist ideology was the integration of all ethnic groups in the territory into one unitary nation-state. However, this could be done only through a process of 'de-ethnicisation'.[22]

In December 1964 the *Majimbo* faction conceded defeat and KADU dissolved itself, and its MPs and leadership joined KANU. Among the first to cross the floor in parliament was the president of the Rift Valley Regional Assembly, Daniel arap Moi.

The speed with which the *Majimbo* faction abandoned its position is noteworthy. In anticipation of a strong unitary state the KADU membership feared exclusion in the allocation of resources. Hence, the speedy co-option into KANU reflected what Jean-Francois Bayart refers to as the "politics of the belly", in which the political elite would try to position itself as close to the pork barrel as possible in order to secure at least some resources for their constituencies.[23]

The independence constitution had provided for a bicameral legislature – a House of Representatives and a Senate – modelled on the British Parliament. The main function of the Senate was to safeguard the *Majimbo* structure. The Regional Assemblies were vested with their own legislative and executive powers, and were designed to take over the functions which had been carried out by the Provincial and District Commissioners under colonialism. The constitution also included a comprehensive Bill of Rights with a special emphasis on minority rights. The

---

[21]  *Daily Nation,* 9 October 1963.
[22]  Cf. Muthahi Ngunyi and Wachira Maina, "Emerging themes in constitution-making in Kenya", draft mimeo, 1995, p. 3ff.
[23]  Jean-Francois Bayart, *The State in Africa. The Politics of the Belly,* London: Longman, 1993.

latter set of rights had been included on the insistence of the settler community. The settlers feared nationalisation of 'their' land, and were able to include a compensation clause.

In conclusion, the constitutional 'compromise' that was achieved through the Lancaster House negotiations was chiefly tactical and temporary as seen from the perspective of the major ethnic groups. KANU rightly anticipated that its future parliamentary majority would make a constitutional amendment easy, and as soon as independence was achieved, a carefully designed strategy of political co-option of the KADU leadership started. However, the KADU leadership accepted the unitary state not out of conviction, but rather as a matter of political survival once the colonial administration had left. The 'national question' had not been resolved, and the constitutional compromise 'imposed' upon the majority party at Lancaster House had been annulled.

This brief review of the decolonisation process suggests that although the sources of authoritarianism and constitutional decay in Kenya are commonly seen as a result of the Moi era, they should rather be seen as stemming from the decolonisation process and its immediate aftermath. Due to the type of politics that evolved in the years after independence, the unitary state was transformed into a 'Kenyatta state' – and the evolution of a 'property relationship' to the state by the ruling elite. This demonstrates that the independence constitution in Kenya was unable to establish a culture of constitutionalism and constitutional legitimacy, based on national unity, identity and trust, and as a corollary, state authority commanding stable national support. This political legacy was taken over and developed further by the regime to follow – that of Moi. According to Barkan this development resulted in the breakdown of effective citizenship and the dismantling of a system of 'legitimate authority and reciprocity', i.e. the governance realm in Kenya. In the words of Barkan, the governance realm concerns two sets of dimensions that determine the relationship between the ruling elite and the citizenry:[24]

> (1) the *actor dimension*, or the personal expectations individuals have for each other's behaviour, and (2) the *structural dimension* – the institutionalised procedures, or rules of the game – operative in a particular polity. Not all systems have established or maintained a governance realm. Those which have, are systems wherein the basis of interaction between the rulers and the ruled is that of legitimate authority or reciprocity, and where the procedures that structure these relationships maintain accountability, trust, or both, between the actors involved. Political systems with a governance realm are thus systems wherein there is a measure of bargaining, compromise, and tolerance among competing interests, and between those who exercise political authority and those who are subject to it.

Barkan argues that a governance realm of sorts was established and maintained under Kenyatta. He asserts that Kenyan politics in the 1960s and 1970s did operate

---

[24] On the concept of 'governance realm', see Goran Hyden, "Governance and the study of politics", in Goran Hyden and Michael Bratton, 1992, *op. cit.* For an application of the concept to the Kenyan post-independence period, see Joel D. Barkan, "The rise and fall of a governance realm in Kenya" in the same volume. The quotation is from the latter piece, p. 167.

in ways that made it fairly predictable, legitimate and competitive. Under the evolving one-party framework, political competition was limited but significant, and this 'semi-competitive' system was able to establish mutually dependent links between the rulers and the ruled through patron-client relationships. For instance, in the 1970s a relatively large number of parliamentary candidates were rejected at the polls, which suggests that the system was able to produce some level of accountability and popular control. Barkan also suggests that the norms, procedures and structures for regulating state-society relations remained predictable and stable over time, in spite of the limitations of the semi-competitive (one-party) system. This produced a governance realm, or a regime which was consciously managed in order to enhance the legitimacy of the public realm. Barkan, in other words, argues that there was significant governance stability during the Kenyatta era, which was 'dismantled' during the Moi era. Thus, he claims that there was discontinuity between Kenyatta and Moi with regard to the governance system.

A divergent perspective on the political developments in post-independence Kenya suggests that "pork-barrel politics was to shape the nature of the nation-state from its most inchoate form to its present state. Under both the Kenyatta and Moi regimes (1963-78, and 1978-present, respectively), it is the nationality/ies of the ruling elite that has/have benefited the most".[25] This perspective submits that the predominant practice throughout the independence period has been to exclude from state patronage altogether those ethnic communities that have expressed opposition to the government, or at least to discriminate against those communities not forming part of the government's core constituency. This became most apparent after multiparty politics was introduced in late 1991, with key cabinet members explicitly threatening – and practising – the "withholding of development" to strongholds of the opposition. In other words, the unitary state, and the corresponding principle of nation-state that was inherent in the amendment of the independence constitution, has hardly worked as proclaimed. The key point is that the destruction of independence *Majimboism*, and the attempt by the new nationalist elite to build a unitary state suggested, moreover, that ethnicity and ethnic association were increasingly seen by the subsequent regimes as illegitimate concerns. Ethnicity was banned from public debate, and condemned as tribalism and anti-Kenyan. Yet, ethnicity permeated real politics in a very consistent way through ethnic favouritism and patronage in political and economic life. The practice of ethnic favouritism and ethnic exclusion emerged under Kenyatta's rule, despite public rhetoric to the contrary about 'non-tribalism' and 'ethnic balancing' of successive cabinets. This practice dates back to KANU's successful attempt to demolish KADU after independence. Barkan's apt interpretation of this process is pertinent: "Rather than suppress KADU during the period immediately before and after independence, Kenyatta starved the party into extinction while incorporating its most important pieces into his regime."[26] Thus, the political developments in the post-independence period have been shaped by the ruling elite's need for forming and adjusting 'useful alliances' in order to retain political and economic

---

[25]  Ngunyi and Maina, 1995, *op.cit.*
[26]  Barkan, 1992, *op. cit*, p. 171.

224

control. In this way ethnic alliances (at the elite level) and re-alignments (at the mass level) have been governed by a symbiotic relationship of ethnicity and class interests in Kenya. "While the elites derive most of their legitimacy from ethnic groupings, and by arousing ethnic sentiment, ethnic communities on the other hand see their elite as their flag bearers pressing for their interests nationally".[27]

## Continuity or discontinuity: from Kenyatta to Moi

Is Barkan's discontinuity thesis an accurate representation of post-independence political developments? Or did growing authoritarianism in the 1980s in fact represent continuity from the previous regime? Are the antecedents of authoritarianism in the 1980s to be found in the process of decolonisation and the failure to establish a legitimate constitutional compromise at independence? It has been argued that the *Majimbo* constitution represented an 'imposed constitutional compromise', which was subsequently reversed through a constitutional reform that was similarly 'imposed' upon the coalition of small ethnic groups in 1964. A compromise is 'imposed' if it does not result from fair and genuine constitutional negotiations between representative parties. In the case of the *Majimbo* constitution the colonial power added weight to the scales in favour of KADU.[28] Only one year after independence, KANU with its dominant parliamentary position scrapped the *Majimbo* constitution in favour of a unitary state without due consideration to the legitimate rights of the minority in a legitimately constructed nation-state. The Constitution of Kenya (Amendment) Act, No. 38 of 1964, similar to the other six amendments passed in the first three years of independence, was rushed through parliament "before the public had had time to consider the matters involved" and that "they were designed to benefit the government in power".[29]

Allegedly in the name of national unity the political leaders of the minority communities were 'voluntarily' co-opted within a year after independence. It seems fair to suggest, however, that the ensuing political decline in the 1970s and 1980s reflected a political culture that had already taken root through the decolonisation process and the establishment of the independence constitution. Indeed, the two 'imposed constitutional compromises' reflected the failure to establish constitutional principles and a system of governance that would enhance democratic political developments in Kenya. To support this view Barkan's discontinuity argument needs to be refuted.

Barkan claims that the system of governance that emerged in Kenya in the first two decades after independence was the combined result of three factors. The first factor was the specific pattern of Kenya's transition from colonialism to independence. At independence, the two contending parties, KANU and KADU

---

[27] Mutahi Ngunyi, "Forces conditioning the transition to multiparty politics in Kenya", paper presented at the first regional conference on law, politics and multi-party democracy in East Africa, Dar es Salaam, 1993, p. 7.

[28] Oginga Odinga, for example, refers to the behaviour of the British in the final constitutional talks as political 'blackmail': "Once again British Government tactics were to force a KADU policy on KANU, or to threaten to postpone independence. It was blackmail, and we said so." Oginga Odinga, *Not Yet Uhuru. An Autobiography*, Nairobi: Heinemann, 1967, pp. 238-9.

[29] C. Gerzel, "Kenya's Constitutional Changes", in *East Africa Journal*, 1966, p. 19.

disagreed on the issue of the form of state to be created. In Barkan's interpretation the establishment in 1964 of a unitary state was one factor which created a legitimate system of governance to which the public was committed. Although this commitment and legitimacy might have been established with respect to the part of the electorate supporting KANU, it is not equally convincing to argue that it also applied to the remaining smaller ethnic groups making up the constituency of KADU.

The second factor suggested by Barkan was the type of leadership that Jomo Kenyatta provided. The nationalist leaders were unable to integrate or absorb the small and large ethnic associations into one organisation. When KADU was dissolved and its leadership co-opted by KANU in 1964, Kenyatta's strategy of power containment was to "rise above the fray and tolerate the activities of local bosses so long as they did not challenge his authority as the head of KANU and later as the head of state".[30] Instead of suppressing local political notables, Kenyatta incorporated them into his own patronage system, and allowed them to maintain their local political following, provided that they supported his regime and were able to secure local support through semi-competitive elections. These elections were another significant characteristic of the Kenyatta regime. After 1969, all parties but KANU were banned in Kenya. But having banned competitive *party* politics, Kenyatta encouraged open contest between multiple KANU *candidates* in national elections. Between 1969 and 1979, therefore, elections in Kenya represented a series of local referenda where the candidates competed in securing resources for their local constituencies. Prospective MPs had to be sensitive to the needs of their local communities, while at the same time remaining incorporated in Kenyatta's system of state patronage. Barkan asserts that this implied accountability and trust, which helped secure regime legitimacy despite the fact that political rights to organise and assemble were circumscribed. But did it really secure legitimacy from all major sections in society – including those without access to the 'pork barrel' of the new unitary state? Or did these sections perceive the state as an organ of and for the ruling coalition of ethnic notables?

With the demise of KADU the rhetoric of the elite was that ethnic politics had been permanently relegated to the garbage dump of history, and that new broad-based alliances would secure a harmonious development of the unitary state. The dissolution of KADU, however, "served to expose the differing personal, ideological and ethnic agendas simmering within KANU itself."[31] Rather than bringing an end to ethno-politics, it nurtured its growth. In spite of different ideologies between the so-called radicals and conservatives inside KANU, the formation and reorganisation of ethnic alliances shaped the political map. While leaders made alliances at the elite level, their ethnic kinfolk at the grassroots realigned correspondingly. A pattern of inclusion and exclusion arose: if a group had access to the state by being associated with the ruling alliance, it reciprocated by providing support and legitimacy for the regime. To be outside the alliance – or excluded – involved high risks. Long-term or permanent exclusion was most

---

[30] Barkan, 1992, *op. cit.*, p. 171.
[31] Muigai, 1995, *op.cit.*, p. 166.

226

serious. In principle, a group that fell out with the regime would aspire for re-integration come the next alliance. Ethnic alignment and re-alignment became a matter of 'distributive politics', yet outside the formal political channels. This pattern of ethnic politics was in place right from independence, and even initiated before that. The guiding principle of this brand of politics has been described as a symbiosis of perceived self-interests on the part of the leaders and their kinsmen of the ethnic group:[32]

> (...) flexing its 'ethnic muscle' as a bargaining chip for key positions in the political space, the elite sought to reproduce both itself and its own position by further promoting ethnic politics. In return for keeping them politically afloat, the ethnic communities received 'development' through harambee projects and various direct development projects providing roads, piped water, schools etc. This relationship between the elite and the ethnic communities provided the *raison d'etre* for ethnic arithmetic in the coalition formation in Kenya.

Kenyatta reshuffled his cabinet infrequently, and upon appointment a minister's tenure was reasonably secure. There was in other words some degree of predictability and space for innovative political activity. Appointments to cabinet and statutory boards meant a wealth of personal benefits that could be traded for support at the local level. This encouraged the pattern of 'pork-barrel politics' with increasing levels of corruption and nepotism. Barkan claims that the Kenyan civil service was characterised by a high degree of professionalism and autonomy and that this contributed to the system of governance. John Okumu, however, stresses that the recruits after independence "were originally attracted to the civil service not out of missionary zeal, but because of the security offered by life appointment with its regular salary and perquisites".[33] In 1980, the Civil Service Review Committee (the Waruhui Committee) concluded: "there has been gross neglect of public duty and misuse of official positions and information in furtherance of civil servants' personal interests."[34] There was also a large degree of over-representation of Kenyatta's ethnic community, the Kikuyu, in the administration and the parastatals. Ethnic favouritism was certainly not inspiring inter-ethnic trust and confidence among those communities that were excluded. Rather, it fuelled ethnic animosity and distrust, although friction and hostility were largely contained by the one-party state. The aborted coup attempt in August 1982 demonstrated, however, the fragility of the apparent political stability in Kenya.

---

[32]  Ngunyi, 1993, *op.cit.*

[33]  John Okumu, "The Socio-Political Setting", in G. Hyden, R. Jackson and J. Okuku (eds.). *Development Administration: The Kenyan Experience,* Nairobi: Oxford University Press, 1970, p. 38.

[34]  Report of the Civil Service Review Committee 1979-80 (Waruhiu Committee), Government of Kenya, 1980, p 39. Cf. also Arne Tostensen and John G. Scott (eds.), *Kenya: Country Study and Norwegian Aid Review,* Bergen: Chr. Michelsen Institute, 1987, p. 100ff. Interestingly, ten years prior to the Waruhiu Committee, the Public Service Structure and Remuneration Commission (Ndegwa Commission), had acknowledged in 1971 that corruption existed in the public service. Nonetheless, it recommended that civil servants be allowed to conduct private business alongside their public office, provided that business interests were publicly declared. Cf. Tostensen and Scott, 1987, *op.cit.*, and Goran Hyden, "Administration and Public Policy", in Joel Barkan (ed.), *Politics and Public Policy in Kenya and Tanzania,* Nairobi: Heineman, revised edition, 1984, p. 116.

According to Barkan, the last factor contributing to the governance system under Kenyatta was the creation of the self-help system (*harambee*), and hence the strengthening of rural civil society.[35] The *harambee* system was seen to mobilise resources for local development projects, conducted by local peasants with the support of rural patrons. Originally, it facilitated a considerable number of self-help initiatives. Funding of local projects, moreover, fell on members of the local community, and in practical terms it became an informal local community tax. Although all members of the community were expected to contribute, the rich were supposed to contribute more than the poor. Increasingly, however, the *harambee* system became a vehicle for local and national politicians to garner legitimacy and support by making contributions to *harambee* projects in their home area, which at election time could be converted into votes. Accordingly, for those with access to state resources the system was used for extending state patronage into local environments. Although this 'distributive system' helped nurture reciprocity and accountability between the patrons and local communities benefiting from the system, the effectiveness of the system relied on the degree of access to state patronage, which was determined by membership in the ruling ethno-political alliance.

The factors of governance discussed above – an arena for limited political competition, a semi-competitive system of patron-client networks knitting the state and civil society together, and the harambee system – may to some degree have enhanced reciprocity and accountability by the rulers to the ruled, and hence contributed to a degree of governance.[36] To some extent the Kenyan state was predictable, and upheld the rule of law, in spite of the final abolition of political pluralism by outlawing the Kenya People's Union (KPU) in 1969.[37] However, a number of factors, including a series of political assassinations in the late 1960s and 1970s, certainly cast doubts on Barkan's predictability thesis. The growing number of serious human rights violations became an increasingly central problem. Thus, rather than representing a break with the developments of the 1960s and 1970s, a high degree of continuity was discernible in the 1980s. Hence, the Moi regime did not dismantle a pre-existing 'governance realm'. Such a realm hardly existed, or only in embryonic form. Under Kenyatta, ethnicity became an integral part of politics. Moi's presidency, however, consolidated this political tradition to serve its own constituency and in the process undermined the 'Kikuyu hegemony' over the state. Parallel to this process, further erosion of government institutions took place. Key features of these developments are discussed below.

## Consolidation of power under Moi and the expansion of ethno-politics

Between 1969 and 1978, Kenyatta had tried to create the semblance of a 'government of national unity', but the dominance of his own ethnic community in government and the economy was beyond question.[38] Proximity to expanding

---

[35] *Harambee* is Kiswahili for 'pull together'.
[36] Barkan, *op.cit.*, p. 168.
[37] Kenya People's Union (KPU) had been formed in 1966 by Oginga Odinga after he became isolated by the governing elites of KANU.
[38] Muigai, 1995, *op.cit.*, p. 172ff.

urban markets and disproportional access to political power added to the advantage, and created a 'proprietary attitude' towards the state.

When Moi took over the presidency after the death of Kenyatta in 1978, he consolidated his power through two strategic moves. During his first 4-5 years in office he reduced considerably the influence of the Kikuyu in the state. At the same time, he created room for his own loyal constituency, which consisted predominantly of key groups in the erstwhile KADU alliance, that is, the so-called KAMATUSA communities (Kalenjin, Maasai, Turkana and Samburu). These communities became the bedrock of his regime. Over time, he was able to enlarge his support to include other 'KADU groups' as well, such as the Abaluhya of Western Kenya and the Mijikenda of the Coast Province.

Within a relatively short time span, Moi had successfully completed a 'de-kikuyuisation' of the state. At the same time, however, he tried to keep the support of the Kikuyu, but as he could not do so through Kenyatta's confidants, he had to create new 'clients' with whom to co-operate. Despite his rhetoric of national unity (cf. his motto 'love, peace and unity'), Moi embarked upon a strategy of 'ethnic engineering', but castigated any public reference to ethnicity as subversive tribalism. Open debate about ethnicity was restricted and regarded with suspicion, yet ethno-politics was widely practised.

Secondly, Moi consolidated his power by passing a constitutional amendment that outlawed political opposition. Although Kenya had become a *de facto* one-party state since the banning of KPU in 1969, Moi saw the need for securing his grip by prohibiting through constitutional amendment the formation of opposition parties. In June 1982, the constitution was amended by section 2a, stating that KANU would be the only political party allowed. The amendment was rushed through parliament in response to the intention of Oginga Odinga to form a new opposition party. The following year Moi felt confident enough to drop his close Kikuyu ally, Charles Njonjo.[39]

Although the removal of Njonjo represented an important step in Moi's break with the Kikuyu power elite, the 'final break' came only after the 1988 elections when he first dropped the influential Kikuyu, Mwai Kibaki, as vice president. In 1989, Kibaki's successor, Joseph Karanja (also a Kikuyu), was replaced after just a few months by a relatively unknown mathematics professor, George Saitoti, ostensibly a Maasai.[40] By choosing Saitoti and the group of Kalenjin advisers that

---

[39] Njonjo had supported Moi in 1976 when the Kiambu faction of the Kikuyu tried to change the constitution in order to prevent Moi, then in his capacity as vice president, from automatically succeeding the president. According to the constitution, the vice president would automatically function as president for a period of 90 days, in case of the incumbent president's retirement or death. Due to the advanced age and ill health of Kenyatta, the succession issue was a subject of political concern (cf. William Ochieng', "Structural and Political Changes", in B.A. Ogot & W.R. Ochieng' (eds.), *Decolonisation and Independence in Kenya 1940-93*, London: James Currey, 1995). The change-the-constitution movement in the mid-1970s did not succeed, however, and Moi became acting president when Kenyatta died in August 1978. He was subsequently elected leader of KANU at a delegates' conference on 3 October, and sworn in as president by the attorney general on 10 October 1978.

[40] Saitoti is born to Kikuyu parents, but grew up among Maasai in Kajiado district where he assumed a Maasai identity and took a Maasai name. In the context of ethnic politics his true ethnic identity has been a source of controversy since he left academia and entered the political arena.

he had included in his 'inner circle', Moi had effectively destroyed what was left of the Kenyatta state and the Kikuyu hegemony. As Muigai writes, "[t]he fall of the last Kikuyu confidants of Moi coincided with the rise of of a Kalenjin-based group of advisers and confidants, led by Nicholas Biwott, a former personal assistant to Moi. This group recreated at Kabarnet, Moi's hometown, and represented a government within the government. ... All major decisions were made by them long before the government or even the party was involved."[41]

In the 1980s, a number of institutional changes and constitutional amendments that undermined the independence of the judiciary were passed. Changes in the electoral code effectively undermined the semi-competitive nature of elections. Through political engineering Moi succeeded in consolidating his support from the former KADU heartland. His support base was secured in most parts of the country apart from the two most populous provinces, Central Province (inhabited mainly by Kikuyu) and Nyanza Province (so-called Luoland). According to Muigai:[42]

> [t]he revived KADU agenda was one of which some form of 'affirmative action' programme was implemented on the basis of a district focus plan. Allocation of development funds was targeted to the districts, as opposed to allocations on the basis of comprehensive national requirements and priorities. The 'affirmative action' programme institutionalised a quota system in schools, colleges, universities and employment opportunities. It resulted in the meteoric rise in a number of 'ethnically correct' persons in all areas of the public service, but particularly in the armed forces, the police and the provincial administration.

Another result was greater control over political and associational life in the rural areas. In the 1980s lack of control over non-governmental organisations, including foreign aid to these organisations, became a major concern of the government. The autonomy of voluntary associations was seriously impaired by new legislation, and some of them were incorporated into KANU, e.g. Maendeleo ya Wanawake.[43] As from 1983 the District Focus Policy became a vehicle for extending control over the districts by the central government. It represented a form of 'centralisation through decentralisation'.[44]

Lastly, human rights violations abounded, reflecting increasing political repression. Crackdown on political opposition, harassment of the press, detention without legal redress, torture and infringement on *habeas corpus* were reported by international human rights organisations, and led to an international outcry.[45] A main reason for the increasingly repressive nature of the regime was its success in

---

[41]  Muigai, 1995, *op. cit.,* p. 175.

[42]  *Ibid.*, p. 174.

[43]  The Co-ordination of Non-Governmental Organisations Act of 1991. For details see Stephen N. Ndegwa, "Civil Society and Political Change in Africa: The Case of Non-Governmental Organisations in Kenya", in *International Journal of Comparative Sociology*, vol. XXXV, no. 1-2, 1994.

[44]  Tostensen and Scott, 1987, *op.cit.*, p. 139ff.

[45]  Cf. Amnesty International, *Kenya. Torture, Political Detention and Unfair Trials*, London: Amnesty International, 1987; and Africa Watch, *Taking Liberties*, London: AfricaWatch, 1991.

dismantling the Kikuyu hegemony over the state. The creation of a Kalenjin-based state meant growing discontent among the Kikuyu and ensuing political instability.

Some of these developments were given a semblance of legality through constitutional amendments and law reforms. For instance, the independence of the judiciary was seriously curtailed, when in 1988, after years of administrative manipulation, an amendment to section 62 of the constitution removed the security of tenure for judges and the attorney general. The amendment also applied to civil servants in general. In a nutshell, these changes reflected an evolving trend of constitutional decay.

## Democratic expansion in the 1990s and the ethnic factor

Towards the end of the 1980s, the repressive apparatus at the disposal of the executive had been enlarged considerably. From 1990 onwards, however, a wave of democratic transitions took place in most one-party or military authoritarian regimes in Africa. Although resistance to authoritarianism had persisted throughout the latter half of the 1980s, the democratic opening in Kenya is commonly seen as having commenced with the 1990 New Year's Day sermon by Rev. Timothy Njoya of the Presbyterian Church of East Africa. He condemned authoritarianism as no longer a viable option for African governments and added that the collapse of the European communist system called for fundamental rethinking of the African one-party system as well.[46]

The speech by Rev. Njoya set in train a process that led to the removal of section 2a of the constitution in December 1991, and hence the re-introduction of a multiparty system in Kenya. The initial transition phase culminated in the conduct of multiparty elections on 29 December 1992. In no sense could the transition, however, be considered complete by the conduct of elections alone. During the five years (1993-97) of the seventh parliament, major issues of democratic rule remained unaddressed. One of these was constitutional reform.

The emerging opposition, however, was characterised by ideological incoherence and lack of a common policy agenda. Gradually, civic institutions and political parties broadened the reform agenda to include the limitation on the duration of presidential tenure from no limit to maximum two five-year terms; repeal of detention laws; and the restoration of security of tenure for judges.

The democratic opening, moreover, was marred by *ethno-political violence* on a scale unprecedented in the country's independence history. From September until October 1991, KANU held a number of political rallies in some of its key support areas in the Rift Valley (Kapkatet, Kapsabet, and Narok). The message conveyed at these rallies, presided over and addressed by senior KANU politicians, was the proclamation of Rift Valley Province as an exclusive 'KANU zone'. All people who did not support KANU should vacate the province.[47] Explicit reference was made to the model of the *Majimbo* constitution.

Immediately after the first rallies, 'ethnic clashes' started to occur in several border areas between Rift Valley Province and Western and Nyanza Provinces,

---

[46] *Daily Nation*, 2 June 1990.
[47] *Daily Nation*, 12 June 1992.

and in places with high numbers of non-Kalenjin inhabitants (mostly Kikuyu who had migrated to the area during colonialism). The rallies incited and lent legitimacy to locally organised violence and attacks on 'foreign communities'. Using traditional weapons, attacks on remote villages and farms were carried out by armed Kalenjin 'warriors' in gangs of up to fifty people. The central issue was land: the warriors were ostensibly 'taking back' the land they claimed belonged to their ancestors, and which had been bought by 'invaders' from neighbouring tribes after independence. The phenomenon was referred to as 'neo-*Majimboism*'. Although this was a misrepresentation of *Majimboism* or the federal model at the constitutional talks before independence, it reflected the pre-eminence of the ethnic factor in political life. Above all, it demonstrated that ethnic claims and interests had not been accommodated during the thirty years since independence, leading instead to aggravation of distrust and enmity. In the following three years, between 1,200 and 1,500 people were killed, and as many as 300,000 displaced from their homes in a process of ethnic cleansing.

Ethnicity in its various manifestations turned out to have become an extremely volatile factor during the initial phase of the reintroduction of multiparty democracy, and was also linked to the constitutional issue. This phenomenon reflected the fragility of national coherence in Kenya and the simmering crisis of the Kenyan nation-state. It is noteworthy that it coincided with the new political pluralism in the country, and the potential for the restructuring of inter-ethnic relations that followed.

The next section addresses more explicitly the demand for constitutional overhaul, and the conditions for establishing a democratic compromise capable of enhancing trust and stability in an environment of deep ethnic divisions.

## PART II: THE ENSUING CONSTITUTIONAL DEBACLE: MINIMUM REFORMS OR COMPREHENSIVE OVERHAUL

It follows from the above analysis that a key challenge to the constitutional reform process in Kenya is the establishment of a democratic and constitutional framework suitable for a deeply divided, multi-ethnic society. This subject has comparative significance in a large number of countries in Sub-Saharan Africa, e.g. Ethiopia, Uganda, Zimbabwe, and Zambia, where the issue has remained incendiary and unresolved. The centrality of the issue demonstrates that ethnicity remains a principal social and political cleavage in African politics.[48] While ethnic division and competition has been contained inside the framework of the authoritarian one-party state for most of these countries' history since independence, the post-authoritarian phase since 1990 has seen the formation of 'ethnic parties', and increasing ethno-political violence.

The failure of the 'nation-state project' in Kenya is to a large extent about the potential centrifugal force of the 'ethnicisation' of politics. The past decade of political liberalisation has demonstrated the fragility of the Kenyan state, and amply underscored the need for integrative institutions and a political culture of trust and reconciliation.

---

[48] Ngunyi, 1995, *op.cit.*, p. 10ff.

For societies confronted by deep-seated socio-cultural conflicts, a basic question is how constitutional provisions may mitigate the centrifugal forces of ethnicity. Again, it is an issue of immense comparative significance in contemporary processes of political and legal reform in Africa. On an optimistic note, constitution-making in South Africa demonstrated how democratic compromises may be reached through an inclusive and participatory process. It proved possible to mobilise the support of the major racial and ethno-regional groupings through a process of negotiation and reconciliation. Nevertheless, the volatility of the transition was demonstrated when the process almost came to a halt as political and ethnic violence erupted in Kwazulu Natal prior to the country's first democratic elections in April 1994.

Other countries where the constitutional issue has been or is presently being addressed include Namibia (independence constitution of 1990), Malawi (1994), Zimbabwe (explosive ethno-regional and sub-ethnic differences), Ethiopia (ethno-regional federation 1993), and Uganda ('non-party' democracy due to fears of ethnic conflict). Although not subject to comparative examination here, the establishment of democratic governance buttressed by constitutional reform has become a chief *developmental* issue where constitutional reform constitutes the legal and moral-institutional break with the past regime, and defines the new democratic political framework.

When Nelson Mandela signed the South African constitution on 10 December 1996, he concluded six years of constitution-making "where competing visions of the new South Africa, formed during the decades of struggle, clashed through paragraph after paragraph".[49] Although the South African constitution has a basically centralist and majoritarian political structure, it gives "significant concessions" to the consociational model, and includes important federal elements.[50] Federal mechanisms are put in place in order to contain centrifugal forces, and include provisions for nine provinces, each with a provincial assembly with legislative as well as executive powers.

Regionalism as a political and constitutional challenge is not peculiar to Africa. It is a well-known phenomenon in most 'old democracies' of Western Europe. Here, one of the toughest institutional challenges has been to establish a functional and legitimate equilibrium of territorial representation, and systems of representation that respect cultural identity and distributive justice when challenged by various types of politicised and explosive 'peripheral' claims. At one end of the spectrum, claims were made for the right to self-determination that:[51]

shook to the core of the concept, held for much of the twentieth century, of the nation-state as the norm for territorial organisation, with Western Europe as its home, and challenged the validity of prevailing theories of social mobilisation, economic

---

[49]  Cf. Siri Gloppen, *South Africa. The Battle over the Constitution*, Aldershot: Ashgate, 1997. p. 215ff.

[50]  *Ibid*, p. 215ff.

[51]  Stein Rokkan and Derek W. Urwin, *Economy, Territory, Identity. Politics of West European Peripheries*, London: Sage, 1983, p. 118.

development, political integration and the successful impact of distributive welfare policies.

The political response typical of West European states to these challenges was a willingness to accommodate demands through constitutional and institutional devices, within existing state borders.

Similarly, constitutional reforms in ethnically divided societies in Africa need to offer accommodation and integration of ethno-regional claims. Yet, how can minority interests be protected? Is constitutional protection adequate to secure *de facto* protection of basic minority interests? Does the constitution garner political legitimacy from minority groups? Under what circumstances is a constitutional compromise among ethnic groups feasible?

## The current process of constitutional change

The democratic opening in Kenya that led to the reintroduction of multiparty politics in 1991 entailed very few political or legal reforms. The repeal of section 2a of the constitution was the only significant reform. Other laws regulating the political system, notably the electoral law that provided for an Electoral Commission, which had been highly politicised, remained intact, or amended only when the need for defusing protest arose.

In 1995, a constitutional lawyer, Pheroze Nowrojee, wrote an article in the *Nairobi Law Monthly* where he argued why the constitution of Kenya needed reform.[52] He cited five reasons for a complete constitutional overhaul:

- There are almost no checks upon the president, and although the presidency is an executive one, the president is also a member of parliament. In a number of areas, e.g., criminal cases and civil litigation he is above the law and cannot be sued in a court (section 14);
- The need for reducing the concentration of power in the Office of the President;
- The need for correcting a number of 'structural deficiencies' in the constitutional and legal structure. These 'deficiencies' include 'repressive laws' left over from the colonial period but still in force. They serve to restrict the freedoms of expression, assembly and association;
- The need for establishing a consolidated and genuine theory of constitutional form and practice. The current constitution is a mixture of several principles, but without the principle of checks and balances;
- The need for constitutional protection of democratic institutions and practises so that the democratic process cannot be subverted unlawfully.

All of the above points addressed democratic procedures, and drew on lessons from the 1992 elections, e.g. gerrymandering and 'ethnic calculation' of constituency boundaries.[53]

---

[52]   *Nairobi Law Monthly*, no. 56, August 1995.
[53]   Cf. Tostensen et al., 1998, *op.cit.*

234

Despite defeat in the 1992 elections, the opposition parties reluctantly decided to use their seats in parliament as a platform for continued pressure for reforms. However, constitutional reform was soon removed from the agenda of party politics. The constitutional question, therefore, was kept alive by civic organisations. In October 1994, the Law Society of Kenya, the International Commission of Jurists – Kenya Section, and the Kenya Human Rights Commission jointly drafted a model constitution in an effort to revitalise the constitutional debate. In January 1995, these organisations launched the Citizen Coalition for Constitutional Change (4Cs), in order to push the process further. The purpose was to involve the population through churches and other institutions in a nation-wide debate on minimum constitutional reform. The initiative of the constitutional debate thus shifted from political to civil society.

The 1995-96 period was one of the most volatile of the transition process in Kenya. A political impasse between the government and the opposition threatened to bring the transition to a complete halt. The government refused to engage in a dialogue with the main architects of the constitutional reform process – the 4Cs and its successors, the National Convention Executive Council (NCEC). The general elections were fast approaching and added urgency to the need for minimum constitutional reform. Without reforms, the opposition would not take part in the elections. Civic institutions were able to launch a national campaign of civil protest. In June 1997 anti-government riots spread in Nairobi.

Under tremendous pressure, the government conceded, and established the so-called Inter-Parties Parliamentary Group (IPPG) as a forum for dialogue between the government and the opposition parties on minimum constitutional reforms. Through negotiations, a package of minimum reforms was concluded and enacted as the revamped Constitution of Kenya (Amendment) Act of 1997 and the Statute Law Act of 1997. The package included several procedural democratic safeguards, such as the removal of restrictions on the formation of parties; amendment of the constitution to allow for a coalition government; enhanced access to the electronic mass media for opposition parties; enlargement of the Electoral Commission by 10 additional commissioners nominated by the opposition parties; and the nomination of 12 members of parliament in proportion to the strength of the respective parties in terms of parliamentary seats.[54]

These reforms, however significant, fell grossly short of the original demands for comprehensive constitutional reform. None of the reforms, for instance, addressed the basic issue referred to by Nowrojee on the structural deficiencies and the theoretical underpinnings of the constitution. Nor were the powers of the presidency addressed. Despite their deficiencies, however, the reforms reflected what was politically feasible at this particular juncture in the transition process.

While causing an outcry among the civil society reformers, the IPPG reforms constituted a compromise, which established a modicum of trust among the antagonists in the political game, and hindered further escalation of mass action and a likely response with brute force on the part of the government. The reforms also facilitated the conduct of general elections in December 1997.

---

[54]    Cf. Tostensen et al., 1998, *op. cit.*, pp. 33-38. However, not all of these 'democratic safeguards' were observed in practice.

However, certain fundamental aspects of the constitutional framework were not addressed. Although the government as part of the IPPG negotiations announced the establishment of a Constitutional Review Commission, confidence-building and reconciliation in a process of national dialogue were not identified as salient issues. National unity, ethno-political competition and lack of mutual confidence as part of the constitutional reform process were not attended to. With reference to *Majimboism* of the independence process and 'neo-*Majimboism*' in the current process of democratic transition, national unity remained elusive. The proprietary relationship to the state of ethnic patrons remained an obstacle to political legitimacy, and a threat to the territorial integrity of the state.

## PART III: REACHING A CONSTITUTIONAL COMPROMISE IN DEEPLY DIVIDED SOCIETIES: THE KEY OPTION

The widening political arena in Kenya in the 1990s provided a new environment for the role of ethnicity in politics. Over the past three decades, the ruling elite had considered the ethnic factor a taboo in the public domain, albeit playing ethnic politics under the surface. With the advent of multiparty politics, however, this factor has assumed even greater significance than previously, and become prominent in public discourse. Multiparty politics has unleashed divisive forces that neither formal political structures nor civil society have been able to contain. Developments during the seventh parliament confirm this observation: the government continued to pursue ethnic politics, e.g., by threatening to punish communities supporting the opposition by 'withholding development'.[55]

In a democracy conflicts must be managed and controlled in ways that sustain the legitimacy of democratic norms and values. This implies that the political system must contain social, economic, or cultural conflicts peacefully. Democracy implies that no individual actor may control the agenda or the outcome of politics. Political outcome is determined by political competition. In other words, the outcome of a democratic process cannot be predetermined *ex ante*; outcomes are uncertain.[56]

Uncertainty and change, however, call for strategies to minimise the risk that follows lack of control over political outcome. Ethnic loyalty and the politicisation of ethnicity have become mechanisms for perceived risk minimisation. Hence, in times of rapid political change ethnicity may be seen as an 'insurance' against the uncertainty and 'anarchy' of democratic competition. Democratic transition, in other words, has increased the significance of ethnicity as an insurance policy in the face of uncertainty.

Furthermore, in Kenya local interests and politics have been tied to the central state through ethnic associations and ethnic notables. Although ethnic groups are not socially homogeneous, ethnic solidarity in politics represents a 'symbiosis' of perceived (class) self-interest on the part of the elite, on the one hand, and the

---

[55] The 'pact' between KANU and the Luo-dominated National Development Party (NDP) may be interpreted in this light. It may be seen as an attempt to secure the survival of the ruling elite, which considers it to be in its interest to negotiate a minimum pact with one or several other parties cum ethnic communities.

[56] Cf. Przeworski, 1991, *op. cit.*, ch 1.

masses, on the other.[57] During Moi's presidency in the 1980s, the KANU government tried to contain ethnic animosity through the use of constitutional and political mechanisms, single-party rule and a policy of regionalism that devolved power and resources to favoured local ethnic leadership (even outside the KAMATUSA core areas). With the advent of multiparty politics, however, the possibility of entering into alliances with ethnic notables outside this KAMATUSA alliance has been blocked by the amalgamation of ethnic and opposition parties in other regions. The result has been that politics in Kenya has remained a zero-sum game for power rather than changing into a positive-sum process of bargaining, growth and distribution. Dichotomous divisions between 'us' and 'them', between 'government' and 'opposition' etc., have been sharpened. The impasse between the government and the opposition that occurred in the mid-1990s can be seen as a product of this type of zero-sum politics, and the failure of political institutions to offer 'broker mechanisms' for political dialogue and co-operation.

From this analysis follows the need for reflecting on prescriptive constitutional and institutional mechanisms for managing and reducing ethnic animosity in Kenya. It remains a problem that the Kenyan state and its constitutional framework is seen as not serving the whole polity. In addition to creating a new constitutional structure, processes for building mutual trust and political legitimacy of the state are needed. The constitutional question in Kenya, therefore, is not just about the theory of the constitution or the principles that underpin it. It is also about *the creation of a constitutional compromise*, i.e., the process of creating legitimacy and ownership to the constitution through the constitution-making process.

Underlying this concern about the constitution are two assumptions. The first is that constitutions matter. This assumption was questioned for many years, referring to the fact that since decolonisation and independence, there have been many constitutions in Africa with little bearing on politics. However, since the mid-1980s, supported by the collapse of authoritarian regimes over the last decade, primarily in Latin-America and Africa, there has been renewed interest in the study of institutions in general, and more particularly in the creation of better constitutional models.

Secondly, the renewed interest in constitutions and constitution-making follows from the assumption that a constitution and compliance with its rules, regulations and regulatory ideas (i.e. constitutionalism), brings fundamental legitimacy to the political system and successful government formation. Whenever a government falls, the basic legitimacy of the *system* remains intact. As is generally acknowledged, legitimacy has a positive impact on political performance, just as political performance also produces legitimacy and political support as a feedback mechanism. The choice of constitutional model and its normative bases, therefore, is highly relevant for transitional politics and democratic consolidation.

---

[57] Cf. Donald L. Horowitz, *Ethnic Groups in Conflict,* Berkeley: University of California Press, 1985.

The principal objective is to identify a model of constitutional structures that may regulate ethnic relations in a society with regional hegemonic ethnic groups.[58] This interest follows from the analysis that in the face of ethnic division Kenya has not yet found institutional mechanisms that may enhance the legitimacy of the polity, and minimise divisive inter-cultural animosity. At the same time, political outcome, stability and human rights observance do not rely only on choice of constitutional model. Rules not adhered to have little political impact. Adherence is critical and requires respect for the rule of law, and a political culture consonant with democratic values and principles.

## Choosing a constitutional model

What constitutional models exist? What decides the choice of constitutional model? Under which conditions do different models work? The basic idea underlying any constitutional design is that the fundamental rules of the game should be constructed in such a way that "the most fundamental problems and conflicts are accommodated and can be solved peacefully within the system."[59] Constitutions, however, differ in a number of dimensions, and in choosing a particular constitutional design, the 'best possible combination' of constitutional components for each political system *sui generis* should be chosen. What constitutes the best possible combination of constitutional components, however, is debated among political and civic actors and reflects their respective interests and preferences. At any rate, the 'best possible constitution' should be reached through democratic negotiation among the interested parties.

The most important dimensions along which constitutional design differs, include the following:[60]

- The electoral system and in particular the choice of electoral formula (the principal difference runs between majoritarian and proportional systems);
- The relationship between the executive and the legislature (parliamentary or presidential systems of government);
- The composition of central political bodies (uni/bi-cameral parliament, collective executive body);
- The requirements on decision-making (decision by consensus, minority vetoes);
- Degree and form of decentralisation/federalism.

These constitutional components may occur in various permutations. Choice of constitutional design is informed by values and interests. Hence, values, interests and different interpretations of social, economic and political realities may lead to different constitutional preferences. As in other African countries, in the current process of democratic transition in Kenya ethnic diversity and conflict may impact

---

[58] A regional hegemonic ethnic group is defined as one enjoying a dominant or majority position in a given region.

[59] Gloppen, 1997, *op. cit.*, p. 49.

[60] *Ibid.*, p. 51.

on the choice of constitutional design. Interpretations of how different institutional set-ups may affect the 'ethnic arithmetic' have a bearing on the choice of constitutional model. In a situation of rising ethnic competition and hatred, as in Kenya's current phase of transition, the constitutional preference of actors may be determined rather by a preoccupation with ethno-regional interest than moderation of ethnic resentment and conflict.

Two issues are particularly important in choosing constitutional models in divided societies: democracy and approach to ethnic pluralism. Democratic ideals reflect different preferences with respect to constitutional models. With reference to South Africa, Gloppen analyses two constitutional models which follow from two different sets of ideal types of democracy: majoritarian versus consensus democracy.[61] Briefly, the majoritarian type of democracy implies 'sovereignty of the majority'. In this type of democracy the electoral majority forms the government. However, depending on the electoral system and the geographical distribution of seats in parliament, the electoral majority may not enjoy the support of the numerical majority of the population. The consensus model, on the other hand, implies that all significant groups in society should be given a say in government. It relies on the assumption that in order to enlist legitimacy, the rights of minorities should be protected and power diffused among various interest groups. In societies with 'permanently excluded minorities' – minorities with little chance of becoming 'a ruling majority' through coalition or alliances – consensus democracy may generally be more representative than majoritarian democracy.

Minority-majority relationships may be (more or less) 'permanent' or alternatively, unstable. When the majority-minority pattern is *unstable*, rival groups are cross-pressured on various issues, and consent (e.g., on a constitutional compromise) may be reached through the disciplining effect of multiple membership or self-restraint. Here, we are not concerned with this type of minority-majority relationships. In the other instance, i.e., when the majority-minority pattern is *stable*, no system of mutual restraint and accommodation is likely to produce consent and cross-sectional accommodation. In these situations institutional devices placing limits on majority powers are required – a variant of constitutionalism – in order to make the minority accept majority decisions. Here, devolution of power from the centre provides essential institutional tools for securing national co-operation and consent, legitimacy and cohesion in divided societies.

The electoral model most commonly found in majoritarian democracy is single-member constituency plurality elections. The consensus model votes, on the other hand, are commonly converted into parliamentary seats through the proportional representation. While the majoritarian model of democracy has been widely practised in African countries, notably in former British colonies, the consensual model has hardly been applied at all, apart from its partial application in the 1994 South African transitional elections. A modified variant of the consensus model suggests that rather than being represented in government, all significant groups should be represented in the legislature. In practical terms this

---

[61]   *Ibid.*, p. 43ff.

requires the application of proportional electoral systems. Proportional elections, however, may imply less stable governments and yet demand consensus-seeking approaches, through compromise and negotiation in order to arrive at majority decisions in parliament. Proportional elections, therefore, more easily imply accommodative politics, but may not secure the interest of every minority fully.

On the other hand, proportional systems provide a potential for party formation along ideological lines inside regions and districts. This is critical. If the compartmentalisation of politics along ethnic lines is potentially dangerous for the unity of the state, the constitutional set-up should include mechanisms for diminishing these effects. One important mechanism is to introduce electoral systems that may encourage alliances across regional and ethnic lines, and provide space for ideological differences based on functional differentiation. Proportional elections may have these types of effect in divided societies.

Another, far-reaching response to pluralism would be to introduce consociational models.[62] They build explicitly on the co-existence of largely autonomous groups who share the power of the centre, but keep the common arena as small as possible, and hence, retain their social and political sectors of society. In terms of national unity, the ambition of the consociational model is modest, and rather establishes co-existing cultural spheres that are given access to the political sphere through power-sharing. Although it aims at enhancing national integration in the long run, its immediate goal is to protect and retain a policy of non-interference and separation of sub-cultures.

What and who decides which model to choose? And what are the implications for efforts to reach a constitutional compromise in a deeply divided society like that of Kenya? The two historically imposed constitutional compromises in Kenya were not able to achieve a unifying accommodation of the ethnic interests prevailing in the country, with a view to establishing a system of governance and to building a political culture conducive to stability. On the contrary, the political transition towards democracy that started in 1990-91 unleashed centrifugal forces, and increased animosity and inter-cultural suspicion and political violence. This raises important issues of principle as well as methodology. The most important include devolution of powers to lower tiers of the political system, and revision of the electoral system to facilitate a fairer distribution of seats in political bodies.

## Institutional mechanism: devolution of power and electoral system

It has often been assumed that constitution-making cannot bridge fundamental group or ethnic conflict. Nonetheless, there is enough evidence to suggest that "where there is some determination to play by the rules, the rules can restructure the system so that the game itself changes".[63] However, identical institutional forms may work differently under varying social, economic, and political conditions. Devolving power may take many forms, ranging from federalism and

---

[62]    The standard reference to the consociational model is Arend Lijphart, *Democracy in Plural Societies. A Comparative Exploration,* New Haven: Yale University Press, 1977.

[63]    Horowitz, 1985, *op. cit,* p. 601.

regional autonomy to local government.[64] The initial attempt to introduce federalism at independence failed, reflecting a failed constitutional compromise. Later, in the 1990s, the issue of federalism or *Majimboism* re-emerged, but this time in a very different political and institutional setting. The term has not been used in serious debate about constitutional devices, however, but rather contaminated the atmosphere by propagating it as an ideological platform for ethnic chauvinism and cleansing. Before the 1992 and 1997 multiparty elections *Majimboism* became the label of emotive ethno-political violence aimed at creating secure 'KANU zones' in the Rift Valley and on the Coast, or to punish localities and voters who had supported the opposition.

On the other hand, local government in Kenya over the last three decades has not been able to play a proper role in effective local development due to the structure of the system and political manipulation. Kenya has a dual local political and administrative system. One is the elected local government structure, which is answerable to the people in periodic civic elections. The other is the provincial administration appointed by the president ('decentralised presidentialism'). Although the elected system is directly accountable to the local electorate, it has in practice been "totally emasculated in favour of the provincial administration."[65] Moreover, the officers of local governments are accountable not only to the local councils, but also to the Ministry of Local Government. Not surprisingly this has caused serious conflicts.

Devolving powers to regional or local tiers of government is a wide subject and a thorough discussion will not be offered here. Yet among the issues which have provoked controversy is the delineation of 'regional borders', that is, the danger of considering regionalism as a route towards 'ethnically homogeneous' regions. This would have traumatic and suicidal effects on 'immigrant minority groups' in most provinces as it would lead to ethnic cleansing. It could lead the country, as some have argued, to the brink of territorial disintegration.

There are a number of other institutional options that would allow for a better division of authority between regions and the state. The actual institutional design, however, can only be reached through a genuine constitutional debate in which national and external experiences are reviewed and analysed with a view to informing a new institutional dispensation. Devolving powers, including local tax collection, is not a *panacea* for inter-ethnic harmony and equity. Yet, it recognises that the current type of a centralised presidential model of governance has

---

[64] This institutional orientation of the constitutional issue reflects the need for identifying structural techniques to reduce ethno-political contention. There is no easy answer to which structural or institutional devises that would best respond to the desire of conflict reduction, and to introduce institutions for a re-orientation of the inter-ethnic relationship. From an institutional and constitutional perspective, the critical issue is to identify constitutionally embedded institutions for a re-structuring of the relationship between the centre (the state) and regional politics. Ethnic conflict is not primarily about cultural differences (the cultural stuff of ethnicity), but about the failure to establish accommodative and tranquil inter-cultural relationships in social and economic life, governed by institutions for conflict management and reduction.

[65] *An Economic and Public Policy Agenda for Kenya*, sub-section entitled "Summary of the prevailing situation", 1998.

promoted a winner-takes-all brand of politics and discouraged political negotiation.

Devolution of power without reallocation of resources from the centre to the local tiers of government, however, will not benefit local development. Similarly, devolution of power in states with regional imbalances of resource endowment requires mechanisms for regional reallocation based on principles of equity and redistributive justice. A key objective of devolution of power in divided societies is to restructure the institutional framework for inter-ethnic communication and interaction by restructuring the state-region dichotomy.

Another objective is to facilitate communication of intra-ethnic differences, and hence promote ideology-based or issue-based politics. Experiences from other African countries (e.g. Nigeria) demonstrate that federalism or other less far-reaching institutional forms of regional government may either aggravate or mitigate ethnic conflict. Increasing the role of the local tiers of government, however, requires structural techniques as well as other measures of 'inter-cultural accommodation'. Of the former type, the electoral system is central. It is striking how little attention has been paid to the electoral system, and its effects on the structure and modalities of the political game in Kenya as, indeed, in most other Eastern and Southern African countries. The notable exception is South Africa, which introduced a proportional electoral formula with party lists in 1994. The main advantage of this system is the enhancement of inter-ethnic interaction and co-operation, more representative government and improved political legitimacy. The main challenge is to identify institutional mechanisms and political incentives for intra-ethnic competition, and at the same time promote functional representation (cutting across conflict constellations) through organisation of functional rather than communitarian interests.

A major institutional and constitutional vehicle for this to take root is a form of proportional representation. Although the accountability factor may be lessened (due to the party list model), this system provides a high degree of representativity. The South African experience suggests that:[66]

> [w]hile the party list system is bound to be conducive to centralist and bureaucratic tendencies in the party system, the present electoral system concurrently (as possibly also as a result of such tendencies) contains the same dynamic and opportunities for smaller parties to actively seek and acquire representation. This was not possible under the previous winner-takes-all system, but it is built into the system of seat allocation in the new system, and it is further facilitated by some low threshold of representation in the system. This is an advantage for any heterogeneous society, as long as it does not develop excessive levels of fragmentation.

In advancing structural techniques for conflict reduction it is critical to apply mechanisms that enhance open competition, and at the same time ensure that the system is not further fragmented. This requires political institutions able to produce effective decisions and cross-sectional political legitimacy and cohesion.

---

[66] Murray Faure, "The Electoral System", in Murray Faure and Jan-Erik Lane, *South Africa: Designing New Political Institutions,* London: Sage, 1996, p. 98.

# CONCLUSION

In Kenya the failed constitutional compromise reached by the national elite negotiating the independence constitution of 1963, introduced a practice of intentionally using ethnicity for political mobilisation, and at the same time making the issue taboo by denying its public role in politics. This practice prevailed in Kenyan politics from the early 1960s until the present process of political liberalisation. By removing the ethnic basis of the regime from the public political discourse, the one-party state was able to claim *nation-wide* legitimacy, while effectively only garnering factional political support. However, in order to retain effective economic and political control, the two post-independent regimes had to rely increasingly on authoritarian means that undermined basic principles of constitutionalism.

Is ethnic diversity a problem for democracy? In Africa this is a pertinent question. The answer suggested is that ethnicity need not by definition be a problem for democracy, but it may in particular circumstances represent a serious obstacle to democracy, and a source of serious social conflict if not properly addressed. The first precondition for minimising the negative effects of ethnicity is to acknowledge that it is a central social and political factor in most African societies, not least in Kenya. It represents a social and political fact that potentially enriches African societies as multi-cultural societies. A second precondition is to avoid a situation in which one ethnic group or an alliance of ethnic communities monopolises the power of the state, and excludes other communities from state resources, governance and development. The vicious cycle of ethnic hegemonic regimes must be broken in order to nurture and support institutionally a consensus model of politics.

It has been argued in this article that among the key issues that need constitutional attention in a severely divided society is how to establish democracy in a multi-ethnic environment. The neo-*Majimbo* project has distracted and corrupted meaningful debate on this issue. At the same time it is increasingly recognised in Kenyan politics that "the greatest threat to polyarchy in this country is ethnic pluralism".[67] In developing a new constitutional design in Kenya, therefore, the various options require careful attention.

This involves two sets of measures. Firstly, devolution of state powers to regional and local tiers of governance in order to enhance popular participation, control and oversight, and to reduce the dominance of the central state in public life. The patrimonial state has survived largely because of 'unlimited' access to state resources, which has been the backbone of its ethno-political patron-client system. Key words in this regard are measures of local autonomy through a multitude of possible institutional solutions; genuine federalism, multicultural regionalism or creation of provinces that cut across ethnic settlement patterns. Models of 'consociational democracy', zoning and rotation of power are also options to be contemplated.

---

[67] Kivutha Kibwana and Wachira Maina, "State and Citizen: Visions of Constitutional and Legal Reform in Kenya's Emergent Multi-Party Democracy", in Joseph Oloka-Onyango, Kivutha Kibwana and Chris Maina Peter (eds.), *Law and the Struggle for Democracy in East Africa,* Nairobi: Claripress, 1996, p. 466.

The second set of measures concerns electoral reform in order to enhance representative and accountable governance. This requires examination of proportional election systems. Proportional representation in political systems where ethnicity is likely to remain a central factor for many years may encourage alliances and coalitions in order to form governments with majority support in parliament. It weakens geographic hegemony, and encourages ideologically founded political competition. It counters the disastrous policy of winner takes all. At the lower tiers of governance, moreover, it requires access and control over resources, and must be seen, therefore, in conjunction with the devolution of state power.

# BOOK REVIEWS

REVIEW ESSAY

## The Shape We're In: Democracy, Rights and Values in the Asia-Pacific

*Kenneth Christie*


James T.H. Tang (ed.): *Human Rights and International Relations in the Asia-Pacific Region*, London: Pinter, 1995.
Daniel Bell et al.: *Towards Illiberal Democracy in Pacific Asia*, Oxford: St. Martins Press, 1995.
David Kelly and Anthony Reid (eds.): *Asian Freedoms: The Idea of Freedom in East and Southeast Asia*, Cambridge: Cambridge University Press, 1998.
Josiane Cauquelin, Paul Lim and Birgit Mayer-König (eds.): *Asian Values: An Encounter with Diversity*, London: Curzon Press, 1998.
Amartya Sen: *Human Rights and Asian Values*, New York: Carnegie Council, 1997 (16th Morgenthau Memorial Lecture on Ethics and Foreign Policy).

> Servitude and oppression are resented everywhere; Asian peoples do not inhabit a separate planet. When they themselves appeal to freedom as a universal standard of political and other values, this can hardly be dismissed as a bourgeois Western, hegemonic invention (David Kelly: 'Freedom – A Eurasian Mosaic', in *Asian Freedoms*, p. 9).

## INTRODUCTION

The volume and controversy surrounding human rights discourse in East and Southeast Asia approached deafening levels in the 1990s. It was here that scholars predicted one of the main challenges to Western versions of liberal democracy, as these countries appeared to combine economic success with authoritarian government. In the Chinese case it was really only after 1989 that some of this discourse began to creep into everyday conversation, although it was and still partially is regarded as a bourgeois theory, dismissed as liberal nonsense. Only after the seminal turning point of Tiananmen square in 1989 did it become more common, entering the dialogue at various levels in society, even if it was in hushed tones.

Western politicians supported the view that democracy and human rights should be promoted as a global agenda (at least rhetorically) in foreign policy. Whereas geopolitical and security considerations provided them with the rationale to support unsavoury right wing authoritarian governments during the cold war, these were now redundant, lacking credence in the 1990s. This new foreign policy impetus in terms of the West asserting a universal human rights doctrine at Asian authoritarian governments was unwelcome for different reasons. Several of these states argued that it was in effect a new form of cultural imperialism, and contrary to established principles of national sovereignty, self determination and non-

247

interference in internal, domestic affairs of states. Moreover, the industrialised West, they claimed, was seeking to undermine their excessively high economic growth because of competition the NICs represented to their declining, stagnant economies. These views have been repeatedly echoed and reinforced by the Prime Minister of Malaysia, Mohammed Mahathir who has declared time after time that they were also trying to undermine Malaysia's economy, the latest vitriolic reserved for currency speculators. At senior levels of leadership in Southeast Asia these fears were expressed audibly, publicly and asserted with great defensiveness. The bookshelves at one stage were overflowing with the notion of a pacific century in which these societies would play a major role in the world economy, moving from peripheral status to core region in only a few decades. It also offered them a different political version removed from the Western liberal model. Asian values were erected by authoritarian governance as a new ideology, to provide the moral and ideological justifications for the success of these societies. Learn from us they argued to a decadent and largely unemployed West. Entire series of books appeared proclaiming the virtues of untrammelled Asian values while explaining how the faltering, industrialised West could learn various lessons for their improvement.

Asian values in that sense was an attempt to deflect criticism from the outside of the lack of human rights policies and democratisation projects in Southeast Asia. In claiming to be different, they were disingenuously covering over the cracks in the political wallpaper of authoritarianism. The question then became for how long would this wallpaper maintain itself? All of these books under discussion are symptomatic of this attempt to portray cultural and political differences between East Asia and the industrialised West and they all try to deal with some of the debates surrounding this nexus of issues.

## THE TEXTS

James Tang's edited book on *Human Rights and International Relations in the Asia-Pacific* is a worthwhile attempt to give the debate an international context. However, it proves to be a bit of a mixed bag. It is a collective attempt to examine human rights problems in the Asia-Pacific following the end of the Cold War and examines the discord that has developed in the region. In March and April of 1993, there was a small turning point in the shape of human rights agendas. Asian governments were able to start redefining their agendas through the Bangkok Declaration, signed by more than 40 countries in the Asia-Pacific region. The credo of universality *per se* as a credo was not rejected but the declaration pointed out that it must be considered within the "context of a dynamic and evolving process of national and regional particularities and various historical, cultural and religious backgrounds" (Tang 1995:2). National sovereignty was highlighted and the right to determine one's own policies independently of outside interference asserted; rights were sometimes universal and sometimes relative to the situation and culture. The force of the document with the ascendant, economic success of East Asia allowed them some moral high ground in the immediate time frame and the first chapter by Tang helps to put these events within a contextual and historical perspective.

In part two of the book there is a section which deals with country perspectives which I feel could have been left out, or possibly changed in terms of country selection. Constantine Pleshakov's chapter on Russia, while providing some valuable insight into Russian and Soviet perspective on human rights fails to really deal with the integral question of how these societies are so different and decide to organise their systems around this difference.

I am surprised that chapters on the latter, the case of Japan and even the Philippines appear; these two in particular are hardly known for their espousal of illiberal democracy or even anti human rights perspectives in their recent pasts. And there is a curious chapter by Paul Taylor, which deals with humanitarian assistance and the United Nations role. The weakest chapter is one on American policy towards Asia which consists of a linear narrative, rather like reading a bureaucrat's account of the problem than any political science analysis. We clearly need the development of a firm neo-realist perspective here: why does the US condemn China and then get into bed with it? This is never really answered. I was also surprised that the most senior advocates of the rights debate vis-à-vis Asian values – Mahathir and Lee Kuan Yew – are never fully represented in a chapter.

One of the most interesting chapters, apart from the material that Tang has contributed, is the piece by Amitav Acharya, one of the brightest scholars in South East Asian politics. He deals with the regional order, specifically how ASEAN has set about managing this order in the post-Cold War period. While there is also some useful discussion of regional economic institutions by Laurence Woods, I found little analysis of the relational impact of these on human rights policy. This is a pity in some ways. The Tang collection is a good piece of work, which would have been enhanced by a few omissions, and perhaps some additional material. There is some effort in a general chapter by Chan and Acharya to note these problems and overall I would recommend it as a solid attempt to deal with conceptual and practical problems relating to the debate. The chapter by Freeman on the Asian challenge to universal human rights is particularly good in summarising much of the debate. In part the basic difference comes down to what Caballero argued: "Southeast Asian states do not have an alternative concept of human rights. What they have is a different approach to the implementation of rights" (p. 50).

*Towards Illiberal Democracy in the Pacific Asia* as the title suggests deals with the ongoing construction of this particular regional political project. It takes to task much conventional wisdom of American political science that liberal democracy derives from processes of economic modernisation. Is this an inevitable and universal process following all forms of economic development and growth, they ask? It is a multi-authored book and Daniel Bell and his collaborators are generally negative in their assessment and argue against this version of reality, suggesting a far more ambiguous and complicated problem at work. To the contrary they argue that the state in modernising East Asian economies is engaged in appropriating democratic practices as a strategy for managing forms of socioeconomic change. The notion that the state acts in a managerial capacity to prevent regime-threatening change is synonymous with a view of the middle classes as beneficiaries not adversaries of authoritarian forms of governance. Why should the middle classes revolt and demand more openness, political liberalism and the development of civic society simply because that has been asserted as a dominant theory to explain the relationship between development and democracy in Western societies? From the perspective of those who promote democracy based on the value of autonomy (central to *liberal* democracies), Daniel Bell argues that it is "far from obvious that most East Asians want to be free and equal with respect to political decisions even in principle – on the bottom, the traditional political culture of the East Asian commoner continues to be one of passivity and dependence on one's betters" (Bell et al. 1995:27-28, quoting also Lucien Pye). Where were the new Chinese middle classes during the Tiananmen square incident for instance? "What then explains the growing presence of liberal social groups clamouring for more freedom and equality, and what is the likely shape of illiberal democracy that may emerge in Asia?" (p. 2) is adopted as the central question of the work. In contrast to liberal democracy the text asserts, East Asian elites believe that the state fulfils both tutelary and disciplinary purposes. Particularly important is the notion of the paternalistic 'interventionist' state, which can justifiably intrude to maintain order, stability and harmony within society, widely cited as one of the major factors in explaining economic success. In this sense the rule of law means nothing more than preparing citizens for the requirements of a national plan formulated by a wise and virtuous bureaucratic elite, rather than a mechanism for the protection of individual rights. The notion of the *law* and the *rule of law* in China and Singapore are devoid of meaning for the protection of individual rights, and more often is wielded as a coercive instrument of state power.

Other characteristics of 'illiberal' or 'Asian' democracy that have come under scrutiny include, patron-client communitarianism, personalism, authority, dominant political party, and strong-state politics. These are typically contrasted with liberal versions of free and fair elections, political participation, multi-party systems and a recognition of political and civil liberties among others. In sum there are three central features of an East Asian 'illiberal' democracy as posed by theorists. These are a non-neutral understanding of the state; second, the evolution of a rationalistic and legalistic technocracy that manages the developing state as a corporate enterprise; and finally, the development of a managed rather than a critical public space and civil society (Bell et al. 1995:163). The text's view is that while Western societies appropriated democratic processes to serve the ends of liberal ideals like freedom and equality, democracy in the Southeast Asia requires the problematic juxtaposition of different sets of alien values and needs to suit their particular context. The contention here is that the liberal democratic project (with its cultural particularity) appears alien in such a context. While processes of democratisation may appear universal to the Western theorists, something very different is happening in this part of the world, according to this text.

However, there is little attempt to locate Gramscian notions of hegemony through ideological formation at the economic and ideational level as a possible alternative to their thesis. Bell and company argue that there is no basis to claims that the bourgeoisie are the hall bearers of political liberalisation in the region. Rather they reverse the equation arguing that the middle classes are actually the prime beneficiaries of authoritarianism, less willing to promote political liberalisation. Political change, then, in East Asia is about the management and effective organisation of state power and stands in contrast to other view of limitation, regulation and control of bureaucratic elites. Jayasuriyia, for instance, supports the argument that the middle classes are not behind political liberalisation. Democracy seems to be about problem-solving in rapidly modernising societies here rather than the accommodation of a plurality of interests. Another alternative that is not considered here is that middle class forms of political opposition who desire more 'space' from authoritarian governments, may not simply espouse liberal democracy or even political liberalism.

Regardless of its problems, *Towards Illiberal Democracy* is an intriguing and interesting effort to reconceptualise the processes of democratisation and its attributes (they draw attention to political economy, ethnic nationalism and traditional culture among others) in this part of the world while eschewing conventional political science perspectives. The view that economic development necessarily prompts the middle classes to seek more democratic freedoms from authoritarian rulers has been challenged by the authors, but to some extent they fail to deal with alternative structural theories to their own perspectives.

## ASIAN VALUES?

*Asian Freedoms* edited by David Kelly and Anthony Reid is an outstanding attempt to deal with difficult concepts that are often imposed upon the region by the Western social scientists with little thought. It traces the complex contexts and sources of the meaning of freedom in various parts of Asia. And a complicated subject it turns out to be. What does freedom mean if you are from Singapore, Thailand, Burma or China amongst others? What role does religion have in promoting freedom? Is it readily transportable across cultures to give it a universal validity? As Kelly notes "nowhere are reports about degrees of freedom – its perilous ascendancy in Taiwan or its suppression in Rangoon, its exuberance in Manila or its mediocrity in Singapore – in greater currency than in this Asian Region" (p. 3). The text combines history and political science in an inventive way, showing how much these disciplines share with each other. There are chapters on Buddhist concepts of freedom, the state and freedom, slavery and modernity interspersed with country studies. Overall, the study finds fairly convincing evidence that key meanings which we attribute to freedom in Western contexts are similarly in place in Asia, perhaps in a different format, but nonetheless they are all the same. There is an emerging common language of freedom, which has specific patterns. Freedom and right may be separate but they hold a position within these societies. There is a general 'social constructivist approach' throughout the book, seen in Orlando Pattersons work from the perspective that "freedom was socially constructed, not discovered – for it was an invented value" (p. 9). However, it is not clung to like a religion; it has its limitations and the authors acknowledge these and adhere to it as a rule of thumb rather than a rigid theoretical framework. The state is important as James Scott notes in defining freedom as is the relative autonomy of the social units within which people live. This relative autonomy to Anthony Reid for instance meant *merdeka*, the Indonesian word for freedom. Where the absence of slavery occurred in Indonesia, *merdeka* had more room to flourish. Similarly in Burma there is no tradition that disavows freedom as Daw Aung San Suu Kyi illustrates throughout her work interpreted by Josef Silverstein. Despite the various transitions in Burmese history, freedom is still a very much sought after value and democracy is prized even if expressing it has been subject to a hard authoritarian government which despises its connotations and practice. Freedom as a concept on the other hand does not have a long historical, intellectual expression as a concept in China. It is a relatively modern response and one that was introduced to China through the West in the 19th century. And it appears to have endured a bifurcated status, in terms of pre-nineteenth century and post nineteenth century in terms of its relevance for Chinese society. It has also been slow to develop in what has now developed into a classified 'hard authoritarian' state in comparison to the 'softer' version of Singapore and some other Southeast Asian states. In fact it appears that China sees Singapore as a model for its 'illiberal' project in the long run in the probability that it cannot sustain the same level of suppression. David Kelly describes a 'stillbirth of freedom' in this Asian colossus; there appears no shared vision over the conceptual underpinnings that characterise a Western liberal version. This does not mean that there are no versions available and clearly some have developed more strongly than others have, after the 1989 incidents. There are various freedoms, he asserts, present in China; what was stillborn was 'their chordal fusion'. He also ends on a positive note saying that there is hope in the long run for this to change. It is a well-written piece of work that provides a very valuable addition to the literature on this fascinating topic. It enables us to place ourselves in the shoes of the average Asian who may be experiencing this kind of change.

The book jacket of *Asian values: Encounter with diversity*, another multi-authored work says that Asian values "is an assertion of an Asia, which has become more self-confident, more sure of itself, on its path of economic ascendance". While one might argue that values and traditions might be important in a country's development, surely this theme is misplaced here. Asian values can really only be understood within the context of socio-political configurations that have emerged out of authoritarian developmentalism. With the crash or under-mining of many of these economies vis-à-vis the continuing currency crisis from 1997, we see that Asian value theorists and propagandists for the most part have retreated and are less willing to assert such ideological claims. Throughout the book we are taken through Buddhist values, Confucian values, Islamic values and Christian values, which is surely an indication that there is little in common amongst 'Asian values'. Four major world religions have had an impact here; it is a mixed bag and values appear simply as a given, rather than a critical formulation. Everyone and every society have them so why not dispense with critiquing them? There appears no attempt to discern a political notion of values; that is to some extent values are created and constructed by society and government to legitimate power relations. How are values invented? How are they managed and how do governments and regimes manage the way in which values change to their own benefit? This might have been more relevant.

The questions are posed problematically (in the preface). "The question [they ask] is, how are ancient cultures and traditional values modified by modern developments, for example, under the impact of market forces, the consumer culture and westernisation?" While there is no doubt that traditional values are modified, so what? What this book does not show us in the same way that *illiberal democracy* does, is how regimes shape values. It is not only markets and consumerism in other words; in many cases it is the actual regime, whether under Sukarnos's Pancasila or Singapore shared values. The best chapter is by Yash Ghai, which dwells on the notion of *duty*, which appears central to any formulation of Asian values; he evokes the communitarian arguments, which conflate state and community and the inevitable erosion of community by market forces. At the heart of modernisation in Southeast Asia lies the difficulty of rapid industrialisation leading to disintegrative societal effects. Asian values have no meaning here. Rising divorce rates, increased drug use, disrespect for family bonds, single parent mothers and many more are not simply the consequence of the declining decadent West but of a particular projects called modernisation, industrialisation and the worship of the development ethos.

This is the most critical chapter of the discourse of Asian values, looking at key concepts such as duties, rights and responsibilities. There is a also a useful chapter explaining Confucianism which in many ways has been wholesale appropriated by various elites bent on their particular project of maintaining power. Yang Baouyan cites three dimensions of Confucianist thought: the moral-ethical, the social and the spiritual values, which emphasise the moral independence of the people. Confucius did believe in independent thinking and it is clear that elites in Southeast Asia, particularly in Singapore, have taken what they want (mainly the patriarchal aspects) and omitted the rest. In this sense Confucius has become a fragmented apologist wheeled out to support authoritarian developmentalism. Good governance, an idea much bandied around by these regimes in government in Southeast Asia and the World Bank became a near philosophical principle for many of these countries in the 1980s and 1990s. It meant sustained economic growth with supposedly clean government but it fell apart with the Asian currency crisis on 1997, which illustrated dramatically the policies of cronyism and corruption that had sustained many Southeast Asian elites.

Practical realities and diplomacy between ASEAN states have also shown how nonsensical the concept of 'saving face' is when applied to contemporary political realities. These can be seen in the case of the convicted Filipino maid, Flor Contemplacion in Singapore, the friction between Malaysia and Singapore over air space and the continual debate over the regime in Burma. In Singapore a law has been passed which allows elder parents to take their children to court if they fail to live up to their 'filial' responsibility. This eschews the idea that all Singaporeans are amenable to supporting their families; the material incentive to avoid court appearances can have a major effect in a society as materialistic as Singapore. In short, this text is a mixture of business, philosophy, history and religious studies and has some flaws in its less than critical construction. One of the problems I had with *Asian Values* is the way in which the authors ignore the political construction of an entire value system with its ultimate goal as one of total control. Rather, this edited collection, again reinforcing the trend, appears to be a historical collection focusing on the traditional, historical and socio-cultural explanations as to why these have emerged. There is little discussion of the political context in which the elites in Singapore, for instance, have planned for years to exercise social control and engineer society. One or two chapters are very good but the rest appears a bit of a mishmash with no real attempt to show how these Asian values fuse into political realities in the present.

In *Human Rights and Asian Values*, a brief booklet based on the 16th Morgenthau memorial lecture in Ethics and Foreign Policy (1997), Amyarta Sen, a well known development economist and philosopher takes on the nexus of Asian values in his effort to explore its nuances. It is an interesting combination. Morgenthau developed a theory of political realism which centred on the notion of power. Certainly Southeast Asian elites, the strongmen of Asia would have no problem with this philosophy, as they have been adept at maintaining, controlling and manipulating power over long periods of time in political leadership. Sen reiterates arguments about the differences between the East and West and finds them lacking. Are Asian values less supportive of freedom and more oriented to order and discipline than Western values? He sets out to answer this and does so in several ways. First, he looks at the question of authoritarianism and economic growth and critiques it. Yes, some states have grown (South Korea, Singapore) but the correlation is far from watertight. One of the fastest global developers, Botswana, is also a beacon of democracy around the world. So the statistical and empirical evidence appears weak.

Second, Asia is enormously diverse; 60 per cent of the planet live here and it is by and large a heterogeneous population. It is an enormous geographical and geopolitical expression to deal with. Third, Asian values or so-called Asian values are not necessary unique. They appear to exist across time, space and culture. Who would not say they believed in hard work and frugality? And as we have seen, contrasts are often drawn between Confucian ideas and Western thought misguidedly. Order versus liberty? It clearly appears as a false dichotomy. As we have seen throughout the essay Confucianism is simply appropriated to serve the elites' political projects. At the heart of order and Confucianism, Sen asks the "real issue is not whether these non-freedom perspectives are *present* in Asian traditions, but whether the freedom-oriented perspectives are present there" (p. 71). In fact Confucius was not as concerned about face as many of the leaders of Southeast Asian states appear to be: when questioned on how to serve rulers, Confucius replied "Tell him the truth even if it offends" (pp. 17-18). This is hardly the stuff of saving face and kow-towing to superior rulers. When I lived in Singapore, telling the truth, however, was tantamount to losing your job and it is unlikely that people can survive in such a difficult academic system unless they pay close attention to face. Sen also covers areas like India and China. Indians, he notes, like to speak, talk, engage in dialogue and argument; hardly the stuff of consensus and harmony. The traditions of India, he notes, are similar to those of China in that they are not at odds with tolerance and freedom as some would like to maintain. Freedom, tolerance and argumentation were as intrinsic to these cultures as they were to the West. It is a clear case of the invention of tradition to discuss Asian values in their political context as substantive. Asian values are not really Asian; they do not survive scrutiny and in the not too distant future they will be swept under the carpet as failed attempts by authoritarians to induce more support.

## CONCLUSION

While the West has written the language of human rights, the notion itself is present in all societies. Indeed, non-western conceptions of human rights abound in the scholarly literature. It is clear there are many differences including societal, ideological and religious variants, representing African, Asian, Russian, Western, Socialist, Marxist, Islamic, Hindu, Buddhist, Judaic, Catholic and Christian and miscellaneous Third World views. The fact that the concept of human rights has arisen from a largely Western discourse does not invalidate the concept's claim to universal applicability. Universalism is not exclusively a Western approach. And international support for the idea of recognising a basic set of general, common human rights is increasing. The authors of the Universal Declaration of Human Rights, for example, strove for a conception that could be accepted as truly universal and not simply a statement of rights conceived only in terms of the values prevalent in the countries of Western Europe and America. Again, however, the question of which rights this universal list ought to include is still of matter of debate. The difficulty of reaching agreement on specific rights is understandable in a region such as East Asia, which includes states as diverse as Myanmar and Japan. All of these books go some way towards illustrating the richness and diversity of views that are being debated concerning these countries.

Liberal democracy, Southeast Asian elites argue is inappropriate to the political and social culture in Asia, a culture that promotes 'order', consensus and harmony over confrontation and adversarial forms of politics. The argument is often made by authoritarians that they do not have the time or the luxury to engage in the debate and dialogue that Western societies do. Moreover, given the erstwhile economic success of what was one of the fastest growing regions of the world economy, many felt they were in a position to resist such intrusions. For those with democratic instincts who hoped that liberal democracy would gain a foothold here, the record was disappointing as authoritarian regimes bucked the trend of the third wave of democratisation described by Samuel Huntington. The region represented 'recalcitrance' in comparison to trends elsewhere. Not only that, these states apparently offered an alternative form and mode of governance. Critics of the modernisation theories also argue that these forms are highly problematic if considered universal. A liberal democratic system is also "informed and justified by the ideas of equality and freedom as well as by a recognition and accommodation of 'the fact of pluralism', [and it] is a culturally distinct, historically contingent artefact, not readily transferable to East and Southeast Asian societies with different traditions, needs and conceptions of human flourishing" (Bell et al. 1995:9). However, it is difficult to accept whether these countries can hold out against democratisation and the basic human rights needs of their societies forever. Already we have seen authoritarian leaders in problems when the economy starts to falter; Suharto in Indonesia, followed by Mahathir in Malaysia. For the people of these countries and lovers of democracy, it may only be a matter of time before the rest come tumbling down.

Akira Iriye: *Cultural Internationalism and World Order,* Baltimore: Johns Hopkins University Press, 1997 (The Albert Shaw Memorial Lectures).

*Helmut Sax*

For this new book review section of the Yearbook *Cultural Internationalism and World Order* offers an excellent opportunity to highlight dimensions of international relations still less explored in the ongoing discussion on the politics of 'power' and 'culture'. Historian by profession, Akira Iriye traces back to the roots the phenomenon of cultural internationalism and undertakes to assert its significance for the development of international relations and world order.

In fact, the book is a collection of essays Iriye presented as Albert Shaw Memorial Lectures at Johns Hopkins University, rewritten and reconceptualised for this publication. The lectures were first delivered ten years ago and one has to concede that most recent developments after the collapse of the Soviet Union still do not receive similar attention as events from the pre-World War II era. However, since the subject is viewed from a historical perspective, covering particularly the earlier decades of this century, there is no need to worry about information being obsolete. The book is a profound historical account and a colourful portrait of cultural internationalist activities over the last one hundred years. Moreover, it has to be noted that owing to its lecture-like origins Iriye's work does not read like some comprehensive general theory of cultural internationalism, but offers an overview of and insights into fascinating, often neglected aspects and trends in international relations history and concepts of war and peace.

*Cultural Internationalism and World Order* contains four main sections, following developments before World War I, during the 1920s, the 1930s and after the Second World War.

In a short introduction to the topic Iriye explains his basic intention for his scholarly interest in the subject, namely to "downplay the theme of power" (p. 2) by emphasising that the usual focus on geopolitical relationships between sovereign states is not an exhaustive perspective of international relations. Regardless of their nationalities, philosophers, artists and scientists engaged in activities across borders, thereby creating "an alternative community of nations and peoples on the basis of their cultural interchanges", with Iriye stating "that, while frequently ridiculed by practitioners of power politics and ignored by historians, their efforts have significantly altered the world community and immeasurably enriched our understanding of international affairs". In general terms, Iriye thus describes his understanding of 'cultural internationalism' as "the inspiration behind these endeavours, as well as the sum of their achievements" (p. 2).

More specifically, the author defines 'internationalism' as "an idea, a movement, or an institution that seeks to reformulate the nature of relations among nations through cross-national co-operation and interchange" (p. 3). In this context

257

the focus is not on formal diplomacy undertaken by states, but on alternative ideas and activities towards a more peaceful and stable world order through transnational efforts. It encompasses *inter alia* international law (legal internationalism), economic co-operation (economic internationalism) as well as concepts of workers' solidarity (socialist internationalism). Still, Iriye's preoccupation in this book is with another aspect, cultural internationalism. The term 'culture' is understood by the author in a comprehensive manner, reaching beyond customs, religion, law or literature. According to Iriye it comprises any "structures of meaning", including "memory, ideology, emotions, life styles, scholarly and artistic works, and other symbols" (p. 3). With regard to its internationalist dimension, cultural internationalism therefore promotes, generally speaking, cultural communication and understanding across national boundaries.

Throughout the book the concept of cultural internationalism is contrasted to geopolitical realism. And it is true, discussion of this topic is permanently oscillating between thinking like "alter ideas and you alter the world" (H.G. Wells, quoted at p. 182) and sarcastic statements on the "naive idea that, in a world of power politics, states co-operate because their populations admire each other" (N. Spykman, p. 144). Of course, Iriye is aware of the complex relations between 'idealism' and 'realism', or matters of 'culture' and 'power', and he provides many examples of e.g. the instrumentalisation of culture for 'Westernisation' or 'Americanisation'. However, as he concludes, most studies on international relations concentrate on national interests of states, thereby neglecting cultural themes underlying internationalist visions. "At the end of the twentieth century the limits of power, whether it be nuclear weapons or localised police force, are quite evident. If power alone cannot maintain order, culture must assume an increasing measure of responsibility" (p. 12). He does not enter the debate on universalist vs. relativist approaches, as he is not as much interested in standards as standard-setting. What Iriye argues for is a cultural definition of international relations, claiming that "cultural internationalist forces may prove to be a key factor in defining the world of the next century". To support this thesis he colourfully portrays such efforts in the course of the following chapters.

Chapter One explores the principal ideas behind "The Internationalist Imagination", the vision of an international community rooted less on excessive nationalism and suspicion of 'the other', but more on interdependence, cooperation and mutual tolerance. A crucial aspect of the French Revolution had been that people started identifying themselves with 'their' nation, and nationalism became a decisive force over the 19th century. Closely linked to increasing militarism in order to be prepared to assert this identity even by force, observers were critical of these threats to a stable and peaceful international order. Already two hundred years before, Grotius and others had laid the foundation for international law and international regimes; now these internationalist views were being complemented through additional dimensions. Iriye presents examples like the vision of the French writer Gustave Hervé, who claimed the idea of *la grande patrie universelle* as the ultimate goal of human development, leaving nation-states behind to have

258

the entire human population live in one single country. Similarly, the sociologist Herbert Spencer proposed his theory of the development of human societies as an evolutionary process, finally leading to 'civilised' societies no longer dominated by considerations of military power. Moreover, through better means of transport cross-border economic activities increased and at the end of the 19$^{th}$ century pioneering efforts started to harmonise national systems of weights and measures, postal mail and national statistics on an international level. Linked to this internationalisation has been the establishment of functional international institutions and agencies to co-ordinate and supervise these activities. Iriye notes that some 400 international organisations were in existence already prior to the First World War.

Finally, the author claims that apart from the legal, economic and other areas the cultural dimension was the last element of internationalism to emerge in the last decades of the nineteenth and in the early twentieth century, "as if to challenge the growing tides of nationalism and militarism" (p. 27). In this context Iriye refers to initiatives such as the Red Cross movement, the rise of women's organisations, increasing international co-operation between artists and scientists, the spread of international exhibitions and 'World Fairs', but also the convening of the world's religious leaders to hold a 'Parliament of Religions' in Chicago in 1893. Another significant endeavour has been the Esperanto movement, promoting the acceptance of a single international language presented by Ludwik Zamenhof in 1887. Also, the Marxist perspective of worker solidarity was based on international co-operation to overcome capitalist state systems.

Still, Iriye notes that cultural internationalism at that time was not yet truly a global undertaking, but limited mainly to the so-called 'civilised' nations, thereby excluding most non-European states except the United States. By waging war against China, Japan started to challenge this order at the beginning of the 20$^{th}$ century with Pan-Asianism as a new concept and an East-West dichotomy emerging. But even within Europe the dominant theme was not cross-border co-operation, but political alliances, nationalism and an ever-increasing preparedness for war. Iriye concludes that cultural internationalist forces at that time lacked political influence to prevent the outbreak of war, but also a consistent concept, because it ignored both the diversity of cultures and racist ideologies then promoted.

The transformation from vision to deliberate strategy is examined in Chapter Two ("The Origins of Cultural Internationalism"), covering the decade of the 1920s. First, Iriye presents striking cases of personalities like Hervé or Urbain Gohier, who initially advocated internationalist ideas, but during the war turned into enthusiastic war advocates, the latter even pleading for expulsion of foreigners from France. Contrasting to the war frenzy Iriye refers also to the "universalising of the particular experience" of individuals during wartime, especially "as if the war had [...] united soldiers of all countries through their shared suffering" (p. 55). In 1928 the Kellogg-Briand Pact outlawed war as an instrument of resolution of international conflicts and in 1932 the Geneva disarmament conference included 'moral disarmament' in its agenda.

This paved the way for renewed and strengthened peace-building efforts on an institutional level, as it became evident that "good intentions were not enough to ensure a peaceful world order", the establishment of the League of Nations being "the most spectacular instance of post-war internationalism" (p. 57). Cultural internationalism now broadened in scope, becoming less confined to the Western world, as reflected in the increasing influence of Asian and Latin American representatives within this global institution. Moreover, through the establishment of the Geneva-based International Committee on Intellectual Co-operation of the League of Nations and various similar institutions and national committees, the idea of peace depending primarily on a 'habit of mind' of the individual was promoted. Iriye quotes a contemporary academic report, stating the necessity to "ensure the recognition of a universal moral doctrine [and] the prevention of the dangerous excesses and warped mentality that are born out of hatred" (p. 105).

Technological advancement created new agents of mass culture, such as telephone, radio and cinema and internationalists prepared (unsuccessfully) drafts for international agreements on "constructive broadcasting" (p. 72), i.e. prohibiting content inciting war and hatred against others. Another core activities became the promotion of exchange programmes for students and teachers alike, the teaching of foreign languages (or alternatively the promotion of Esperanto) and the rewriting of textbooks for students e.g. in regard to the depiction of other countries. International seminars did not shy to "tackle even the thorniest issues" (p. 80) like national immigration policies.

At the same time Akira Iriye describes the United States as the emerging new centre for popular mass culture, backed by Mount Rushmore-patriotism and influential scholars propagating "Americanism as a social ideal" (Horace Kallen) and predicting a "common culture and a common historical life" for all the peoples of the earth (Robert Park).

Chapter Three continues by explaining the "Separation of Culture from Internationalism" during the 1930s. The Great Depression beginning in 1929 in the US proved to be a major challenge for internationalist efforts. Increasingly, lack of confidence in the economy and capitalism as a concept favoured attitudes, such as stressing the "American way of life", but also support for ideas of neutralism, non-interventionism and pacifism. On the other hand, the earlier 1930s saw totalitarian tendencies in Europe, racism and military confrontation in the East, whereas the League of Nations was rapidly losing impact on the international level. Nevertheless, Iriye again presents admittedly "scattered examples" of still ongoing educational exchange programmes, which could be easily dismissed "as expressions of dilettantism or at best naive idealism", but which are "as much part of the historical record as the Japanese aggression in China, the German decision to rearm, and other events that were steadily undermining the structure of the world community" (p. 103).

Within this context Iriye stresses the most important aspect of the developments in 1930s, the instrumentalisation of culture for national politics – which is true not only for the totalitarian regimes of that time, but also for the democracies. In 1934 the British government founded the British Council,[1] as an agency for promoting cultural exchange, including the maintenance of libraries abroad, but, in fact, serving British cultural propaganda. Four years later a separate division of cultural relations was set up in the US State Department. This controversial step signalled a major shift in US policy towards cultural activities. Now, they were no longer regarded as private affairs of some universities or enthusiastic individuals, but as a government-sponsored instrument of foreign policy. "Cultural diplomacy, rather than cultural internationalism, might be the correct term to use for such activity" (p. 114).

The Japanese war of conquest of northern China was repeatedly couched in terms like 'cultural operations'. However, at the same time the democracies, too, prepared to fight for "their culture" by force, similarly claiming that their war was different to previous wars. Iriye affirms that "[f]or cultural internationalists, this was as serious a challenge in the 1930s as the rise of fascist cultures". He goes on quoting Aldous Huxley who stated that "the military defence of democracy in contemporary circumstances entails the abolition of democracy even before the war starts", arguing that "the results of war are always identical ... people are slaughtered and a passionate sense of wrong and desire for vengeance are created in the survivors – feelings which make yet further wars inevitable" (p. 128). Iriye thus pleads for the importance of culture to keep its autonomy from power and at the same time "to assert, more strongly than ever, the essential distinction between totalitarian and democratic cultures" (p. 129).

The consequences of the Second World War on the cultural internationalist movement as well as current challenges to it are finally dealt with in the fourth chapter of the book, "The Cultural Foundation of the New Globalism". Iriye observes three main challenges for internationalism in the post-war era.

First, there was the need to overcome the wartime nationalisation of cultural pursuits through the use of culture as an instrument for national identity, which was evident not only in Germany or Japan, but in the US as well. An important step to counter this process has been the creation of the United Nations Educational, Scientific and Cultural Organisation (UNESCO), which by its mandate covers not only cultural activities, but also scientific exchange and educational co-operation based on the efforts of the League of Nations Intellectual Co-operation Committee. Moreover, the new United Nations itself established an Economic and Social Council, thereby reflecting the need to conceptualise post-war peace on a more comprehensive approach, including economic co-operation, social standards and welfare on an international level.

Related to this development Iriye states as a second challenge to cultural internationalism the question how to cope with matters of national and international security as the new major concern of the super-powers, particularly

---

[1]  Japan established a similar institution in the same year.

during the Cold War. In this context he observes that throughout the confrontation with the Soviet Union the US succeeded in establishing a symbiotic relationship between US nationalism and internationalism. "Cultural internationalism in the guise of Americanisation [...] was destined to survive the geopolitically defined cold war" (p. 160).

Another major challenge to cultural internationalism was proposed through the rise of the countries of the so-called Third World. Adding even more complexity to the discussion the new independent states were primarily concerned with nation-building frequently forced into 'multiculturalism' complemented by nationalism.[2] The crucial task remains to combine acceptance of the diversity of cultures with shared values and concerns. "If such an environment could be fostered, then cultural internationalism and multiculturalism would be made compatible; indeed, the two would reinforce each other" (p. 170).

Finally, Iriye also mentions two other recent developments providing new impetus for cultural internationalism. First, there is the emergence of non-governmental organisations (NGOs) as major actors in the international arena. They are now able to significantly challenge state authority without pursuing economic or other national interests as their primary objective. Second, Iriye refers to the "politically sensitive issue" of cross-national migration of refugees, minorities and economically marginalised people, arguing that "to the extent that multiculturalism and cultural internationalism are mediated through the influx of migrants, one may talk of global and domestic multiculturalism as a positive force for internationalism" (p. 173).[3]

In the last section of the book, Akira Iriye comes to the conclusion that there is a need for a new concept of international relations, which includes the cultural dimension. He strongly advocates "to explore further possibilities for a cultural definition of international relations as a way to link national developments to world developments" (p. 182). Any nation being a cultural construction, its implications within the international context would only be adequately understood if the latter, too, were conceptualised in cultural terms. Today this is to include a wide variety of aspects, ranging from environmental protection to matters of human rights. Iriye affirms that such a definition is particularly useful to analyse "the alleged chaos that is said to have ensued in the aftermath of the cold war" (p. 183). To him, "it simply means that, now that military power, strategy, mobilisation for war, and alliance diplomacy have lost their once dominant roles in defining international relations, other forces, social and cultural, are coming to the fore".

Iriye completes his portrait on cultural internationalist visions and achievements by stressing the importance of three principles for observance – the universality of shared values and concerns, the commitment to cross-cultural communication and co-operation and independence from the dictates of national/geopolitical interests.

---

[2]  Iriye also notes that internationalist aspects of the Arab/Islamic community still await further research.

[3]  Of course, the argument holds similarly true in regard to migration within national boundaries.

*Cultural Internationalism and World Order* is an important book, because it focuses on cultural dimensions of international relations, which have received much less attention than other aspects of the role of culture – aspects less conducive for international peaceful coexistence.[4] Iriye's strong support for a localised, self-reflective approach to any evaluation of developments, concentrating less on decision-makers, but on the surrounding setting and those affected by the decision also makes it a relevant book for anyone engaged in human rights and development assistance issues. Finally, it is a challenging book, simply because it poses more questions than it provides answers.

---

[4] Such as distinguishing criteria for establishing a battlefield for some 'clash of civilisations'.

# CONTRIBUTORS AND EDITORS

*Bård-Anders Andreassen* is a political scientist and a researcher at the Norwegian Institute of Human Rights in Oslo, Norway. He was co-editor of the 1990, 1991, and 1993 editions of the Yearbook.

*Kenneth Christie* is Associate Professor in the Department of Comparative Politics at the University of Bergen, Norway. He is currently working on a book on the politics of human rights in East Asia.

*Stener Ekern* is a social anthropologist and researcher at the Norwegian Institute of Human Rights in Oslo, Norway. He was co-ordinator of the Norwegian Programme for Indigenous Peoples 1992-96, and contributed to the 1997 edition of the Yearbook.

*Kai Grieg* is a social anthropologist and a research assistant at the Chr. Michelsen Institute in Bergen, Norway. He is the current chair of the Board of the Thorolf Rafto Foundation for Human Rights, which awarded the Rafto Prize to Aung San Suu Kyi in 1990.

*Hilde Hey* is a political scientist and a human rights consultant, based in the Netherlands. She contributed to the 1990, 1996 and 1997 editions and was co-editor of the 1994 and 1995 editions of the Yearbook.

*Alf Morten Jerve* is a social anthropologist and director of advisory services at the Chr. Michelsen Institute in Bergen, Norway.

*Carol Lasbrey* is a graduate of the London School of Economics and works as a freelance researcher, based in Guatemala. Between 1994 and 1998 she worked for the United Nations Mission in Guatemala, monitoring the implementation of the Peace Agreements.

*Lone Lindholt* is a jurist and a researcher at the Danish Centre for Human Rights in Copenhagen, Denmark.

*Birgit Lindsnæs* is a social anthropologist and deputy director of the Danish Centre for Human Rights in Copenhagen, Denmark.

*Zaw Oo* is co-ordinator of a Research Group for the Economic Development of Burma, based in Washington D.C. and Hurst Scholar at the School of International Service, American University in Washington D.C.

*Helmut Sax* is a jurist and a researcher at the Boltzmann Institute for Human Rights in Vienna, Austria. He contributed to the 1997 edition of the Yearbook.

*Hugo Stokke* is a political scientist and a research fellow at the Chr. Michelsen Institute in Bergen. He has contributed to several previous editions of the Yearbook and was co-editor of the 1997 edition.

*Arne Tostensen* is a sociologist and a senior research fellow at the Chr. Michelsen Institute in Bergen. He contributed to the 1995 edition of the Yearbook and was co-editor of the 1997 edition.